The politics of the public sphere
in early modern England

MANCHESTER
1824
Manchester University Press

Politics, culture and society in early modern Britain

General editors

PROFESSOR ANN HUGHES
DR ANTHONY MILTON
PROFESSOR PETER LAKE

This important series publishes monographs that take a fresh and challenging look at the interactions between politics, culture and society in Britain between 1500 and the mid-eighteenth century. It counteracts the fragmentation of current historiography through encouraging a variety of approaches which attempt to redefine the political, social and cultural worlds, and to explore their interconnection in a flexible and creative fashion. All the volumes in the series question and transcend traditional interdisciplinary boundaries, such as those between political history and literary studies, social history and divinity, urban history and anthropology. They contribute to a broader understanding of crucial developments in early modern Britain.

The politics of the public sphere in early modern England

Edited by
PETER LAKE *and* STEVEN PINCUS

Manchester
University Press
Manchester and New York

distributed exclusively in the USA by Palgrave

Published by Manchester University Press
Oxford Road, Manchester M13 9NR, UK
and Room 400, 175 Fifth Avenue, New York, NY 10010, USA
www.manchesteruniversitypress.co.uk

Distributed exclusively in the USA by
Palgrave, 175 Fifth Avenue, New York, NY 10010, USA

Distributed exclusively in Canada by
UBC Press, University of British Columbia, 2029 West Mall,
Vancouver, BC, Canada V6T 1Z2

British Library Cataloguing-in-Publication Data
A catalogue record for this book is available from the British Library

Library of Congress Cataloging-in-Publication Data applied for

ISBN 978 0 7190 5317 7 *hardback*

First published 2007

16 15 14 13 12 11 10 09 08 07   10 9 8 7 6 5 4 3 2 1

Typeset in Scala with Pastonchi display
by Koinonia, Manchester

Printed in Great Britain
by Biddles Ltd, King's Lynn

Contents

List of contributors

Alastair Bellany is Associate Professor of History at Rutgers University and the author of *The Politics of Court Scandal in Early Modern England* (2002). He has edited with Andrew McRae *Early Stuart Libels: an Edition of Poetry from Manuscript Sources* (2005), and is working with Tom Cogswell on a book about the assassination of Buckingham.

Richard Cust, Reader in Early Modern History at the University of Birmingham, has published a range of books and articles on the politics and political culture of early Stuart England, including *Charles I: a Political Life* (2005).

Paul E. J. Hammer teaches in the School of History at the University of St Andrews and is the author of numerous publications, including *The Polarisation of Elizabethan Politics: the Political Career of Robert Devereux, Second Earl of Essex, 1585–1597* (1999) and *Elizabeth's Wars: War, Government and Society in Tudor England, 1544–1604* (2003). He is completing a book on the earl of Essex and the late Elizabethan crisis of 1598–1603.

Ann Hughes is Professor of Early Modern History at Keele University. Her latest book is *Gangraena and the Struggle for the English Revolution* (2004). She is completing with Tom Corns and David Loewenstein an edition of the works of Gerrard Winstanley.

Mark Knights is Reader in British History at the University of East Anglia, Norwich. He has published *Politics and Opinion in Crisis, 1678–1681* (1994), *Representation and Misrepresentation in later Stuart Britain: Partisanship and Political Culture* (2005) and has edited one of the volumes of *The Entring Book of Roger Morrice, 1677–1691* (2007). He also helps to direct a project to create a 'virtual research environment' for early modern texts.

Peter Lake is Professor of History at Princeton University. He has published on a wide variety of subjects in the history of early modern Britain, most recently, with Michael Questier, *The Antichrist's lewd Hat* (2003). He is completing a book on Shakespeare's history plays and the politics of the 1590s.

Anthony Milton is Reader in History at the University of Sheffield. He is the author of *Catholic and Reformed: the Roman and Protestant Churches in English Protestant Thought, 1600–1640* and, most recently, *The British Delegation and the Synod of Dort, 1618–1619* and *Laudian and Royalist Polemic in Seventeenth Century England: the Career and Writings of Peter Heylyn*. Among future projects is a study of perceptions of royalism and a monograph provisionally entitled *The Battle for the Church of England, 1636–1662*.

Steven Pincus is Professor of History at Yale University. He has written widely on later seventeenth-century politics, culture, religion and society. He is completing a book on the Revolution of 1688–89 called *The First Modern Revolution*.

List of contributors

Ethan H. Shagan is Professor of History at Northwestern University, Evanston IL. His first prizewinning book was *Popular Politics and the English Reformation*. He is working on a study of the ideological work performed by the notion of 'moderation' in early modern English politics and culture.

Rachel Weil is Associate Professor of History at Cornell University. Her first book, *Political Passions: Gender, the Family and Political Argument in England, 1680–1714*, was published by Manchester University Press in 1999.

Acknowledgements

This book has been a long time in the making. The editors would like to thank the contributors and Manchester University press in general and Alison Welsby in particular for their patience. We should also like to thank Roger Pooley, Ann Hughes and Julie Sanders for organizing a conference at Keele on the public sphere in which many of the arguments advanced in the book were first aired.

We should also thank the organizers of the North American Conference of British Studies for putting on a special session at which an early version of Chapter 1 was circulated and discussed. Subsequent versions owed a great deal to the commentators at that session (Julia Adams, John Marshall and Kevin Sharpe) and indeed to the wider discussion that took place there. A revised version of that paper was subsequently published in the *Journal of British Studies* and we owe a considerable debt to the editor, Anna Clark, for her kindness, comments and advice.

P. G. L.

S. P.

Chapter 1

Rethinking the public sphere
in early modern England

Peter Lake and Steven Pincus

I

The 'public sphere' has become ubiquitous in the historiography and in
historically oriented literary criticism of early modern England. In this
chapter we argue that the phrase does have real efficacy in discussions of the
period. However, we want to use 'public sphere' in slightly different ways than
most scholars have done. In particular we argue that a narrative of the emergence of the public sphere, in the ways we will define it, can be used to talk
coherently about the entire period from the Reformation into the eighteenth
century.

The 'public sphere' has been moving backwards in time. The term 'bourgeois public sphere' originally referred to a particular kind of Enlightenment
discussion. However, 'public sphere' now appears frequently in articles and
monographs referring to the Restoration, the Interregnum, the Civil War, and
is now even invading the Elizabethan and early Stuart periods.[1]

Why should this be the case? Some of it no doubt has to do with scholarly
fashion. Some more, we are sure, is because scholars are always anxious to
ascribe important conceptual developments to their period. We have all been
chastened by debates over the emergence of the middle class, the rise of the
gentry, or the development of separate spheres. Nevertheless, in this instance
the reasons for the increasing deployment of the term have wider and more
interesting causes than mere academic mimicry.

It seems fair to say that for many scholars working on the period before
1660 the impulse to deploy the term 'public sphere' stemmed from the impact
of revisionism. Revisionism presented both sets of scholars with substantive
and methodological challenges.[2] Substantively, revisionists described the
political process as court-centred, elitist, and consensual. Interestingly these
interpretative concerns are exactly replicated in the Whig account of the later
seventeenth century.[3] This is why one prominent revisionist of the early seven-

teenth century has been able to endorse Trevelyan's account of the Revolution of 1688–89.[4] Thus a similar set of issues has pushed scholars working on the period after 1660 to concern themselves with the public sphere.

Methodologically revisionists have insisted on the primacy of manuscript materials. This was because, even when they insisted on the importance of the local, their emphasis was always placed on a kind of high politics. The high politics they described admittedly often took place outside of Westminster, but it was nearly always about the struggles and discussions of the landed elite.[5] This view prompted an all-out assault on a historiography that had privileged printed sources.[6] On the revisionist account historians studied what had really happened, rather than what contemporaries claimed or perceived had happened. Only manuscript sources gave access to such knowledge, while the printed sources privileged by the likes of Hill and Manning did not.

Such distinctions between manuscript and print, between what actually happened and contemporary perceptions and claims about what happened, greatly facilitated the marginalization of ideological conflict as a major feature of this period. It became unclear what to do with the great printed sources of the seventeenth century, whether the Thomason Tracts, the vast swath of Exclusion era broadsides and ephemeral pamphlets, or later seventeenth-century memoirs, and there was a tendency in some quarters to dismiss such material as self-justificatory white noise. When revisionist historians did address printed materials they tended to do so under the rubrics of the irrational, the irreducibly religious, or as mere propaganda.[7]

Revisionist emphasis on contingency and high politics also tended to break up the early modern period, by bracketing off the crisis years of the 1640s and 1650s from the events that preceded and followed them. The outbreak of the Civil War became the end point of many accounts, while 1660 retained its canonical status as the starting point for a host of monographs and overviews. This made good sense, given the revisionist emphasis on high political contingencies and the relative absence of long-term structural causes for the great events of the period. The result was, of course, that the mid-century convulsion ceased to be conceived as a coherent or cumulative process and became a series of contingent crises, cut off from what had come before and from what was to come later. If, as Blair Worden has pointed out,[8] nineteenth-century British historians had fought fiercely over whether the English Revolution occurred between 1640 and 1660 or in 1688–89, some revisionists appeared to deny that there had ever been an English Revolution.[9]

We propose in this chapter that a modified and more historically grounded conception of the public sphere allows us to reconfigure the English early modern period in ways analytically distinguishable from both revisionist and older Whig/Marxist accounts. In doing so, we want to deploy methodological insights from both groups. We want, in short, to explore the interactions of print and manuscript, and the relationship between what 'really happened' and the stories people told about what was happening. The result is to place a depiction of communication, the relaying of accounts of political processes to different audiences, at the centre of our history of the period. In particular our deployment of the notion of the public sphere allows us to give an account of religious conflict as a major motor for political conflict and change that goes beyond that provided by the revisionists. It enables us to provide an analysis of the modes of communication and action created by religious conflict and thus to integrate religion into a wider account of political, social and economic change without in the process collapsing religion into other categories or social and political interests.[10] Similarly, we are able to recover political economy neither as an irreducible cause of social and political change nor as a category easily subsumed in the political or religious, but as an autonomous area of contestation in its own right. Political economy, in our account, can be understood in terms of socially anchored ideological conflict.[11]

II

Jürgen Habermas distinguishes four phases of the public sphere: the ancient, the medieval (what he terms representative publicness), the bourgeois, and the degraded or transformed.[12] While we find Habermas's periodization a useful heuristic device, a conceptual starting-off point, neither his rigidly stadial account nor his categories fit the patterns of historical development of early modern England as we outline them below. What follows, then, is best seen as some variations on and applications of some basic themes and categories from Habermas, rather than a rigid application of his scheme to early modern England. In what follows we offer a rather different account and chronology. In particular, we introduce the notion of a post-Reformation period and mode of political manoeuvre and public politics. This period stretches from the 1530s through the 1630s.[13] The formative period for this mode was the reign of Elizabeth I. In the period after the Reformation issues of religious identity and division came together with issues of dynastic and geopolitical rivalry to create a series of public spheres. The most spectacular examples of such behaviour were often overtly oppositional, the work of Protestant opponents of the Catholic regime and then of Catholic opponents of a Protestant one, or of puritan critics of the national church.[14] However, as recent research has revealed, many of the first and most sophisticated attempts to appeal to and mobilize various publics emanated from the centre of the regime itself. These appeals were intended either to induce the Queen to take actions that she did not wish to do, or to prevent her from doing things that she wanted to do. Thus opinion was mobilized both in and outside parliament to persuade her, amongst other things, to marry, settle the succession, kill Mary Stuart, restrain her Catholic subjects, and reform her church. In the late 1570s similar attempts were launched to prevent her from marrying the duke of Anjou. Traditionally such activities were seen as the product of an often puritan opposition.[15] More recent (revisionist) scholarship has seen them, quite rightly, as largely orchestrated by central members of the regime and their clients. This change of perspective locates the likes of William Cecil as well as the erstwhile puritan Thomas Norton at the centre of the development of novel techniques of political manoeuvre and communication that, we argue, helped to frame the post-Reformation public sphere.[16] The repeated willingness of members of the establishment to resort to these novel and potentially destabilizing techniques is explained by the hothouse atmosphere attendant upon Collinson's Elizabethan Exclusion crisis (and arguably the succession crisis that followed it).[17]

These appeals by elements of the regime to the people, or to the Protestant Nation, were prompted in large part to meet the threat posed to the state by Catholicism. Accordingly they elicited from a variety of Catholics replies in kind; challenges through the pulpit, press, circulating manuscript, and rumour to the legitimacy of the regime and its treatment of its Catholic subjects. These challenges were met in their turn not merely by repression – although repression in plenty there was – but also by replies in kind, using the same media and the same styles of argument.[18] Similarly both in opposing Catholicism and in mobilizing opinion in and outside parliament to influence the queen the regime had used as agents and intermediaries persons of a markedly puritan cast of mind. Arguably the puritan movement itself was a product of such men and *their* often rather more radical friends and allies freelancing. In effect the puritans were turning back against central elements in the regime the same techniques of argument and propaganda that they habitually used to defend that regime against Catholicism.[19] Very often at stake in the resulting exchanges were appeals to the notion of the commonwealth. Under that rubric a range of issues concerned with the workings and maintenance of the social order were also discussed.[20] A number of 'revisionist historians' of the Elizabethan parliament have been at pains to point out that amongst that institution's most central functions was the transmutation of a variety of local, private, and conciliar complaints and concerns into legislation about commonwealth matters. In our conception such activity can usefully be seen as in itself constitutive of a sort of public sphere. We are describing, then, is a series of exchanges not so much between the rulers and ruled as between elements within the regime and their allies, clients and connections. These exchanges varied from the quotidian to the controversial and even the allegedly seditious. Nevertheless they all involved the same polemical and communicative strategies, and in that sense constituted a post-Reformation public sphere.[21]

The legitimation for these political interactions came from two sources. It came in the first instance from notions of counsel giving, deliberation, political participation, the right to petition, and the service of the common weal, all of which were established elements in the political culture of the late Middle Ages. These notions, we now know, were significantly modified – in large part by the use of classical tropes and rhetorical forms –for deployment in Elizabethan politics.[22] As Richard Cust's contribution to this volume shows, definitions of active political virtue and its discharge in the service of the common weal based on such classical sources were very often mixed and merged with puritan or hot protestant notions of the godly magistrate to form an ideal of the commonwealthsman or patriot, the public performance of whose service to his 'country', commonwealth and monarch in a number of arenas did a great deal to bring the local to the national and the national to the local, in the process helping to construct an arena for the public discussion of political and religious issues.[23] The second source of legitimation derived from religious disputation or controversy and polemic. The disputes conducted therein centred on publicly canvassed argument, conducted within certain conventions about what counted as effective or legitimate argument and in terms of certain commonly accepted proof texts and sources of authority. The conviction was that discussion conducted within these rules would allow error to be identified and truth to prevail. At stake were certain acknowledged public goods – the interests of the commonwealth, of true religion, the defence of orthodoxy or legitimate authority. These public ends were to be furthered through different parts of the commonwealth talking to one another; as the subject, in reality diverse interest groups, petitioned for redress of grievances; as elements within the establishment appealed for support to further their own versions of the polity and the public good.

The post-Reformation public sphere that we are describing, then, provided the arena for discussion of both religious and non-religious issues. Nevertheless we maintain that commonwealth talk in the Elizabethan period is conceptually distinct from discussions of political economy in the 1690s. Comparison between discussions of public welfare in the 1590s and the 1690s reveals both that the Elizabethan period marks the beginning of a long-term trend but also that the volume and range of such activity were so much greater in the later period as to constitute a different form of political practice.[24]

While concerned with the public or common good, such discussions should ideally have taken place 'in private'; that is to say, in closely controlled arenas of public discussion closed off from the gaze of the multitude. The institution of parliament is perhaps the crucial example of the paradoxes involved here. The quintessentially public institution where the representatives of the realm discussed and transacted the business of the commonwealth, its discussions were, notionally at least, entirely private. Only members of the House could contribute or even witness the debate and it was an offence to spread news of the institution's proceedings outside that charmed circle. Here and in the privy council, state and commonwealth matters were supposed to be discussed, policy formulated, and counsel given. Increasingly, of course, throughout the period these conventions and rules were obeyed almost as much in the breech as in the observance. For instance, from the Elizabethan period on, the supposedly private proceedings in parliament were brought to wider and wider audiences through the circulation of manuscript separates and news-letters, accounts of speeches often disseminated by the speakers themselves, the oral and manuscript accounts of their doings rendered by the members to their constituents and others. By the early Stuart period such texts were being collected in manuscript accounts of particular parliaments.[25] Moreover, during moments of perceived crisis or emergency, religio-political controversy and public pitch making were conducted both by members of the regime, its supporters, loyal opposition and overt critics and opponents. A variety of media – print, the pulpit, performance, circulating manuscript – was used to address promiscuously uncontrollable, socially heterogeneous, in some sense 'popular', audiences. Such activity implied the existence of – indeed, notion-ally at least called into being – an adjudicating public or publics able to judge or determine the truth of the matter in hand on the basis of the information and argument placed before them.

This post-Reformation period can fairly be said to have fostered public spheres of sorts; spaces for or modes of communication or pitch making in which appeals to a general audience were made through a variety of media, appealing to a notion of the public good (or religious truth). These appeals were justified as much by the quality of the pronouncements as by the status of the pronouncer and, necessarily called into being an adjudicating public (or publics). The legitimacy of such activities was always in question; they were never assumed to be a normal or regular feature of political life. Rather, they represented emergency measures, resorted to, in extremity, by a variety of groups anxious to push their case with the prince and/or the people. When adopted by one's opponents or those of whom one disapproved such matters represented a form of 'popularity', a dangerously seditious appeal to the people inimical to good order and monarchical rule.[26] When resorted to by one's self they represented either the continuation of loyalty and obedience by other means or accidents, occasions when private documents, letters, apolo-gias, position papers, intended for restricted circulation, spilled out into the public domain and sometimes even into print. As Paul Hammer's chapter shows, the earl of Essex, for one, became an expert in the circulation and manipulation in manuscript of such ostensibly private documents for what were public political purposes. Indeed, in this period the leaked and circu-lated 'private letter' became an acknowledged means of surreptitiously going public.[27] Such transactions took place through the circulation and scribal publication of manuscript material, alerting us to the fact that print was not necessarily central to the public sphere being delineated here. In fact when material intended for circulation in this mode found its way into print it often indicated the failure of the initial polemical strategy; a breach of decorum that could prove fatal to the initial political project.

Accordingly, recourse to such methods was very often accompanied – indeed, legitimated – by a variety of conspiracy theories. For it was only the incipient triumph of some conspiracy of (papist, puritan, or corrupt, court-based) evil counsel that could justify recourse to political methods and appeals that so transcended the normal boundaries of counsel giving and legitimate religio-political communication. In each case the notional end of such actions was not to instantiate such appeals to the public as either normal or norma-tive, but rather, having saved orthodoxy or the commonweal, vindicated truth and vanquished error, to return to a consensual, deferential, and hierarchical normality in which any such recourse to the public would again be regarded as seditious and deviant.[28] The nature of the post-Reformation politico-religious scene in Western Europe, the contingencies of English politics, and the struc-ture of the English state – in its capacity to generate conflict about the nature of and relationship between public and private interest – ensured that a return to this normality never quite happened.

The result was that this mode of political pitch making, of manoeuvre and legitimation, came to play an unacknowledged but central role in the politics of the Elizabethan and early Stuart period. However its role was by no means normalized, and recourse to such methods, particularly at moments of crisis that prompted such recourse, could prove dangerous or counterproductive. As Alastair Bellany's analysis of the continuing instability of contemporary atti-tudes to and deployments of the libel shows, there were emerging protocols and controls, conventions to be observed when having recourse to the politics of popularity, but they remained hazy and ill defined and it was always horribly easy to fall over the edge into sedition. The recourse to cheap print and popular modes of discourse by Martin Marprelate, designed to rescue the Presbyterian cause, in fact provoked the authorities into the final suppression of the Pres-byterian movement. Similarly, as Hammer shows, the earl of Essex's resort to increasingly 'popular' methods to promote his cause, coerce or convince the queen, backfired fatally. These actions confirmed his reputation for 'popu-larity' and ambition, thus alienating the queen and playing into the hands of his rivals. But again, as Hammer demonstrates, just as with Campion and Marprelate, in dealing with the threat posed by Essex the regime did not rely only on punishment or repression but resorted to precisely the same 'popular' methods – print, performance, the spread of rumour, indeed in effect the dissemination of counter-libels – as those used by the earl himself.[29]

Significantly even when the exclusion and succession crises that helped to form this mode of political practice under Elizabeth I had been dissipated by the accession of James I the practices themselves did not fall into abeyance. Indeed, the new reign opened with a renewed outbreak of petitioning and pitch making from a variety of groups, both Catholic and puritan, as well as the bearers of a variety of commonwealth grievances, all eager to secure the new king's attention and support. Statesmen and even monarchs like James I himself, whose structural position and political principles committed them to the view that such activities were inherently illegitimate, indeed subversive, also became skilled players of precisely this sort of communicative political game.[30] Even Sir Robert Cecil, a man to whom the denunciation of 'popularity' came as second nature, framed the most daring political initiative of his career in terms of the exploitation of 'popular' and parliamentary grievances against the fiscal policies of the crown. Taking such grievances as read, he set up the Great Contract as a bargain between the crown and the subject whereby the prerogative rights of the crown would be surrendered in return for regular parliamentary taxation. This manoeuvre prompted and foundered upon the public consultation by the parliament men of their constituents' opinions of the proposal. The consequence of Cecil's initiative was enhanced public discussion of the prerogative rights of the crown and, after his demise, of the *arcana imperii* of crown finance and royal extravagance. For, as Pauline Croft has shown, one of the responses to the wave of scurrilous libels that greeted Salisbury's death was the scribal publication of a number of internal memoranda written by the earl to the king in a vain attempt to convert James to the path of financial retrenchment and reform. Thus did the circulation of the most disreputable of genres – the libel – prompt the release to 'the public' of some of the most respectable and private of state papers. Such were the complex interrelations between the private and the public, the workings of court and conciliar politics and the dynamics of the 'public sphere' under the early Stuarts.[31] Again interest groups, like the East India Company, that were dependent on, but not coterminous with, the public authority of the crown used a range of techniques to appeal to a variety of publics when trying to get the crown to do what they wanted. Anthony Milton's article about the company's carefully modulated attempts to exploit the Amboyna massacre reveals a sophisticated appreciation of the possibilities and limitations of various appeals to a variety of different publics, using a wide variety of media, in a context in which the commercial urge to exploit such contentious issues and spectacular events made the control of which messages were sent to what audiences deeply problematic.[32]

Thus while the practices and techniques that constituted the public sphere we are describing became normal, though unacknowledged, parts of the political process, the level of pitch making in public debate and petitioning was neither constant nor incrementally growing. Rather, the size and nature of the post-Reformation public sphere were intensely dependent on political circumstance. Even during what Andrew Thrush has termed 'the personal rule of James I', as Alastair Bellany has shown, ostensibly private court scandal could generate a series of exchanges conducted through manuscript libel, public performance – trials, executions, and the performance of royal mercy – and cheap print.[33] However, it was not until the late 1610s and 1620s, when the heady mixture of international confessional conflict, domestic religious dispute, royal marriage, war and the rise to power of a classic evil counsellor combined to create a sustained pitch of public political discourse equal to that achieved in the 1590s.[34] In turn, as Kevin Sharpe has shown, it was the very intensity of the political crisis of the 1620s that shaped the peculiar cultural politics of the 1630s. With its reform of the court, performance of royal power in a number of settings and ritual centred reform of the church this amounted to a series of linked manoeuvres engineered to shut down the public sphere opened up in the previous decade.[35]

III

This post-Reformation public sphere was a prerequisite for the creation of the post-revolutionary public sphere. The transitional moment, we suggest, started with the outbreak of England's civil wars. The Civil Wars broke out and took the form that they did, in part, because the recurrently episodic instantiations of the post-Reformation public sphere helped to change the nature of politics and expand the political nation. Once the war had started, both royalists and parliamentarians struggled to generate the resources necessary to secure military and ideological victory. These were wars of words as well as guns. There was unprecedented proliferation of newsprint, polemic, propaganda, and petitioning. Almost from the outset, contemporaries of all ideological stripes resorted to the now familiar if previously irregular techniques of popular and public political manoeuvre. Petitions, now not merely circulated and presented in manuscript but increasingly printed and produced to further nationally co-ordinated propaganda campaigns, were used not merely to express or organize opinion but to appeal to and manipulate it.[36] Under the pressure of events, both sides further divided into series of competing ideological factions. As Ann Hughes's chapter shows, there were any number of different versions of what the public interest might be and what it was to defend such an interest and a series of unstable lines dividing the public from the private. In these circumstances the claim to be a public person dedicated to the defence of the public good, an 'honest' servant of the state, rather than a corrupt or malignant furtherer of private interests, became both very hard to sustain and open to a vastly extended range of political actors, of both sexes. This process of fragmentation created by the unprecedented events of the 1640s and 1650s in turn reinforced the sustained market for news and comment. This new situation became virtually self-sustaining, as individual actors might now enter the public sphere for narrow political advantage, economic self-interest, or desire to achieve ideological hegemony.[37] Constant and constantly increasing demand for news, information, and political comment ushered into being new forms of literary production, such as the printed newspaper. Similarly texts that had previously been restricted to the realm of manuscript were now routinely printed. Petitions became forms of propaganda. Libels and rumours, that earlier circulated in manuscript, were now routinely printed. Theological disputes that had earlier been 'publicly' conducted only in the private circles of the godly, through the circulation in manuscript of a variety of position papers, challenges, and responses, now went public, making the transition from the pulpit into print with dizzying speed.[38]

Arguably by the 1650s this situation was no longer perceived as episodic, but had come to be seen by many as unavoidable, even to some as normal.[39] It is perhaps possible, and in some readings of the period necessary, to begin to speak of *a* single unified as opposed to multiple public spheres. In other words the different kinds of political, religious, and economic gestures that emerged at different points in different episodes before this period tended now to all become regular features of political communication. Many of the strategies being deployed in the 1640s and 1650s had antecedents in the earlier period. There were once again appeals for popular support from rival factions within each camp; interventions, unprompted by the great and the good, by an increasingly varied range of dissident and radical groups; struggles between grandees and their often more radical supporters and clients for control of the political or ideological agenda; the strategic releasing of private correspondence, as well as the scurrilous circulation of scandalous libel and rumour. All these had been present during the Elizabethan period, but now they were happening in public and in print at a rate and intensity that were completely unprecedented.[40] Unlike the earlier periods all these modes were almost simultaneously deployed with ever increasing rapidity. What was new, we suggest, was the intensity, speed, and sheer volume of popular and public political discussion. At this point, it seems fair to conclude, that the post-Reformation public sphere was well on the way to becoming something else.

The type of public sphere that was emerging was socially and ideologically distinct from what went before. While a range of contemporaries still hoped to eliminate the public sphere, or at least return to a chastened version thereof, a number of other developments made this impossible. First, the vast cost of the Civil Wars themselves, as Mike Braddick has shown, required both sides in raising revenue to rely upon mobile rather than exclusively upon landed wealth.[41] The new apparatuses necessary to create an infrastructure capable of fighting and sustaining professional armies and navies forced the state to tap new social resources. Since the English had learned by experience that money provided the sinews of war, debates over the best ways to raise money became an essential part of the public sphere. Economic and fiscal issues – conceived as an increasingly autonomous area of activity and concern – which we will refer to as 'political economy' – were becoming an increasingly central topic for public discussion.[42] Second, the scale of warfare that came into being in England in the 1640s and 1650s forced the state to recognize its permanent reliance, on a scale hitherto unimaginable, upon financiers, merchants, and tradesmen.[43] Of course, the early Stuart state had been episodically compelled to turn to just these classes of people for financial assistance and expertise. From the 1650s, however, this reliance became an increasingly normal, indeed routinized, feature of the state. In effect the post-1650 state came to depend on a differently configured and broader set of social groups.

These political and institutional changes need to be set alongside social and economic shifts in the second half of the seventeenth century. While most of the rest of Europe was undergoing a process of de-urbanization in the last two-thirds of the seventeenth century, England was rapidly urbanizing. Whereas 10–12 per cent of English people lived in towns in the early sixteenth century, the most recent estimates suggests that as many as 40 per cent lived in urban areas by 1700.[44] England's cities and towns were setting the economic and cultural agenda. Just as important, later seventeenth-century England was more attuned to the market as a central medium of exchange. There is good reason to believe that the English had more disposable income in the later seventeenth century. Whereas over 80 per cent of the population were primarily employed in agriculture in the early sixteenth century, less than 60 per cent of the population were so employed in the later seventeenth century.[45] Those not employed in agriculture were necessarily paid in wages rather than in kind. These new wage earners were economically able to consume actively the exponentially increasing amounts of broadsides, pamphlets, sermons, and news sheets generated during and after the Civil Wars. All these factors can be seen coming together in the coffee house, famously the social site in which Habermas located his rendition of the bourgeois public sphere. Coffee houses had become spaces in which merchants, tradesmen, aristocrats, and clerics assembled in urban settings to discuss news, politics, and trade – political economy – while purchasing and consuming the newly fashionable exotic drinks of coffee, tea, and chocolate.[46]

The Restoration period, of course, did not always exhibit the feverish levels of public discussion characteristic of the 1640s and 1650s. The public sphere continued to ebb and flow. While it is true that as in the earlier period crises – for example, the Exclusion crisis or the Anglo-Dutch Wars – generated spikes in public discussion, we see a qualitative shift. Even at its lowest points public discussion never returned to the relative quiescence of the mid-1630s.[47] Issues of religion, the constitution, the national interest, and political economy were constantly under public scrutiny. More important, many royalists/Tories, leading members of precisely the group we might expect to be keenest to suppress the public sphere, recognized the importance of appeals to the public.[48] In the early 1670s, as he contemplated a declaration of indulgence, Charles II intervened to prevent the censoring of Andrew Marvell's *A Rehearsal Transposed*, because one of the prime objects of Marvell's satire, Samuel Parker, 'has done him [the king] wrong' and Marvell, the author, 'hath done him right'. Only after Charles gave over the policy of indulgence was Marvell's book subjected to effective censorship.[49] There could scarcely be a clearer example of the way in which high politics, indeed court politics, was integrally related to the production and circulation of satires, polemics and libels, in both manuscript and print, and of how dependent on immediate political circumstance the control of the press had become. So normal were such connections and manoeuvres by the 1670s that even the king himself can be found having casual resort to them to effect his ends. Even at the height of the Tory reaction in the 1680s, for example, it was a period characterized not by press silence but rather by the shrill tones of Roger L'Estrange's *Observator*. Had James II succeeded in his plan to recast the English state, the public sphere as we are describing it here would almost certainly have been severely attenuated.[50] James at various times did call for the suppression of all false news, did deploy a vast network of spies and informants to chill public criticism, did create new institutions such as the Ecclesiastical Commission to silence religious debate, and did use an increasingly professional and brutal standing army to discourage dissidents in the localities.[51] However, all indications are that James would have relied not on a court-centred polity like his grandfather but rather on a culture of incessant public adulation coupled with a sophisticated print-based propaganda regime like that of Louis XIV.[52] James deployed an army of Catholic propagandists based at St James's Palace, made use of Quaker news networks, and routinely resorted precisely to the kinds of political manoeuvres pioneered episodically in the post-Reformation public sphere.[53]

IV

In later seventeenth-century England the public discussion of political economy had emerged as a distinguishing characteristic of the public sphere. As Steve Pincus argues in his chapter, it was clear by the 1680s that two competing visions of England's economic future had emerged.[54] Pamphlets, broadsides, economic periodicals, widely circulated company position papers outlined increasingly demarcated positions on political economy.[55] Tories, and supporters of James II, worked out in the committee rooms of the Royal African and East India Companies a political economic vision in which England needed to acquire and maintain a territorial empire in order to achieve and maintain a major role in European geopolitics. Because James II and his economic fellow-travellers believed wealth was ultimately based on land, they were convinced that the world's property was limited. States thus competed in a vicious game to amass as much of the world's scarce resources as possible. The alternative economic vision, enunciated most prominently in the 1680s by East India interlopers (opponents of the joint-stock company's trade monopoly) and England's manufacturers, was that England's best hope was as a manufacturing nation. The proponents of this view, mostly Whigs, argued along with John Locke that the basis of wealth was human labour. Therefore wealth was potentially infinitely expandable. Each of these visions had clear implications for describing the contours of the public sphere. If wealth was finite, then public discussion of political economic data was itself a scarce and valuable commodity. Knowledge of the location of valuable commodities – spices, minerals, or other raw materials – needed to be hoarded by competitive states. By contrast, those who believed that manufacturing held the key to economic success needed economic information to be readily available. Only by having information about regional price variations, labour supplies, and local political constraints could manufacturers maximize commercial efficiency. When the Whig political economic vision triumphed after the Revolution of 1688–89, leading eventually to the creation of the Bank of England (1694), England's government was ultimately constrained to limit its interventions against the public sphere. Occasional interventions to limit forms of political activity were imaginable, but only within legally defined limits.[56]

It was only after the Revolution of 1688–89, then, that what we refer to as the fully fledged post-revolutionary public sphere had become a permanent feature of English public life. Even then, the victory of Whig political economy remained fragile in the several decades following the Revolution of 1688–89. The East India Company, Royal African Company, and eventually the South Sea Company continued to advocate a land-based political economy. Tory politicians working hand in hand with Jacobite activists such as John Briscoe had many opportunities to regain the political economic upper hand. Economic initiatives such as the Land Bank, or political success (including the various Jacobite plots up to and including the '15) could easily have restored a Jacobite political economic vision. In this sense England's Age of Revolution came to an end only when the South Sea Bubble had finally discredited Jacobite political economy soon after the Hanoverian succession had made the possibility of Jacobite political restoration appear remote.[57]

Even at this late date public rationality appeared as an ideal to be aspired to rather than as description of public discourse. In the earlier period the model of rational discussion had been in large part provided by religious controversy. This controversy, of course, presupposed commonly known standards of argument, sources of authority and proof text. In some quarters, at least, the existence of heresy and the need for public debate were regarded not only as necessary evils inherent in a fallen world, but as positive goods; means whereby error could be publicly confuted and truth refined and even discovered.[58] However, the underlying model remained that of the ultimate triumph of truth over heretical error, in which the end result of controversy was an agreement on orthodoxy, a return to consensus and an end to further discussion. Given the non-negotiable nature of post-Reformation religious difference and the fragmentation of the 1640s and 1650s, such expectations had, naturally, been consistently frustrated throughout the period. Even into the eighteenth century many contemporaries retained such expectations of closure and quiescence. However, during the post-revolutionary period some began to develop a genuinely open-ended notion of deliberatively discovered truth. For these men and women – and there is no evidence that they had in any sense triumphed by 1720 – public discussion was a means to discover truth, not through the victory of one side over the other, but through the cut-and-thrust of argument and the dialogic interrogations of plausible hypotheses.[59]

The Reformation, socio-economic change, and state formation were all European as much as they were British problems. The narrative we have traced here, the transition from the post-Reformation public sphere to the post-revolutionary public sphere, naturally begs for comparisons. The two obvious points of comparison are France and the United Provinces of the Netherlands. We have neither space nor the requisite expertise to do anything like full justice to the comparisons called for. What follows is an attempt to provoke reflection and debate.

In France, like in England, religious struggles of the sixteenth century generated an episodic yet recurrent series of public spheres.[60] The level of polemical excitement and conflict reached in France during the religious wars far exceeded anything experienced in Elizabethan England. Similarly the political energy and public controversy produced during the Fronde arguably rivalled in intensity if not in form contemporary developments in England.[61] Unlike in England, however, those public spheres did not morph into anything like what we are describing as the post-revolutionary public sphere. Rather what emerged after the Fronde was the greatly strengthened monarchy of Louis XIV.[62] This outcome starkly emphasizes the role of political contingency in shaping the contours of the public sphere. The French monarchy, unlike the English, was able to finance itself despite its remarkable growth without recourse to a newly configured social class. Intendants, it is true, provided the state with new wealth, but they were invariably co-opted into a traditional hierarchical framework as the English merchant and trading classes were not.

The French monarchy was thus able to feed its own ravenous state without creating a dynamic class organized around mobile wealth.[63]

The United Provinces of the Netherlands, like England and France, had fierce, vibrant, and episodically robust post-Reformation public spheres in the sixteenth and seventeenth centuries. Religious controversies, ranging from debates between Catholics and Protestants to debates between Remonstrant and Counter-remonstrant Protestants periodically engaged the Dutch in town squares and in *grachten spraken.*. The Dutch Republic itself was formed in the crucible of war – in this case an eighty-year struggle for independence against Spain. While that struggle did not, perhaps, ever create the centralized state that emerged in France or England, this should not blind us to the massive accretion of state-like bureaucracies in all of the seven provinces. If England had to turn to mobile wealth to remain a major player on the European scene in the second half of the seventeenth century, the Dutch had to turn to mobile wealth much earlier. The Netherlands were and are land-poor.[64] At the instant in which the post-Reformation public spheres in the Netherlands succeeded in creating an independent state, the Dutch were faced with the constant and difficult problems of finance and economic survival that the English did not have to face until the Civil Wars or thereafter. In the Dutch Republic, then, the post-Reformation public spheres gave rise to something like what we are describing as the post-revolutionary phase more rapidly than in England.

These heavily schematized comparisons are included for two reasons. First, we want to underline our belief that the English case is best understood by making comparisons with the histories of other European polities. And, second, we wish to emphasize that the account we are advancing here is not intended to revert to an old Whiggish story of English triumphalism and exceptionalism.[65]

V

By now it should be clear how our narrative differs substantively from both the revisionist and the Whig accounts of early modern England. Unlike the revisionists, our narrative is a story of conflict as well as the drive towards consensus; it is a story that locates politico-religious conflict beyond as well as within the court, and it is an account that highlights the importance of the creation of, and appeals to, publics beyond the landed elite. By deploying the concept of the public sphere we are able to tell a dialectically coherent story of cumulative change that runs from the later sixteenth century through the eighteenth century. We are able to establish meaningful contact between histories and historiographies that have long been severed. The concept of the public sphere allows us to connect court-based political manoeuvres, religious controversy, and then political economic debate, with wider socio-economic and institutional change. One of the great virtues of this narrative, it seems to us, is that we do not need to accord causal primacy to any one factor. We highlight the interaction of ideas, political and factional manoeuvre, socio-economic, and institutional changes.[66]

We want to make clear, however, that ours is a project that hopes to build upon rather than merely to refute the historiographical claims of the revisionists. We take seriously the revisionists' emphasis on religious conflict as a cause of political instability; their insistence on dynastic issues and the politics of the court as a central element in the politics of the period; their problematization of the categories of government and opposition; and, perhaps most important, their insistence on contingency. Our emphasis is on the modes of political communication and manoeuvre deployed by a variety of actors both inside and outside the establishment to deal with the potentially explosive consequences produced by the combination of confessional division, geopolitical crisis, and political economic controversy. By focusing on the methods and strategies of political communication rather than solely on the ideas communicated or the political ends pursued, we can identify and perhaps even start to explain changes in both popular politics and governance that are occluded by revisionist accounts of the same periods. Our account of the transformations of the public sphere makes clear that apparent political repetitions, whether in the form of baronial revolt or crises of popery and arbitrary government, must be understood as historically distinct events. On our account, the changing nature of political communication and action ensures that, despite the persistence of political slogans or aims, the structure of the event and the nature of its outcome(s) necessarily could not be the same.[67]

Our narrative also differs substantively from the Whig account popularized by Macaulay and Trevelyan. It is worth recalling that for both of these Whig historians England avoided the fate of continental Europe in the nineteenth century because it achieved religious toleration and parliamentary supremacy in the seventeenth through a bloodless, consensual and aristocratic 'revolution'. 'The English have for the last century and more been insistent that their revolution [of 1688–89] was unique – so unique as to have been practically no revolution at all,' notes Crane Brinton, summarizing almost two centuries of Whig scholarship. [68] Unlike these accounts, we emphasize the importance of politics out of doors, the centrality of social and institutional change in shaping the nature of political discussion, and the frequently intensely partisan nature of politics. Whereas the Whigs highlight English exceptionalism to explain the unique (and unContinental) nature of English political development, our account emphasizes that the public spheres developed in England in ways not so different from the Continental experience. In our view, had James II succeeded in completing his reconfiguration of the English state in the 1680s,

English public political culture would have been remarkably similar to the political culture of Louis XIV's France.

We are, therefore, advancing a very different understanding of the emergence of 'modernity' from that produced in Whig narratives. We agree with the Whig account that the early modern period in general, and early modern England in particular, was a transitional moment in European history. But we disagree with the Whigs that there was one path to 'modernity' and one kind of 'modernity'. Instead we see modernization as necessarily contingent on a number of religious, political, economic, and institutional factors. The central characteristic of the modern state was bureaucratic capacity and local extension rather than the achievement of political liberty. The state as it emerged in France in the later seventeenth century or that was imagined by James II accorded with no Whig definition of modernity. It was, however, decidedly new and indeed in its own ways decidedly 'modern'. It had the resources to fight wars on a scale unimaginable in the sixteenth century; it had new mechanisms to manipulate and agitate public opinion (the newly extensive Post Office, for example); and it had a large bureaucracy that professionalized and nationalized governance. Such a state was easily distinguishable from the sort of state that had long existed in the United Provinces or the one that came into being in England after 1689. Both the Williamite state and the Jacobite state, we maintain, could be described as 'modern'. Each had a possible future in England as late as 1720. That the Jacobites failed to regain political dominance in England in the eighteenth century was by no means predictable or inevitable. Political contingency remains central to this account.

Methodologically we want to go beyond revisionist accounts in two ways. First, we want to reappropriate the deployment of contemporary printed materials. While we appreciate the force of revisionist criticisms of the use of printed sources by a previous generation of historians to give them unmediated access to contemporary social and political reality, we do not accept their consequent privileging of a certain sort of manuscript source. The notion of the public sphere, and the modes of political communication and action appropriate to it, provide us with the means to relate the contents of a variety of different kinds of polemical text to social and political contexts. Printed works are a central, but by no means the only, form of polemical text with which historians of the public sphere should concern themselves. We need to remember the central role played by a variety of circulating manuscripts and images, of performances and collective political actions.[69] In particular the concept of the public sphere allows us to connect these polemical texts to the sorts of political narratives which revisionist historians were so keen to produce exclusively out of manuscript materials. In interpreting these sources, we insist on locating their deployment with social and political specificity. Printed works and political performances were unleashed in the public sphere at specific moments, in specific locations, with specific political, religious, or economic aims in mind. In making this point we are merely drawing on the work of a range of historians and literary critics who have worked with the history of the book, the history of reading, and popular politics.[70] We want, in short, to reconfigure what we take to have been an overly rigid distinction that revisionists drew between representation and reality. We take the first task of the historian to be to situate socially and politically the stories contemporaries told about their circumstance rather than to evaluate immediately the truth-value of those stories.

Second, whereas one of the basic moves of revisionism was to separate firmly political history from social and economic history, our approach tends in the opposite direction.[71] One of revisionism's achievements was to restore autonomy to the political domain and to study it on its own terms. Our insistence on understanding the period in terms of the developing public sphere forces us to integrate political history with the histories of commercialization, literacy, institutional development, and extra-English affairs. By focusing on political communication, rather than narrowly on politics, we are compelled to consider historically relevant socio-economic conditions that constrained and enabled communication, the institutions that facilitated (and even necessitated) different modes of communication, as well as the ideological content of the messages being sent out. Political communication was shaped by emerging markets and developing infrastructures of communication.[72] While we insist that social and cultural conditions shaped the contours of political communication, we are not saying that socio-economic developments determined political conflict in any straightforward and over-determined way.

VI

Our narrative, organized around the concept of the public sphere, then, is one of transformation.[73] However, it is not one that points to the causes or consequences of a single revolutionary political event. Nor is it a narrative that insists that this revolutionary transformation was inevitable. Indeed, by separating the development of England's public sphere into various phases we are bringing the contingency of those developments into sharp relief.

What then were the most important aspects of the transformations in the public sphere that we've been describing? First, we are emphasizing the sheer quantitative increase of public discussion. There was an exponential growth in the number of pamphlets, broadsides and poems produced. Political gossip and news circulated over a much broader geographical and social domain. More and more people were brought into public discussion. The intensity and extent of political activity during the Civil Wars and Exclusion crisis have no parallels prior to 1640. Whereas the Elizabethan Bond of Association in the 1580s generated dozens of signatures in individual counties, that number pales in comparison with the hundreds of thousands of people that signed the 1696 Bond of Association in Lancashire alone.[74] A quantitative change of this magnitude represents, in fact, a profound qualitative change.

Second, the distinction we draw between the earlier and later public spheres is the difference between the episodic and the regular. The post-Reformation public sphere began as occasional and opportunistic opening and shutting-down of debate on a limited set of issues. In many cases this was initiated by the regime, or sometimes by elements within it, in order to generate support for its policies. Increasingly, the state was unable to put the genie back in the bottle, both because other more or less oppositional forces saw the public sphere as a stage upon which they could air their grievances and circulate their complaints, and because the public increasingly demanded information. In the 1640s and 1650s the regularity that both sides (and factions within each group) appealed to the public transformed the occasional into the normal. This regularity created political actors with an increasingly conscious and sophisticated sense of the way to play politics in this new public arena.[75] This in itself made certain that political struggles in the second half of the century were conducted differently from political struggles in the first half. Many appreciated the political value of appeals to the public while denying that free and open public political discussion was inevitable or desirable. James II and various members of his political circle, for example, were adept at advertising their policy initiatives to the public while at the same effectively clamping down on political communication initiated by their critics. Only after 1688–89 with the vastly expanded financial institutions of the government, and the need that the government had to keep open channels of political economic communication in order to maintain the health of those very institutions, was the state compelled to accept a regular, public sphere.

Third, our account points up the shifting geographical and social location of the public sphere. The quantitative expansion of the public sphere in England's early modern period necessarily meant that an increasingly wide array of people was brought within the nexus of political communication. This quantitative shift meant that people below the level of the landed elite gained access, both because they wanted that access, and because political factions had much to gain from mobilizing them, to various forms of political information. While London had always been at the centre of networks of political information, political communication outside of London was not limited to the towns. News sheets and separates were more likely to be circulated through the country houses of the landed elite.[76] Religious controversy could surface not only in rural parish churches but also in the myriad voluntary associations and networks of the godly, both Protestant and Catholic.[77]

The growth in the size and number of towns over the course of the seventeenth century created new centres of the public sphere. The proliferation of the coffee house indicated one way in which London's urban culture permeated the provinces. The emergence of a variety of urban amenities in the period after the Civil Wars has led one scholar to describe an English urban renaissance.[78] Critics have demonstrated the specifically urban character of the new literary genre of the novel.[79] While the majority of English men and women still lived in rural areas in the later seventeenth century, there can be little doubt that a great deal of the cultural energy in this later period came from England's towns.

Fourth, while participants in the post-Reformation public spheres considered political communication to be a necessary evil, by the end of our period many (though by no means all) political actors understood relatively unfettered public discussion to be normatively desirable.[80] Controversialists opened post-Reformation public spheres as a means of establishing the truth against imperfectly reformed or politically degraded opponents. Once polemical and political victory was achieved these actors imagined that the public discussion had served its ephemeral purpose. In the post-revolutionary period not only did actors perceive the existence of the public sphere as the normal state of affairs, some came to see that state of affairs as a positive good. Religious, political, and political economic dispute in the view of commentators such as John Locke and Daniel Defoe could lead, in itself, to the discovery of a truth distinct from the positions initially enunciated by the disputants.

As both Mark Knights and Rachel Weil make clear, participants in this public sphere were under no illusion that each individual utterance in that sphere would be rational – indeed, under the licence of public partisanship the political slur reached new quantitative and qualitative heights in the period – but at least some contemporaries maintained the normative illusion that the cut-and-thrust of debate would reveal better political options.[81] Political and religious conspiracy theories did not disappear in the period (nor have they now), in fact the anxieties created in part by the pace of change in the public sphere and by the intensity of increasingly party-based political conflict caused many contemporaries to resort to them with increased fervour.[82]

Fifth, the later period was distinguished from the post-Reformation public sphere by the emergence of 'political economy' as a central autonomous element in public controversy. The claim is not that discussions of commerce emerged for the first time after the Civil Wars but rather that their quantitative ubiquity in the later period infused the language of politics so as to create a qualitative shift in political communication. By the latter end of the seventeenth century the public sphere was suffused with pamphlets, broadsides, and the circulation of company stock, that not only appealed to notions of the public good, but did so to publics beyond parliament, the privy council or members of the joint-stock companies. 'Political economy' did not replace discussions of religion or geopolitics. These issues remained, and still remain, crucial elements of public discussion. But it was the addition of 'political economy' to public discourse that in part demarcated the post-revolutionary period.

While our notion of the public sphere is influenced more than merely nominally by the work of Jürgen Habermas, our aim is not to apply his notion of the public sphere slavishly to early modern England or merely to claim that it emerged earlier than he suggested. Instead our discussion of the public sphere modifies Habermas's story in a number of important ways. First, we suggest that a necessary prerequisite for the emergence of what we term here the post-revolutionary public sphere, not only in England but throughout Europe, were the practices and procedures that constituted the post-Reformation public sphere. The existence of the post-Reformation public sphere did not make the later developments sketched here inevitable, but did make them possible. The mid-century crisis itself would not have taken the form it did without the previous existence of the political forms of manoeuvre and communication of the post-Reformation period. The robust discussion of political economy characteristic of the post-revolutionary public sphere depended on these earlier developments.

This, at the least, suggests that the crisis of capitalism of the sort described by Habermas could not in and of itself have generated the kind of post-revolutionary public sphere described here. Our post-revolutionary public sphere emerged out of a series of successive and dialectically related crises and conjunctures. Habermas argues that a crisis of capitalism, a bitter struggle between finance and manufacturing interests, forced each side to appeal to and create publics to settle their differences.[83] In the period after 1688 it is hard to find a conflict between manufacturing and finance capitalism. Instead the supporters of the Bank of England and England's manufacturing interest, by and large, aligned themselves together in print and polemic behind the notion of an infinitely expandable political economy based on labour. Their opponents, supporters of the East India and African Companies – and various agrarian interests aligned against the growing manufacturing sector – defended a vision of a finite political economy based on land. In both cases economic self-interest was melded with a sophisticated geopolitical, socio-political, and (at times) religious vision. This ideological contest was always near the centre of the political controversies of the 1680s, 1690s and the early decades of the eighteenth century.[84]

Finally, unlike Habermas's account, our story insists on the central role played by an increasingly powerful state. In the earlier period we see a state, perceiving itself to be under dynastic, confessional, and socio-economic threat, resorting to various modes of political communication and the invocation of various publics to shore up its position. It was, then, the division of the state at mid-century, both instantiating regular invocations of the public sphere, and placing larger and larger demands on an ever widening public, that arguably began the transformation from the post-Reformation to what we have been calling here the post-revolutionary public sphere. Even at this point, we want to caution that the public sphere had a tenuous existence still tied to the ebb and flow of political conflict and crisis. It was only in the 1690s and thereafter that the political struggle over how best to feed the voracious appetite of a now greatly expanded state apparatus rendered public discussion of the sort we have been describing a permanent feature of political life.[85]

We conclude with a final paradox. We see different paths to, and indeed different political modernities or public spheres emerging out of, the circulation (in part) of conspiracy theories and more or less unsubstantiated political rumours. It was these conspiracy theories, and the ideological passions upon which they fed, that created the political energy that exploded in the crisis of mid-century. It was also different but related sorts of conspiracy theories – in this case competing claims about French and Dutch aspirations to universal dominion – that gave force to the political economic conflict that so influenced the replacement of James II with William III.[86] As both Knights and Weil show, in their different ways, it was out of the need to navigate their way through the consequent welter of claim and counter-claim, plot and counter-plot, conspiracy and counter-conspiracy, that contemporaries developed and deployed standards and expectations about rational argument and proof, credibility and civility, even as their own political and discursive practices and manoeuvres continued to contravene, and perhaps even to subvert, those very standards.

NOTES

This chapter had its origins as a position paper presented at the North Atlantic Conference on British Studies at Philadelphia in 2004. A version will appear in the *Journal of British Studies* in 2006. We are grateful for the criticism and suggestions of those present at the NACBS session, especially of the respondents John Marshall, Kevin Sharpe and Julia Adams, the two anonymous readers, and Anna Clark. We are also grateful for discussions with Bill Bullman, Tom Cogswell, Richard Cust, Alan Houston, Ann Hughes, and Anthony Milton. Intended as a schematic overview, a critique of recent historiographical trends, and a suggestion for further research, it is presented here as one framework within which the contributions to this volume may be read. It speaks to the contents of the following chapters and seeks to relate them to an overarching vision of the early modern period. But while we think that the argument presented here is compatible with, and is certainly informed by, the contents of this volume, there is no sense in which this introduction represents the collective wisdom of the contributors, but rather the particular views of the two editors. Indeed, even a cursory reading of the volume will show that the chapters that follow contain much material for an extended critique of the views expressed here.

1 For example: Joad Raymond, *Pamphlets and Pamphleteering in Early Modern Britain* (Cambridge, 2003); Raymond, 'The newspaper, public opinion, and the public sphere in the seventeenth century', *Prose Studies* 21:2 (1998), 109–40; David Zaret, *Origins of Democratic Culture: Printing, Petitions, and the Public Sphere in Early Modern England*

(Princeton NJ, 2000); Sharon Achinstein, *Milton and the Revolutionary Reader* (Princeton NJ, 1994); David Norbrook, *Writing and the English Republic: Poetry, Rhetoric, and Politics, 1627–1660* (Cambridge, 1998); Nigel Smith, *Literature and Revolution in England, 1640–1660* (New Haven CT, 1994); Ann Hughes, *Gangraena* (Oxford, 2004); Brian Cowan, 'Mr Spectator and the coffeehouse public sphere', *Eighteenth Century Studies* 37:3 (2004), 345–66; Steve Pincus, '"Coffee politicians does create": coffeehouses and Restoration political culture', *Journal of Modern History* 67:4 (1995), 807–34; Peter Lake and Michael Questier, *The Antichrist's Lewd Hat: Protestants, Papists and Players in post-Reformation England* (New Haven CT, 2002); Alexandra Halasz, *The Marketplace of Print: Pamphlets and the Public Sphere in Early Modern England* (Cambridge, 1997); Harold Love, *Scribal Publication in Seventeenth-Century England* (Oxford, 1993); Adrian Johns, *The Nature of the Book* (Chicago, 1998); Natalie Mears, *Queenship and Political Discourse in the Elizabethan Realms* (Cambridge, 2005). There are countless others.

2 In fact for later seventeenth-century scholars the revisionist challenge was more methodological than substantive, since the revisionist account fitted snugly with old Whig interpretations of that period.

3 Thomas Babington Macaulay, *The History of England from the Accession of James the Second* (8 vols, New York, 1849); G. M. Trevelyan, *The English Revolution, 1688–1689* (Oxford, 1938).

4 John Morrill, 'The sensible revolution', in Jonathan Israel (ed.), *The Anglo-Dutch Moment* (Cambridge, 1991), 73–104.

5 Conrad Russell, *Unrevolutionary England, 1603–1642* (London, 1990); Russell, *Parliaments and English Politics, 1621–1629* (Oxford, 1979); Alan Milner Everitt, *The Community of Kent and the Great Rebellion, 1640–1660* (Leicester, 1966); Mark Kishlansky, *Parliamentary Selection* (Cambridge, 1986); David H. Hosford, *Nottingham, Nobles and the North* (Hamden CT, 1976).

6 Brian Manning, *The English People and the English Revolution, 1640–1649* (London, 1976). Such a rigidly sceptical view of the printed sources of the period was a major underpinning of Mark Kishlansky's *The Rise of the New Model Army* (Cambridge, 1979). The attack on printed sources was not, however, limited to revisionists, see J. H. Hexter, *On Historians: Reappraisals of Some of the Makers of Modern History* (Cambridge MA, 1979), in particular 'The historical method of Christopher Hill', 227–51. For some critical comments on these issues, upon which we are attempting to build, see Kevin Sharpe and Peter Lake, 'Introduction' to their edited collection *Culture and Politics in Early Stuart England* (Stanford CA, 1993); Hughes, *Gangraena*.

7 John Morrill, *The Revolt of the Provinces* (rev. edn, London, 1980); Conrad Russell, *The Causes of the English Civil War* (Oxford, 1990); Tony Claydon, *William III and the Godly Revolution* (Cambridge, 1996); Jonathan Scott, *England's Troubles* (Cambridge, 2000); Jonathan Clark, *English Society, 1660–1832* (2nd edn, Cambridge, 2000). On religious prejudice, paranoid fantasy, and myth, see Anthony Fletcher, *The Outbreak of the English Civil War* (New York, 1981); J. P. Kenyon, *The Popish Plot* (London, 1972). Jonathan Scott certainly privileges confessional conflict and English fear of popery as the motor behind political change. However, Scott is careful to distinguish his position from that of Kenyon. See Scott's 'England's troubles: exhuming the Popish Plot', in Tim Harris, Paul Seaward and Mark Goldie (eds), *The Politics of Religion in Restoration England* (Oxford, 1990), 107–32.

8 Blair Worden, *Roundhead Reputations: The English Civil Wars and the Passions of Posterity* (London, 2001).

9 Russell, *Unrevolutionary England*; Morrill, 'Sensible revolution'; William A. Speck, *Reluctant Revolutionaries: Englishman and the Revolution of 1688* (Oxford, 1988). Speck argues that there was a narrowly political, and quite conservative, revolution in 1688, but emphatically denies that there was a social revolution in the period. Kevin Sharpe, while adopting a revisionist account of the causes the Civil War, attributes genuinely revolutionary political and cultural effects to the regicide. See his 'A commonwealth of meanings', in *Politics and Ideas in early Stuart England* (London, 1989); also see his *Reading Revolutions* (New Haven CT, 2000).

10 This builds on the accounts of puritanism as a political movement given by Patrick Collinson, *The Elizabethan Puritan Movement* (London, 1967), for the Elizabethan period and, for the outbreak of the Civil War, by Conrad Russell in his *Causes of the English Civil War* and the *Fall of the British Monarchies* (London, 1990). For an account of the multiple media used by puritans, see Lake and Questier, *Antichrist's Lewd Hat*.

11 D. W. Jones, *War and Economy in the Age of William III* (Oxford, 1998); Steve Pincus, 'The making of a great power? Universal monarchy, political economy, and the transformation of English political culture', *The European Legacy* 5:4 (2000), 531–45; Pincus, 'Neither Machiavellian moment nor possessive individualism: commercial society and the defenders of the English Commonwealth', *American Historical Review* 103:3 (1998), 705–36.

12 For an explication of this periodization in Habermas see Steve Pincus's chapter in this volume. This argument in turn relies on a reading of Jürgen Habermas, *The Structural Transformation of the Public Sphere*, trans. Thomas Burger (Cambridge MA, 1989), especially 52, 178.

13 The notion of a long post-Reformation period is based on the research of revisionist historians of the Reformation and the notion of a long-term working out of the tensions created by the spread of Protestantism amongst a populace wedded to traditional ways until well into Elizabeth's reign. The problematic envisaged here draws heavily on the work of Patrick Collinson. See especially his *Birthpangs of Protestant England* (New York, 1988). Also see Ethan Shagan's chapter in this volume.

14 The classic study of this is Patrick Collinson's account of Presbyterian attempts to reform the English church from within in *The Elizabethan Puritan Movement*.

15 J. E. Neale, *Elizabeth I and her Parliaments* (London, 1957–58).

16 Michael Graves, 'Thomas Norton the parliament man', *Historical Journal* 23:1 (1980), 17–35; Graves, 'The common lawyers and the privy council's parliamentary men of business, 1584–1601', *Parliamentary History* 8 (1989), 189–215; Graves, 'The management of the Elizabethan House of Commons: the council's men of business', *Parliamentary History* 2 (1983), 11–38. But also see Patrick Collinson, 'Puritans, men of business and Elizabethan parliaments', *Parliamentary History* 7 (1988), 187–211.

17 Patrick Collinson, 'The monarchical republic of Queen Elizabeth I', *Bulletin of the John Rylands University Library of Manchester* 69:2 (1987), 394–424; Collinson, 'The Elizabethan Exclusion crisis and the Elizabethan polity', *Proceedings of the British Academy* 84 (1994), 51–92.

18 Peter Lake and Michael Questier, 'Puritans, papists and the "public sphere" in early modern England', *Journal of Modern History* 72:3 (2000), 587–627; Lake and Questier, 'Agency, appropriation and rhetoric under the gallows', *Past and Present* 153 (1996), 64–107.

19 See Peter Lake's chapter in this volume and his essay 'The monarchical republic of Elizabeth I redefined (by its victims) as a conspiracy', in Barry Coward and Julian Swann (eds), *Conspiracies and Conspiracy Theory in Early Modern Europe* (London, 2004).

20 David Dean, *Law-making and Society in late Elizabethan England* (Cambridge, 1996). Comparison between such activity in say the 1590s and the 1690s reveals both that this is the beginning of long-term trend but also that the volume and range of such activity were so much greater in the later period as to constitute a different from of political practice. See Perry Gauci, *The Politics of Trade* (Oxford, 2001), 211–12.

21 Paul Slack highlights the change in talk about the public good in the 1640s and 1650s in *From Reformation to Improvement: Public Welfare in Early Modern England* (Oxford, 1999), 82–101. See also Joan Thirsk, *Economic Policy and Projects: The Development of a Consumer Society in Early Modern England* (Oxford, 1978). The way in which the older commonwealth discourse is substantively and analytically transformed over the course of the period is the subject of Blair Hoxby's *Mammon's Music* (New Haven CT, 2002).

22 Markku Peltonen, *Classical Humanism and Republicanism in English Political Thought, 1570–1640* (Cambridge, 1995); Stephen Alford, *The Early Elizabethan Polity* (Cambridge, 1998); David Colclough, *Freedom of Speech in Early Stuart England* (Cambridge, 2005).

23 See Richard Cust's chapter in this volume and Richard Cust and Peter Lake, 'Sir Richard Grosvenor and the rhetoric of magistracy', *Bulletin of the Institute of Historical Research* 54 (1981), 40–53. The two types of character and discourse, the puritan zealot and the classicizing self-appointed public man, were separated out and viciously satirized by Ben Jonson in *Bartholomew Fair* through the characters of Zeal of the Land Busy and Adam Overdo. Commentary upon the developments discussed in this introduction on the public stage played a crucial part in the creation of the public sphere we are describing. Lake and Questier, *The Antichrist's Lewd Hat*, especially chapter 14.

24 Gauci, *The Politics of Trade*, 211–12.

25 See the discussion of the issues by Harold Love in his *Scribal Publication*, 9–22. On the wider issue of public access to parliament see C. Kyle and J. Peacey, '"Under cover of so much coming and going": public access to parliament and the political process in early modern England', in Kyle and Peacey (eds), *Parliament at Work: Parliamentary Committees, Political Power and Public Access in Early Modern England* (Woodbridge, 2002), 1–23.

26 The increasing use of the term 'popularity' as a boo-word to describe the political practices being described here is a sure sign that something significant and novel was happening and that contemporaries had noticed. On popularity see Richard Cust, 'Charles I and popularity', in Thomas Cogswell, Richard Cust and Peter Lake (eds), *Politics, Religion and Popularity in early Stuart Britain: Essays in Honour of Conrad Russell* (Cambridge, 2002), 235–58, and Peter Lake, 'John Whitgift, puritanism and the invention of popularity', forthcoming in a volume of essays on the monarchical republic of Elizabeth I.

27 See Paul Hammer's chapter in this volume. Also see Peter Lake and Kenneth Fincham, 'Popularity, prelacy and puritanism in the 1630s', *English Historical Review* 11:443 (1996), 856–65.

28 Lake, 'The monarchical republic of Elizabeth I redefined'; Colclough, *Freedom of Speech*, 211–12.

29 See Paul Hammer's chapter below.

30 Kevin Sharpe, 'Royal authors and royal authority in early modern England', in Kevin Sharpe and Peter Lake (eds), *Culture and Politics in Early Stuart England* (Stanford CA, 1993); Peter Lake, 'The king (the queen) and the Jesuit: James Stuart's *True Law of Free Monarchies* in context/s', *Transactions of the Royal Historical Society*, 6th ser., 14 (2004), 243–60.

31 A. G. R. Smith, 'Crown, parliament and finance: the Great Contract of 1610', in Peter Clark, Alan Smith and Nicholas Tyacke (eds), *The English Commonwealth, 1547–1640*, (Leicester, 1979), 111–27; Pauline Croft (ed.), 'A collection of several speeches and treatises of the late Lord Treasurer Cecil', in *Camden Miscellany* 29, Camden Society, 4th ser., XXXIV (1987), and Croft, 'The reputation of Robert Cecil', *Transactions of the Royal History Society*, 6th ser., 1 (1991), 43–69.

32 See Anthony Milton's chapter in this volume.

33 Andrew Thrush, 'The personal rule of James I', in Cogswell, Cust and Lake, *Politics, Religion and Popularity*, 84–102. Alastair Bellany, *The Politics of Court Scandal in Early Modern England* (Cambridge, 2002).

34 Thomas Cogswell, '"Published by Authoritie": newsbooks and the duke of Buckingham's expedition to the Ile de Ré', *Huntington Library Quarterly* 67:1 (2004), 1–25; Cogswell, '"The People's Love": the duke of Buckingham and popularity', in Cogswell, Cust and Lake, *Politics, Religion and Popularity*, 211–34; Cogswell, 'The politics of propaganda: Charles I and the people in the 1620s', *Journal of British Studies* 29:3 (1990), 187–215; Cogswell, 'England the Spanish match', in Richard Cust and Ann Hughes (eds), *Conflict in Early Stuart England: Studies in Religion and Politics, 1603–1642* (London, 1989), 107–33.

35 Kevin Sharpe, *The Personal Rule of Charles I* (London, 1992), 1–63 and *passim*.

36 David Wootton, 'From rebellion to revolution: the crisis of the winter of 1642/3 and the origins of Civil War radicalism', *English Historical* Review 105:416 (1990), 654–69; Peter Lake, 'Puritans, popularity and petitions: local politics in national context, Cheshire 1641', in Cogswell, Cust and Lake, *Politics, Religion and Popularity*, 259–89; Zaret, *Origins of Democratic Culture*; Achinstein, *Milton and the Revolutionary Reader*, 27–70.

37 Hughes, *Gangraena*; Raymond, *The Newspaper*; Raymond, *Pamphlets*; Zaret, *Origins*; Jason Peacey, *Politicians and Pamphleteers: Propaganda during the English Civil Wars and Interregnum* (Aldershot, 2004).

38 Joseph Frank, *The Beginnings of the English Newspaper* (Cambridge MA, 1961); Joad Raymond, *The Invention of the Newspaper* (Oxford, 1996); Smith, *Literature and Revolution*, 21–92; Zaret, *Origins*; Bellany, *Politics of Court Scandal*, 261–78. On theological dispute compare the account given of the pre-war situation in Peter Lake and David Como, '"Orthodoxy" and its discontents', *Journal of British Studies* 39:1 (2000), 35–70, with the situation described in Hughes, *Gangraena*.

39 Steve Pincus, *Protestantism and Patriotism: Ideologies and the Making of English Foreign Policy, 1650–1668* (Cambridge, 1996).

40 For instance, Kate Peters's account *Print Culture and the early Quakers* (Cambridge, 2005) shows a movement learning the rules of this new game with lightning speed, compressing the developments and lessons of the previous century or so into a few years.

41 Michael Braddick, *Parliamentary Taxation in Seventeenth Century England* (Woodbridge, 1994), 297–8.

42 See Paul Slack, 'Government and information in seventeenth-century England', *Past*

and Present 184:1 (2004), 65–6, for a defence of the use of the term 'political economy' in the period.

43 Braddick, *Parliamentary Taxation in Seventeenth Century England*; Braddick, *The Nerves of State* (Manchester, 1996); James Scott Wheeler, *The Making of a World Power* (Stroud, 1999); Steven Pincus, 'From holy cause to economic interest', in Alan Houston and Steve Pincus (eds), *A Nation Transformed* (Cambridge, 2001), 272–98.

44 C. G. A. Clay, *Economic Expansion and Social Change* I (Cambridge, 1984), 165; John Langton, 'Urban growth and economic change: from the late seventeenth century to 1841', in Peter Clark (ed.), *The Cambridge Urban History of England* II, *1540–1840* (Cambridge, 2000), 462. This is not far from William Petty's estimate of 33 per cent: William Petty, 'Essay about Analysis of Property', Temp. James II, British Library, Additional Mss 72866, fol. 54r.

45 Clay, *Economic Expansion* I, 165, II, 102; Carole Shammas, *The Pre-industrial Consumer in England and America* (Oxford, 1990), 28.

46 Pincus, 'Coffee houses'; Cowan, 'Mr Spectator'.

47 This clearly shown by Mark Knights, *Representation and Misrepresentation in later Stuart Britain* (Oxford, 2005), 16; Knights, *Politics and Opinion in Crisis, 1679–1681* (Cambridge, 1994), Part 2, which demonstrates that petitioning and addressing had become highly competitive modes of propaganda dissemination; Pincus, *Protestantism and Patriotism*, 199–268, 276–318; John Miller, *After the Civil Wars* (Harlow, 2000).

48 Tim Harris, *London Crowds in the Reign of Charles II* (Cambridge, 1987); Knights, *Politics and Opinion*; Susan J. Owen, *Restoration Theatre and Crisis* (Oxford, 1996); Philip Harth, *Pen for a Party* (Princeton NJ, 1993).

49 Martin Dzelzainis and Annable Patterson (eds), *The Prose Works of Andrew Marvell* (2 vols, New Haven CT and London, 2003) I, 22–33. We owe this reference to Nigel Smith.

50 John R. Western, *Monarchy and Revolution* (Basingstoke, 1985).

51 The extent and power of James's absolutist regime are discussed more fully in Steven Pincus, *The First Modern Revolution* (New Haven CT, forthcoming).

52 See, for example, the similarities between the strategies deployed by Louis XIV – detailed by Peter Burke, *The Fabrication of Louis XIV* (New Haven CT, 1992) – and those used by James II's chief publicist, Henry Care, explored by Lois Schwoerer, *The Ingenious Mr Henry Care* (Baltimore MD, 2001).

53 Steve Pincus, 'The European Catholic context of the Revolution of 1688–1689', in Allan MacInnes and Arthur Williamson (eds), *Shaping the Stuart World* (Leiden, 2005), 79–114; Pincus, *First Modern Revolution*. This view is at odds with currently conventional views of James II's rule, which are largely based on the scholarship of John Miller, *James II: a Study in Kingship* (Hove, 1977).

54 For the emergence of these views, see Robert Brenner, *Merchants and Revolution* (Princeton NJ, 1993). For the political consequences of these divisions, see Gary De Krey, *A Fractured Society* (Oxford, 1985); and Bruce Carruthers, *City of Capital: Politics and Markets in the English Financial Revolution* (Princeton NJ, 1996); Steven Pincus, 'Whigs, political economy, and the Revolution of 1688–1689', in David Womersley (ed.), *Cultures of Whiggism* (Newark DE, 2005), 62–85.

55 For one example of a political economic periodical from the 1690s, with its origins in the

1680s, see Natasha Glaisyer, 'Readers, correspondence and communities: John Hough-ton's *A Collection for Improvement in Husbandry and Trade* (1692–1703)', in Alexandra Shepard and Phil Withington (eds), *Communities in Early Modern England* (Manchester, 2000), 235–51.

56 William Letwin, *Sir Josiah Child: Merchant Economist* (Cambridge MA, 1959), 22; W. J. Ashley, 'The Tory origin of free trade policy', *Quarterly Journal of Economics* 11:4 (1897), 353; K. G. Davies, *The Royal African Company* (London, 1957), 103–29; K. N. Chaudhuri, *The Trading World of Asia and the English East India Company, 1660–1760* (Cambridge, 1978), 116; Tim Keirn, 'Monopoly, economic thought, and the Royal African Company', in John Brewer and Susan Staves (eds), *Early Modern Conceptions of Property* (New York, 1996), 427–66; D. W. Jones, *War and Economy in the Age of William III and Marlbor-ough* (Oxford, 1988), 12–13, 296–301; Douglass North and Barry Weingast, 'Constitutions and commitment: the evolution of institutions governing public choice in seventeenth century England', *Journal of Economic History* 49:4 (1989), 803–32.

57 Daniel Szechi, *The Jacobites: Britain and Europe, 1688–1788* (Manchester, 1993); Paul Monod, *Jacobitism and the English People, 1688–1788* (Cambridge, 1989); Eveline Cruick-shanks, *The Glorious Revolution* (New York, 2000); Paul Hopkins, *Glencoe and the End of the Highland War* (Edinburgh, 1986). In the interim the continued survival of the post-revolutionary public sphere had to be ensured by occasional coercive state action. Even then, the extent of Jacobitism frustrated the episodic attempts of the post-revolution state to silence its political enemies.

58 Peter Lake, 'Anti-popery: the structure of a prejudice', in Richard Cust and Ann Hughes (eds), *Conflict in Early Stuart England* (London, 1989), 72–106.

59 Pincus, '"Coffee politicians does create"'; Knights, *Representation and Misrepresentation*, Part 2. Also see Rachel Weil's chapter in this volume.

60 J. H. M. Salmon, *Society in Crisis: France in the Sixteenth Century* (New York, 1975); Mack Holt, *The French Wars of Religion, 1562–1629* (Cambridge, 1995).

61 We are not meaning to suggest that France witnessed public controversy and debate only during these two episodes. See, for example, the lively discussion in Jeffrey Sawyer, *Printed Poison* (Berkeley CA, 1990).

62 Orest Ranum, *The Fronde: a French Revolution* (New York, 1993).

63 We are aware that French historiography, like its English counterpart, has had its revi-sionist moment. However, we have been persuaded by the more recent literature on the powers of the crown: Fanny Cosandey and Robert Descimon, *L'Absolutisme en France* (Paris, 2002); Marie-Laure Legay, *Les Etats Provinciaux dans la construction de l'Etat moderne* (Geneva, 2001); Julia Adams, *The Familial State* (Ithaca NY, 2005).

64 Jonathan Israel, *The Dutch Republic* (Oxford, 1995); Jan De Vries, *Nederland, 1500–1815* (Amsterdam, 1995).

65 We are arguing that the English case is best understood in a European context. We are emphatically not telling a British story. Developments in Ireland and Scotland deserve their own narratives using the terms and concepts we have developed here if and when they are appropriate. Such narratives could then be juxtaposed. One study has made such comparisons: Tim Harris, *Restoration: Charles II and his Kingdoms, 1660–1685* (London, 2005). We would also argue that the comparative approach needs to be applied within the conventional narratives of English history, with crisis decades like the 1590s and the 1620 or the 1670s being compared against one another as a means to gauge the

nature and pace of change as well as to establish continuity or longer-term patterns of repetitions. See here Scott, *England's Troubles*.

66 Our dialectical approach bears strong similarities to the method deployed by Michael McKeon, *The Origins of the English Novel* (Baltimore MD, 1987), especially 1–22.

67 Jonathan Scott, *Algernon Sidney and the Restoration Crisis* (Cambridge, 1991), 6.

68 Crane Brinton, *The Anatomy of Revolution* (rev. edn, New York, 1965), 19. Brinton originally made this claim in 1938.

69 Polemical texts in our period did not remain narrowly in one media form or another. Much recent work shows texts moving freely between printed and non-printed media, from the pamphlet or printed ballad, into petitions, oral tradition, or crowd behaviour, and back again. See, for instance, Harris, *London Crowds*; Zaret, *Origins*; Hughes, *Gangraena*; Adam Fox, *Oral and Literate Culture in England, 1500–1700* (Oxford, 2000). An awareness of these movements provides us with a broader context in which to situate printed materials. In our usage the concept of the public sphere, as opposed to the conventionally deployed dichotomy of politics and society, allows us to capture fully the impact of the early modern polemical text in its various forms.

70 For example, see Thomas Cogswell, *The Blessed Revolution: English Politics and the Coming of War, 1621–1624* (Cambridge, 1989); Bellany, *The Politics of Court Scandal*; Peacey, *Politicians and Pamphleteers*; Harris, *London Crowds*; Knights, *Politics and Opinion*.

71 Our complaint here runs parallel to Keith Wrightson's concern about the direction of the new social history in 'The enclosure of English social history', in Adrian Wilson (ed.), *Rethinking Social History* (Manchester, 1993), 59–77.

72 For instance, forthcoming work by both Susan Whyman and Lindsay O'Neill on the postal system and letter writing in early modern England will illuminate a vital element of English infrastructure. Here developments in the earlier period provided a crucial underpinning for the later burgeoning markets and more highly developed infrastructure for the distribution of news and cheap print. See Craig Muldrew, *An Economy of Obligation* (Basingstoke, 1998); Tessa Watt, *Cheap Print and Popular Piety* (Cambridge, 1991); Margaret Spufford, *The Great Reclothing of Rural England* (London, 1984); Spufford, *Small Books and Pleasant Histories* (Athens GA, 1982). For the role played by communication in the public sphere in another national context, see Richard John, *Spreading the News: the American Postal System from Franklin to Morse* (Cambridge MA, 1995).

73 In some ways we are filling out the account first advanced by Lawrence Stone in 'The results of the English Revolutions of the Seventeenth Century', in J. G. A. Pocock (ed.), *Three British Revolutions* (Princeton NJ, 1980), 23–108.

74 Pincus, *First Modern Revolution*, epilogue.

75 Nigel Smith is describing exactly this phenomenon when he highlights the emergences of new literary genres between 1640 and 1660: *Literature and Revolution*.

76 Susan Whyman, *Sociability and Power in late Stuart England* (Oxford, 1999).

77 The prophesyings of the Elizabethan church were suppressed because they allegedly provoked popular debate and therefore disorder. David Como's account of the Grindletonians locates the growth of this sect in a remote jurisdictionally complex part of the Pennines connected directly with London through cloth trade routes cloth trade and the personal networks of the godly: David Como, *Blown by the Spirit* (Stanford CA, 2004), chapter 8. Patrick Collinson's remarks on the Protestant town as a centre for socia-

bility and communication in *Birthpangs of Protestant England* are also suggestive on this subject.

78 Peter Borsay, *The English Urban Renaissance* (Oxford, 1989).

79 Ian Watt, *The Rise of the Novel* (Berkeley CA, 1957); J. Paul Hunter, *Before Novels* (New York, 1990); McKeon, *The Origins of the English Novel*.

80 John Brewer, *Party Ideology and Popular Politics at the Accession of George III* (Cambridge, 1976).

81 See Knights, *Representation and Misrepresentation*; Rachel Weil, '"If I did say so, I lyed": Elizabeth Cellier and the construction of credibility in the Popish Plot crisis', in Susan Amussen and Mark Kishlansky (eds), *Political Culture and Cultural Politics in Early Modern England* (Manchester, 1995), 189–209.

82 See Rachel Weil, 'The politics of legitimacy: women and the warming pan', in Lois Schwoerer (ed.), *The Revolution of 1688–1689* (Cambridge, 1992), 65–82.

83 Habermas, *Structural Transformation*, 14–20, 57–8, 144.

84 Pincus, Chapter 9 of the present volume; Pincus, *First Modern Revolution*.

85 John Brewer, *The Sinews of Power* (New York, 1988); Michael Braddick, *State Formation in Early Modern England, c. 1550–1700* (Cambridge, 2000).

86 Steve Pincus, 'From butterboxes to wooden shoes: the shift in English popular sentiment from anti-Dutch to anti-French in the 1670s', *Historical Journal* 38 (1995), 333–61; Pincus, 'The English debate over universal monarchy', in John Robertson (ed.), *A Union for Empire* (Cambridge, 1995), 37–62; Pincus, '"To protect English liberties": the English nationalist revolution, 1688–1689', in Tony Claydon and Ian McBride (eds), *Protestantism and National Identity: Britain and Ireland c. 1650–c. 1850* (Cambridge, 1998), 75–104.

Chapter 2

The Pilgrimage of Grace and the public sphere?

Ethan H. Shagan

I

In November 1536 the ambitious young humanist Richard Morison penned a tract against the Pilgrimage of Grace entitled *A Remedy for Sedition*. As part of his explanation for the wave of disloyalty that had swept across northern England, Morison gave voice to the commonplace assumption of early modern intellectuals that the common people had no business even discussing matters of state. Using the standard metaphor of the commonwealth as a political body with the commons as its feet, Morison condemned as monstrous any body in which 'the heels make unlawful requests and very mad petitions' to the head. Displaying his considerable classical learning, he cited Demosthenes's story of the city of Locri, where anyone who suggested changing the law came to dispute the matter 'with a cord around his neck'; if he could not convince the magistrates of his opinion, he was 'forthwith trussed up'. Most forcefully, Morison paraphrased Plato's plea for the exclusion of the majority from the business of government: 'No man shall dispute any law in the presence of youth or common people, that hath little judgement in such things. It is no part of the people's play to discuss acts made in parliament.'[1]

In recent years, Morison's view of sixteenth-century politics as the sheltered domain of the governing elite has acquired an influential ally in Jürgen Habermas, whose treatise *The Structural Transformation of the Public Sphere* has taken Anglo-American intellectuals by storm since its belated translation in 1989.[2] Habermas described the 'public sphere' as that zone of social interaction where private persons conduct 'rational-critical debate' and thereby constitute a 'public' that can present its beliefs as the freely constituted will of the populace. Habermas argued that no 'public sphere' existed in Europe before the seventeenth century. 'Publicness' in the preceding 'feudal' system, he suggested, consisted only of the display of power for an audience without that audience in any sense constituting a 'public' that might critically respond:

'As long as the prince and the estates of his realm "were" the country and not just its representatives, they could represent it in a specific sense. They represented their lordship not for but "before" the people.'[3] On this view, a true 'public sphere' developed only in the seventeenth and eighteenth centuries as a result of new developments in European (and particularly British) culture, most importantly the development of 'the press'. Habermas suggested that earlier media that 'indiscriminately spread the news of religious wars, campaigns against the Turks, and papal decrees as well as news of rains of blood and fire', especially news sheets that were meant to be 'declaimed or sung' rather than simply read, were not truly constitutive of a 'public sphere' since they 'permitted merely passive acceptance incapable of independent interpretation'.[4]

Both Morison and Habermas constructed their arguments within well defined philosophical systems – one classical and patriarchal, the other Kantian and liberal – and both were clearly describing ideal types. Morison, furthermore, was a propagandist, while Habermas was intervening in post-war debates over the failures of German civil society. It therefore might seem perverse to criticize the two writers on grounds of historical inaccuracy, yet in Habermas's case it has become something of a cottage industry, or at least a parlour game, for historians to do just that, revising to earlier and earlier dates the point at which a 'public sphere' allegedly emerged. This revisionism is often practised with little understanding of Habermas's Kantian categories or engagement with his ideal vision of civil society; historians simply point to the vast numbers of pamphlets published in any given period (especially the civil wars of the 1640s) and argue that the production and reception of those pamphlets constituted a 'public sphere', Q.E.D. Never mind that Habermas believed that, without a space free from domination, individuals could not transcend their role as private persons and contribute to a 'public'.[5] Never mind that Habermas's 'public sphere' was by definition entirely separate from state authority. Never mind that Habermas's concept of the 'public sphere' presupposed the primacy of the public good. Wherever there was political disputation among the people, in other words wherever Morison's elitist presuppositions were self-evidently incorrect, there (we are told) was the 'public sphere'.

This chapter no doubt seems poised to topple from the same precipice. By asking if we can locate a 'public sphere' in the Pilgrimage of Grace, a popular rebellion that occurred a century and a half before the rise of the coffee house or the salon, it seems inevitable to bowdlerize Habermas's categories and wreak havoc with his philosophical assumptions. Surely political communication in the Pilgrimage of Grace was predicated on the force of arms, for instance, so it must have fallen far short of the 'rational-critical' ideal. Surely modes of argument employed by the rebels were punishable by death and thus hardly free from domination. Surely the Tudor state at several points forcibly injected its own opinions into popular debates, rendering those debates decidedly 'unpublic' in the Habermasian model.

Rather than criticizing or revising Habermas, then, I want to suggest that we can profitably study the same issues that interested Habermas (e.g. political communication, the universalizing of politics, and the space of civil society) *without* reference to his Kantian categories or teleological narrative. I want to examine the spaces for political communication that were available in the sixteenth century without imagining them as incomplete bourgeois 'public spheres' in the process of rising. Within this approach, however, I want to appropriate philosophical terms-of-art like 'public sphere' and 'civil society', reclaiming them from an academic discourse that has made it difficult or impossible to describe issues of socio-political interaction outside a Habermasian framework. I use these terms (in inverted commas, both literally and figuratively) not as mere place-holders but to make a crucial point: while philosophers use terms to define and delineate ideals, historians use them to comprehend and taxonomize the decidedly non-ideal behaviour of real human beings. In other words, I want to argue that because in practice there never was an ideal Habermasian public sphere, it is not a useful exercise for historians to ask when one first emerged. However much neo-Kantian philosophers are enamoured of the literary salon and the printed newspaper as agents of 'rational-critical' debate, in reality all social situations are laden with inequalities of power and distortions of communicative transparency.[6] It is therefore the historian's task not to search for the moment at which perfect 'rationality' or 'publicness' was achieved but rather to ask how different sorts of communication in different settings acted as infrastructures for politics, always channelling and distorting messages but doing so in interesting and productive ways.[7]

This chapter is a preliminary attempt to do just that. By looking at political communication in the sixteenth century and its ability to foster spaces analogous to 'civil society', we can gain new insights into both the practical functioning of politics and the theoretical ways in which English subjects imagined their own competence to comment 'publicly' on affairs of state. By examining these subjects during the political emergency of the Pilgrimage of Grace, we can see aspects of contemporary opinion formation and the assumptions behind them, usually hidden from our sources, rising briefly to the surface. I will suggest from this evidence that there were two spheres of 'public' debate in Tudor politics, sometimes antagonistic to one another and sometimes reinforcing, each energized by the same overarching phenomenon: the Reformation. The elaborate dance of these two 'public spheres', one legitimated by traditional ideals of good government and the commonwealth, the other legitimated by new ideals of scripturalism and the priesthood of all believers, would shape the engagement of English people with their government for more than a century.

II

Any discussion of 'public' politics and 'civil society' in Tudor England must begin with notions of legitimation. If Richard Morison and his elite contemporaries believed that 'it is no part of the people's play to discuss acts made in parliament', how and why did so many people come to do just that in 1536–37?

The Pilgrims of Grace claimed competence to comment upon and intervene in national politics through the ideology of the commonwealth. Michael Bush has shown the importance of the 'society of orders' in the rebels' self-representation, taking advantage of a widely available belief system in which the 'commonwealth', which literally denoted the collective prosperity of the nation, could be guarded only when commons, gentlemen, priests, nobles, and crown all co-operated for the common good. By insisting that gentlemen and priests actively participate in their uprising, then, the commons constructed the Pilgrimage as a rising of the estates of the realm against a central government that had been corrupted and thus could no longer fulfil its divinely mandated role in maintaining social harmony. The rebellion thus metaphorically recreated a properly functioning society of orders that could be put up as a mirror to the ills of the realm. As Bush put it, 'With the clergy and gentlemen unable to curb the government's tyrannical and heretical ways, it was now up to the commons to rise to the occasion'. Similarly, elite rebels, by playing 'popularity' politics and describing themselves as fulfilling their proper patriarchal role as 'good lords' and petitioners on behalf of the commonalty, rationalized their own treason on the grounds of 'public' interest.[8]

But how could the voice of 'the commons' be convincingly constituted as a political actor when no *individual* commoner could claim competence in political affairs? To answer this conundrum, the Pilgrims constructed their rebellion in such a way that they could claim to speak for the common or public good rather than their own self-interest, using quasi-republican techniques in their organization and decision-making processes and employing mass meetings, votes, and representative councils to construct their programme. The use of these techniques did not imply that Tudor subjects were applying classical republican ideas to their own governance, but rather that, as Patrick Collinson has shown for a slightly later period, the experience of community co-operation and public dispute resolution in local life provided the English commonalty with a remarkably participatory political model that they could import into national politics when the occasion arose.[9]

From the initial outbreak of violence in Lincolnshire, rebel leaders felt obliged to have their decisions ratified by the commonalty. When the Lincolnshire gentlemen finished drawing up their articles of grievance, for instance, according to Nicholas Leach, parson of Byrchforde, the following scene occurred:

At length they [the gentlemen] brought forth certain articles touching diverse of their griefs, whereof one was that the king's highness should remit the subsidy and another article was that his grace should let the abbeys stand and diverse other articles ... which articles George Staines openly in the field in presence of diverse of the said gentlemen with a loud voice did proclaim. And the sheriff and he said to the commons, 'Masters, ye see that in all the time we have been absent from you we have not been idle. How like you these articles? If they please you say yea, if not ye shall have them amended.' And then the commons held up their hands with a loud voice, saying, 'We like them very well.'[10]

Many similar examples can be found of rebel leaders publicly requesting the support of the commons and accepting, at least rhetorically, the commons' capacity to speak for the 'commonwealth'. Francis Bigod began his rebellion, for instance, by standing upon a 'hillock' and haranguing the multitudes. Bigod cried out at the end of his speech, 'If ye will take my part in this and defend it, I will not fail you so long as I live, to the uttermost of my power. And who will so do, assure me by your hands and hold them up.' The response to this call for support was that 'they with that held up their hands with a great shout and said whosoever would not so do, strike off his head'.[11] On 9 January 1537 the gentleman Robert Aske gathered the inhabitants of Beverley to explain why they should put down their arms and end their rebellion. Remarkably, Aske actually accepted questions from the audience after his address, resulting in his being caught off guard by the radical John Hallom, who undermined the proceedings with frightening new information about renewed royal attempts to gather taxes.[12] When the rebels arrested a man called Robert Wetlay in January 1537 on suspicion of carrying the king's letters to northern gentlemen, they 'brought him to Cockermouth into the market, where did assemble all the whole country' to decide what should become of him.[13] When messengers from Lincolnshire arrived at Westwood Green in Yorkshire to read a letter to the assembled host, the gentleman Sir Ralph Ellerkar suggested that it be vetted privately 'to four or five apart' who could then 'amend' its contents before reading it aloud; the messengers refused and instead read the letter openly to the commons.[14]

If too much of this public participation appears to be merely an obligatory cry of assent rather than active opinion formation, it should be remembered that the rebels themselves were far from united over the details of their grievances, and in practice a wide variety of competing proposals were canvassed. While some rebels demanded the restoration of all dissolved monasteries, for instance, others demanded in highly equivocal fashion 'all the houses of religion that are suppressed to be restored again except such houses as the king hath suppressed for his pleasure only', while Francis Bigod demanded that 'the money of the suppressed abbeys should feed the poor soldiers that were not able to bear their own charges'.[15] While some rebels demanded the abolition of clerical taxes instituted by the Act of First Fruits and Tenths, Robert Aske distinguished between first fruits, which he called 'a decay to all religion', and clerical tenths, which he said could 'be borne well enough'.[16] While some rebels wanted to abolish the feudal payments known as gressums, others suggested that gressums become fixed payments equal to rents, while the Pontefract articles cautiously demanded that gressums become fixed payments of no more than double rents.[17] There was also significant class tension within the Pilgrim ranks, and as Michael Bush has shown, regardless of the rhetoric of the 'society of orders' that permeated the rebellion, in practice the commons were often loath to relinquish control to their social superiors. At Penrith, for instance, a gentlemen called Anthony Hutton was briefly a rebel captain but was replaced by Robert Mownsey because, as he himself put it, 'the commons would have no gentlemen to be their captains'.[18] Throughout the rebellion, then, issues of concern to the rebels were not merely pronounced but constantly canvassed, refined, and debated.[19]

The methods through which the rebels constituted their meetings and councils, furthermore, were highly participatory, reflecting an ethos of open debate and participation that characterized local government. A partial list of delegates to the Pontefract council, for instance, included not only 'worshipful men' but also eight commoners from Cumberland, six commoners from Kendal and Lonsdale, three yeomen from Cartmel, six commoners from the city of York, six commoners from Ainsty, and so on; many of these 'commoners', moreover, were 'chosen by election'.[20] The rebel council at York, convened on 21 November 1536 to consider information brought from London by Ralph Ellerkar and Robert Bowes, boasted over 800 delegates.[21] Even after the main body of the Pilgrimage collapsed those who tried to re-spark the rebellion employed the same conciliar techniques. A woolman of Kendal called John Nycholson, for instance, received an anonymous bill in January 1537 telling parishioners 'that two [persons] of the same parish should meet at Richmond for a council to be had there on the next Monday after, at their peril'.[22] Indeed, the rebels were so consistent in their attachment to popular representation that some opponents of the Pilgrimage singled out the practice for ridicule. The evangelical Yorkshire gentleman Wilfrid Holme, for instance, mocked the democratic aspect of the rebel delegation sent to meet the duke of Norfolk at Doncaster:

> To this [summons] the commons agreed universal,
> And so the day was set at Doncaster to meet,
> Whereunto the commons appointed men several,
> By the baronage's advise whom they thought discrete,
> Thus they appointed their number whole complete.[23]

The most remarkable 'public' representation of the rebels' competence to comment on affairs of state was the great rebel council that began at Pontefract on 2 December 1536. While one might expect this council to have been little more than a rubber stamp for Aske, Darcy, and other rebel leaders, this was far from the case. In fact, the very essence of the Pontefract council was that it was consciously performed as a *parliament*, representing the combined will of the estates of the realm before the king in quasi-legal fashion. Aske, for instance, described the council as a place where 'the lords, knights and esquires and the commons there appointed should meet ... to the intent to decide to the particulars of the articles'.[24] That the meeting really did give full ear to all the grievances brought by the delegates is attested by the remarkable shopping list of complaints that was eventually ratified, which included such special pleadings as complaints against the heresies of John Oecolampadius, demands that 'the statutes of handguns and crossbows' be repealed, and complaints 'against escheators for finding of false office and extortious fees'.[25] Once grievances were on the table, moreover, the council approved them by parliamentary process: 'After the said articles [were] read and agreed upon amongst the lords, knights, and gentlemen, on every article agreed upon was set on the head "fiat". And after[wards] the said articles were read and declared to the commons, who wholly condescended to every article. And in like manner the said Aske received the opinion of the clergy.'[26] The remarkable openness of these proceedings was stated most succinctly by a surprised Marmaduke Neville: 'As touching a council, I never knew none which was privy, but after most open sort, and in those were as many gentlemen and commoners as might be in the places where they sat.'[27]

The extent of conscious parliamentary symbolism at Pontefract can be seen most fully in the fact that from 4–5 December, alongside the larger rebel council, a 'convocation' of divines met in Pontefract Priory to debate a series of spiritual questions put to them by Robert Aske.[28] The members of this convocation were mostly the same abbots, chancellors, and archdeacons who would have sat in a proper convocation of the province of York; in addition, the rebellion's leaders solicited written theological advice from a number of northern divines who could not attend the proceedings. Convocations were ordinarily clerical appendages to *parliaments*, and significantly, it was a source of much anger in the north that the Ten Articles of 1536 had not been put before a northern convocation. The convocation at Pontefract was thus in an important sense a quasi-legal attempt to convene a legitimate body of divines to refute Reformation policies, an indigenously created northern convocation to replace the ordinary northern convocation whose authority the government had ignored. Concomitantly, the very existence of a rebel convocation was an explicit statement that the gathering of commons, gentlemen, and lords at Pontefract was in essence a parliament, convened by the emergency powers of the estates of the realm.

This remarkable convening of a pseudo-parliament was the height of the rebels' attempts to represent their own legitimacy and was the epitome of the creation of something very much like a 'public sphere' in northern England in the autumn of 1536. Large numbers of individuals, having heard about alleged royal and ministerial abuses from the media available to them, had in 1536 debated the meaning of those abuses and staged an elaborate protest. Later, those private individuals sent their representatives to quasi-legal councils, armed with specific instructions as to local grievances. These rebel councils systematically debated the various grievances put to them and then, in the conscious form of a parliament, put their decisions to the king for his assent, trusting that both their moral authority as representatives of the estates of the realm and the brute force that underlay their existence would force a fundamental change in government policy.

Clearly we can see here a sphere of private individuals constituting a 'public' through their politicization and debate over policy, energized by a set of cultural assumptions that granted people outside the institutions of government a surprising competence to construct the 'common' good. Of course, this was not a Habermasian 'public', since it occurred under threat of government reprisal, and Habermas argued that without a space free from domination individuals cannot transcend their role as private persons. Yet given the *weakness* of the Tudor government, and given the prominence of notions like the 'commonwealth' that were only partially embedded in the institutions of the state, in the sixteenth century spaces akin to 'publicness' could sometimes coalesce despite official opposition. Ordinarily, the Tudor government and its subjects engaged in a constant series of negotiations over the boundaries of acceptable illegality, with law enforcement almost entirely dependent upon local informants and the willingness of local leaders to co-operate with the royal government. In times of extreme unrest like the Pilgrimage of Grace, when the hegemonic imperatives of community self-censorship collapsed under the weight of popular disaffection, the willingness of ordinary people to debate public policy far outstripped the ability of the state to repress that debate. Social spheres could thus be formed where subjects debated the details of their grievances and then performed those grievances before both the government and their neighbours in the ritualized language of social protest.[29]

III

If notions of 'commonwealth' enabled the Pilgrims of Grace to claim a voice in 'public' affairs in 1536, it remains to be seen what form of legitimation enabled Richard Morison, despite his claim that 'it is no part of the people's play to discuss acts made in parliament', to propagate his defences of royal policy through the promiscuous and inherently open-ended medium of English-language print. In other words, in what sort of spaces did *loyalism* operate, and could that loyalism become sufficiently separate from the voice of the state to constitute its own 'public' discourse on politics?

Clearly in Morison's case legitimation was over-determined, since his writings were in fact authorized, encouraged, and perhaps even commissioned by the government. Yet we must not imagine Morison's anti-Pilgrimage tracts as mere government productions. In the autumn of 1536 the king wrote several replies to the rebels that between them constituted an 'official' position on the Pilgrimage.[30] Remarkably, despite the overtly spiritual nature of the rebels' grievances, these official replies contained virtually no discussion of the royal supremacy over the church, the dangers of papistry, the role of priests and monks in the rebellion, or any other overtly religious issues. The king instead painted the rebellion as a mere *jacquerie* perpetrated by the 'rude commons', a sub-ideological manifestation of popular ignorance wholly divorced from 'public opinion'. Not surprisingly, however, the regime found itself dependent upon religious reformers to provide a reliable bulwark against what it knew perfectly well was religiously motivated opposition, and the king grudgingly allowed people like Morison, with views of the Pilgrimage considerably different from the 'official' view, to present their opinions 'publicly' so long as they unambiguously condemned the rebellion.

Thus in 'public' commentaries on the rebellion like Morison's we can locate an unofficial legitimation for 'public' engagement: the same evangelical, Word-centred critique of the Catholic church (and the government's role in maintaining it) that had had its shaky beginnings in England in the writings of Simon Fish and William Tyndale. The participants in this evangelical 'public' believed that their opinions were legitimate in the highest possible sense, reflecting the divine will, while their claim to competence in affairs of state was grounded in scripture: even the weakest human being could be an appropriate vessel for the Holy Spirit, and the Bible was filled with examples of poor men and women criticizing prelates and princes. Partakers of this intellectual system had argued since the break with Rome that all religious 'conservatism' was by definition infected with popery, since its theological errors had been introduced by the bishop of Rome precisely to keep people ignorant of Christ's Gospel and True Religion. Now suddenly with the Pilgrimage of Grace the connections between conservatism, popery, and treason were manifest, and evangelicals moved quickly to legitimize their position. While technically no more licit in the months after the Pilgrimage of Grace than it had been in the months before, then, evangelical rhetoric suddenly became a recognizable part of a legitimate political discourse, a way of talking about events in the north that, because of its emphasis on loyalism, was difficult to oppose. As such, while evangelical rhetoric did not necessarily change, the sphere in which it operated shifted significantly, becoming markedly more 'public' as it was interjected into political debates over the meaning of rebellion.

There is no better place to observe this transformation than in the work of Richard Morison himself, a Cromwellian protégé and future Marian exile who wrote two responses to the 1536 revolts: *A Lamentation in which is Showed what Ruin and Destruction cometh of Seditious Rebellion* and *A Remedy for Sedition wherein are contained Many Things concerning the True and Loyal Obeisance that Commons owe unto their Prince and Sovereign Lord the King.* Both have been seen by historians as 'official' propaganda productions, and indeed in some senses they were: they were written on instructions from Cromwell, they were printed by the royal printer, and they may even have been read by the king himself prior to publication.[31] Yet, unlike the writings attributed to the king, Morison's tracts show clear evangelical leanings. While they remained within the bounds of official religious policy, the two tracts constructed the rebellion in terms reminiscent of the evangelical polemic that had flowed from English controversialist pens in the previous decade. Thus while Henry VIII may have found nothing particular in these pamphlets to criticize, he may not have noticed that his own efforts to cast the rebels as ignorant and greedy peasants were substantially undermined by Morison's obsessive references to corrupt monks and papists.

The *Lamentation*, written hastily in response to the Lincolnshire revolt before the north had risen, was built around a series of entirely standard condemnations of rebellion. The pamphlet was in fact an extended gloss on the question 'What folly, what madness is this to make an hole in the ship that thou sailest in?' with proof texts ranging from the Old Testament to Ovid.[32] Yet, rather than focusing on ignorant peasants, Morison wrote that *monks* were 'the ringleaders of these traitorous rebels' because 'their pope, their puppet, their idol, their Roman god will not [get] out of their hearts'.[33] In a striking passage, he mocked the use of the term 'spirituality' to describe monks who so willingly disobeyed their divinely sanctioned sovereign:

> So indeed these spiritual traitors that are in harness against their country call themselves, who have none other than their father the devil hath inspired unto them. If these be spiritual, put a cowl on Cataline's back, is not he then a religious monk and a good spiritual man? If these be religious and spiritual men who do all they can to destroy both the laws of God and of man to bring this realm in desolation, why may not Jack Cade, Jack Straw, Will Wawe, Wat Tyler, Jack Shepherd, Tom Miller, and Hob Carter – a barber sent for – be shorn into religion? If they be spiritual that consume the day either in idleness or in another thing worse than that, sowing seed in other men's furrows, whom shall we call carnal?

This last reference to monastic homosexuality was further pursued by Morison, who cited ecclesiastical visitations to show 'how young novices may stand instead of young wives'.[34] He thus argued that monks should be grateful that they suffered no worse punishment than the dissolution of their monasteries, since 'the civil law putteth such not out of their house but with the sword putteth them to death'.[35] At the end of the pamphlet Morison took a parting shot at clerics who were lukewarm on the royal supremacy: 'Sorry I must needs be to see monks, friars, and priests who so long stood doubting whether they might acknowledge our sovereign lord the king to be their head, so without any staggering to have made a cobbler their head'.[36]

Similar rhetoric continued in Morison's much longer tract, the *Remedy for Sedition*. Morison argued that the cause of the rebels' treason lay not in their material condition but in their poisoned upbringing:

> Some say poverty is the cause that men come to be thieves, murderers, rebels; but I think nothing so. For I know diverse realms where poverty reigneth much more than in England, yet rebels there be none. The root is lower; dig deeper, ye may perchance find it. Education, evil education, is a great cause of these and all other mischiefs that grow in a commonwealth.[37]

By 'evil education' Morison meant not the conventional meaning of the term but rather its revised meaning within the lexicon of evangelical Protestantism, where a good education referred to the Gospel and an evil education referred to popery. He explained his terms in more detail later in the tract:

> If the nobles be evil taught in points concerning religion, as if they be popish (to put one example for many), how can their servants choose but be so too? How can their tenants, who must have their lord's favor, be of another religion than their lord is? How can they agree with their neighbors if they both be not of one faith and one belief? The king's grace shall never have true subjects that do not believe as his grace doth. For how can they love him (as they should do) who, being in error themselves, in darkness and ignorancy, suppose his grace to be in a wrong faith?[38]

In short, Morison blamed the rebellion on the popish education of the common people and the consequent lack of godly preaching and teaching; as Morison put it in response to traditionalist complaints about the potential radicalism of evangelical sermons, 'Preaching of the Gospel is not the cause of sedition, but rather the lack of preaching of it.'[39] Morison's seemingly unimpeachable critiques of 'popular rebellion', in other words, were grounded in highly controversial critiques of the religious practices of the northern nobility and clergy, and these critiques were legitimated not merely by Morison's semi-official role as a voice for the government but by his unofficial role as a 'voice in the wilderness' against popery in defence of True Religion.

This broader mode of legitimation could be brought to bear even without explicit permission from the government, and at least one evangelical subject penned his own explanation for the Pilgrimage. Wilfrid Holme completed his massive evangelical poem, *The Fall and Evill Success of Rebellion*, in July 1537.[40] This frightfully written epic of more than sixty pages is a dialogue between the author and the rhetorical figure of Anglia, who asks Holme to recount for her the story of the rebellion. Whereas Morison took time to reach the conclusion that papists were responsible for the rebellion, Holme began with that assumption; the first lines of the section entitled 'The Insurrection' are 'Then briefly I declared how the old Leviathan/Whispered with the papists, this region to divide.'[41] Holme's anti-monasticism was also easily worthy of Morison's; he called monastic life 'a vile abomination', condemning the hypocrisy of those whose pretence to holiness only 'cloaks their deeds libidinous and incest fornication'.[42]

These reformist statements were only a prelude, however, to blatantly evangelical rhetoric. When writing of Christian faith, for instance, Holme defended supralapsarian predestination: 'But this faith hath no man but by inspiration/Though they can speak Hebrew, Greek, Latin, or Caldie/For they are born of God, and elect in creation/And trust not to their works like to a Pharisee.'[43] Of priests he wrote, 'They be free to wed or not, it is at their liberty,' since 'it is better to wed than burn'. He argued that all monastic vows were abrogate, since 'their vows are like Jews' vows'.[44] He denied the infallibility of general councils, since one council had 'believed not Christ's justification/But mired it with works, the which made properly/Their council to be naught to Christ's derogation'.[45] He also argued against saints' worship, purgatory, and penance, and he defended an extremely liberal reading of the royal supremacy in which Christ gave spiritual authority directly to princes.

Most remarkably, Holme's evangelical interpretation of the rebellion was presented *as a gloss on the king's own words*. Much of the tract, especially the more radical sections, was a line-by-line explication of the king's *Answere* to the Yorkshire rebels, twisting even the most insignificant references to religion in the king's tract into a clarion call for evangelical reform. In the king's defence of the dissolution of the monasteries, for instance, he had not defended himself on theological grounds but rather invoked historical precedents like Henry V's suppression of 'above one hundred monasteries, taking the great benefit of the same to his own proper use'.[46] In Holme's tract this explanation is quoted but then expanded and glossed so that Henry VIII's dissolution becomes an ectype of Christ's expulsion of the moneylenders from the Temple in Jerusalem.[47] Similarly, in his *Answere* the king had responded to claims that he had failed in his maintenance of the church by asking what 'church' the rebels meant, thus drawing a significant distinction between the Church of Rome and the Church of England.[48] Holme glossed this royal statement with the remarkable claim that, just as the laws of the Jews were abrogate after Christ's deliverance of the new dispensation, so the physical, stone-and-mortar churches in which people worshipped were merely 'convenient', carnal representations of the true spiritual church, and that those churches might legally be confiscated or destroyed by any temporal ruler.[49] Perhaps most significantly, the king's *Answere* had responded to accusations of 'innovations' in government policy with the argument that he and his council had learned from experience over the twenty-eight years of his reign, and that any changes in law were the result of their ever-increasing understanding of how the commonwealth should best be ordered.[50] Holme used this blanket admission as an excuse for openly advocating a wide variety of evangelical innovations; after all, if the king admitted that he had been wrong in his earlier support for the pope and the monasteries, might he also admit having been wrong about clerical marriage, salvation through works, and oracular confession?[51] Holme's poem, then, was not only an explicitly evangelical interpretation of the rebellions, but it was also an attempt to recast the king's own position in a decidedly evangelical light. By refracting the king's words in this way, Holme both gave his own ideas legitimacy and took part in a recognizably 'public' debate in which the king's authority, far from being 'represented ... not for but 'before' the people', was interpreted, discussed, and used.

None of this reformist rhetoric was new to England, but what made it so important was the air of legitimacy it enjoyed in the context of a Catholic revolt. In such an environment, with the government frighteningly dependent upon religious radicals as its most zealous defenders, anyone who saw themselves as upholders of Christ's Gospel might explicitly claim competence to comment on affairs of state, so long as they defended the government's religious innovations against the 'superstitious' majority. The Suffolk priest Thomas Wylley, for instance, wrote to Cromwell in early 1537 asking for his aid because 'the most part of the priests of Suffolk will not receive me in their churches to preach, but have disdained me ever since I made a play against the pope's counsellors, "Error, Coal Clogger of Conscience and Incredulity"'. The aspiring playwright's criticisms were not limited to Rome, moreover. Wylley also informed Cromwell that he had 'made a play called "A Rude Commonalty"', presumably a response to the Pilgrimage of Grace, and that he had written (although not performed) other plays called 'The Woman on the Rock in the Fire of Faith Assigning' and 'A Purging in the True Purgatory'.[52] Here the priest was not only willing to present his interpretations of religio-political issues before a heterogeneous audience, but he was willing to implicate his parishioners in these performances by using them as actors. Plays, moreover, were an increasingly common medium for presenting radical ideas to a heterogeneous 'public'; by 1550 one conservative social critic, complaining of the common people 'discoursing of the affairs of state at their liberty', would lament that 'players play abroad in every place every lewd, seditious fellow's device, to the danger of the king and his Council'.[53]

The potential effects of these 'public' linkages between government policy, the suppression of revolt, and religious innovation can be seen in an incident from London in October 1536. In the fraught environment of a Catholic revolt, the London watchman Thomas Multon dared to express to his fellow watchmen the blatantly heretical opinions that 'holy bread and holy water was nothing worth', that 'confession is naught', and that 'Our Blessed Lady was no better than his wife'. By uttering these beliefs 'publicly' Multon exposed himself to the law's fury, but ironically it seems that he did so exactly because he believed himself to be a loyal subject rooting out hidden traitors in his midst. He had gotten into an argument with the other watchmen in which he vigorously supported the king's exclusion of a London alderman called William Hollis from the mayoralty of the city, arguing that Hollis had connections with the Lincolnshire rebels. The other watchmen not only supported Hollis but also let it be known that they were unhappy with the king's abrogation of holy days. Multon answered that 'they that do not hold with the same be traitors' and that 'half London be traitors' since only those who supported the king's religious innovations were truly loyal subjects.[54] If 'newfangled' beliefs could be glossed as upholding the safety of the king against rebellion, it seems, there was no limit to how 'publicly' they could be debated.

IV

These two legitimations of 'public' competence in affairs of state – one grounded in commonwealth ideology, the other grounded in evangelical ideals – each created spheres of social interaction where generalized notions of the 'public good' were debated and competing versions of 'public opinion' were canvassed. If we turn to the media through which these 'publics' were constructed, moreover, we find that their different legitimations and different relationships to state power dictated that political communication within them would operate very differently.

The 'public' grounded in notions of the commonwealth – in other words, the 'public' that participated in the Pilgrimage of Grace – employed a wide variety of media to convey news and information, from rumour to prophecy to symbolic public ceremony. But, most interestingly for our purposes, it also employed an arcane mode of communication that turned out to be uniquely suited to its needs: manuscript transmission. This aspect of contemporary opinion formation has not been well studied by historians, both because it has been imagined as an embryonic and ineffectual 'press' rather than as a medium of communication in its own right, and because its requirements of literacy are presumed to have made it marginal in a 'popular' rebellion. As historians like Adam Fox have taught us, however, writing provided an important interface between the English commonalty and their social superiors, and even for the illiterate the written word carried significant authority. Hearing manuscripts read was commonplace, and nearly every community had an educated minority who routinely copied texts or took dictation for a small fee and read documents aloud to their illiterate neighbours.[55] This system was perfectly suited to the spread of more bluntly ideological manuscripts when they became available. As early as 1431, for instance, Lollards posted bills in Salisbury, Oxford, Northampton, and Coventry describing their plans to disendow the church, while just before Jack Cade's rebellion in 1450 London walls were covered with bills describing the realm's ills.[56] In the Pilgrimage of Grace this mode of communication served the difficult tasks of conveying various versions of northern 'public opinion' to people outside rebel-controlled territory, and of organizing vast quantities of news and opinion into coherent statements that could serve as the bases for local debate.

From the outbreak of the Pilgrimage, posted bills were an important means of communication for the rebellion's leaders. The commons north of York, for instance, were raised partially by means of a letter nailed to church doors, written in the name of 'Chief Captain' Robert Aske, asking the people to rise to oppose heresy and the decay of the commonwealth.[57] Another bill echoed rumours of new taxes, claiming that 'no infant shall receive the blessed sacrament of baptism unless a tribute be paid to the king'.[58] After the formal structure of the Pilgrimage collapsed, moreover, there was a remarkable proliferation of bills expressing a wide variety of ideas and recommended actions. Sir Ralph Sadler reported in mid January 1537, for instance, that:

diverse bills and scrolls [were] set up on posts and church doors throughout the bishopric [of Durham] and lost and scattered abroad in the country ... and by such means it was put into the heads of the people that my lord of Norfolk came down with a great army and power to do execution and to hang and draw from Doncaster to Berwick in all places northward notwithstanding the king's pardon.[59]

One bill included a list of reasons why the treaty at Doncaster was 'but feigned policy to subdue the commoners withal', including the fact that no parliament had been held at York, the fact that Cromwell was still in the king's Council, and the belief that 'Captain Aske was at London and had great reward given to betray the commoners'.[60] A bill that defended traditional agrarian customs and advised the commons to 'stick ye together' was written largely in rhyme, ending with the cryptic endorsement: 'Maker of this letter, pray Jesu be his speed. He shall be your captain when that ye have need.'[61]

In addition to posted bills, letters could also be sent direct to interested parties, often with instructions to read the letters aloud or spread their message throughout the locality. On the second day of the rebellion in Lincolnshire, for instance, the blind parson of Sotby heard a monk at Louth Cross angrily read a letter declaring that 'the king's pleasure was that there should be but one parish church standing within six miles one from another'.[62] Lord Hussey received a letter at roughly the same time asking if he would 'aid the commonalty in their service to God, the king, and the commonwealth of this realm' and informing him that if he refused, the 'commonalty will in all haste come and seek [him] as their utter enemy'.[63] The sending of letters became such a common feature of the revolt that by 18 January 1537 Robert Aske, who by this point opposed renewed attempts at rebellion, could report to the king, 'As I am informed, the commons of one country hath posts to commons in other countries and quarters'.[64] In other words, written communication between rebels was so routine that there were standardized postal routes with extra horses so that messengers could reach their destinations quickly.

Written bills became most significant when they were copied and circulated. In the north there are numerous examples of people copying out key rebel texts such as the Pilgrims' oaths, their articles of grievance, and Robert Aske's declarations. William Talbot and the abbot of Pontefract, for instance, wrote out 'the copy of the oath that the commons swear men by, and the articles of their petition, and the articles of their convocation' and gave them to a servant of the abbey of Whalley, who delivered them to his master.[65] Richard Bowier, who according to his own testimony acted as a loyalist spy at the rebels' Pontefract conference, had no trouble obtaining written copies of 'our safe conduct, pardon, and commission, with other things made and done at Pontefract', including the acts of the rebel convocation.[66] According to Robert Aske, when the rebellion first spread from Lincolnshire to Yorkshire the commons of Marshland assembled after they 'had attained the articles of Lincolnshire', clearly a reference to the arrival of a written document.[67] Similarly, John Hallom reported that when the Lincolnshire men Guy Kyme and Thomas Dunne first brought to Beverley, Yorkshire, a list of 'the articles that they rose for in Lincolnshire', 'every man strove to have the sight or a copy of the same'.[68] In January 1537, the prior of Malton showed a copy of 'the articles given at Doncaster' to Sir Francis Bigod, who desired a copy for himself and paid the prior's servant two groats to make it for him.[69]

The most remarkable manuscript circulation, however, was in the south, where rebel leaders sent numerous documents hoping for their rapid scribal publication. The gentleman George Lumley, for instance, reported that 'he heard Robert Aske say at my lord Darcy's house called Templehurst that he had delivered or sent a copy of the oath to a gentleman of Norfolk, whose name he cannot tell, which would set, as he trowed, the matter forward in the south parts'.[70] This story may or may not be directly related to the report of the Norfolk gentleman Richard Southwell on 23 December that he had 'apprehended and taken two priests which both hath taken and given copies of the late traitorous and rebellious oaths, regests, and opinions of the late rebels of the north'.[71] There is no question that the penetration of rebel manuscripts into Norfolk was widespread. For instance, Richard Fletcher, keeper of the common gaol in Norwich, travelled briefly northwards and acquired a bill 'of all the news in the north parts'. Fletcher read the bill aloud to several merchants at the Bell in Lynn, and the keeper of the house, George Wharton, was so intrigued that he asked to have two copies made. Wharton then showed copies of the bill to a variety of persons around Lynn, including the bailey of Gaywood. Upon his return to Norwich, Fletcher gave a copy to John Manne, showed it to a man called Thetford, showed it to Lord Morley, and sent a copy to 'one Rogers, merchant of Norwich'.[72]

An interesting postscript to this story, discovered by Madeleine and Ruth Dodds, is that George Wharton also gave a copy of the rebel manuscript to some Cornish soldiers, who were coming from the north on a pilgrimage to Walsingham.[73] It happens that in Cornwall in April 1537 there was a small attempted rising at the village of St Keverne which bore striking similarities to events in Yorkshire: a banner portraying the five wounds of Christ, a plea to the king to have holidays restored, the swearing of a rebel oath, and so on.[74] It seems at least plausible that this 'copycat' rebellion, hundreds of miles from the farthest reaches of the Pilgrimage itself, was encouraged by the arrival of those same manuscripts from Norfolk in the hands of Cornish soldiers.[75]

In Reading, much farther than Norwich from rebel territory, William Wyre, innkeeper of the Cardinal's Inn, was given 'a bill made and devised in the name of one Robert Aske' by his brother, a fletcher, and then read the bill aloud in the presence of a number of men. There was such interest in its contents that Wyre gave one of his guests, Sir Nicholas Wagstaff, 2*d* to make him a copy. When Wyre was interrogated as to how he obtained the bill, he reported that a man from Shrivenham, Berkshire, called Geoffrey Gunter stayed at his inn and brought the bill with him, showing it to at least three other persons while staying there.[76] Here the plot thickens, since Gunter was a servant of Sir William Essex, who was himself in trouble for circulating rebel manuscripts in London (see below).[77] Moreover, at least three leading men of Reading soon acquired copies of their own, although each later claimed that he had intended to report the existence of the bill all along. Richard Turner, a man of considerable local reputation, acquired a copy from one John Bourne. Some days later a servant of the local priest John Eynon came to Turner requesting a copy for his master. Turner did not make a copy, but rather lent his own copy to both Eynon and the vicar of St Giles', Richard Snowe; however, since the copy was returned to Turner by 'one Whytbourn, clerk of St Giles', it seems likely that at least one other copy was made. Only several days later, on 30 November, did Snowe report the existence of the bill to one of the bailiffs of the town (he made another copy for the bailiff and kept his own), while Turner did not report the existence of the bill until the same day because he claimed the local JPs were all out of town. Given the 'coincidence' that both men belatedly reported the existence of the bill on 30 November, something must have occurred on that date to give them pause for thought.[78] Regardless, for at least a week rebel manuscripts circulated to dozens of people in Reading, giving locals an unfiltered view of Aske's 'letters and demands' which they could then use as the basis for their own discussions and opinions.[79]

Manuscript circulation was not limited to larger towns. In the small town of Bromsgrove, Worcestershire, for instance, a letter was received that had been 'made by Robert Aske traitor, directed to the commons, wherein he persuadeth them against their prince under the color of a pretended pilgrimage'. A husbandman called Richard Parks, who had just returned from London, heard about the letter from a friend called Richard Cross and asked him how he might get his hands on it. He had to follow a trail of readers which included a servant, a gentleman, and a priest, however, before he was able to track down the letter, read it himself, and finally turn it in to the authorities. While it is unclear just how many copies were made of the letter in Bromsgrove, it is clear that copying was a standard procedure, since the priest reported that Parks promised when he borrowed the letter to 'take a copy of it and bring the letter again'.[80]

In London, always the prime clearing house for English news, rebel manuscripts were particularly widespread. The parish clerk of St Leonard Eastcheap, for instance, received several rebel manifestoes from a chaplain called Richard Scarlet, including a copy of the rebel oath and an exhortation for the rebels' cause.[81] More noteworthy is the story of Sir William Essex, who was given a rebel bill by Sir George Throckmorton at a Fleet Street tavern. Essex took the bill back to his chamber, and two days later, when Throckmorton asked for it to be returned, he arranged to have his own copy made by Throckmorton's servant.[82] This story becomes more enlightening when we examine Throckmorton's version of events. He claimed to have arrived in London on 18 November and the next day to have had a conversation at 'the Horse Head in Cheap' in which his friend Sir John Clarke expressed surprise that he had not seen the rebels' demands. That same night Clarke sent Throckmorton a copy of the rebels' articles, which Throckmorton read and did not bother to hide: 'I read them over and then cast them in my chamber window where I lay, little regarding them who looked upon them for that I heard say they were so common'.[83] When Throckmorton returned to Berkshire in December, moreover, he spread word around the countryside that rebel manuscripts were everywhere in London and that people should not worry about possessing them. When he arrived in the vicinity of Reading and learned that 'diverse men of the town and priests' had angered king and council by having 'made out copies of the rebels' demands and Aske's letters', Throckmorton told a crowd of men, 'I marvel of that, for they be universal at London and so even that no man passeth upon them.' He similarly told his brother at Englefield that rebel manuscripts 'were so suffered at London, for in manner everybody had them there'.[84]

It thus appears that the ideas of the northern rebels circulated with remarkable ease, ideas both produced through, and in turn producing, debate over the legitimacy of the government's policies. The circulation of these ideas, it is true, was not 'public' in a Habermasian sense, since it was bound by fears of government reprisal and was embedded in an armed uprising. But, that being said, we should not underestimate the complexity of the debate that was in practice facilitated when the government, largely deprived of its local collaborators, effectively lost control over political communication. Some idea of the vigour of debate over the rebellion's aims, for instance, can be gleaned from a controversy that arose in Dent when William Breyar, a servant of the king, found himself in a crowd of rebels. One man, identified as a smith, heard that Breyar wore the king's livery and told him, 'Thy master is a thief, for he pulleth down all our churches in the country'. The smith had evidently heard or read the commonly circulating reports that parish churches were under attack, and he glossed those reports as attacks on the king's legitimacy. Others in the crowd, however, argued angrily against the smith's opinion: 'It is not the king's deed but the d[eed] of Crumwell, and if we had him here we would crum him [and crum] him that he was never so Crummed, and if thy master were [here] we would new crown him.'[85] Here, then, the pre-modern media, far from 'permitting merely passive acceptance incapable of independent interpretation', as Habermas suggested, were instrumental in the formation of a complex, fluid, 'public' opinion.

V

England's evangelical 'public sphere', too, was not without recourse to media like circulating manuscripts, rumours, and print. The last will and testament of William Tracy, for instance, circulated throughout England in manuscript in the early 1530s and in print after 1535, providing a template to show nascent evangelicals what a properly reformed will might look like.[86] But, more than earthly media, the evangelical 'public' centred on the divine medium of the Word preached. Exactly because it was based on the notion that the Holy Spirit could endow sinful human beings with the ability (or even the duty) to confront negligent authorities, the evangelical 'public sphere' came to depend heavily on sermons, where the Word of God was most obviously translated into human words. In sermons preached against the Pilgrimage of Grace, then, political legitimacy could be claimed for the evangelical cause and various suggestions for English religious policy, with their concomitant criticisms of current policy, could be put forward.

The most important sermon against the Pilgrimage of Grace, preached from the nation's leading pulpit at St Paul's cross, was delivered by Hugh Latimer on 5 November 1536. Like Morison's pamphlets, Latimer's sermon stated unambiguously that popery was at the heart of the rebellion, drawing an extended metaphor of the devil as a military captain with popes as his artillery pieces, evil bishops as his ordnance, and so forth.[87] The usual armour of

Christians against the devil, moral purity, had been largely forfeit owing to the sexual hypocrisy of the religious orders, leaving people unable to defend themselves against evil and hence easily seduced by Aske and the rebels.[88] The other piece of armour that protected Christians, the Gospel, was allegedly promised to the people by the king but then kept from them by 'certain gentlemen, being justices'.[89]

These loyalist and orthodox anti-papal sentiments then provided an opening through which Latimer imparted bluntly evangelical ideas to his audience. When defending the 'setting forth of the gospel' as a way of preventing rebellion, for instance, Latimer preached, 'But, ye say, it is new learning. Now I tell you it is the old learning. Yea, ye say, it is old heresy new scoured. Nay, I tell you it is old truth, long rusted with your canker, and now new made bright and scoured.' Later he preached that Christians needed not only a shield against the devil but a sword to slay him, the Word of God:

Christ himself gave us example to fight with this sword; for he answered the devil with the scripture, and said, 'It is written.' With this sword he drove away the devil: and so let us break his head with this sword, the true word of God, and not with any word of the bishop of Rome's making; not with his old learning, nor his new learning, but with the pure word of God.

Buried within these statements was a well defined theology of *sola scriptura* in which the pope's edicts were wrong not merely because they were in error but because they were accretions to a scripture already sufficient for the foundation of the visible church.[90]

Latimer's sermon was not well received by some of his listeners at the court, and he was prevented from preaching again until the emergency in the north was over. As such, he occupied a liminal space between the 'state' and the nation at large where a highly contested version of 'public' authority could be performed for a heterogeneous audience. In other words Latimer's listeners, both evangelical and conservative, were offered a version of 'official' policy that not only portrayed the government as evangelically minded but also encouraged other preachers to repeat and elaborate Latimer's interpretation of the rebellion. It seems reasonable, then, to link Latimer's controversial sermon with the crisis that erupted among London evangelicals over the subsequent two weeks. On 14 November, the prominent evangelical citizen Robert Packington was shot and killed in Cheapside on his way to church. Although an evangelical was at first accused of the crime, most contemporaries assumed that Packington was killed by religious conservatives who sympathized with the northern rebels. In response to the murder, at Packington's funeral the following day Robert Barnes preached an extremely inflammatory sermon against the conservative establishment; while we do not know its precise contents, it was radical enough that over the next two days Barnes and four other leading evangelical preachers and writers were arrested under orders from their patron, Thomas Cromwell, apparently for their own protection.[91]

Quite apart from these unabashedly radical sermons, some discussions of the rebellions and their meaning seemed on the surface to be standard exhortations to obedience, but actually used this generic form to sneak evangelical rhetoric into 'public' discussion. For instance, one sermon from late 1536 lambasted the sin of rebellion and begged its listeners not to listen to self-proclaimed 'prophets' who claimed to know by 'inspirations, revelations, and dreams' that God had ordered subjects to 'rise against the king and put him down for his sin'. The preacher's rationale for denying these claims, however, was the evangelical argument that 'the time wherein God used to speak to men by inspiration, revelations, and dreams is now past' and that instead the Word of Christ as represented in scripture is sufficient for every man's salvation: 'We are not bound upon peril of our damnation, but only to the belief of the Gospel and of all truths contained therein.'[92] This position should not have been uttered 'publicly' in 1536, but when used to defend king and country it became difficult for religious conservatives to gloss it as beyond the pale of 'public' discourse.

Similarly, an anonymous preacher in Oxford who described himself as 'no graduate' delivered an apparently anodyne sermon of thanks for Queen Jane's pregnancy in the spring of 1537. He argued that the devil, no longer able to make Englishmen 'put trust and confidence in pardons, nor to live under the feigned religion of the bishop of Rome', had given up stealthy seduction and now instead 'biddeth open battle, raising up a sort of rascals and of such as secretly were never true men, making open traitors'. Nonetheless, 'the merciful goodness of God proved that devilish invention folly', and now God's favour on the king had been manifested in the queen's pregnancy. Once again, however, this seemingly orthodox sermon stepped once or twice over the edge of heterodoxy before climbing back again. For instance, the preacher mocked the idea that the bishop of Rome could, through his works, 'bring a soul out of the pope's purgatory'. The attack on papal dispensations evident here was entirely orthodox in 1537, but the idea that purgatory was a papal invention fell well afoul of the king's prohibitions against controversial preaching and depended upon a selective and heavily idiosyncratic reading of the Act of Ten Articles. Moreover, the last part of the sermon contained a stinging rebuke against its mostly clerical audience for 'shearing' and 'fleecing' their flocks rather than feeding them with spiritual food. This sort of attack against the corruption of the clergy was all well and good when directed against Rome and its minions, but when directed against Oxford dons it was likely to cause talk.[93]

Another evangelical who took it upon himself to defend the government's policies was Richard Croke, who wrote to Cromwell in March 1537 that 'since the time of my licence given me by your lordship to preach' he had delivered 'six score sermons' in a total of thirty-seven churches in Northamptonshire, Oxfordshire, Hertfordshire, and Buckinghamshire. In every one of these sermons, he claimed, he had preached 'against the usurped power of the bishop of Rome', and from his claims that both laymen and priests came to him after his sermons 'lamenting their ignorance and long lack of instruction' it would seem that he provided at least a plausible bulwark against disloyalty in the Midlands in the midst of the northern rebellion. Like Latimer, however, Croke played loosely along the boundaries of orthodoxy in these sermons, taking advantage of his new-found legitimacy to inject radical language into public discourse. While arguing against the superiority of the bishop of Rome, for instance, he included extremely heterodox suggestions about the equality of all clergy: 'In *primitiva ecclesia* ... the name and authority of bishop and priest were all but one thing, until the time that man's policy to avoid schisms devised the pre-eminence amongst priests by the name of a bishop'.[94]

If the pre-existing space of manuscript circulation became the site of one 'public sphere' in the Pilgrimage of Grace, then, the pre-existing space of pulpit and pew became the site of another. Debate within this sphere was not 'rational-critical', of course, since its primary appeals were to scripture rather than reason, and its conceptions of the 'common good' were based in God's ineffable plan for the world, which subordinated this-worldly happiness to next-worldly salvation and inevitably consigned many or even most human beings to eternal damnation. Yet a 'public sphere' founded on theological axioms is certainly analogous in many respects to a 'public sphere' founded on reason, as even Habermas has admitted.[95] The debate contained within that sphere, moreover, was not limited to the mere reception of sermons any more than the debate contained within Habermas's 'public sphere' was limited to the mere reception of newspapers; both constituted grounds for further discussion and debate, since both shared the dual goals of presenting a point of view yet also fostering deeper meditation on the issues at hand. As long as political circumstances made aggressive anti-popery mainstream, then ideas ordinarily considered too heretical to discuss in polite company could be grafted on to the quintessentially orthodox language of loyalty to the sovereign and divinely ordained hierarchy. Thus an increasingly 'public' sphere of evangelical, Word-centred critique of public policy, already almost two decades old by 1536, became for the first time a significant voice within the commonwealth in the crucible of the Pilgrimage of Grace.

VI

While the Enlightenment may have enthroned reason and freedom as *ideals* for 'public' debate, this chapter has shown that the Reformation energized *practices* of 'publicness' with very different legitimations. Lurking within the belief system bequeathed to Tudor England by its classical and medieval ante-cedents were two potentially explosive rationales through which the closed boundaries of 'the political nation' could be penetrated and subverted. One of these rationales was the notion of the 'commonwealth', an extrapolation from Aristotle's mixed polity in which all subjects of a realm helped to constitute, and thus in some sense were competent to comment upon, the common good. The other rationale was the Christian and biblical notion that God could breath knowledge of His will into even the most humble Christian soul. Both of these fault lines had been activated in England at certain times and places before the sixteenth century; in 1381, for instance, both had been important in moulding popular anger into coherent and comprehensible forms of protest.[96] But the Reformation, by exposing central contradictions within the social order and by providing a coherent theology of a priesthood of all believers, energized these nascent forms of civil society to an unprecedented degree, making them the central modes through which people navigated the dangerous political crises of early modern England.

In the Pilgrimage of Grace it happens that these two 'public spheres' opposed one another. Indeed, one might argue that an important and unex-pected consequence of the 'public' debate over the commonwealth in the Pilgrimage of Grace was the accidental and almost ironic manifestation of an intellectual, evangelical 'public' bent on suppressing it. Yet in other times and places throughout the sixteenth century, ideas of 'commonwealth' and Protestant evangelism could go hand in hand: in 1549, for instance, rebels in East Anglia combined the two modes of legitimation in a particularly explosive mixture.[97]

The point, then, is not that two 'public spheres' competed for support and participation in Tudor England. Rather, I want to suggest that these two 'public spheres' provided an infrastructure for popular politics that would help to shape English society for decades to come. If politicians wanted to appeal to the populace in support of their policies, from the 'Good Duke' of Somerset in the 1540s to 'King Pym' in the 1640s, they could legitimate those appeals through the rhetoric of the commonwealth, the rhetoric of the Saints, or both. Conversely, popular-political activists from Robert Kett to John Lilburne could amplify their political voices by appealing to these same fonts of legitimacy. This political infrastructure in turn helped shape the development of news media (Alexandra Walsham's providential pamphlets, for instance, appealed precisely to the intersection of these two 'public spheres') and helped delineate the political options available in times of crisis (Charles I's *Answer* to parlia-ment's nineteen propositions, for instance, utilized commonwealth ideas as the only available 'public' rationale for absolute prerogative). In other words, by looking at the quintessentially Habermasian issues of political communi-cation and participation without imagining those issues as leading inevitably to 'rational', 'enlightened', 'liberal' civil society, we can reclaim a great deal of the political dynamism and *de facto* 'public' debate that characterized the early modern polity.

NOTES

I would like to thank Peter Lake, Anthony Grafton, and Ian McNeely for reading drafts of this chapter. Versions were also presented at the Princeton University British Studies Colloquium in 2000 and the Cornell University Early Modern Colloquium in 2003, and I would like to thank the participants for their comments.

1 D. S. Berkowitz (ed.), *Humanist Scholarship and Public Order: Two Tracts against the Pilgrimage of Grace by Richard Morison* (Washington DC, 1984), 117–18.

2 J. Habermas, *The Structural Transformation of the Public Sphere: An Inquiry into a Category of Bourgeois Society*, trans. T. Burger with F. Lawrence (Cambridge MA, 1989). For works of early modern history utilizing Habermas's concept of the public sphere, see for instance A. Halasz, *The Marketplace of Print: Pamphlets and the Public Sphere in Early Modern England* (Cambridge, 1997); J. Sawyer, *Printed Poison: Pamphlet Propaganda, Faction Politics, and the Public Sphere in Early Seventeenth-Century France* (Berkeley CA, 1990); D. Zaret, 'Religion, science, and printing in the public spheres in seventeenth-century England', in C. Calhoun (ed.), *Habermas and the Public Sphere* (Cambridge MA, 1992); S. Pincus, '"Coffee politicians does create": coffeehouses and Restoration political culture', *Journal of Modern History* 67:4 (1995), 807–34.

3 Habermas, *The Structural Transformation of the Public Sphere*, 7–8.

4 *Ibid.*, 254 n. 35 and 16–7.

5 This phrasing is from J. M. Bernstein's gloss of Habermas in Bernstein, *Recovering Ethical Life: Jürgen Habermas and the Future of Critical Theory* (London, 1995), 39.

6 Craig Calhoun made a similar point about the ahistoricism of Habermas's model: 'Habermas tends to judge the eighteenth century by Locke and Kant, the nineteenth century by Marx and Mill, and the twentieth century by the typical suburban television viewer' ('Introduction', in Calhoun, *Habermas and the Public Sphere*, 33).

7 On these issues see I. F. McNeely, 'Writing, Citizenship, and the Making of Civil Society in Germany, 1780–1840', Ph.D. dissertation, University of Michigan, 1998.

8 M. Bush, *The Pilgrimage of Grace: a Study of the Rebel Armies of October 1536* (Manchester, 1996), quote on p. 409. R. W. Hoyle has challenged Bush's interpretation of the 'society of orders' in the rebellion; his critique, which I do not accept, would reject my description of 'elite rebels' but would not, I think, disagree with my interpretation of the commons. See R. W. Hoyle, *The Pilgrimage of Grace and the Politics of the 1530s* (Oxford, 2001).

9 P. Collinson, 'The monarchical republic of Queen Elizabeth I', *Bulletin of the John Rylands Library* 69:2 (1987), 394–424; D. MacCulloch, 'Kett's rebellion in context', *Past and Present* 84 (1979), 36–59.

10 PRO, E 36/119, fos 15v–16r. (This MS is calendared in J. S. Brewer *et al.*, eds, *Letters and Papers, Foreign and Domestic, of the Reign of Henry VIII, 1509–1547* (hereafter cited as *LP*), London, 1862–1932, XII, i, 70.) Another witness reported that Staines read the articles 'openly in the field, saying to the people holding up his hands, "Sirs, how like you these articles, doth they please you or no?" And to that the people held up their staves, saying, "Yea, yea, yea"' (PRO, E 36/119, fol. 9v [*LP*, XII, i, 70]).

11 PRO, SP 1/115, fol. 215r [*LP*, XII, i, 369].

12 PRO, E 36/119, fols 21r–22r [*LP*, XII, i, 201].

13 PRO, SP 1/114, fol. 259r [*LP*, XII, i, 185].

14 PRO, E 36/118, fol. 77r [*LP*, XII, i, 392].

15 PRO, E 36/121, fol. 116v [*LP*, XI, 585]; PRO, SP 1/115, fol. 215r [*LP*, XII, i, 369].

16 M. Bush, '"Enhancements and importunate charges": an analysis of the tax complaints of October 1536', *Albion* 22:3 (1990), 403–19, at 413–14.

17 M. Bush and D. Bownes, *The Defeat of the Pilgrimage of Grace: a Study of the Postpardon Revolts of December 1536 to March 1537 and their Effect* (Hull, 1999), p. 267. A. Fletcher and D. MacCulloch, *Tudor Rebellions* (4th edn, London, 1997), p. 136; see also Bush, *The Pilgrimage of Grace*, 171–2.

18 Bush, *The Pilgrimage of Grace*, 332.

19 For policy debates and disagreements within the Pilgrim ranks, see Ethan Shagan, *Popular Politics and the English Reformation* (Cambridge, 2003), chapter 3.

20 PRO, SP 1/111, fols 237r–239r [*LP*, XI, 1155(2)].

21 PRO, E 36/119, fol. 69r [*LP*, XII, i, 466].

22 *Ibid.*, fol. 128v [*LP*, XII, i, 914].

23 Wilifride Holme, *The Fall and Evill Successe of Rebellion* (London, 1572), sig. H1v.

24 M. Bateson (ed.), 'The Pilgrimage of Grace and Aske's examination', *English Historical Review* 5 (1890), 340.

25 Fletcher and MacCulloch, *Tudor Rebellions*, 135–7.

26 Bateson, 'The Pilgrimage of Grace and Aske's examination', 340.

27 PRO, E 36/118, fol. 119r [*LP*, XII, i, 29].

28 M. H. Dodds and R. Dodds, *The Pilgrimage of Grace, 1536–1537, and the Exeter Conspiracy, 1538* (Cambridge, 1915) I, 382–4.

29 On the political nature of popular disorder in the early modern period, see C. Holmes, 'Drainers and Fenmen: the problem of popular political consciousness in the seventeenth century', in A. Fletcher and J. Stevenson (eds), *Order and Disorder in Early Modern England* (Cambridge, 1985), K. Wrightson, 'Two concepts of order: justices, constables and jurymen in seventeenth-century England', and J. Walter, 'Grain riots and popular attitudes to the law: Maldon and the crisis of 1629', both in J. Brewer and J. Styles (eds), *An Ungovernable People: the English and their Law in the Seventeenth and Eighteenth Centuries* (New Brunswick NJ, 1980). The *loci classici* of this mode of analysis are of course N. Z. Davis, 'The rites of violence: religious riot in sixteenth-century France', *Past and Present* 59 (1973), 51–91, and E. P. Thompson, 'The moral economy of the English crowd in the eighteenth century', *Past and Present* 50 (1971), 76–136.

30 Henry VIII, *Answere made by the Kynges Hyghnes to Petitions of the Rebelles in Yorkeshire* (London, 1536); Henry VIII, *Answere to the Petitions of the Traytors and Rebelles in Lyncolnshyre* (London, 1536); PRO, E 36/121, fols 23r–28r [*LP*, XI, 1175].

31 Berkowitz's suggestion that Henry VIII contributed to the writing of these tracts appears to have no evidentiary basis (*Humanist Scholarship and Public Order*, 43–4).

32 *Ibid.*, 91.

33 *Ibid.*, 92.

34 *Ibid.*, 93.

35 *Ibid.*, 94

36 *Ibid.*, 98.

37 *Ibid.*, 128.

38 *Ibid.*, 129.

39 *Ibid.*, 134–5.

40 While it was apparently not printed until 1570s, when the crisis over the Revolt of the Northern Earls and the Ridolfi Plot made it again topical, there is reason to believe that it may have circulated previously. Not only was a copy mysteriously available for printing in London thirty-six years after it was written, but the last stanza contains a device that Renaissance authors often included in manuscripts intended for circulation, a pseudo-modest claim that the author was 'unlearned'.

41 Holme, *The Fall and Evill Successe of Rebellion*, sig. C1v.

42 *Ibid.*, sig. E1r.

43 *Ibid.*, sig. D2r.

44 *Ibid.*, sigs E2v and E3v.

45 *Ibid.*, sig. G1r.

46 Henry VIII, *Answere made by the Kynges Hyghnes to Petitions of the Rebelles in Yorkeshire*, sig. A3r.

47 *Ibid.*, sig. D2v–D3v.

48 *Ibid.*, sig. A2r–v.

49 Holme, *The Fall and Evill Successe of Rebellion*, sig. D2v–D4r.

50 Henry VIII, *Answere made by the Kynges Hyghnes to Petitions of the Rebelles in Yorkeshire*, sig. A3v.

51 Holme, *The Fall and Evill Successe of Rebellion*, sigs E2v–F1r.

52 PRO, SP 1/116, fol. 158r [*LP*, XII, i, 529].

53 BL, Egerton Ms 2623, fol. 9r–v.

54 S. Brigden, *London and the Reformation* (Oxford, 1989), 250–1, 255–6. Despite the appearance of Lollardy in Multon's view, he claimed to be of the 'new fashion'.

55 See A. Fox, 'Custom, memory, and the authority of writing', in P. Griffiths, A. Fox, and S. Hindle (eds), *The Experience of Authority in Early Modern England* (London, 1996); A. Fox, 'Ballads, libels and popular ridicule in Jacobean England', *Past and Present* 145 (1994), 47–83. One good example of political communication crossing the written/oral barrier occurred in 1537, when a man called Richard Bishop, of Bungay, Suffolk, told Robert Seymon that he knew 'where was a certain prophecy which if the said Robert would come to Bungay he should hear it read, and that one man had taken pain to watch in the night to write the copy of the same, and if so be as the prophecy sayeth there shall be a rising of the people this year or never' (PRO, SP 1/120, fol. 102v [*LP*, XII, i, 1212]).

56 I. M. W. Harvey, *Jack Cade's Rebellion of 1450* (Oxford, 1991), 25–6, 70.

57 Bush, *The Pilgrimage of Grace*, 197–8.

58 T. N. Toller (ed.), *Correspondence of Edward, Third Earl of Derby*, Chetham Society, new ser., XIX (Manchester, 1890), 49–50.

59 BL, Cotton Ms Caligula B.II, fol. 361r.

60 PRO, SP 1/114, fol. 191r [*LP*, XII, i, 138].

61 PRO, SP 1/114, fol. 228r [*LP*, XII, i, 163(2)].

62 PRO, SP 1/110, fol. 188r [*LP*, XI, 973].

63 PRO, SP 1/106, fol. 255r [*LP*, XI, 539].

64 PRO, SP 1/114, fol. 189v [*LP*, XI, i, 136].

65 PRO, E 36/122, fol. 28v [*LP*, XII, i, 853].

66 PRO, SP 1/115, fols 164v–165r [*LP*, XII, i, 306].

67 Bateson, 'The Pilgrimage of Grace and Aske's examination', 334.

68 PRO, E 36/119, fol. 27r [*LP*, XII, i, 201].

69 PRO, SP 1/116, fol. 165r [*LP*, XII, i, 534].

70 PRO, SP 1/115, fol. 213r [*LP*, XII, i, 369].

71 PRO, SP 1/113, fol. 25v [*LP*, XI, 1356].

72 PRO, SP 1/112, fols 169r–171v [*LP*, XI, 1260].

73 *Ibid.*, fol. 170r–v [*LP*, XI, 1260].

74 PRO, SP 1/118, fol. 245r [*LP*, XII, i, 1000]; PRO, SP 1/118, fols 247v–248r [*LP*, XII, i, 1001].

75 Dodds and Dodds, *The Pilgrimage of Grace, 1536–1537, and the Exeter Conspiracy, 1538* II, 170–1.

76 PRO, SP 1/112, fol. 110r [*LP*, XI, 1231].

77 PRO, SP 1/113, fols 68r–71r [*LP*, XI, 1406].

78 PRO, SP 1/112, fols 110r–111r [*LP*, XI, 1231]

79 PRO, SP 1/113, fol. 69r [*LP*, XI, 1406].

80 PRO, SP 1/112, fol. 209r–v [*LP*, XI, 1286]; PRO SP 112, fo. 214r [*LP*, XI, 1292].

81 Brigden, *London and the Reformation*, 251.

82 PRO, E 36/121, fol. 83r–v [*LP*, XI, 1405].

83 PRO, SP 1/113, fol. 68r–v [*LP*, XI, 1406].

84 PRO, SP 1/113, fols 69r–71r [*LP*, XI, 1406].

85 *LP*, XI, 841.

86 J. Craig and C. Litzenberger, 'Wills as religious propaganda: the testament of William Tracy', *Journal of Ecclesiastical History* 44 (1993), 415–31.

87 G. E. Corrie (ed.), *The Works of Hugh Latimer, Sometime Bishop of Worcester, Martyr, 1555* (Cambridge, 1844–45) I, 27.

88 *Ibid.*, 29.

89 *Ibid.*, 30.

90 *Ibid.*, 30–2.

91 Brigden, *London and the Reformation*, 252–4; D. MacCulloch, *Thomas Cranmer: a Life* (New Haven CT, 1996), 171.

92 PRO, SP 6/13, fols 50v–52v [*LP*, XI, 1215].

93 PRO, SP 1/120, fols 265r–268v [*LP*, XII, i, 1325].

94 PRO, SP 1/117, fols 160r–162r [*LP*, XII, i, 757].

95 The idea of 'rational' debate founded in theological axioms as constitutive of a public sphere is discussed in D. Tracy, 'Theology, critical social theory, and the public realm', in D. S. Browning and F. S. Fiorenze (eds), *Habermas, Modernity, and Public Theology* (New York, 1992). Habermas himself largely accepts this notion in his conclusion/response in the same volume, 'Transcendence from within, transcendence in this world'.

96 See S. Justice, *Writing and Rebellion: England in 1381* (Berkeley CA, 1994).

97 E. H. Shagan, '"Popularity" and the 1549 rebellions revisited', *English Historical Review* 115 (2000), 121–33.

Chapter 3

The politics of 'popularity' and the public sphere: the 'monarchical republic' of Elizabeth I defends itself

Peter Lake

I

This chapter is about the often inadvertent, even accidental, creation of spaces (both conceptual and practical) for 'public' debate and discourse about subjects central to the future and preservation of the Elizabethan regime. These spaces, I will argue, were created by a number of interactions between the purposes of different groups and actors (many of them situated within the regime) and the peculiar politico-religious circumstances in which that regime found itself during the central years of the reign. Our starting point, expressed in the terms set by the recent historiography, and in particular by a series of brilliant articles by Patrick Collinson, is certain modes of political manoeuvre adopted by the 'monarchical republic' of Elizabethan England as it tried to defend and perpetuate itself amidst the exigencies of that long 'Elizabethan exclusion crisis' that Collinson sees stretching from the 1560s at least until the execution of Mary Queen of Scots.[1] The result was a mode of behaviour in which, using a motley collection of different agents and men of business, of collaborators and hangers-on, and a variety of media, both the regime (or rather different groupings within it) and its critics, members of both the Protestant and Catholic 'loyal opposition', addressed and sought to mobilize a variety of publics.

More often than not the topics under discussion were ones upon which the ordinary subject was supposed to be silent and even the discussions of insiders were supposed to be private (that is, restricted to an in-group of privileged participants and most certainly not for general consumption). At the very least we are dealing here with subjects upon which public comment was supposed to be strictly regulated and controlled. Juxtaposing the term 'public' against the privacy of the *arcana imperii*, I want to attribute four (and a bit) main characteristics to the notion of publicness in play in this chapter. First, we are dealing with messages sent through a variety of media – the full gamut of print (formal polemic, sermons, cheap tracts, printed proclamations, parliamentary legislation), circulating manuscripts, public performance of a variety of types (sermons, show trials, disputations, executions and even, at times, plays), and rumour – to an ultimately uncontrollably general audience. Second, the message sending or case making in question is legitimated either explicitly or implicitly in terms of some general public interest defined socially (as in appeals to the commonweal) or religiously (true religion) or politically (the nation, England, or the person, safety or interests of the monarch, taken in their public, representative rather than in their private, personated senses). The pitch was often made in conscious opposition to what was taken to be the necessarily corrupt pursuit of private interest by a variety of third parties, groups often depicted as treasonable or heretical factions, bent, for their own purposes, on subverting the current religio-political state. Third, the message or pitch being thus generally broadcast is cast in terms of generally knowable principles or criteria of truth or interest, thus assuming and, in a sense, calling into being and invoking, a body or bodies of opinion, a public or series of over-lapping publics, both legitimately interested in and able to consider and even to decide (in terms of such criteria of truth and common interest) the question or issue at hand. The purpose in so doing is to garner general support for some policy or initiative, or to make a public and popular fuss sufficiently great that the queen's hand would be forced or at least certain policy options and outcomes would be pushed off limits. Fourthly, the appeals thus made to the public or people did not depend so much on the personal authority, institutional standing or political connections of those making them as on the cogency of the message being sent and on the closeness of the fit between that message and the general criteria of truth mentioned above.

Central to these developments and transactions were religious and confessional conflict and, on the Protestant side, at least, the notion of popery. Popery in its foreignness and otherness threatened, and hence, of course, helped to constitute, an essentially Protestant England. Here the demands of national interest and true religion intersected. Here the personal powers of the monarch, as head of the church and defender of the Gospel, shaded very quickly into the need to defend, at all costs, an essentially transpersonal notion of a Protestant regime and nation. That, after all, was what the personal, divinely ordained, prerogative powers of the crown were for. Again, as a miasma of superstition and religious error, popery could best be dispelled through the preaching of the self-evidently true, as it were, 'rational', principles of true religion contained in the Bible, principles that were assumed, in a fair fight, to be able to cut through popish error like a knife through butter. Accordingly, many conviction Protestants held, such principles should, as a matter of some urgency, be communicated to each and every member of the commonweal to enable them the more effectively to resist the blandishments of Antichrist. Again, as a form of corruption, grounded in human sin and the fleshly lusts and impulses of a fallen humanity, popery could do duty as a symbol for all sorts of corruption, all sorts of threats to the commonweal. Thus the ideological imperatives of anti-popery helped to introduce and underwrite the public, national and common interests and purposes that rendered what I am referring to here as 'the post-Reformation public sphere' genuinely 'public'.[2]

There were, of course, Catholic equivalents to anti-popery. These could be found in Catholic accounts of the deleterious moral and political effects of schism and heresy. The Calvinist sort of heresy adopted in England was inherently divisive and antinomian, leading inevitably to moral chaos and religious division. Worse still, on certain *politique* Catholic readings, the change in religion had been prompted not by Calvinist principle so much as by factious ambition. The result was a form of political atheism, a Machiavellian rather than a Protestant regime, instituted by upstart politicians and *politiques*, who used religious change and worries about the security of the regime in the face of an invented Catholic threat to elbow aside the ancient nobility, the natural rulers of the land and councillors of the monarch. Monopolizing the favour and patronage of the queen, they proceeded to create a form of tyranny. This monstrous regime (alternately styled either as Cecil's or Leicester's commonwealth) was then sold to the people through a barrage of lies and half-truths, deliberately spread through the pulpit, the press and rumour, at the behest of the regime, to convince the people that, for instance, the duke of Norfolk was a traitor; Mary Stuart a popish whore, determined to gain the throne by any means; that Catholics were all potential traitors who were only ever punished for political crime rather than religious belief; that the king of Spain was the nation's natural enemy and that the pope was Antichrist. Such accounts of the nature of the Elizabethan regime amounted to replies to, indeed in some ways inversions of, the Catholic conspiracy theories with which elements in the regime and their agents and supporters sought to type the Catholics as enemies to the realm, to their prince and to God.[3]

None of the developments under discussion here originated as the work of some radical Protestant, puritan (or indeed Catholic) opposition. Rather, following the insights of recent revisionist and post-revisionist historians, I want to suggest that the construction of and appeal to various notions of the public and public opinion need to be set not in the context of a dichotomous juxtaposition of state and society, still less of government and opposition – with a resultant 'public sphere' defined always as standing autonomously apart from the state – but rather in terms of struggles within an ideologically, politically and even institutionally variegated establishment or regime for the ideological and political initiative. The model adopted here for the internal workings of that regime is not one dominated by 'faction', but rather, following on the seminal work of Simon Adams, one which posits, as the most significant political division within the high Elizabethan regime, a series of disagreements between the queen and her council over how best to secure and preserve the realm or the Protestant state.[4] Certainly, as we shall see below, the modes of action and communication I am discussing here could be and were used by both the Catholic opponents and the puritan critics of the regime, but, under Elizabeth at least,[5] these practises and techniques originated in the actions of groups or factions located at or near the centre of the establishment rather than in the actions of any radical opposition (either Catholic or Protestant).

II

Rather than try to present a continuous history of these developments, a process which, since it would involve a retelling of virtually the entire political history of the reign, is far beyond both my capacities and the compass of this chapter, I will instead analyse the nature and sketch the development of the modes of political action under discussion here through a number of loosely linked case studies, each of them chosen to illustrate a different element or strand within the style popular or public politics at the centre of the current discussion.

I want to start with two projected matches, the first between Mary Stuart and the duke of Norfolk, and the second between Elizabeth herself and the duke of Anjou.[6] They represent the two occasions when prolonged political manoeuvres/negotiations (both of which originated from deep within the establishment) seemed set fair fundamentally to alter both the political and religious complexion of the regime, the first by establishing and domesticating, within the Elizabethan political establishment, what threatened to become a largely Catholic Stuart reversionary interest, the second by marrying the queen herself to a Catholic. Both got a variety of political and particularly Catholic hopes up, only rapidly thereafter to dash them again. For that very reason both provoked a range of different appeals for public or popular support, appeals which emanated both from the centre of the regime as elements therein sought to protect themselves from the Catholic threat and from various Catholics, seeking to counter the propaganda assault launched by the regime and make their own pitch for support and the political initiative.

Famously, the meltdown of the first such machination produced the revolt of the northern earls and then the Ridolphi conspiracy.[7] The revolt in the north and the subsequent papal bull excommunicating Elizabeth were greeted with a barrage of anti-Catholic tracts, proclamations and even ballads, all dedicated to proving the evils of rebellion and the inexorable connection between rebellion and popery. Many of these were written by Thomas Norton.[8] For our current purposes the most interesting was the astonishingly indiscreet *A Discourse*

touching the pretended Match between the Duke of Norfolk and the Queen of Scots.
This was a remarkable tract of some twelve pages which not only ran through
the arguments against the match but sought to build a case against the parties
to it. Organized methodically under a series of headings – 'A consideration
of the Queen of Scots person', 'A consideration of the match' 'of the present
state', of 'what groweth by this match', the pamphlet pilloried Mary's character
and political track record. She was either 'a papist, which is evil, or an atheist,
which is worse'. Her past 'horrible acts', as well as her parentage – on her
mother's side she 'is descended of a race that is both enemy to God and the
common quiet of Europe' – proclaimed her moral character. As 'a competitor
of this crown', the Queen of Scots was also a professed enemy of Queen Elizabeth and England. As for the duke, his questionable religious affiliations,
weak character, high birth, noble connections and popularity – the latter based,
Norton contemptuously claimed, on 'his familiarity' with the people 'in public
sport as in shooting and cockfighting' – made him all too likely and dangerous
a dupe for the sinister purposes of 'the Scottish idolatress'.[9]

This was strong stuff to be broached through the pamphlet press to the
people but, after the disclosure of the Ridolfi Plot, the volume got turned
still higher as elements on the council decided now to press for the trial and
condemnation of both Norfolk and Mary. The denunciation of rebels was
one thing, the legitimation of the execution of the leading peer in England
and of the heir to the throne was quite another, particularly in a situation in
which the queen herself was extremely unwilling to act with the ruthlessness
which many of her councillors desired. The result was a whispering campaign
designed to tar both Norfolk and Mary with the brush of foreign conspiracy
and treason and to force the queen's hand.

This, of course, was a ticklish business in which the leaders of the anti-
Mary party, councillors like Burghley or Bacon, could not appear publicly to
be involved. It was conducted accordingly by surrogates: men like Thomas
Norton and William Fleetwood, subsequently identified by Michael Graves,
precisely because of their facilitating role in such affairs, as 'council men of
business'. Something of the involved chains of complicity, of nudging and
winking, of heavy hint dropping combined with the creation of all sorts of
plausible deniability which this ticklish situation produced can be gleaned
from events in London in the autumn of 1571. On 12 October the lords of the
privy council called before them in Star Chamber the Lord Mayor of London,
six aldermen, six leading citizens and the recorder, William Fleetwood, and
briefed them on what Fleetwood tactfully described as 'such matters touching
the queen's majesty and her estate now in hand'. The meeting took place on
the queen's express instructions (at 'her majesty's pleasure', as Fleetwood put
it) and he claimed that the privy councillors disclosed only 'such matter as they
had by her majesty's own mouth given them in charge to publish'.

The following Monday the lord mayor and aldermen called before them at the Guildhall all the wardens of the city companies 'with a great multitude of other citizens' and recorder Fleetwood gave the assembled multitude an edited version of what the privy council had told the city authorities. Clearly everyone had heard of 'persons [i.e. Norfolk, who had been rearrested after the disclosure of the Ridolfi conspiracy] as for great causes be apprehended and committed to custody'. The queen, Fleetwood reassured them, had had 'just cause to do the same and a great deal more', a claim he justified with reference not merely to the northern rebellion but to events much closer to home. The 'great trouble and unquietness' in the north 'hath laid an egg of most dangerous rebellion' which, carried south 'to this city ... hath been hatched and hath brought forth a brood of most vile and horrible treason'. For, as the privy councillors had explained, a plot had been hatched with foreign backing, that very month, to land a force 'at some place near to the city of London' and then 'to destroy the queen's most royal person ... to tumble up her government, to overthrow the state of this realm and to spoil and undo this noble city'. 'The richest persons and such as God hath blessed with fortunes and worldly goods should have been robbed, rifled and spoiled' and 'the bodies of the chief governors and most notable men should have been apprehended and murdered'. The result of all this was an appeal to all the citizenry 'in your companies and in your households and in every place, time and opportunity to look about you' for any signs of subversion or conspiracy. For there were those 'not of the best, substantial and honest sort of you but rascals and of the worst degree' who had spread and were spreading 'rumours' and 'lewd and seditious papers and letters' 'giving away the honour of her majesty's good government to other, and transferring great praises to some singular persons' and thus, 'as much as in them lieth', seeking 'to strengthen the party of her majesty's enemies'. Fleetwood accordingly appealed to the assembled multitude to turn in to the mayor anyone found 'either by writing, ciphering, printing, speaking or otherwise' defaming 'the queen's majesty's government, and doings' or 'the state of the realm' or encouraging or favouring 'dangerous persons'.

Quite who these dangerous persons might be was never made entirely explicit, for, remarkably, Fleetwood never identified the parties to the plot. A nameless 'they', a group of 'untrue and unnatural subjects', were said to have 'conspired with the queen's foreign enemies the pope and the duke of Alva' to ruin the nation and sack the city. Thus, while the authenticity and legitimacy of Fleetwood's speech, and the ensuing pamphlet (again published by Day) in which these events have come down to us, were derived ultimately from a chain of contact and command that led directly, via the city authorities, to the privy council, from the Guildhall to Star Chamber and thence, less distinctly, to Whitehall and the queen herself, that same hot line to authority (both conciliar and royal) meant that for Fleetwood discretion had had to remain the better part of valour.[10]

But just in case the point had been lost on the audience, Fleetwood's performance and printed text were almost immediately glossed by a second anonymous pamphlet by one R.G. Entitled *Salutem in Christo*, this crossed the t's and dotted the i's left indistinct by the recorder, running over recent events once again and this time identifying the villains of the piece by name. Thus the reader was told that 'it was not unknown' that 'the Scottish queen hath been the most dangerous enemy against the queen's majesty our sovereign lady that lived'. 'It was also said and credibly avowed that the Scottish queen was the greatest cause of the rebellion lately in the north.' It was similarly 'not unknown' that she and Norfolk had 'secretly practised' to marry without the queen's knowledge or permission. Having been discovered, both duke and queen had promised to give up the scheme, only to continue to intrigue throughout the duke's imprisonment in the Tower and subsequent period under house arrest. How dangerous this attempt had been to the realm had been rendered crystal-clear, the author claimed, by the plots and conspiracies that had attended it. He now repeated Fleetwood's account of a rebellion designed to seize the city and then, combining with foreign forces from the Low Countries, to 'proceed to further things than is expedient (as I hear) to be spoken of at this time'. This plot was accompanied with other plans to spring Mary from prison by either fraud or force, to proclaim her Queen of England and Scotland and to spirit her son out of Scotland and into Spain. This time, Mary and Norfolk were clearly named as parties to these conspiracies; the messenger sent to Rome and Spain had been given letters of credit from both and 'several letters were speedily written [in reply] to the said queen and to the duke of Norfolk'.

Where Fleetwood, writing under his own name at the end of a clear chain of command and information that led straight back to the council, had had to keep mum, the author of this pamphlet was quite happy to use the freedom conferred by anonymity to name names. Then, having done so, he proceeded to drop some very heavy hints that he was acting at the behest of authority.

> It may be that some will say that many of these things are doubtful and percase wrested in report, either by malice or by overmuch credulity. But truly in such credible sort are all the things above mentioned with sundry others to me reported to be very true by such as have cause to know them and use not to report untruths, as I do boldly avow them to be true. And if they shall be found otherwise, then it is likely that some of the queen's majesty's council will cause them to be reprehended, who upon this my writing shall report them and thereupon I will patiently suffer correction for my hasty credit, for it is most likely that such matters of estate as these are will not be suffered to be communicated without reprehension.

Nor did the author stop there; in an afterword allegedly written after his text was completed on 13 October he cited the briefing 'this very day' of the lord mayor and aldermen in the Star Chamber, which, he claimed, 'more boldened him to think all these things true', thus in one smooth movement freeing his own text from any suspicion of collusion in a wider official propaganda effort and claiming official confirmation that what he said was indeed true.[11]

If anything still more extraordinary was the publication some time in November or December 1571 of *A Detection of the Doings of Mary Queen of Scots*. The book bore no printer's name, nor date or place of publication. It comprised a translation of Buchanan's Latin denunciation of Mary and of the *Actio contra Mariam*, which had been appended to an earlier edition of that work. Also included were all eight of the notorious casket letters. The book was translated not into English but into Scots and accompanied by another, shorter tract entitled *The Copy of a Letter written by one in London to his Friend concerning the Credit of the late published Detection of the Doings of the Lady Mary of Scotland*. This introduced the longer piece as something 'of late' 'published out of Scotland' 'detecting the foul doings of some that have been dangerous to our noble queen' 'by which detection is induced a very excellent comparison for all English men to judge whether it be good to change queens or no'. The book was thus given an entirely Scottish provenance. Its author Buchanan was described as 'one privy to the lords of the king's secret council there, well able to understand and disclose the truth'. The book 'was written by him not as of himself, nor in his own name, but according to the instructions to him given by common conference of the lords of the privy council of Scotland'. It represented official justification for their conduct offered by the Scottish lords to 'our sovereign lady or her highnesses commissioners in that behalf appointed'. The queen, the tract argued, had been convinced by all this evidence, otherwise she would have helped Mary regain her throne, just as she had previously helped her against the French and indeed as she had helped the French king against his Catholic rebels. Elizabeth would never have 'lived in such good amity with the young king of Scotland, the regents and the true lords maintainers of that side, if these heinous offences alleged on that part had not been provable or if the young king had been a usurper or his regents and other lords of that faction traitors, as they must have been all if all be false that is objected against the said lady Mary'.[12]

Not only could Elizabeth's *bona fides* and Mary's malignity be confirmed by the text, so too could Norfolk's depravity and ambition. For he had had a Latin copy of the work, which must mean that he was well aware of Mary's character. That in turn must mean that

> the duke could not so well like the woman, being such a woman, as for her persons sake to venture the overthrow of such a flourishing state, wherein he stood before, but that some other greater thing it might be that he liked, the greediness whereof

might temper his abhorring of so foul conditions and of so great a danger to him self to be sent after his predecessors.

If Norfolk's possession of this knowledge damned him in the sight of public opinion, so too would the response of the English people to this information display their affections and loyalties as the queen's true subjects. For, lamented the author, there were many 'who would fain seem indifferent judges' that 'they will credit nothing till they hear both parties'. Worse still, others, 'more open fellows, say flatly that all is false, the book hath no credit, the author is unknown, obscure, the matter counterfeit and all is nothing'. And all this despite the fact that in this book the cases of both parties were readily visible, and the Scottish queen's infamy was rendered plain for all to see in her own letters. All of which meant that if the reader were to come across any such sceptics he or she was to draw the conclusion 'thou art also one of them'. 'God disclose these hollow hearts or rather grant her majesty and those that be in authority under her an earnest will to see them, for they will disclose them- selves fast enough.'[13]

We do not know who did the translation but on 8 November 1571 Thomas Wilson wrote to Cecil enclosing a copy of the book 'translated', as he put it, 'into handsome Scottish' and desiring Cecil to send him 'Paris closely sealed and it shall not be known from whence it cometh'. This last refers to the declaration of Hubert Paris, produced after the hearing about Mary at West- minster and not included in the Latin version of Buchanan's text.[14] Wilson's almost offhand remarks make it certain that, for all the considerable efforts made in the framing materials to make this book look like an exclusively Scottish production, written and validated entirely by the Scots, translated by them into Scots, not English, and presumably printed abroad, this book was produced with Cecil's full knowledge, approval and connivance. It was printed in London (probably by John Day, a close associate of Cecil and the same man who produced the collection of Norton's recent writings on popery and the succession in *All such Treatises as have been lately published by Thomas Norton*).[15]

This campaign against Mary and Norfolk – just like that conducted by Thomas Norton before it – used the (alleged) plethora of rumours and stories, the popular debate and division, circulating around the duke and the Scottish queen as a justification for its own populist methods. On this view, the need to go public – to broach 'matters of estate' in print before 'the people' – was rendered plain by the seriousness and ubiquity of the lies being spread by the regime's enemies and all too readily believed by the ill affected (the two-thirds of the population that Norton had claimed fell under the headings of atheism and popery). Now fire was to be met with fire as the regime and its agents used the full range of contemporary media – cheap print, performance (the meeting at the Guildhall) and planted rumour – to convince a promiscuously popular audience of the righteousness of its increasingly strident, not merely anti-popish but now pointedly anti-Marian cause.

Here, then, is a regime anxious to control and prime popular opinion and report and happy to do so through a variety of media – printed pamphlets, ballads, the planting and circulation of 'news' and rumour, a fairly straightforward trail which led straight back to the privy council and its agents, who like R.G. were anxious both to preserve their own anonymity and plausible deniability for their patrons, while at the same time parading the semi-official status of their version of events. Moreover, all of this activity *in foro publico* was designed not merely to prepare the people for the trial of the duke of Norfolk but as a preliminary to the full court press put on in parliament the following year, the main purpose of which was to force the queen to take fatally definitive action against not only the duke but the Queen of Scots as well. As Michael Graves has shown, this exercise in loyal opposition to a too merciful queen – as the author of *Salutem in Christo* noted, Elizabeth was so 'void of a revenging nature' that 'some sort of wise men have noted it a fault for a prince'[16] – was run at the council's behest and managed in the Commons by the likes of Thomas Norton. As John Guy has pointed out, one of the central and most sinisterly threatening political *aperçus* in *An Detection* – the contention that 'desperate necessity will dare the uttermost' – was actually quoted by Norton himself in the course of the debates.[17] And, in the course of the ensuing exchanges between parliament and crown, the final attributes of publicness, as we defined it at the outset, were set in place, as hints and prompts, information and advice, disseminated through the pseudo-official and anonymous means described above and represented there as having a pseudo-official, semi-conciliar, indeed even regal, provenance, were now handed back to the queen in the form of the unsolicited, zealously loyal and fiercely independent counsel of a free parliament.[18]

But this official recourse to what we might describe, perhaps slightly (but only slightly) in advance of contemporary usage, as the politics of 'popularity' had its down side. For what was sauce for the goose proved to be sauce for the gander as well. These pamphlets (and, in particular, *Salutem in Christo*) provoked a response from the Catholic side. I refer, of course, to the famous tract *The Treatise of Treasons*. This, too, was anonymous (although it is conventionally attributed to John Lesley, the bishop of Ross and a leading Marian)[19] and it too took advantage of its anonymity to name names, only now the names being named were those of William Cecil and Nicholas Bacon, the queen's two 'machiavel Catilines'. Here were the real traitors who were trying to turn the queen against her true heir, Mary Stuart and the ancient nobility (represented, of course, by the northern earls who had been forced to take arms by the oppressions of Cecil and Bacon and the hapless duke of Norfolk). Theirs was the real plot against the crown and the realm, the *Treatise* claimed. It was Cecil and Bacon who were behind 'these public and extraordinary speeches in the Star Chamber and Guildhall and these unwonted libels published in print to defame them [Mary and Norfolk] of conspiring rebellions'.[20] Cecil and Bacon were 'the privy publishers of these pamphlets'. 'By other men's pens' they were hoping to ruin Norfolk and Mary 'as the principal objects likely to frustrate their pestilent purpose'.[21] Nor was the recent barrage of official disinformation emanating from the regime anything new; there had been 'infinite numbers of impudent lies published by authority in the time of these men's government', the *Treatise* claimed, appealing to the reader to 'review the sundry printed pamphlets, proclamations, libels, letters, rhymes and other like things sent out among you'.[22]

Against this barrage of lies, the *Treatise* claimed to be telling its audience the truth by laying bare before the public the real traitors whose court-based plots were designed to change the nation's religion and, on that basis, take over the regime. Having established a virtual monopoly over high public office and royal patronage, Cecil and Bacon had exploited the same for their own private gain. To maintain their hold on power they had, through the invention of various popish threats to her rule, misled the queen, in the process alienating her from the ancient nobility, her loyal Catholic subjects and legitimate heir. Combined with their successful persuasion of Elizabeth not to marry, all this was intended to culminate in the ultimate treason, the diversion of the succession away from the legitimate heir to the Greys. And all to advance the corrupt, private purposes and interests of a small faction of low-born new men of no religion, 'Catilines' and 'Machiavels' indeed.

Thus the author of the *Treatise* was able to invoke the regime's appeals to the people and the public to legitimate his own similar appeals and to use his own lack of connections with what he portrayed as a thoroughly corrupt regime as the determining condition, the clinching evidence, of his own veracity and trustworthiness. Yet as much as the author of the *Treatise*, who constructed himself throughout as a foreigner, deeply familiar with, yet untainted by, English politics,[23] might declare his distance from the regime, the structure of the pitch he was making closely paralleled the official versions: their libels, their allegations of desperate plots, their accusations of treason, were countered by his; where Norton or Fleetwood (and behind them Cecil) claimed to be unmasking the corrupt popish treason, the personal avarice and ambition, of Mary and Norfolk and the northern earls, he claimed to be unmasking the equally treasonable private plots of the low-born heretics Bacon and Cecil. Each side's case was, of course, the mirror image of its opponent's; in each case the highly unusual, seemingly seditious and libellous course of broaching the doings of the great and the good, the royal and the noble, before the people was legitimated by the activities in doing precisely that of the other side. The privacy, corruption, the tell-tale combination of Machiavellian policy with religious error, that prompted the other side's attempts, also rendered yours necessary and, almost by definition, orderly, orthodox and loyal.[24]

III

We can see many of the same impulses and forces at work in the fuss over the next great marital crisis of the reign, that involving Elizabeth herself and Anjou. Again this intrigue/negotiation threatened, albeit briefly, fundamentally to reorient the religious and political structure of the regime. But this time the impulse towards the match emanated from even closer to the centre of the regime than had the projected match between Mary and Norfolk. For the most recent commentators on the Anjou affair are agreed that it was the queen herself who most wanted the match to proceed. This considerably complicated matters, since while the dynamics of the affair and of 'the public politics' through which it was in part conducted shared many features with the fuss over Norfolk and Mary, now it was the often hot Protestant opponents of the match who were forced, first, to go public, with some interesting consequences for the resulting line-up of ideological forces and political styles.[25]

Elizabeth's unwonted enthusiasm in the face of the prospect of matrimony divided her councillors. Some (most notably Sussex)[26] were relatively enthusiastic, others (like Burghley, whose position as always remained finely balanced and difficult to judge) were prepared to at least appear to go along with the scheme, and still others, the most forward Protestants, those viscerally committed to English intervention in the Low Countries, were vehemently against. Crypto-catholic peers on the edge of the court were, on the contrary, understandably elated by the prospect of the queen's marriage to a Catholic.[27] Persuasion at court and in council having failed to deflect the queen from her purpose, the issue was taken 'out of doors', through a series of sermons preached both in London and elsewhere, through any number of rumours spread about both Anjou and his agent Simier and through the press. Most notoriously John Stubbes's *Gaping Gulf* rehearsed, for the benefit of a public restricted only by the circulation of the book and of oral reports and rumours based upon it, many of the arguments used in council against the match.[28]

The extent and nature of the resulting furore can be gleaned from a remarkable letter of September 1579 from Bishop Aylmer of London to his patron Sir Christopher Hatton. Aylmer's letter recounts an attempt by the regime to counter Stubbes's arguments by tuning the pulpits. The bishop recounts the contents and response to what appears to have been a Paul's Cross sermon by one Mr Bond. Bond had been briefed on what to say beforehand by Hatton and Aylmer and Aylmer reported that 'I thank God your travail and mine with the preacher hath taken good effect'. Bond in short had said what he had been told to say, accusing the author of the 'seditious pamphlet' of 'arrogancy and lack of charity': arrogancy in 'that being a private man durst so far presume to look into the secret bosom of princes' counsels' and 'lack of charity' in that, despite the queen's track record as a supporter of the Gospel 'ever since her first entry into her most gracious reign', he had dared to cast aspersions on her future protection of or adherence to the true religion. Bond also accused some of the people of 'curiosity and unkindness' in that they could 'not read in the book of her majesty's dealing in government written by experience of twenty years sweet peaceable years to confirm' her continued 'love and care for them' now and in the future. Whenever the preacher defended the queen in such terms, Aylmer reported, the people 'seemed, as it were with a shout, to give god good thanks and, as far as I could perceive, took it very well that she was commended for her zeal and constancy'. However, every time he turned his attention to Stubbes they

> utterly bent their brows at the sharp and bitter speeches that he gave against the author of the book of whom they conceive and report that he is one that feareth God, loveth her majesty, entered into this cause being carried with suspicion and jealousy of her person and safety, whereby I perceive that any that bend their pen, wit, knowledge or speech against foreign prince is of them counted a good patriot and pius subditus.

Aylmer then went on to give Hatton some good news and some bad news. As for 'the people of London', he surmised, 'I hope well that by the good instructions of the preachers they will stay themselves from all outrages'. However, 'abroad in the country (and the further off the worse)' things were rather different. There the preachers were denouncing Monsieur and the people were lapping it up. Aylmer wanted to call some of the offenders before him but was unwilling to go too far in that direction lest 'by sending for them in the country the Londoners should understand of the grudging and groaning abroad' and that 'would make them the worse'. Stubbes, in short, had struck a nerve, and his pamphlet had caused a very considerable echo effect, reverberating through myriad sermons, conversations and rumours, stirring up the people to something like open opposition to the match. As Aylmer summed up the state of opinion in and around London, 'there is a singular love towards her [Elizabeth] and great heart burning towards him [Anjou]', and there was little or nothing that the authorities could do about it.[29] At a popular level, at least, the image of the queen as a Protestant heroine, an inveterate enemy of popery and protectress of the Gospel, even in the face of 'the misliking of the greatest potentates in Europe' – an image which the regime pushed at every opportunity to legitimate her rule – had succeeded to such an extent that (whatever Elizabeth's personal wishes or intentions may have been) marriage to a foreign papist now seemed entirely incompatible with 'the queen's person and safety', and any opponent of such a project must by definition be a 'good patriot' and a 'pious subject'.

Stubbes's pamphlet sought to exploit this paradox by deploying at every turn the heightened language of the rabid anti-popery and anti-foreigner sentiment that constituted perhaps the central link between the godly and 'the people'. While this move made the case against the match that much easier to make, it also served to heighten the already considerable tensions inherent in Stubbes's position as a hot Protestant defender of the queen and of Protestant England against the queen's own policy. The consequent difficulties forced him into a number of positions very like those adopted by the author of the *Treatise of Treasons*.

For Stubbes it was axiomatic that marriage to a papist and a foreigner could not be in the nation's interests; it would necessitate, at the very least, official sanction for the presence of idolatry in the midst of Protestant England and very likely something like *de facto* if not *de jure* toleration of papists. Either would be certain to bring down the judgement of a jealous God upon the nation. On one level, this should have been a clinching argument, its force obvious to all right-thinking English Protestants and rendered all the greater by the notorious opposition of the French royal house to the cause of the Gospel. But Stubbes could not leave the matter there; he needed both to explain how, despite this, the policy had won so much royal favour and to find a way to engage with the other more *politique* arguments adduced in the match's support without being seen himself to subjugate the dictates of God's law and the cause of true religion to the demands of mere human policy. To his rescue came the presence at court of a group of 'half taught Christians and half hearted Englishmen', 'discoursers that use the word of God with as little conscience as they do Machiavelli, picking out of both indifferently what may serve their turns'.[30] These men were 'flatterers' who told the queen what she wanted to hear, rather than the truth;[31] they were ne'er-do-wells and malcontents, 'such as find themselves not advanced in this state according to that desert which they conceive in themselves and therefore disdain at others' good estate, or else such as are past hope here and having nothing know they can lose nothing, what change or tumbling soever come'. 'Politics', they were guided by 'policy' rather than by conscience, by the works of Machiavelli rather than the word of God,[32] except that while Machiavelli ever 'wrested his ungracious wit to the maintenance of the present state' 'these foolish scholars put forth their gross conceits to the overthrow this present in hope of I wot not what future commonwealth of their own head'. To that end they argued more 'like Basciaes to the great Turk than Christian commonwealthsmen', preferring 'the honour that comes to the prince' to the interests of 'the nation'.[33]

In all these characteristics such people were more private than public, more Catholic than Protestant, more French than English. For the quintessence of these qualities, Stubbes argued, was to be found in France. 'This is that most

Christian court where Machiavelli is their New Testament and atheism is their religion, yea, whose whole policy and government seems to set the Turkish tyranny as a pattern, and they draw as near to it as their ancient laws will any ways suffer'.[34] But English they were, and, having established the presence of such people at court, Stubbes was then able to use that fact as an excuse to engage in an extended debate about policy, broaching in print and before the people a full discussion of the geopolitical pros and cons of the match. All of which was laced throughout by a whole series of very personal arguments about both the queen and Anjou. On the queen's side, these concentrated on her age, and the consequent likelihood of her dying in childbirth, or, having failed to conceive, of her being deserted by the much younger Anjou, now desperate for an heir and, as a papist, well able to abandon the marriage, having obtained a dispensation for that purpose from the ever obliging pope.[35] As for Anjou, much play was made with his depraved character ('his marvellous licentious and dissolute youth'),[36] his past political failures, his inveterate popery ('in France he haunts the mass and is haunted only of papists') and his evil following, 'the scum of the French court, which is the scum of France, which is the scum of Europe'.[37]

There was, of course, more than a passing resemblance between Stubbes's picture of the group of nameless evil counsellors who were pushing the Anjou match and the *Treatise of Treasons* portrait of those two Machiavellian Catilines, Cecil and Bacon. And the two portrayals played a parallel role in both books, legitimating recourse to public discussion of the *arcana imperii* as the only way to frustrate the machinations of a private, court-based faction or conspiracy. Just as the *Treatise* spoke out in defence of the ancient nobility, traditional religion and the integrity of the monarchical state and succession, so Stubbes pictured himself as 'a Christian commonwealthsman'. He was telling the queen the unvarnished truth and thus championing the interests of her 'civil body', which he presented as simply coterminous with those of 'the commonwealth', as opposed, with the self-serving flatterers and Machiavels, to pandering to the potentially destructive wilfulness, the private interest and vainglory, of her 'natural body'.[38] The difference, of course, was that while the targets of the *Treatise* were pillars of the regime, in so far as they existed at all, the objects of Stubbes's criticism – a group of crypto-Catholic noblemen, some of them very close to Mary Stuart – were peripheral to the Elizabethan establishment, their hopes of real power and influence tied very closely to the success of the Anjou match, after the failure of which they receded back into disgrace or exile, on their way producing in *Leicester's Commonwealth* the second instalment, as it were, of the *Treatise of Treasons*. This tract started with an explanation of the failure of the Anjou match in terms of the sinister dominance of the regime by the earl of Leicester, who, just like Cecil and Bacon before him, was pictured as the leader of a nominally 'Protestant', but in fact

Machiavellian, plot to monopolize royal favour and patronage, subvert the monarchical state and divert the succession.[39]

A lawyer, Stubbes was also Thomas Cartwright's brother-in-law – by any standards a puritan. Wallace MacCaffrey has argued that in thus having recourse to the public prints Stubbes was in effect acting as the agent of the forward Protestants on the council. Allowing such men plausible deniability, as the secrets of the *arcana imperii* were seditiously broached before 'the people', Stubbes took the risks and the can, while helping to create precisely the sort of public stir against the match that his erstwhile backers at court could then innocently cite to the queen as yet another reason not to proceed. More recently, Natalie Mears has argued that, far from acting as the catspaw of Leicester and his mates, Stubbes was in effect freelancing. Mears's case rests firstly on the lack of any substantive ties of patronage linking Stubbes with the forward Protestant party on the council. Rather his ties were with Burghley and his secretaries Vincent Skinner and Michael Hickes. Secondly, she makes much of a distinction between the view of counsel adopted by privy councillors like Burghley or Leicester and that animating Stubbes's activities. It is, however, not altogether clear that Burghley and Stubbes had different theories of counsel. Stubbes clearly thought that, all things being equal, the role of counselling the monarch belonged to a group he addressed as 'you noblemen and high counsellors', to 'bishops and others who sometimes speak in the ear of our prince' and 'whosoever in court' was 'honoured by her majesty with any special favour and grace'. He also held that it was the duty of 'the meaner sort throughout the land, and all private ones' to 'know your place' and remain 'in all subjection and peaceable patience'. For such, tears and prayers were the only recourse. It was just that in the present conjuncture, with those charged with the duty of counselling the queen having failed to 'render to the queen that faithful counsel which she may well challenge for advancing of you to honour', and with the queen having fallen under the influence of the flatterers and evil counsellors denounced in his tract, Stubbes had felt the need, 'as a true Englishman' and 'a sworn liegeman to her majesty', to speak out, by 'gathering these necessary consequences by their reasonable causes'. This, then, was an emergency, and Stubbes's act, while necessary, was extraordinary; like, he admitted, to 'cost me my life'.[40] What is at stake here, then, is not so much a different theory of counsel as a different estimation of the seriousness of the crisis confronting the Elizabethan state, interacting with Stubbes's sense of vocation and duty, in an emergency, to speak truth to power, whatever the consequences. Here again Stubbes's analysis of the situation, and construction of his own role within it, was very like that of the author of *The Treatise of Treasons*.

Mears sees the council as largely united in opposition to the match (although not necessarily in their reasons for that opposition) and, following Simon Adams, argues that, after page upon page of pro and con argument, in the last analysis even Burghley himself remained cool on the issue.[41] Here it is worth noting that Burghley's qualified assent to the match, given at a meeting of the privy council on 6 October 1579, was predicated on 'the cause of religion' being 'provided for' and on 'all other things requisite' being 'assented to by parliament'.[42] He repeated what was in effect the same caveat in council the next day when he observed that 'there is no benefit such by the marriage, but except there be also provisions accorded and wisely established to withstand certain apparent perils' – presumably another reference to, among other things, religion 'being provided for' and the approval or ratification of the marriage treaty by parliament being obtained – 'no wise man can make the marriage beneficial'. Given that Burghley must have fully appreciated the difficulties involved in achieving a settlement of the religious issues and in obtaining parliamentary approval, and given that he had concluded his remarks of the previous day with the admission that 'except her majesty would of her mind incline to this marriage he would never advise her to',[43] putting him down simply as a supporter of, and still less as an enthusiast for, the match seems precipitate.

Ultimately, if they were to retain their places on the council, let alone the queen's favour, in the matter of a royal marriage, privy councillors had to concede the queen the final say, restricting their role to the provision of arguments for or against the match. The very furthest members of the inner circle could go in publicizing their opinions or appealing to wider bodies of opinion was Sir Philip Sidney's letter to the queen against the match.[44] This circulated in manuscript but in very tight circles and Sidney, who was not a councillor, of course, but who may be thought to have been acting as the catspaw or surrogate of men, like his uncle Leicester, who were, managed to retain the queen's favour despite having written and circulated it.[45]

Thus were the proprieties of counsel giving observed but, as Susan Doran has pointed out, in thus refusing collectively to endorse the match the councillors were denying Elizabeth the support she needed to get the proposal through what was sure to be an assertively Protestant and hostile parliament.[46] The difficulty of that task could only be increased, of course, by the briefing of both popular and parliamentary opinion being conducted in Stubbes's book, where, as we have seen, all the major arguments for the match were confuted and its proponents denounced as crypto-Catholic or Machiavel francophile courtiers on the make. The resulting combination amounted to a one–two punch, with councillors scrupulously observing the proprieties in private while in public, through print, rumour and the pulpit, opinion was aroused in ways designed to further pressure the queen to act (or, in this case, not to act) as they desired. This is an outcome and a *modus operandi* reminiscent of nothing so much as the campaign against Mary and Norfolk described above: a campaign that, as we have seen, had been co-ordinated by none other than Burghley himself.

As Stubbes languished in prison after his condign punishment at the hands of the public hangman, he petitioned both the privy council in general and one councillor in particular for mercy. It is the letter to the unnamed individual councillor that is of especial interest here. Stubbes sought particular favour from this man because, he claimed,

> even as the lord God directed the first examining of me to your lordship, so I hope it will please him, by the same, to give me good issue of my troubles; and, as before the matter found out, he then gave you the diligent endeavour of a vigilant magistrate, to examine and resist, by timely foresight, anything that might fall out perilous to this common-weal, whereof you have not the least charge, as well in counsel of state as for administration of justice, even so, now the matter is nakedly revealed, and the worst thereof fallen upon myself, without any disturbance to her majesty's common peace, whereof I thank God more than my life, I hope verily, and with much comfort, to find in your lordship that noble disposition which delighteth in procuring mercy, and that Christianity that taketh pleasure in comforting oppressed hearts.[47]

Behind the very considerable complexity of Stubbes's syntax we can surely discern in this petition clear evidence that one councillor at least knew of the book 'before the matter found out' and now, 'the worst thereof' having 'fallen' upon Stubbes, with no damage done either to the common peace or to the common weal, there remained a residual obligation on that same councillor to do something to help Stubbes himself out of his current predicament. For all the elaborate humility of tone, there is an element of moral blackmail here that suggests levels of complicity the nature of which is likely forever to remain hidden. Given the constraints inherent in the political situation with which we are dealing here, this is as close to a smoking gun as we are likely to get. Certainly, by 1587 Burghley himself can be found employing Stubbes to produce a reply to Cardinal Allen's attack on Burghley's own tract *The Execution of Justice in England.* [48] At the very least, we can say that, however much they may have offended the queen, over the long haul, Stubbes's efforts to stymie the match had done his relations with the lord treasurer no harm at all.

Similarly striking is the case of Thomas Norton. Imprisoned in the Tower, it seems, for talking out of line about the Anjou match, Norton placed all his hopes of release and rehabilitation on his old patron, Burghley. (As he told his wife, 'next unto God . . . I have rested myself upon the goodness and media-tion of my Lord Treasurer'. 'My Lord Treasurer,' he claimed, was 'the only man in whom I have chief earthly confidence'.) While in prison, Norton was also employed by Walsingham to write 'commonwealth' tracts about how best to protect the realm from 'popery'.[49] And certainly the role played in distrib-uting fifty copies of Stubbes's pamphlet in the West Country by William Page, a parliament man and secretary of the earl of Bedford, makes it clear that Stubbes did not lack sympathizers and accomplices in relatively high and well connected places.[50]

The precise extent to which Stubbes acted alone or with the connivance or even at the instigation of greater men at court or on the council is likely to remain unknowable. For the purposes of the present argument this ultimately does not matter. What is clear is the existence of a political conjuncture in which appeal to bodies of opinion outside the inner circles of counsel giving was likely to be crucial to the outcome and was therefore both in the interests of certain elements within the regime (Leicester, certainly, but also, on this account, Burghley) and of interested parties, on the fringes of the court and the establishment, with their own ideological commitment to averting the match, like Stubbes or indeed Norton. There was also an established *modus operandi*, a political style or set of manoeuvres, perfected in the course of earlier such conjunctures, and now available to be deployed here. Stubbes deployed them and paid the penalty. Either way, as his gruesome public punishment shows, in writing the *Gaping Gulf* Stubbes had gone a large step further than Graves's 'council men of business', Fleetwood and Norton, usually went. But the difference was one of degree rather than of kind.[51] Their activities, while less overtly oppositional or 'popular' than those of Stubbes, were also designed to massage, manage and manipulate both parliamentary and, as we have seen in the case of Mary Stuart, popular opinion in ways that were intended to force the queen's hand on issues on which many of her councillors desired action and about which she, at best, wished to prevaricate or delay. The list of such topics is, of course, entirely familiar to students of the period, comprising, most obviously and recurrently, the succession, marriage, the both domestic and international threats of popery, intervention in the Low Countries, further reform of the church, Mary Queen of Scots. All of these topics, differently structured and posed by changing political circumstance, retained their urgency and salience from the 1560s through what Professor Collinson has memorably christened the Elizabethan exclusion crisis of the 1580s.

As Sir John Neale, in his perhaps rather overly Whiggish way, noted years ago, it was through parliament that many of the most famous attempts to force the queen's hand on these issues were undertaken. Where Neale tended to see the machinations of a puritan opposition behind these events, it is remarkable how often, even in Neale's own narrative, the figures of Burghley and his clients and creatures feature at the centre of these manoeuvres; manoeuvres which more recent, consciously revisionist, writers have recategorized as largely the work of 'council men of business' like Norton and Fleetwood.[52] (Here we might take as paradigmatic Graves's extended analysis of the campaign against Mary Stuart in 1572.[53]) While, in the end, parliament played no role in the Anjou debacle, it is surely significant that both Burghley and Stubbes assumed that the queen could not successfully conclude a match with Anjou without first consulting parliament.[54] Again, on Doran's reading of events, the difficulty of getting any version of the match through parliament was a major factor in the calculations of both the queen and her councillors.

IV

Parliament, viewed both as an institution and an event, a law-making body and a debating chamber, stands somewhere near the centre of the ambiguities and contradictions of the notion of the public with which we are dealing here. In what sense was parliament a public institution? Was it part of 'the state' or not? To ask that question is to advert to the difficulty, even the impossibility, of distinguishing clearly between the 'state' and 'civil society' or 'a public sphere' in this period. For, at one level, as Geoffrey Elton never tired of telling us, parliament was a part of the monarchical state, its proceedings privileged and secret, its central function the transaction of the monarch's business.[55] Yet, on another level, parliament was the ultimate 'public' arena, its business that of the commonwealth. For it was in parliament that private interest – the claims of individuals, of particular localities, corporate bodies or interest groups – were transmuted, through the rhetoric of the commonweal and the public good and the procedures of the house, into genuinely public acts.[56] Parliament was also a privileged sounding board or arena where things unsayable in public elsewhere could be uttered in a context likely to garner them the rapt attention of a very generously defined political nation. As Pauline Croft has argued, the floating of proposals for legislation there (bills) and the completion of actual legislative action (acts) have to be seen as part of a broader manipulation of and appeal to public opinion.[57] And, of course, as Graves has shown, it was precisely because of their skill, judgement, standing and independence as parliament men that the likes of Norton and Fleetwood were so useful to the council or individual councillors as men of business and instruments of parliamentary management.

For, just like Stubbes, when Fleetwood or Norton acted in that role, they were acting (formally, at least) as independents. As Graves has insisted, neither man ever took office from the crown. Rather they remained employees of the city of London.[58] Not only did this give their backers in high places plausible deniability, just as important for their role as parliamentary managers, men of business and political agents, it also conferred on them an aura of independence. Not catspaws or creatures of the great, here were parliament men and lawyers, persons of judgement, skill and independence, in Stubbe's phrase, 'Christian commonwealthsmen', speaking out in defence of what they saw as the interests of queen and commonwealth, of church, state and true religion.[59]

We are seeing here the development of a series of forms of political action and manoeuvre which were both oppositional and public, in the senses that they often flew in the face of the royal will and entailed appeal to wider bodies of public, parliamentary and/or popular opinion. And yet they can scarcely be taken either to have characterized or denoted the presence of an opposition, puritan or otherwise, in the classic Nealean sense of that term – a notion against which, of course, both Graves and Collinson, in their different ways, are writing in revolt and reaction. For many (if not most) of these manoeuvres and moves proceeded from within the establishment, indeed very often from within the circle of none other than William Cecil, who may well deserve to be regarded as, if not the originator of, then certainly as a past master at, this particular style of political manoeuvre.[60]

At this point, it might be tempting to conclude that what we are seeing here is the product of a certain interaction or confluence between the two major ideological strands – 'perfect Protestantism' and what has been termed the 'classical republicanism' – in terms of which recent scholarship has shown many of the leading members of the high Elizabethan regime (and their clients and men of business) saw or interpreted the world.[61] On the one hand, we have the vision of the English polity as a mixed monarchy or even polity, with the monarchical element provided, of course, by the queen, the aristocratic element by the council and the democratic by the parliament.[62] Animating the workings of the polity thus conceived was a vision of political virtue and participation, of government and order, the bearing of office and discharge of duty under the crown, to which the giving and taking of counsel were central. But while the business of giving (and, for that matter, of taking) counsel was inherently 'public', in the sense that regard could only be had to the public good of the commonwealth (rather than to the furtherance of any private interests), it was also an intensely private affair, to be conducted, for the most part, behind closed doors at court and in council, between the queen and her chosen councillors. Sometimes, of course, it took place in parliament – parliament again providing the limiting case, the exception that proved the rule. Since one of that institution's major functions was to provide the monarch with counsel, all the members of that institution, while it was in session, might consider themselves to be, in some sense, counsellors if not councillors. Here, on certain readings (but not, of course, on that favoured by the queen), the notion of counsel could reach its greatest extent, stretching out, through the parliament men and their relations with their counties or constituents, to the wider political nation. And yet parliament was subject to rather stringent versions of the conventional limits placed upon the process of giving and taking counsel. At least notionally, its proceedings were secret, its role in the operation of the polity episodic and the nature and the extent of its privileges of free speech the subject of intermittent but often sharp disagreement and dispute.

Taken on its own, then, the 'civic republicanism' described by scholars like Alford and Peltonnen was quite compatible with, indeed arguably rather conducive to, decidedly constricted versions both of the extent of the counsel-giving political nation and of the political initiative left to the individual royal councillor. As Stephen Alford and Natalie Mears have both pointed out, it was precisely such a constricted view of the counsellor's role that Burghley himself espoused and at least outwardly observed in his conduct as privy councillor.[63] There was, then, no necessary connection between a 'civic republican' view of the polity and the sort of public and popular political style under discussion here.

At this point, of course, we might have recourse to certain attitudes or tendencies central to, perhaps even distinctively inherent in, the Protestant impulse, propensities which we might see working themselves out in and through the process whereby a Protestant establishment sought to construct and defend itself against the ideological and political threat represented by its Catholic other. After all, a causal link could easily be posited between a whole series of 'Protestant' attitudes and attributes and both the sort of publics being imagined and appealed to here and the media being mobilized to make those appeals. The aggressive certainties of Protestant scripturalism, the obsession with the potency of the Word preached and the iron conviction that the cause of true religion must and would be best vindicated and spread through open public dispute and assertion, conducted before the widest possible audience, in terms of known (purportedly) scriptural criteria of truth and purity, might well be taken to be conducive to precisely the sort of actions and attitudes here described.

Again, the notion of England as a nation in some sort of covenantal relation with a demanding God, a God who might respond to any backsliding in the prosecution of the cause of true religion or reformation with punishment delivered at the hands of the very papists against whom the nation was supposed to be uniting – such, after all, had been the fate of the first English try at reformation under Edward VI – provided, whenever danger loomed, legitimation for extraordinary actions, in the shape of direct, indeed prophetically inflamed and intemperate, appeals to prince, magistrate and people to both repent and act before all was lost. Here action to defend or preserve the 'state', i.e. the current distribution of office and favour, merged together with the defence of the Gospel both at home and abroad, and, on certain views, the pursuit of various sorts of 'reformation'.[64]

Through the notion of the thing to be preserved as the commonwealth and an identification between the perpetuation of the current regime, its personnel and policies, and the wider cause of the Gospel, both at home and abroad, might come into being a transpersonal political and moral entity (a Christian commonwealth or Protestant state) whose interests had to be protected, even against the personal whims and fancies, the mistakes and miscalculations, of the present incumbent of the throne and, indeed, whose protection might confer legitimacy on actions taken against or in order to frustrate the preferred policies of the monarch, actions often taken using 'popular' means the legitimacy of which, in more normal circumstances, would have remained in the

most serious question. Thus could reasons of state, the demands of an escha-
tologically charged providentialism and what became known as the politics of
'popularity' come together. (Small wonder that some Catholics claimed that
what was going on here was the practice of an atheistical Machiavellianism,
with religion providing a legitimating screen for the pursuit of private, secular
self-interest.) Perhaps, therefore, in the confluence between such perfect Protestant impulses and imperatives and the counsel-centred notions of political
virtue and participation central to the 'monarchical republic' we have the
ideological origins of the emergent style of political action under discussion
here.[65]

Certainly, the strength and salience of the supposed connections and corre-
lations cannot but seem all the greater when we recall that we have been
talking, for the most part, about the activities of hot Protestants and puritans
(Stubbes, Fleetwood, Norton) – men who were acting not merely or perhaps
even mainly as the instruments, 'the men of business', surrogates and intermediaries of other, greater persons but also as autonomous agents, commonwealthsmen, keen to push their own particular visions of the common good
and of true religion to the forefront of royal concern in a struggle against
what they took to be the world historical threat of Antichristian popery. In
conventional or traditional accounts of the developments under discussion
here, puritanism would almost certainly have played a more prominent role
than it has or will in this chapter. The reasons for that are twofold. Firstly, on
the view being put forward here, the lobbying and organizing activities that, in
Patrick Collinson's classic account, constituted 'the Elizabethan puritan movement' are best conceived as a continuation and development of the efforts of
the Protestant regime in church and state to define and defend itself against
the popish other. Starting out as willing participants in officially sponsored
or patronized efforts to further the course of reformation and preserve the
Protestant regime as they understood it, as further reformation not only failed
to happen, but episcopal authority, acting at the behest of the queen herself,
clamped down on certain of its outward forms or signs, zealous Protestants
became (intermittently) involved in something like open opposition to royal
policy and overt criticism of the liturgy, governing structures and policies of
the church. Thus men as loyal and obedient as Norton or Fleetwood or indeed
John Stubbes became or could become, on certain issues and at certain times,
'puritans', and preachers as ambitious and well connected as Edward Dering
could be driven into open criticism not only of the queen and her church but,
in Dering's case, of his erstwhile patrons as well. Thanks largely to the work of
Patrick Collinson the outline of how and when that happened, and the chronological ark of puritan campaigns for further reformation, is one of the best
known, most exhaustively researched and well told aspects of the whole reign.
There is, therefore, no need to retell that story here.[66]

Secondly, and more important, to give too great a prominence to 'puritanism' and 'puritans' in the development and deployment of the political techniques, the attitudes and assumptions, at the core of this chapter would be to give a quite distorted and misleading impression. It is certainly true that, both early and late in the reign, when royally sponsored efforts to crack down on the godly produced moments of perceived crisis – and here the Vestiaran controversy and the subscription crisis of 1583–84 spring to mind – various coalitions of zealous clergy and their lay supporters pushed the style of public politicking being described here to its highest peaks of coherence, radicalism and risk. In so doing they provoked an ideological and political reaction against what became known as the politics of 'popularity' and thus inadvertently played a central role in the subversion of many of the core assumptions and characteristics of Collinson's 'monarchical republic'.[67] But it would be wrong to attribute to 'puritanism' the origins and initial development of the political style under discussion here merely because that style, and the assumptions and techniques that underpinned it, were subsequently pushed to breaking point and beyond by the likes of John Field and Martin Marprelate.[68] For that style owed its origins and indeed its initial, and perhaps most subtle and skilful, deployments to elements located very close to the centre of the Elizabethan establishment.[69] On this view, it is no accident that leading 'puritans' – men like Dering or Field or Walter Travers, or indeed Stubbes, Norton and Fleetwood – had all been protégés and clients, allies and dependants of the likes of Burghley or Leicester. For, at the level of political action or technique, even at its most radical, all the 'Elizabethan puritan movement' amounted to was the turning back against (often episcopal and clericalist) elements in the establishment, of a political mode or style that had first been perfected and deployed in the defence of that establishment, at the behest or with the connivance of some of the most powerful men in England. But, having said that, the proliferation of these techniques and assumptions, and their deployment to criticize and pressure the regime, as it were, from without as well as from within, were developments crucial to the emergence of the political scene, of the mode of communication and manoeuvre, being described in this article and here 'puritanism', conceived as both a movement and an ideology, was a crucial factor. Again, however, to place too much emphasis even upon this aspect of the case would be to run the risk of another sort of distortion.

V

For, for all its affinities with perfect Protestantism, defined both as a political interest and as a nexus of ideological affinities and attitudes, as the *Treatise of Treasons* proved, Catholics could and did play this game with great gusto and effectiveness. To illustrate and amplify that point let us turn now to the mission to England led by Robert Parsons and Edmund Campion in 1580–81. As Michael Questier and I have argued at length elsewhere, that mission was not only or simply evangelical in its purposes.[70] That is to say, it was not concerned solely with the provision of the word Catholically preached and of the mass and the sacraments to English Catholics both fully separated and schismatic. That certainly was a good part of the point, but the mission conceived thus took place in a certain political context and in consequence took certain forms that meant that it was always much more than such a description might lead us to assume.

Crudely put, the political context, the backdrop against which their mission took place, was that provided by the Anjou match and its attendant political consequences and fantasies. For the match led Catholics and crypto-Catholics to hope for precisely what Protestants like Stubbes most feared; for Catholics many of Stubbes's central arguments against the marriage were, in fact, reasons to want it. For to many on both sides of the confessional divide, marriage to a Catholic seemed to offer the all but certain prospect, if not of overt toleration, then certainly of much improved terms and conditions of allegiance for all but the most politically rabid and hispanophile of English Catholics.

Into this context Campion and Parsons proceeded to insert themselves. They operated not covertly as missionaries, mere doctors of the soul, anxious to reconcile schismatics and administer the mass and the word. Rather they conducted what can only be called a public propaganda campaign, using the full gamut of available media: semi-public meetings, rumours, circulated manuscript and illicit print. Through Campion's famous brag and then through the products of their secret printing press they challenged the regime to engage them in open debate about the real theological and legal issues at stake in the showdown between the regime and its Catholic subjects. What this amounted to was a calling of the regime's bluff on the issue of whether Catholics were being persecuted in England for religion or not. They were here, the two Jesuits claimed, not for any political reason but merely as missionaries; they were religious men fulfilling a purely religious mission. If, as the regime claimed, Catholics were not subject to persecution for their religion, then it followed that the regime must allow such men room to perform their purely religious functions or, at the very least, allow them to argue their case in public before the queen. The Elizabethan state was thus being challenged to answer a religious case, religiously and peacefully made, not with accusations of treason, with the rack, the rope and the disembowelling block, but with counter-arguments and scripture.

As they issued this challenge the two men also upped the ante in the Catholic stand-off with the Elizabethan state, by arguing, both in private meetings with their fellow Catholics and in (illicit) print, that no true Catholic could in good conscience attend any service of the national (heretical) church. In so doing, as McKoog has shown, they were both taking an altogether harder line than even the pope and flying in the face of a good deal of indigenous English Catholic opinion.[71] The underlying polemical – indeed, political – logic of this stance is clear. If Catholics were precluded by merely conscientious religious reasons and obligations from attending church, they could not be accused of political disloyalty in so doing. But the more Catholics in fact became principled and consistent recusants the greater the campaign of religious disobedience that would attend both Campion and Parson's campaign for a public hearing of the Catholic case and the conclusion of the Anjou match.

A proper appreciation of both the effectiveness of this challenge and indeed of the prevalence of the mode of political manoeuvre and pitch making under discussion here can be gleaned from the nature of the regime's response. This consisted not of an attempt to close down the space for public discussion opened by the two Jesuits activities but rather by further opening it, the more readily to manipulate the resulting arena for their own propagandistic purposes. Admittedly, this was not their preferred option. First, they tried to undermine Campion's personal standing as a holy man, a potential martyr and saint, by trying to turn and then to break him. In interviews with Leicester he was offered preferment and honour if he would just change sides. Later resort was had to torture and the claim was spread that he had shopped his friends and erstwhile supporters. But it was a sign of just how effective the public challenge represented by the brag had been that when these manoeuvres failed the regime then allowed Campion an admittedly rigged series of theological debates in the Tower. Subsequently, his trial become a showcase not only for Campion and his fellows' status as traitors, agents of an international Catholic conspiracy, but also for the Catholic contention that they were being persecuted solely for religion. Again Campion's execution became the occasion for a very public demonstration of the same two cases; for there Campion was presented, according to your tastes, interests and perspective, either as a traitor deservedly dying the distinctively dreadful death reserved for such or as a martyr-saint suffering for his convictions.

As Michael Questier and I have argued elsewhere, such public performances were inherently glossable.[72] Catholic accounts of the Tower disputations, and of Campion's trial and death, all circulated by word of mouth, manuscript and print. The regime responded in kind, glossing Campion's career, opinions and fate via rumours, cheap print, published formal refutations of the printed propaganda of mission, and a printed account of debates in the Tower expressly designed to refute Catholic versions of the same event. The process culminated famously with Burghley himself entering the debate over the persecution issue.[73] Thus we can conclude that the confrontation with Catholicism precipitated by the Parsons and Campion affair took place as much in the public sphere of argument and assertion as it did in and through the dumb-show of capture, imprisonment and a traitor's death. The whole debate about the state's relation to and treatment of English Catholics was played out in public, in court, on the scaffold and in print, before a series of overlapping 'popular' audiences. The very arenas, stages and audiences called into being by the state to dispatch its Catholic victims in fact allowed those same victims to put their own spin on the proceedings and thus to make a pitch for popular support. The variegatedly public nature of the state's response shows how effective Campion and Parson's calling of the regime's bluff on the treason/religion issue had been. The regime's concerted response to this challenge provides a marked contrast with its response to, say, the *Treatise of Treasons*, when, despite voluminous notes towards a reply being drawn up by Cecil himself, discretion proved to be the better part of valour and the libel was met, not with a formal reply, but rather with a formal rebuke, in the form of a proclamation denouncing, dismissing and suppressing the book as a seditious libel.[74] This firstly suggests a developed sense on the part of the regime, and in particular of William Cecil, of the dynamics, the pros and cons, of this mode of political and communicative action and secondly provides vivid testimony to the extraordinary effectiveness of Campion and Parsons' assault on the legitimacy of the regime. For, by its very nature, their challenge had virtually forced the monarchical state to answer back in public, and in so doing it had created the grounds of possibility for Catholics to make their case, both at home and abroad, to a series of wider and wider Catholic, Protestant and ideologically indeterminate audiences.

The enormous brio, courage and skill with which the two Jesuits deployed all the techniques and media crucial to this mode of political pitch making – circulating manuscript, rumour, various genres of print and public performance – to challenge some of the central legitimating claims of the regime must render any claim that this was a peculiarly Protestant, or still less a peculiarly puritan or indeed a 'republican', mode exceedingly doubtful. Rather than to properties or potentials inherent in either English Protestantism or monarchical republicanism, then, it is to the interaction of those ideological strands and the course and dynamics of inter-confessional dispute and controversy, in the extremely unstable political context provided, in general, by the geopolitics of post-Reformation Europe that we should turn if the phenomenon under discussion here is to be properly understood. As Collinson has pointed out in a series of ground-breaking articles,[75] almost throughout the reign, the Elizabethan establishment (and its Catholic enemies) viewed an always already hostile geopolitical environment through the lens provided by the peculiar situation in which the subjects of Elizabeth Tudor perforce found themselves: ruled by an unmarried woman, without an heir of her body and saddled (until 1587) with a reversionary interest of the opposite confessional colouring and thereafter with what looked to many contemporaries like a succession crisis waiting to happen. It was the dynamics of this situation that prompted those at the centre of the regime to have repeated recourse to the modes of political manoeuvre and manipulation, the appeals to a variety of publics, described above. Thus were the populist potentials latent within perfect Protestantism and 'monarchical republicanism' released and channelled into what had become, by the late 1570s and early 1580s, an established, recurring, almost reflexive, mode of political manoeuvre.

VI

This chapter stops, then, in many ways, *in medias res*, before Collinson's 'monarchical republic' reached its highest pitch of coherence and daring in the Bond of Association; before the politics of popularity were pushed to a similar pitch, first by the Elizabethan puritan movement, and then by the earl of Essex; before the incipient succession crisis of the 1590s combined with the dissolution of the high Elizabethan regime at the hands of the grim reaper to enable both the absolutist reaction and the ideological cacophony of the Elizabethan *fin-de-siècle*. But it also stops at a point at which all the constitutive parts and defining characteristics of what has been referred to in Chapter 1 of this book as 'the post-Reformation public sphere' had emerged into plain sight.

That 'public sphere' and the modes of political and communicative action that structured and produced it were in turn the product of the interaction between a number of forces and factors. First, of course, we have the dynamics of post-Reformation ideological and geopolitical conflict. In the English case the impact of that conflict was refracted through the status of Elizabeth Tudor as an unmarried regnant queen, devoid of an heir of her body and lumbered with a next successor of the opposite confessional colouring. This was compounded by what we might term the internal, both political and interpersonal, dynamics of the regime; the series of personal and political relationships that bound the queen to her councillors and courtiers and her councillors and courtiers, sometimes despite themselves, one to another. These dynamics ensured that a number of issues, upon which the queen and the majority of her councillors remained largely in disagreement, stayed unresolved throughout the central decades of the reign. The result was a series of attempts to appeal to and mobilize various bodies of opinion, or publics, as elements within the regime tried to protect both themselves and the Protestant state, as they understood it, from the popish threat at home and abroad. Very often the aim in so doing was also to persuade or induce the queen to take action at which she recoiled – to marry, to settle the succession, to bear down ever more relentlessly on her Catholic subjects, to reform her church, definitively to remove Mary Stuart from the scene – or, rather less frequently, to abandon action – like the marriage to Anjou or the sacking of Grindal –

that she seemed bound and determined to take. Even when the origins of these manoeuvres could be found at the very centre of the regime, they were launched and sustained by second-order figures, men (like Thomas Norton, John Stubbes and even John Field) attached to elements in the establishment by links of patronage or ideological affinity, but who were also, in important senses, acting independently.

Thus, at moments of perceived crisis, appeals were made to wider bodies of opinion through the full gamut of available media or modes of communication – print, performance, the pulpit, circulating manuscript, rumour. No doubt the preferred audience nearly always remained a modestly expanded version of the counsel-giving political nation – what we might term the parliamentary classes, a collection of 'public men', as John Stubbes almost put it. After all, even Stubbes himself had consigned those he termed 'private ones' or the 'meaner sort' to passive recourse to tears and prayers in the face of the doings of their rulers and betters. However, all too often what recourse to such methods meant was that appeals, concerning issues that were central to the *arcana imperii*, were in effect addressed to what the proclamation denouncing Stubbes's book called 'the simpler sort and the multitude',[76] that is to say, to promiscuously uncontrollable, both socially and ideologically heterogeneous, audiences. In short, these appeals were 'public' in all four of the senses of that term outlined at the start of this chapter and they called into being, even as they sought to mobilize, a series of publics who were taken to be integrally involved in both the political and the religious issues of the day.

Such appeals were scarcely ever, in the period under discussion here, regarded as licit, as either normal or normative, even by those most centrally involved in making them. The element of deception, of behind-the-scenes manoeuvre and manipulation, described above in section II, and absolutely essential to the maintenance of plausible deniability for the major players at court, shows that. But even John Stubbes, at the conclusion of his pamphlet, did not (quite) justify his action as based on his right to free speech or on his capacity or right, as not 'a private' but a 'public man', as an 'Englishman', to counsel his queen. Certainly he claimed to speak as such – 'a sworn liegeman to her majesty'[77] – but he spoke up only in an emergency: an emergency created by the failure of those obliged to counsel the queen properly to discharge their duties as counsellors and by the incipient capture of the queen by the conspiracy of evil, Machiavellian and Frenchified counsel that his book outlined and denounced. In this, as we have seen, Stubbes's pitch was very similar to that made by the author of *The Treatise of Treasons*, who, in turn, presented his recourse to print as a response to the most extreme of political circumstances – circumstances, just like those to which Stubbes claimed to be reacting, structured by a triumphant conspiracy of Machiavellian and atheistical evil counsel.

These, then, were always already emergency measures; transgressions of the bounds of the normal and the conventional, prompted by the extremity of the situation with which the author in question, and indeed the commonwealth, found themselves confronted. No doubt we should imagine the likes of Burghley having recourse to a similar logic of the extreme and the exceptional to justify their recourse to such methods and intermediaries, when the queen just would not do what was necessary to perpetuate or secure the Protestant state as he and his allies and clients conceived it. Certainly members of the puritan movement used precisely such arguments to justify their campaign for further reformation, carried on in the teeth of royal displeasure. Here was a kingdom threatened, both at home and abroad, not only by popery, but also by the incipient judgement of God, for its continued failure properly or fully to reform itself. And here was a queen subject to the evil counsel of a sinister claque of bishops and their self-serving, place-seeking clerical hangers-on, men who systematically misled her both about what the Bible said about the government of the church and what the discipline meant for the exercise of royal power.[78]

But, we might enquire, how many times does the 'exceptional' response to an 'emergency' have to be repeated before it becomes something like normal? After all, the confessional divisions inherent in the post-Reformation dilemma ensured that one person's normality almost always constituted someone else's emergency. Moreover, each recourse to such methods and claims constituted a challenge, indeed an invitation, to those intended to be excluded or marginalized by it to reply in kind. Thus did what was always legitimated as exceptional and extreme enter the realm of the normal, if not of the normative or the fully licit. And thus did the inherently dialogic nature of such appeals to the public – compounded, of course, by the inherently heterogeneous, indeed potentially bitterly divided, nature of the public/s being appealed to – ensure that (in the short to medium term, at least,) no one was going to get the last word.

Thus what began, in intention at least, as reasonably decorous attempts to get relatively limited versions of an emergent 'Protestant nation' to talk to itself, in the process inducing the queen to do the right thing, became something else entirely. Not only did the nature of the audiences being brought into that conversation become difficult to control, the boundaries of the 'Protestant nation', the border between 'private' and 'public' men, prove difficult both to draw and to police, other groups muscled in on the conversation. Here, of course, the prime example was the Catholics; the very group intended to be excluded not only from the conversation but from the contours of the state that that conversation was intended to construct. Unwilling to suffer passively on the receiving end of that process, various groups of Catholics took up the challenge and directed the same techniques and appeals back against the regime that the regime was using to marginalize and exclude them. Similarly, as further reformation refused to arrive and, at the behest of the queen and an emergent faction of determinedly anti-puritan clerics, official policy took turns inimical to the interests and aspirations of the *soi-disant* Protestant 'godly', erstwhile supporters and agents of the regime ('puritans') did the same thing, creating, as they did so, the 'Elizabethan puritan movement'. The result, with all its ragged edges and contested boundaries, was 'the post-Reformation public sphere' delineated in this chapter.

NOTES

Versions of this chapter have been given at London, Oxford, Johns Hopkins, and Yale. I would like to thank the participants at all those seminars and at the conference held at Keele on the public sphere in 2003 for their suggestions and criticisms and in particular Michael Questier, Richard Cust, Ann Hughes and Tom Cogswell for their comments and advice.

1 P. Collinson, 'The monarchical republic of Queen Elizabeth I', in his *Elizabethan Essays* (London, 1994), 31–57; Collinson, 'The Elizabethan exclusion crisis and the Elizabethan polity', *Proceedings of the British Academy* 84 (1995), 52–94.

2 P. Lake, 'Anti-popery: the structure of a prejudice', in R. Cust and A. Hughes (eds), *Conflict in early Stuart England* (Harlow, 1989), 72–106. For the origins of Elizabethan anti-popery see C. Davies, *A Religion of the Word: the Defence of the Reformation in the Reign of Edward VI* (Manchester, 2002), chapter I.

3 I summarize here the argument of *The Treatise of Treasons* (1572). On this general strand of Catholic analysis see P. Lake, '"The monarchical republic of Elizabeth I" revisited (by its victims) as a conspiracy', in B. Coward and J. Swann (eds), *Conspiracies and Conspiracy Theory in Early Modern Europe* (Aldershot, 2004), 87–111.

4 L. Adams, 'Faction, clientage and party: English politics, 1550–1603' *History Today* 32 (1982), 33–9. Also see Adams, 'Eliza enthroned? The court and its politics', in C. Haigh (ed.), *The Reign of Elizabeth I* (Basingstoke, 1984), 55–77, and Adams, 'The patronage of the Crown in Elizabethan politics: the 1590s in perspective', in J. Guy (ed.), *The Reign of Elizabeth I: Court and Culture in the last Decade* (Cambridge, 1995), 20–45.

5 If the real 'origins' of this mode of political action and manoeuvre were to be sought, we would have to go back to the first age of the English Reformation: to the 1520s and 1530s and not only where the conventional account would have us look, in the 'progressive' 'proto-Protestant' circles around Thomas Cromwell in the 1530s, but also, for example, in the circles around John Fisher or Thomas More which orchestrated the opposition to Lutheranism, to Henry's divorce and even the breach with Rome, on which see Richard Rex, 'The English campaign against Luther in the 1520s', *Transactions of the Royal Historical Society*, 5th ser., 39 (1989), 85–106; G. R. Elton, 'Sir Thomas More and the opposition to Henry VIII', in his *Studies in Tudor and Stuart Politics and Government* (Cambridge, 1974) I, 155–72. Also see Ethan Shagan, *Popular Politics and the English Reformation* (Cambridge, 2003), part I and especially chapter 2, and his article 'Print, orality and communications in the Maid of Kent affair', *Journal of Ecclesiastical History* 52 (2001), 21–33. Also see Shagan's chapter in this volume.

6 Again, if one were to begin, as it were, at the beginning, even in Elizabeth's reign, one would have to start with the various agitations around the succession and the queen's marriage during the 1560s, which formed the back story to the assault of Mary Stuart

and Norfolk with which the present discussion begins. This is a topic to which I hope to return elsewhere. The most authoritative account is still Mortimer Levine, *The early Elizabethan Succession Question* (Stanford CA, 1966).

7 The most recent account of the innerness of these events is S. Alford, *The early Elizabethan Polity: William Cecil and the British Succession Crisis, 1558–1569* (Cambridge, 1998), *passim*, and especially chapter 8.

8 They were collected together and printed by John Day as *All such Treatises as have been lately published by Thomas Norton*, of which there were two editions, one in 1569 and the other in 1570. On the propaganda generated by the revolt of the northern earls see J. K. Lowers, *Mirrors for Rebels: a Study of the Political Literature relating to the Northern Rebellion of 1569* (Berkeley CA, 1953).

9 Thomas Norton, *A Discourse touching the pretended Match between the Duke of Norfolk and the Queen of Scots*, separately printed by John Day and also included in Day's 1570 edition of *All such Treatises*.

10 William Fleetwood, *The Effect of the Declaration made in the Guildhall by M. Recorder of London, concerning the late Attempts of the Queen's Majesty's evil, seditious and disobedient Subjects* (London, 1571), quotations at sigs A4v, A2r, Bv, B2r, B2v, B3r–v, B4r–v, Cr.

11 *Salutem in Christo* (London, 1571), quotations at sigs A3v, A4r, A5r–v, A7r–v.

12 *A Detection of the Doings of Mary Queen of Scots* (1571). Quotations from *The Copy of a Letter*, sigs A2r, A3r–A4v.

13 *The Copy of a Letter*, sigs A4r, A2v, Bv.

14 Wilson's letter is printed in W. Murdin, *A Collection of State Papers relating to Affairs in the Reign of Queen Elizabeth* (London, 1759), 57. On this affair and Day's involvement see J. Guy, *My Heart is my Own: the Life of Mary Queen of Scots* (London, 2004), 467.

15 The involvement of Day in the printing of nearly all these tracts adds to the sense that what we are dealing with here was a concerted propaganda campaign emanating from the very centre of the regime. For the closeness of Day's links with Norton and with Cecil at this point see Liz Evenden and Tom Freeman, 'Print, profit and propaganda: the Elizabethan privy council and the 1570 edition of Foxe's *Book of Martyrs*', *English Historical Review* 119 (2004), 1288–307; E. Evenden, 'The Michael Wood mystery: William Cecil and the Lincolnshire printing of John Day', *Sixteenth Century Journal* 25 (2004), 3873–94; also see T. Freeman, '"The reformation of the church in this parliament": Thomas Norton, John Foxe and the parliament of 1571', *Parliamentary History* 16 (1997), 132–47.

16 *Salutem in Christo*, sig. A4r–v.

17 M. Graves, 'The management of the Elizabethan House of Commons: the council's "men of business"', *Parliamentary History* 2 (1982), 11–38; also see, more generally, Graves's article 'Thomas Norton the parliament man: an Elizabethan MP', *Historical Journal* 23 (1980), 17–35, and his *Thomas Norton the Parliament Man* (Oxford, 1994). Graves's conclusions fit perfectly with John Guy's account of Cecil's determination, during this period, to bring Mary to the block; see his *My Heart is my Own*, *passim*. For the quotation of *A Detection* in the parliamentary debates, see *ibid.*, 469.

18 In the ensuing debates some very radical arguments, culled from the resistance theories of the previous reign, were deployed, in particular by the bishops in the upper house. See Gerry Bowler, '"An Axe or an Acte": the parliament of 1572 and resistance theory in early Elizabthan England', *Canadian Journal of History* 19 (1984), 349–59, an article which

informs much of Collinson, 'Monarchical republic' and 'Elizabethan exclusion crisis'.

19 *The Treatise of Treasons* (1572). On the question of authorship see T. H. Clancy, 'A political pamphlet: the *Treatise of Treasons*, 1572', in G. J. Eberle (ed.), *Loyola Studies in the Humanities* (New Orleans LA, 1962).

20 *Treatise*, 80.

21 *Ibid.*, 84.

22 *Ibid.*, 99a–b.

23 *Ibid.*, preface, sig. A6v, where the author describes himself as 'a stranger that hath lived in this country, for the most part, above thirty years'.

24 On all this see Lake, 'Monarchical republic revisited'.

25 Among the best and most recent accounts of this affair are Wallace MacCaffrey, 'The Anjou match and the making of Elizabethan foreign policy', in N. Tyacke, P. Clarke and A. G. R. Smith (eds), *The English Commonwealth* (Leiceister, 1979), pp. 59–75; S. Doran, *Monarchy and Matrimony* (London, 1996), chapter 7; Blair Worden, *The Sound of Virtue* (London, 1996), *passim* but especially chapter 6; Natalie Mears, 'Love-making and diplomacy: Elizabeth I and the Anjou marriage negotiations, *c.* 1578–1582', *History* 86 (2001), 442–66; and Mears, 'Counsel, public debate and queenship: John Stubbs's *The Discoverie of a Gaping Gulf*', *Historical Journal* 44 (2001), 629–50.

26 For Sussex's enthusiasm for the match see a long letter to the queen of August 1578 in the Cecil manuscripts at Hatfield House, vol. 10, fols 30r–33v. I should like to thank Simon Adams for many discussions of this document.

27 J. Bossy, 'English Catholics and the French marriage, 1571–1578', *Recusant History* 5 (1960), 2–18.

28 Lloyd Berry (ed.), *John Stubbs' Gaping Gulf, with Letters and other relevant Documents* (Charlottesville VA, 1968).

29 BL, Additional Mss 15891, fols 5r–6r, Aylmer to Hatton, 28 September 1579.

30 Berry, *Stubbs' Gaping Gulf*, 5, 12.

31 *Ibid.*, 30–3.

32 *Ibid.*, 39.

33 *Ibid.*, 67, 39, 50, 53.

34 *Ibid.*, 76.

35 *Ibid.*, 72–3.

36 *Ibid.*, 71.

37 *Ibid.*, 28, 46.

38 *Ibid.*, 68–9.

39 Dwight C. Peck (ed.), *Leicester's Commonwealth* (Athens OH, 1985). For the failure of the Anjou match see 73–9.

40 *Ibid.*, 91–2.

41 Mears, 'Counsel, public debate and queenship'.

42 Notes on the discussion of the match in council in the Hatfield Mss, vol. 140, fols 6r–7v; quotation at 7v.

43 *Ibid.*, and Murdin, *Collection of State Papers*, 331.

44 Sidney's letter is printed in K. Duncan-Jones and J. Van Dorsten (eds), *Miscellaneous Prose of Sir Philip Sidney* (Oxford, 1973), 46–57.

45 Thus Worden reports Languet's remark that Sidney had been 'ordered to write as you did by those whom you were bound to obey' and speaks of Sidney 'risking political suicide on his uncle's behalf' in the crisis of 1579. Languet also commented that Sidney's decision to circulate the letter in manuscript was 'by no means a safe proceeding' (Worden, *Sound of Virtue*, 42, 48, 20). On the circulation of Sidney's letter see Peter Beal, *In Praise of Scribes* (Oxford, 1998), chapter 4.

46 Doran, *Monarchy and Matrimony*, 173–4.

47 John Harington, *Nugae Antiquae* (2 vols, London, 1804) I, 162–3.

48 Berry, *John Stubbs's* Gaping Gulf, xlii–iii.

49 Norton's letters from prison are to be found in BL, Additional Mss 48023, quotations at fols 32v, 42v.

50 Doran, *Monarchy and Matrimony*, 166–7.

51 Here, of course, we broach Patrick Collinson's famous distinction between the 'forward' and the 'froward'. As Collinson himself observes this is perhaps not best seen as a firm distinction between different character types, or still less between distinct ideological positions or even proclivities – between, say, 'moderate' and 'radical puritans' – although it could operate as such. Rather it is probably best regarded as an often ill defined and shifting line, on the wrong side of which even the most practised insider or 'council man of business', like Thomas Norton, could intermittently find himself. See P. Collinson, 'Puritans, men of business and Elizabethan parliaments', *Parliamentary History* 7 (1988), 187–211.

52 J. E. Neale, *Elizabeth I and her Parliaments, 1559–1581* (London, 1953) and *Elizabeth I and her Parliaments, 1584–1601* (London, 1957). Indeed, if one simply excises Neale's incessant and insistent references to 'the puritan opposition' and 'our puritan choir' his narrative lends itself quite nicely to the sort of post-revisionist reading of events being suggested here.

53 Graves, 'Management of the Elizabethan House of Commons'.

54 Berry, *John Stubbs'* Gaping Gulf, 68. Here Stubbes claimed that 'according to the laws of all well-ordered realms and manner of all good princes' it behove the queen 'not to conclude her marriage before she parle in parliament with her subjects, before she consult with the laws and call the commonweal as it were to common council'.

55 G. R. Elton, 'Parliament in the sixteenth century: functions and fortunes', *Historical Journal* 22 (1979), 255–78; Elton, 'Parliament', in C. Haigh (ed.), *The Reign of Elizabeth I* (Basingstoke, 1984), 79–100; Elton, *The Parliament of England, 1559–1581* (Cambridge, 1986).

56 See, for instance, G. R. Elton. 'Piscatorial politics in the early parliaments of Elizabeth I', in N. McKendrick and R. B. Outhwaite (eds), *Business Life and Public Policy* (Cambridge, 1986), 1–20; I. Archer, 'The London lobbies in the later sixteenth century', *Historical Journal* 31 (1988), 17–44; D. Dean, *Law-making and Society in late Elizabethan England* (Cambridge, 1996); and D. Dean and N. Jones (eds), *The Parliaments of Elizabethan England* (Oxford, 1990).

57 P. Croft, 'The parliament of England', *Transactions of the Royal Historical Society*, 6th ser.,

7 (1997), 217–34. Also see C. Kyle and J. Peacey, '"Under cover of so much coming and going": public access to parliament and the political process in early modern England'; and D. Dean, 'Public space, private affairs: committees, petitions and lobbies in the early modern English parliament', both in Kyle and Peacey (eds), *Parliament at Work: Parliamentary Committees, Political Power and Public Access in early modern England* (Woodbridge, 2002), 1–23, 198–78.

58 M. Graves, 'The common lawyers and the privy council's parliamentary men of business, 1584–1601', *Parliamentary History* 8 (1989), 189–215.

59 Cf. Collinson, 'Puritan, men of business and Elizabethan parliaments'.

60 Conyers Read, 'William Cecil and Elizabethan public relations', in S. T. Bindoff, J. Hurstfield and C. H. Williams (eds), *Elizabethan Government and Society* (London, 1961), 21–55.

61 On the 'civic republicanism' of the Elizabethan period see M. Peltonen, *Classical Humanism and Republicanism in English Political Thought, 1570–1640* (Cambridge, 1995), and Alford, *The early Elizabethan Polity*, and in a rather different key A. McClaren, *Political Culture in the Reign of Elizabeth I: Queen and Commonwealth, 1559–1585* (Cambridge, 1999). For a discussion of some of these themes for a slightly later period now see A. McRae, *Literature, Satire and the early Stuart State* (Cambridge, 2004), and D. Colclough, *Freedom of Speech in early Stuart England* (Cambridge, 2005). Both McRae and Colclough pay scant attention to the sort of confessional and dynastic conflicts and anxieties (not to mention the Catholic libels) from the Elizabethan period that alone make sense of the subsequent developments they describe. For a discussion of some of these themes untainted by the rhetoric of republicanism see Richard Cust's chapter in this volume.

62 This was the view of the English polity held both by Thomas Cartwright and Lord Burghley; see my review of Michael Mendle's book *Daungerous Positions* in *Parliamentary History* 6 (1987). Also see P. Lake, *Anglicans and Puritans? Presbyterianism and English Conformist Thought from Whitgift to Hooker* (London, 1988), 53–64.

63 Mears, 'Counsel, public debate and queenship'.

64 For the origins of such attitudes in the reign of Edward VI see Davies, *Religion of the Word*. Puritanism was, of course, one obvious product of this chain of argument or development. At some point, or rather points, perfect Protestantism slipped from being the ideology of an emergent and embattled Protestant 'establishment' to that of an equally embattled puritan 'opposition' – except that, despite the best efforts of generations of anti-puritan polemicists, such moments of shift or slippage never quite became a definitive or once-and-for-all transition or transformation. For an account of the extraordinarily close fit between the underpinning assumptions of the 'monarchical republic' and presbyterian theory see P. Lake, 'Presbyterianism, the idea of a national church and the argument from divine right', in P. Lake and M. Dowling (eds), *Protestantism and the National Church in Sixteenth Century England* (Beckenham, 1987), 193–224, and for somewhat different accounts of the resulting ambiguities and antinomies see P. Collinson, *The Religion of Protestants* (Oxford, 1982) and P. Lake, *Moderate Puritans and the Elizabethan Church* (Cambridge, 1982).

65 For an account of what the resulting synthesis might look like see P. Lake, 'Constitutional consensus and puritan opposition in the 1620s: Thomas Scott and the Spanish match', *Historical Journal* 25 (1982), 805–25, and R. Cust and P. Lake, 'Sir Richard Grosvenor and the rhetoric of magistracy', *Bulletin of the Institute of Historical Research* 54 (1981), 40–59, and Richard Cust's chapter in this volume. Also see P. Lake and M.

Questier, *The Antichrist's lewd Hat* (London, 2002), chapter 14, for Ben Jonson's satirically hostile account of the same distinct but often coagulated ideological strands in *Bartholomew Fair.*

66 P. Collinson, *The Elizabethan Puritan Movement* (London, 1967); on Dering see Collinson's essay 'A mirror of Elizabethan puritanism: the life and letters of "Godly master Dering"', in his *Godly People* (London, 1983), 289–323.

67 On this see P. Lake, 'John Whitgift, puritanism and the invention of "popularity"', forthcoming in a book of essays on *The Monarchical Republic of Queen Elizabeth I.*

68 Lake and Questier, *The Antichrist's lewd Hat*, 505–76.

69 The point emerges with renewed force when we recall that, shortly after the Field–Marprelate combination had pushed the politics of popularity way past the point of enlightened self-interest, destroying the Elizabethan puritan movement as it did so, the trick was repeated, with, if anything, even more disastrous results, by that ultimate Elizabethan insider, the earl of Essex. On the collapse of the classis movement see Colllinson, *Elizabethan Puritan Movement*, part 8. On Essex and popularity see Paul Hammer's chapter in this volume.

70 P. Lake and M. Questier, 'Puritans, papists and the "public sphere" in early modern England: the Edmund Campion affair in context', *Journal of Modern History* 72 (2000), 587–627. What follows is based upon the argument of that essay and the evidence adduced therein.

71 T. McKoog, *The Society of Jesus in Ireland, Scotland and England, 1541–1588* (Leiden, 1996), 145 n. 56.

72 P. Lake and M. Questier, 'Agency, appropriation and rhetoric under the gallows: puritans, Romanists and the state in early modern England', *Past and Present* 153 (1996), 64–107.

73 Robert M. Kingdom (ed.), *The Execution of Justice in England by William Cecil* (Ithaca NY, 1965).

74 For Burghley's most extensive set of notes on the *Treatise* see PRO, SP 53/11/637; for a letter from Mathew Parker to Burghley of 11 September 1573 urging him not to reply, see Murdin, *Collection of State Papers*, p. 259. I owe these references to the kindness of Tom Freeman. For the proclamation see P. L. Hughes and J. F. Larkin, *Tudor Royal Proclamations* (3 vols, Cambridge, 1969) II, *The later Tudors*, proclamation No. 598, 376–79.

75 Collinson, 'Monarchical republic' and 'Elizabethan exclusion crisis'.

76 Hughes and Larkin, *Tudor Royal Proclamations* II, 447.

77 Berry, *John Stubbs's Gaping Gulf*, 91.

78 Lake, *Moderate Puritans and the Elizabethan Church*, chapter 3, especially 25–35; and Lake, *Anglicans and Puritans?*, chapter 2.

Chapter 4

The smiling crocodile: the earl of Essex and late Elizabethan 'popularity'

Paul Hammer

In the late 1590s, English politics were riven by controversies surrounding the actions of Robert Devereux, second earl of Essex, the chief royal favourite, whose repeated efforts to reshape England's strategy in its war with Spain increasingly polarized opinion at court and across the realm. Ultimately he also lost the trust of the queen herself, with disastrous consequences. One of the chief accusations against Essex by his enemies was that his aristocratic style of politics had a deliberately populist appeal, which he fostered by relentlessly seeking public endorsement for his actions. Such 'popularity' was regarded as a sign of the earl's boundless ambition, but it also required the Elizabethan regime to wage its own propaganda campaigns in response. In this struggle against one of its own leading members, the government was forced to expose 'mysteries of state' to the light of public scrutiny, violating its own basic principle about the secrecy which should accompany royal government. In this public manoeuvring by Essex and his rivals, the whole of the queen's regime was opened up to discussion and criticism by subjects in ways which even the best efforts of official censorship could not control.

I

In early 1599 an ambitious civil lawyer, Dr John Hayward, published a history book which recounted events in England precisely 200 years before. Entitled *The First Part of the Life and Raigne of King Henrie IIII*, Hayward's work described the political failure of Richard II and his deposition in 1399 by Henry Bolingbroke, earl of Derby, who usurped the throne as Henry IV. The book quickly proved a best-seller because its subject matter seemed extraordinarily topical in the forty-first year of Elizabeth I's reign – a childless sovereign troubled by rebellion in Ireland, facing widespread discontent over heavy taxation, and buffeted by bitter factionalism at court and accusations that key royal councillors lacked sufficient respect for martial honour and the status of the peerage. The parallels between 1399 and 1599 were further accentuated by the work's fulsome dedication (albeit in Latin) to the earl of Essex, who had built his career upon the conspicuous display of aristocratic virtue and was then about to lead a large army to Ireland. Although he failed to emphasize the curious parallel between Bolingbroke's promotion to the dukedom of Hereford and Essex's junior title of Viscount Hereford, Hayward's dedication explicitly connected Essex with 'our Henry' ('Henrici nostri') and praised him as great 'both in present judgement and in expectation of future time' ('magnus siquidem es, & presenti iudicio & futuri temporis expectatione').[1] Given the intense speculation about the disposition of the crown when the elderly Elizabeth I finally died, this praise implicitly ascribed to Essex the role of a future king-maker. However, the direct comparison with Henry Bolingbroke might be seen as implying even more – that, like Bolingbroke, Essex would return from overseas and seize the throne from a failing and childless monarch for the sake of national stability.

Regardless of whether Hayward intended to ventilate this second possibility, some of his readers certainly made the connection. Essex himself – who was allegedly too busy preparing for his Irish expedition to pay any attention to the book before its publication – suddenly recognized the danger of such praise in late February and complained to Archbishop Whitgift about the dedication. On Whitgift's order, the dedication was physically cut out of unsold copies of the book, which remained on sale in this mutilated form until it sold out. According to its publisher, John Wolfe, 'never any booke was better sould or more desired, that ever he printed, then this book was'. Although about 1,200 copies had been sold, a revised second edition was hastily prepared and printed, 'the people callinge exsedinglie for yt'.[2] However, publication of this new edition was forestalled by an order from the crown's chief censors of the press, the archbishop of Canterbury and the bishop of London, on 1 June. Although it only made specific reference to a range of satirical works by authors like Edward Guilpin and John Marston, the order was also enforced against Hayward's book. This 'bishops' ban' also restricted the printing of plays and required that works of English history receive approval directly from the privy council.[3] The unsold copies of Hayward's book (like the other banned works) were burned. After Essex returned from Ireland at the end of September to face disgrace and arrest, Hayward suddenly found himself under intense official scrutiny about his relationship with the earl and the 'real' purposes of his writing. Although the storm subsided while Essex seemed likely to die or face extreme punishment by the queen, Hayward faced a fresh round of questioning in July 1600, when Essex's rivals on the privy council sought evidence which might convince the queen not to treat the earl mercifully. In essence, Hayward was suspected of writing his book at the direction of Essex, or his friends, and with the express intention of airing the earl's claims to 'greatness' and testing the public reaction to his association with the usurper Bolingbroke/Henry IV. Hayward consistently denied these claims, but spent the remaining three years of Elizabeth's reign in the Tower.[4]

The fate of Hayward and that of his book have long attracted scholarly attention. For many years, this academic interest was chiefly driven by possible connections between Hayward's book and Shakespeare's *Richard II*, especially given the long-standing (but unproven) assumption that the latter play was performed for some of Essex's friends at the Globe theatre on the day before his disastrous insurrection of 8 February 1601.[5] Scholars have also shown interest in the Hayward affair as evidence of the political potency of history in early modern England, especially in connection with the late Elizabethan vogue for 'politic history' modelled upon the style of Tacitus.[6] Much less attention has been paid to the reasons why the council believed so insistently that Hayward was a stooge for Essex and that his work was intentionally subversive. In so far as answers have been offered to this question, they focus chiefly on the eagerness of Essex's rivals to find political ammunition which they could use against him. After Essex's highly suspicious conduct in Ireland, the efforts of his factional opponents to maintain his exclusion from power – and the desperation of the earl and his supporters to break their rivals' influence over the queen – became increasingly intense.[7] Although Sir Robert Cecil and the lord admiral may have been content to see Essex trapped in the political wilderness, more bitter enemies of the earl such as Sir Walter Raleigh, Lord Cobham and Sir Edward Coke were bent upon his destruction and were apparently eager for evidence to support charges of treason against him. However, personal enmity towards Essex cannot explain Elizabeth's own intense suspicion of Hayward. According to Francis Bacon, she even talked about having Hayward racked because she 'would not be perswaded it was his writing whose name was to it'.[8]

II

The most important reason for Elizabeth and key privy councillors to believe that the nature and circumstances of Hayward's publication were much less innocent than he claimed lay in their estimation of Essex himself. Essex was well known as an *aficionado* of history and regularly asserted its value for understanding contemporary politics. One of his secretaries, Henry Cuffe, acquired considerable notoriety for his 'dangerous' expositions of classical history texts. Indeed, Essex's final insurrection was supposedly prompted by Cuffe's interpretation of a tag from Lucan. Such 'politic' readings of history were most closely associated with the study of Tacitus, whose style Hayward consciously emulated – Francis Bacon quipped that Hayward was guilty not of treason but of 'very apparant theft' from Tacitus.[9] In 1598, Richard Grenewey had dedicated his translation of Tacitus's *Annals* and *Germania* to Essex because 'this author [is] well knowen unto your Honor'.[10] This may be an allusion to the contemporary belief that Essex himself wrote the epistle to the reader by 'A.B'. for Henry Savile's Tacitist text *The Ende of Nero and Beginninge of Galba*, which was published in 1591 and appeared as a second edition in 1598. Elizabeth and the council were also thoroughly familiar with Essex's frequent use of Cambridge graduates like Hayward in sensitive political tasks. Dr Henry Hawkins (a civil lawyer like Hayward) was sent to Venice as a political agent for the earl in 1595, while Robert Naunton (the university orator) was diverted from his plans for European travel to serve the earl's interests at the French court. Bacon himself also wielded his intellect and pen on Essex's behalf for the best part of a decade.[11]

Elizabeth and the councillors also knew that Essex often sought to disguise his political actions behind uncontroversial appearances or the names of others. As he privately confessed to one of his secretaries in 1596, 'I must like the watermen rowe one waie and looke an other.'[12] One document which circulated widely in manuscript and showcased Essex's credentials to become the queen's next dominant councillor was adapted from a letter of travel advice to the young earl of Rutland.[13] Essex's long and uncompromising response to those who 'jealously and maliciously tax him to be the hinderer of the peace and quiet of his country' in mid-1598 (best known as his 'Apologie') was framed as a private letter to Anthony Bacon. When the circulation of this inflammatory document came into question, Essex claimed that it had 'escaped' from his chamber, variously blaming the negligence of servants or of his friend and 'cousin' Fulke Greville.[14] Essex's assertion that an individual nobleman's honour should outweigh the unfair demands of the sovereign – a justification for his refusal to compromise with Elizabeth during their 'great quarrel' in the late summer of 1598 – also circulated in manuscript form as copies of a supposedly private correspondence between himself and the lord keeper, Sir Thomas Egerton. Similarly indirect political tactics were employed even after the Hayward affair broke. A letter ostensibly from Essex to Greville about research techniques and hiring a scholar from Cambridge may well have been drafted as part of the effort to re-establish Essex in the queen's favour during 1600. Francis Bacon certainly drafted two letters for this purpose – supposedly to the earl from his brother Anthony and the earl's reply – in mid-1600.[15]

Essex had also been in trouble over printed works before. In early November 1595, the queen became aware of *A Conference about the next Succession to the Crowne of Ingland*, a tract published abroad under the pseudonym 'R. Doleman' which debated the merits of the queen's various potential successors and featured a glowing dedication to Essex which prefigured Hayward's praise for the earl: 'no man [is] like to have a greater part or sway in deciding of this great affaire (when tyme shall come for that determination) then your Honour, and those that will assist you & are likest to follow your fame and fortune'. Although Essex finally convinced her that this dedication was a hostile act designed to embarrass him, it is telling that Elizabeth's immediate reaction was to suspect he had some part in the publication of this notorious treatise: when she first confronted him about the matter, her anger left him visibly 'wan and pale'.[16]

If Essex succeeded in allaying Elizabeth's suspicions about the Doleman book in 1595, his actions during the following autumn surely revived them. Following the capture of the Spanish city of Cadiz in June 1596, Essex attempted to publish an account of the expedition which glorified his own role in the victory at the expense of the lord admiral and subordinate officers. Written at Cadiz by Cuffe according to the earl's own 'large enstructions' and given finishing touches by Essex himself, the manuscript of this 'True relacion' was secretly sent back to England for publication. Another secretary, Edward Reynoldes, was to draft a preface and arrange the pamphlet's printing under a false name:

> conferre with Mr Grivill whether he can be contented to suffer the 2 first lettres of his name to be used in the inscription, which, if he graunt, he must be entreated not to take notice of the author but to give out that indeede he receved it amongst other papers by the first messenger ... the subscription may [be] DT or some other designed name as you shall thinke good ... If he be unwillinge, you may put RB, which some noe doubt will interpret to be Mr Beale, but it skills not[17]

Significantly, although Essex hoped for assistance in this matter from his friend Fulke Greville, he was prepared to imply a false connection with Robert Beale, a clerk of the privy council who had fallen out with Essex over the advancement of yet another of the earl's secretaries during 1595.

In the end, news of Essex's plans reached the queen and the 'True relacion' was banned from publication, along with potential rival accounts of the victory. Nevertheless, manuscript versions of Essex's pamphlet were circulated among his supporters, as were copies of Essex's earlier letter to the privy council which announced his intention to ignore the queen's instructions for the Cadiz expedition, which he had left behind to be delivered only after the fleet was beyond recall. Circulating scribal copies in this manner circumvented official controls on the press, but also limited the audience for these documents to gentlemen who had connections with Essex's circle of friends or the means to purchase a copy. A correspondent of Sir Thomas Kitson, for example, 'came by this [Essex's letter to the council] by great chance' in July 1596 and asked Kitson to 'kepe yt very private & ret[urn] yt safe enclosed in a sheete of paper when your Worshippe may conveniently'.[18] Ironically, the scarcity value of such coterie manuscript publications gave these documents a cachet which perhaps meant they retained a longer 'shelf life' than printed works. Many of the numerous surviving manuscript copies of Essex's 'Apologie' seem to have been made long after his death, even though it became freely available in printed form in 1603.[19]

III

Essex's covert attempt to publicize his own heroism at Cadiz and whip up public support for fresh attacks on Spain infuriated the queen and many of his colleagues on the privy council. It seemed especially shocking that Essex would seek to go outside the confines of the court and appeal directly to a public audience for endorsement of an aggressive war strategy when he knew that Elizabeth disliked this policy and most of his conciliar colleagues directly opposed it. However, Essex's desire for public acclaim – relentless self-aggrandizement, as his critics saw it – was far less surprising. Robert Devereux had succeeded to the earldom of Essex at the age of ten and lived most of the rest of his life in a blaze of public attention which went far beyond the ceremony which attached to other peers. Thanks to the creative pen of a family servant and skilful use of the printing press, the messy death of his father from dysentery in Ireland was transformed into a famous model of Protestant piety, against which Essex's own actions would be measured. The remarriage of Essex's mother to Robert Dudley, earl of Leicester, meant that he was not only a cousin of the queen but also the stepson of her greatest favourite. The Dudley link also made Essex a cousin (by marriage) to Philip Sidney. Essex won a knighthood for his bravery in the famous skirmish at Zutphen where Sidney was mortally wounded in 1586 and subsequently played a central role in the great propaganda campaign which elevated Sidney's death to the status of Protestant martyrdom. Essex had been educated to prize aristocratic 'virtue' and to believe that he had a godly 'calling' to live a public life for the benefit of the state. The myth of Sidney – that he had made 'a conquest of death by fame in his life' – reinforced Essex's commitment to the conspicuous display of virtue, to the extent that he even married Sidney's widow, despite the queen's angry disapproval. This was not merely a grand romantic gesture, but a statement that he regarded himself as the new Sidney – but as the mythic Sidneian paragon of virtue, not the real flesh-and-blood Sidney.[20]

Essex's identification with the Sidney myth deepened his propensity to see himself as a public person who lived his life under a spotlight, even though the burden of such attention sometimes became almost unbearable. On the one hand, it meant that he consistently aspired to be the best at whatever he undertook – to be the best and bravest soldier, the ideal councillor, the most generous lord or friend, the most honest courtier, the most illustrious aristocrat who retained the common touch. On the other hand, these self-conscious and exhausting efforts to embody perfection were performed in the expectation of public acclaim and Essex made sure they were as widely known as possible – his whole life, in effect, was conceived as a display of virtue, which necessitated the attention of an audience.[21] It is perhaps not surprising therefore that he repeatedly used metaphors of acting and the theatre to describe the world in which he saw himself living. His passionate interest in French affairs, for example, reflected his belief that 'ffraunce is at thys daye the theater and stage wheron the greatest actions are acted'.[22]

Essex displayed himself to the world in a variety of ways which showcased his various qualities for a range of different audiences. His extraordinary athleticism and energy in the Tiltyard, for example, where he dominated proceedings during the 1590s, were intended to become the talk of the court and the inhabitants of London and Westminster. When the thousands who packed into the Tiltyard at Whitehall went home in the evening, Essex wanted to be the chief subject of the reports which these spectators made to those who had not been there. While the commons thrilled to his martial skill and the entertainments which he staged between jousts, the cognoscenti were better able to ponder the deeper meanings of the mottoes which were displayed upon his entrance into the arena and the potential political allusions in the entertainments.[23] Essex's conspicuous wearing of a great plumed hat and insistence on fighting in the foremost rank in any battle similarly made him the focus of attention for the armies which he commanded. As Sir Walter Raleigh noted of the victory at Cadiz, 'the best wilbe that ther was 16,000 witnesses'. These witnesses to Essex's derring-do included the gentlemen officers, common soldiers drawn from across virtually the whole realm and many enemy soldiers, all of whom would go home and talk about the great battle at Cadiz for years to come.[24] At the universities, Essex's reputation as a great patron of learning was nurtured by high-profile visits to Oxford in 1588 and 1592 and Cambridge in 1595. Even more important, he excited great enthusiasm among academics and students by regularly recruiting notable scholars into his service as chaplains and secretaries and sponsoring others for travel on the Continent. Essex also made use of conspicuous gifts. When the queen recognized the lord admiral's part in the victory at Cadiz by making him earl of Nottingham in 1597, Essex responded by presenting a large psalter which had been seized at Cadiz to King's College, Cambridge, where it was placed on prominent public display with a Latin dedication which praised him as 'greater than Hercules' ('Hercule maior').[25]

Essex also repeatedly paraded his credentials as a supporter of puritan-leaning Protestantism. He offered conspicuous patronage to prominent religious dissidents such as William Hubbocke and Stephen Egerton, regularly attended public sermons, and willingly received the dedication of numerous godly books and treatises. Some of these publications, such as Nicholas Bownde's sabbatarian tract *The Doctrine of the Sabbath*, carried Essex's coat of arms as proof of his personal endorsement of the contents. The frequency with which religious works were dedicated to Essex helped to make him the most common dedicatee for books published in England during the 1590s, outstripping even Elizabeth herself.[26] Such dedications were testimony to the earl's reputation for liberality to authors (a point which undoubtedly attracted Hayward), but they also served to make his name and renown seem increasingly ubiquitous to a reading public. While most of these dedications trumpeted Essex's image as a Protestant crusader, a few publications (especially works of music) offered more subtle clues that Essex was also prepared to countenance toleration for loyal Catholics.[27]

Essex's self-promotion was so successful that his name and reputation became commodified. When he undertook some conspicuous task, such as when he left London to take up his command in Ireland in March 1599, writers and publishers sought to cash in by selling pamphlets to commemorate the event. According to the (self-exculpatory) testimony of Hayward's publisher, Wolfe, this was also the reason why *The First Part* was dedicated to Essex – because 'the booke treated of Irishe causes'. Whether true or not, publications connected with Essex were sufficiently marketable to make this explanation seem at least plausible.[28] Even in 1589, when he returned from the disastrous Portugal expedition, Essex's comings and goings were seen as a commercial opportunity.[29] In 1596, his success at Cadiz would undoubtedly have provoked a flood of pamphlets if he had not provoked the queen into banning all publications on the subject.[30] However, the very marketability of Essex's name also meant that he could not always control the circumstances in which it was invoked. Although the dedication by 'R. Doleman' in 1595 was almost certainly a mischievous attempt by Catholic exiles to smear his reputation, the attempt by publishers to capitalize on Essex's fame by producing a pirate edition of his 'Apologie' in May 1600 proved acutely embarrassing.[31] The sale of an engraving of Essex in equestrian pose shortly afterwards was perhaps even more worrisome because the portrait bore a caption which epitomized the public image which he had sought to cultivate ('Vertue's honor, Wisdome's valure'), but carried it further by associating him with the distinctly royal style of 'God's elected'. Both publications were hastily suppressed, but they provided unwelcome ammunition for his political enemies just as their attention was returning to Hayward and his book.[32]

Essex's success in projecting himself as a 'public person' was also reflected in the criticism and mockery which his behaviour elicited in some quarters. In *Skialetheia*, one of the books suppressed under the 'bishops' ban' of 1599, Everard Guilpin satirized Essex in the character of 'great Foelix', who 'passing through the street,/Vayleth his cap to each one he doth meet'. According to Guilpin, such conspicuous courtesy to social inferiors could be interpreted only as a Machivellian 'mumming trick':

with curtesie
T'entrench himselfe in popularitie,
And for [i.e. by means of] a writhen face, and bodie's move,
Be barricadode in the people's love.[33]

Essex's excessive desire to be admired by all and sundry therefore seemed like a deceptive ploy to 'barricade' himself 'in the people's love' for his own malign purposes. Other writers made the same point. Guilpin's friend John Marston (whose work was also banned in 1599) equated 'the perfect image of Curtesie' with the pretence of 'a damn'd Machevelian', while an anonymous writer explicitly mocked Essex after his death as a man who was so eager to win the admiration of 'the vulgar sorte' that he 'would vaile his bonnett to an oyster wife' when he walked through the streets of London. Significantly, such criticisms of Essex can be seen as echoes of a strikingly similar description of Bolingbroke's behaviour in Shakespeare's *Richard II*, when Richard reflects bitterly on Bolingbroke's 'courtship to the common people ... with craft of smiles' – even to the doffing of his bonnet 'to an oysterwench'. Although Essex, Raleigh and Cecil apparently shared a joke about allusions to Richard II in July 1597, it seems that comparison with Bolingbroke was already established as a means of criticizing Essex's behaviour well before Hayward chose to dedicate his book to the earl, which makes his choice of dedicatee all the more striking. Whether or not it was his intention, the effect of Hayward's dedication is publicly to contest the nature of this identification between Essex and Bolingbroke.[34]

IV

It is perhaps not surprising that criticisms of Essex's courting of popular acclaim seem to cluster in the latter half of the 1590s. Although he had cultivated public approbation virtually from the moment he attained his majority in late 1586, the political purpose and significance of Essex's actions underwent a marked shift during 1595–96. Instead of merely promoting himself as a man whom Elizabeth should rely upon in matters of state, Essex actively sought to mobilize public support for aggressive war policies which the queen disliked and his rivals opposed. By the end of 1595 Essex could no longer believe that he would eventually win the queen over to his viewpoint simply by making a convincing argument. As he confided to one of his secretaries before his departure for Cadiz, 'I know I shall never do her service butt against her will.'[35] Rather than accept political defeat, however, Essex raised the stakes by trying to force the queen's hand. Although he failed in his attempt to maintain a garrison at Cadiz, he hastily launched the Elizabethan equivalent of a multimedia campaign to pressure the queen into using the army which returned from Cadiz for offensive operations elsewhere. In addition to producing the

'True relacion', he sought to promote national celebrations for the victory, required that the 'True relacion' be translated into French for dissemination abroad, and launched overtures to the French and Dutch ambassadors to apply diplomatic pressure on the queen. He also ordered discreet lobbying of the City of London for an offer of financial support to the crown on condition that Elizabeth used the returning army to attack Calais: 'but he must doe it as onlie sollicited by the occasion itself and, above all thinges, none of mine must ever be seene or named in this motion'. After his return to England, Essex had himself painted wearing the beard which he had grown during the voyage to Cadiz. The beard subsequently became a distinctive feature of his appearance and the image presented in the new portraits by Oliver and Gheer-aerts subsequently found its way into cheaper and more widely disseminated engravings.[36]

Although it is unclear if Elizabeth appreciated the full extent of Essex's manoeuvres in 1596, neither she nor his rivals on the privy council harboured any illusions about the earl's political ambitions thereafter. Essex's willingness to whip up public support for new expeditions in an attempt to apply pressure to the queen and his conciliar colleagues seemed infuriating and infringed the requirement that affairs of state should remain secret – a principle embodied in the very institution of the 'privy' (i.e. secret) council. In light of this brazen behaviour, Essex's habit of advertising his 'virtuous' behaviour for the sake of public affirmation – which had previously been merely irritating to other court-iers – now seemed distinctly ominous. In early October, Francis Bacon explic-itly warned Essex about the impression which his actions were creating:

> But how is it now? A man of a nature not to be ruled, that hath the advantage of my affection, and knoweth it; of an estate not grounded to his greatness; of a popular reputation; of a military dependence: I demand whether there can be a more dangerous image than this represented to any monarch living, much more to a lady and of her Majesty's apprehension? ... I cannot sufficiently wonder at your Lordship's course.[37]

Although they were usually intended to mock Essex, the allusions to Boling-broke – who was, after all, a usurper – implicitly attributed an ulterior polit-ical motive to his 'craft of smiles'. In Guilpin's satire on 'great Foelix', 'like a swartrutter's hose his puffe thoughts swell/With yeastie ambition'.[38] Hayward's portrayal of Bolingbroke in *The First Part* also directly emphasizes the connec-tion between political ambition and the pursuit of 'great reputation and regarde, especially with those of the meaner sort'.[39] Shakespeare's *Richard II* is even more pointed. Noting Bolingbroke's 'courtship to the common people', the king remarks that he behaved 'as were our England in reversion his,/And he our subjects' next degree in hope'.[40] Essex's combination of zealous regard for public acclaim and consistent advocacy of a military strategy which would

guarantee his own political indispensability therefore made him seem dangerously ambitious – to the extent that he might even harbour regal pretensions.

Essex himself always poured scorn on any suggestion that he might aspire
to the crown and claimed – probably in all sincerity – that his goal was merely
to ensure the succession of James VI of Scotland. Nevertheless, his actions
stirred deep suspicions among his political opponents. In particular, Essex
was accused of seeking 'popularity'. This charge meant that he sought political
support from outside the realm's governing élite and, in doing so, interposed
himself between the queen and her subjects, challenging the monopoly which
a sovereign supposedly enjoyed over their subjects' 'love'. The pursuit of
'popularity' was therefore an offence of *lèse-majesté* and, in the eyes of Essex's
critics, betokened political ambitions of a distinctly royal nature. The full
force of these accusations can be seen most explicitly during his disgrace in
1599–1600 and in the aftermath of his failed rising in February 1601, but the
attitudes expressed then clearly reflected opinions which had been hardening
since 1596. Typical of the tone of these bitter accusations is Serjeant Christopher Yelverton's attack on Essex at the opening of his trial in 1601:

> Noe man advaunced younger to place in counsell, nor to more dignities, all which
> the earle abused, makinge his cheife companions of sword men and affecting
> popularitie. He declared the insatiablenes of ambicion, which never resteth untill it
> attaine as high as it can reach, comparing it to the crocadile that is said to grow soe
> long as it liveth.[41]

Although judicial convention required expressions of outrage from the crown's
prosecutors, the intensely personal manner in which Essex was denounced
after 1599 suggests that his accusers genuinely believed they were unmasking a
crocodilian ambition which had always motivated the earl's public posturing.

For his part, Essex consistently claimed that 'I have no ambition but her
Majeste's gratious favour & the reputation of well serving her'.[42] Elizabeth
herself was inclined to believe Essex until he finally forfeited her trust by
arranging a truce in Ireland with the rebel earl of Tyrone in September 1599.
However, Essex's arrest upon his return to England created an acute political
problem: how should a government which insisted that 'matters of state' must
remain secret deal with the fall of a popular hero? The most obvious response,
already seen in the treatment of Hayward's book and the other targets of the
'bishops' ban', was to suppress publications which drew public attention to
Essex. One conspicuous victim of this anti-Essex purge was Richard Hakluyt's
vast new edition of his *Principal Navigations*, the first volume of which contained
an account of the victory at Cadiz in 1596. Even though it had been published
before Hayward's *The First Part* and its Cadiz account was based upon that
written by the lord admiral's physician, the book was recalled in September
1599 and banned from sale until the offending pages were cut out.[43]

However, such clumsy censorship merely increased popular suspicions that the government had something to hide in its treatment of Essex and that he was the innocent victim of factional rivalry. In the end, the privy council was forced to respond to public criticism by a public statement of its own. On 29 November 1599, members of the council addressed a gathering of justices and gentlemen JPs in the Star Chamber at the end of the Michaelmas law term. One after another, the councillors warned their audience about the evils of rumour-mongers and 'popular' politics and systematically sought to dismantle Essex's reputation as a great soldier and the aristocratic embodiment of English patriotism. 'Such ys the iniquitye of theise dayes,' claimed the lord keeper, 'that the taverns and ordinaries are filled with tales of governement and matters of state, and they so farr proceede that they scatter libells which doe falcely and trayterouslye slaunder her Majestie and her whole counsell.' In the lord treasurer's opinion, libellers 'deserve death better then open enemies', while Sir Robert Cecil claimed that 'these slaunderous libellers that raise infamies be the children of the divell'. 'And though princes are not bounde to discend to particularities', successive speakers also listed the failings of Essex's expedition to Ireland, detailing the numbers of men he commanded, the sums of money which he received and even the quantities of supplies made available to him: 'the armye was so furnished with apparell that they had 20,000 shirtes & were but 13,000 persones'.[44] Essex's 'affecting [of] popularitie', therefore, compelled Elizabeth's government to respond at least partially in kind: although the councillors addressed an élite audience and condemned talk of state affairs in taverns, their sudden willingness to reveal 'mysteries of state' was startling. As one gentleman who was caught up in 'the thronge and presse' reported, 'I did not expecte to have hard any such matter in the Starchamber and therefore came not in tyme to take a place where I might convenientlie here all suche matters as were there declared.'[45]

V

Essex's efforts to mobilize political support in the late 1590s – and especially his 'courtship to the common people' (to borrow Shakespeare's description of Bolingbroke) – challenged both the conventions of late Elizabethan government and the political standing of his personal rivals who actually ran the government on the queen's behalf. Although it is unlikely that Essex sought the throne for himself, the lengths to which he went in his efforts to force his own policies through and outflank his opponents made him an increasingly dangerous political maverick. These actions were all the more disquieting because they raised the prospect of unpredictable interventions in national politics – whether by Essex's own aristocratic clique or by the urban masses of London which he seemed bent upon politicizing – just when the uncertainties surrounding the disposition of the throne after Elizabeth's death were becoming most urgent. Although open discussion of the succession remained a taboo subject, Essex's behaviour seemed to cast him as a king-maker, or even a potential king. For Essex's enemies, most of whom lacked aristocratic status and depended entirely upon Elizabeth's favour for their political standing, the earl's future prospects represented a deadly threat for the period which would follow the queen's death.

More immediately, Essex's behaviour was inimical to the exalted image of royal authority which his rivals sought to foster in order to buttress their own political status. Driven by a powerful need to contrast the earl's 'ambitious' conduct with their own 'dutiful' obedience to the queen, Essex's rivals insisted upon an elevated view of royal authority which maximized their own political power (since they exercised that authority on her behalf) and sought to deny any thought of the queen's mortality (which would see that authority pass into unknown hands). In his exchange of letters with Lord Keeper Egerton, Essex asked, 'What, cannot princes err? Cannot subjects receive wrong? Is an earthly power or authority infinite?' Egerton contended that true honour required submission to the royal will. In 1601, Sir Edward Coke went even further, arguing that 'all the nobillitie drawe their honour & dignitie immediatlie from the queene, as the starres take their light from the sunne' – instead of possessing an autonomous personal honour, as Essex and his friends insisted, even aristocrats were merely satellites orbiting a sovereign star.[46] In this cosmic order of quasi-divine royal authority there was no place for subjects to pursue 'popularity', and spreaders of rumours and libels merited exemplary punishment.

Essex's destruction in 1601, following the failure of his insurrection in London on 8 February, represented the Elizabethan regime's attempt to shatter his public reputation and to uphold the new conventions of elevated royal supremacy which the earl and his friends had so embarrassingly challenged. This multi-media campaign involved a series of show trials (that for Essex involving a specially constructed temporary courtroom to accommodate the huge audience), public sermons to denounce the 'wickedness' of Essex's treason against his 'natural' sovereign, stage-managed executions and the publication of William Barlow's Paul's Cross sermon and Francis Bacon's official declaration of the Essex affair, the latter complete with scores of pages detailing excerpted confessions and other testimony to 'prove' the government's case.[47] However, this massive effort to deface Essex's public image and utilize his fate in the service of the elevated late Elizabethan conception of royal authority proved at best a limited success. This was partly due to Essex's own behaviour at his trial and execution, when he publicly played out the sharply contrasting roles of aristocratic constancy and self-flagellating Protestant *dévot*. Some of the government's charges against Essex, such as the attempt to portray him as conspiring with the king of Spain, were also so extreme and unreal that they undermined the credibility of the whole effort. Elizabeth herself apparently believed that Barlow's sermon was a gross distortion of the truth and Essex's enemies found themselves facing accusations that they had railroaded the earl to his death for years to come.[48] As early as December 1599, Francis Bacon felt obliged to defend himself against rumours 'shaped ... in the London forge that beats apace at this time' about his dealings against Essex by writing a letter which deplored such libels, but which he apparently circulated in the same manner as the libels themselves.[49] By 1604, Bacon felt obliged to write a more elaborate 'Apologie' about his dealings with Essex, which consciously echoed the format of the earl's pamphlet in its claim to be a private letter to the earl of Devonshire.[50] Sir Robert Cecil was plagued by bitter smears over his treatment of Essex until his death in 1612, while Sir Walter Raleigh felt obliged to defend himself against similar accusations even as he took his turn on the scaffold in 1618.[51] Government efforts to counter Essex's public reputation with its own propaganda therefore encouraged public cynicism and fuelled fresh libels against individual councillors and courtiers, opening the late Elizabethan regime to the sort of criticism which was directly contrary to its authoritarian royalist pretensions. Elizabeth herself seems to have recognized this bitter irony. If contemporary descriptions of her final years are to be believed, it was precisely in the destruction of Essex that she saw the puncturing of her own regal aura – despite the extravagant praise with which her councillors and courtiers still hailed her – and the souring of her subjects' affection. In this light, Elizabeth's famous comment to William Lambarde in August 1601 must reflect her bitter recognition that she and her regime had won a decidedly pyrrhic victory over Essex, becoming defined by what she sought to deny: 'I am Richard II, know ye not that?'[52]

VI

The struggle between Essex and his political rivals which was played out so openly in the late 1590s can be seen as a contribution to the growth of a 'public sphere' in early modern England. In strictly formal terms, Essex's bravura performance of all the qualities which Elizabethans expected and desired of a great nobleman can be seen as a classic embodiment of the pre-modern 'representative publicness' which Jürgen Habermas identifies with medieval and Renaissance society. Nevertheless, Essex might also be seen as part of a transitional process in early modern English history towards the emergence of Habermas's 'modern public sphere', in which 'the state-governed public sphere was appropriated by the public of private people making use of their reason and was established as a sphere of criticism of public authority'.[53]

Peter Lake and Michael Questier have argued for the existence of an

Elizabethan 'public sphere' by shearing off those elements of the Habermasian concept which seem incompatible with sixteenth-century government and society, especially the emphasis upon bourgeois capitalism, modernity and the 'public sphere's' function as an expression of strictly rational public criticism of state actions and authority. They correctly argue that it is difficult to talk about an Elizabethan 'state' when much of the evidence of public discourse in this period reflects elements within the regime manoeuvring for their own advantage or the promotion of their own particular views.[54] Lake and Questier have therefore charted 'the emergence of something like a rudimentary "public sphere" in Elizabethan England' by considering the ideological challenge posed to the queen's regime by Jesuit missionaries, beginning about 1580.[55] This public challenge to the Elizabethan government to prove the legitimacy of its laws against Catholics – and more generally, the authority by which Elizabeth reigned as queen – forced the government to respond in kind, just as Essex's challenge ultimately required a similar response in 1599–1601.

By the 1590s, however, when an elevated model of royal authority became increasingly pervasive, the Elizabethan regime supposedly no longer permitted the kind of ideological dissent which had been aired in earlier years. What Patrick Collinson characterized as the 'monarchical republic' of mid-Elizabethan England was displaced by an increasingly intolerant and demanding regime with absolutist pretensions which John Guy has described as representing virtually a 'second reign' of Elizabeth I.[56] Just as Catholic missionaries were banished from the realm on pain of death in 1585 and their works banned, the affair of the 'Martin Mareprelate' tracts in 1588–89 also roused the government against extremist Protestants and their disrespect for the established church. Those who had once been valued as 'the most diligent barkers against the popish wolf' now found themselves facing repression 'too much savouring of the Romish inquisition'.[57] However, after the events which Lake and Questier describe, it seems that the quelling of dissent was no longer possible without resort to the very 'public sphere' from which the challenges to government authority had originated. Elizabeth's furious reaction to the printed Martinist abuse of ecclesiastical authorities not only prompted Archbishop Whitgift to crack down on leading Presbyterians, but also encouraged him to give Richard Bancroft and others a free hand to publish outspoken attacks on puritan extremists.[58] The censorship of the press (which Whitgift oversaw, later with Bancroft's assistance) and the prosecution of individual puritan radicals were therefore accompanied by a sustained polemical campaign which the government itself – or, more precisely, a specific clique of 'high church' clerics who worked under Whitgift's protection – conducted through the press. Although this campaign was waged in the name of obedience to royal and ecclesiastical authority, many of the works were scurrilous in tone and some of the professional writers permitted to assist in the effort proved distinctly embarrassing. The work of Thomas Nashe, for example, was specifically included in the 'bishops' ban' of 1599. By the late 1590s, Bancroft's campaign against troublesome puritans was also joined by another government initiative, spearheaded by Bancroft and Sir Robert Cecil, to permit the publication of Catholic anti-Jesuit polemics in order to stigmatize Jesuits as unpatriotic hispanophiles and promote division within the English Catholic community.[59]

In light of these developments, perhaps the key contribution of the public struggle played out around Essex was to broaden the terms of debate about dissent and legitimate authority away from religion. Unlike Catholics or radical puritans, Essex was not an outsider but the ultimate embodiment of an Elizabethan establishment insider – an earl by birth, a royal cousin and favourite who was also the stepson of the queen's greatest favourite. The controversy which swirled around him consequently raised issues not of religion but of personality, policy and the legitimacy of the crown's lofty new pretensions. Essex's 'Apologie', for example, which trenchantly argued against peace with Spain in 1598, was only the most prominent contribution in a vigorous debate about war and peace – mostly expressed in the form of anonymous manuscript treatises – which the earl helped to fuel during the final years of Elizabeth's reign. While Essex and his supporters urged the cause of martial honour and the impossibility of trusting a 'tyrannical' Catholic Spain, proponents of peace principally couched their arguments in terms of trade and national economic advantage. Both views would echo through the decades which followed, prefiguring the public debate about political economy which Habermas regards as central to the emergence of the 'modern political sphere' in late seventeenth-century England.[60] The dissemination of printed and manuscript works by and about Essex also pointed to a growing commodification of politics – the 'people callinge exsedinglie' for the latest controversial work meant frantic 'gaping' by printers eager to capitalize on such commercial opportunities. However 'rudimentary' the 'public sphere' which emerged in this period may have been, it was strongly influenced by the dictates of commerce.

The importance of the market is emphasized very forcibly by Alexandra Halascz, who has argued that pamphlets and printing created a 'public sphere' in the late Elizabethan period, albeit in a manner which Habermas did not predict: 'the problem that Habermas identifies as an incursion of commercial interests into the public sphere is present from the moment a public sphere becomes imaginable'.[61] One of the pioneers of this 'paper stage' was John Wolfe, the publisher of Hayward's *The First Part*.[62] It is perhaps not surprising therefore that the example of Essex seems to support Halacsz's claim. Not only were Essex and his government rivals unable fully to control the ways in which their names and ideas were used, but the products of their late Elizabethan clash – and the comments of third parties upon it – remained available for print and manuscript publication as long as a market for this material existed. Thanks to the lustre of Essex's name and the notoriety surrounding the affair with Hayward, six new editions of *The First Part of the Life and Raigne of King Henrie IIII* were printed between *c.* 1604 and 1642, each complete with a false date of '1599' and a copy of the suppressed dedication to Essex.[63] However, commercial interest also dictated that such Elizabethan materials could be deployed in new ways which reflected the business opportunities created by Jacobean and Caroline politics. The early 1620s therefore saw ghostly representations of Essex and Raleigh – deadly rivals in the late 1590s – jointly enlisted as paragons of Elizabethan militarism and hispanophobia to cast a critical light on government policies under James I and Charles I.[64] On the 'paper stage' which emerged in the late sixteenth century, as these later pamphlets and the controversy surrounding Hayward's book showed, what mattered was not historical accuracy but the uses to which historical ideas and characters could be convincingly redeployed and sold.

NOTES

1 J. J. Manning (ed.), *The First and Second Parts of John Hayward's The Life and Raigne of King Henrie IIII*, Camden Society, 4th ser., XLII (1991), 61. *The First Part* was registered for printing on 9 January 1599, but published some weeks later.

2 Public Record Office (hereafter PRO), SP 12/275/28. The printed *Calendar* to the State Papers Domestic gives the erroneous impression that not all of the first edition were sold, but the original manuscript makes it clear that 'the residew, beinge 5 or 6 houndred ... sould ... also within a very short tyme'.

3 Manning, *First and Second Parts*, 24–5; E. Arber (ed.), *A Transcript of the Registers of the Company of Stationers of London, 1554–1640* (5 vols, priv. pr., London, 1875–94) III, fol. 316r. For discussion of 'the bishops' ban', see C. S. Clegg, *Press Censorship in Elizabethan England* (Cambridge, 1997), chapter 9.

4 Manning, *First and Second Parts*, 21 ff. See also R. Dutton, '"Buggeswords": Samuel Harsnett and the licensing, suppression and afterlife of Dr John Hayward's *The First Part of the Life and and Reign of Henry IV*', *Criticism* 35 (1993), 305–39. Hayward was remanded to the Tower on 13 July 1600: J. R. Dasent *et al.* (eds), *Acts of the Privy Council*, new ser. (46 vols, London, 1890–1964), XXX, 499 (hereafter *APC*).

5 This debate has been reignited by Blair Worden, who posits a more direct connection between Hayward's book and the play of February 1601: 'Which play was performed at the Globe theatre on 7 February 1601?', *London Review of Books* 25:13 (10 July 2003), 22–4. For subsequent correspondence, see *ibid.* 25:18 ff.

6 For example, S. L. Goldberg, 'Sir John Hayward, "politic" historian', *Review of English Studies*, new ser., 6 (1955), 233–44; F. J. Levy, 'Hayward, Daniel and the beginnings of politic history in England', *Huntington Library Quarterly* 50 (1987), 1–37. A related argument – that Hayward's civil law practices were misread because they were interpreted in terms of 'politic history' – is advanced by Rebecca Lemon: 'The faulty verdict in "The crown v. John Hayward"', *Studies in English Literature* 41 (2001), 109–32. Note that, despite the allusion in Lemon's title, Hayward was not formally indicted. Alzada J.

Tipton is one of the few scholars to argue that Hayward actively planned his history as a piece of political advice for Essex and did not simply stumble into trouble as he claimed: "'Lively patterns ... for affayres of state": Sir John Hayward's *The Life and Raigne of King Henrie IIII* and the earl of Essex', *Sixteenth Century Journal* 33 (2002), 769–94.

7 By August 1599 the potential existed for an Elizabethan civil war: P. E. J. Hammer, *Elizabeth's Wars: War, Government and Society in Tudor England, 1544–1604* (Basingstoke, 2003), 214–16.

8 Francis Bacon, *Sir Francis Bacon his Apologie in certain Imputations concerning the late Earle of Essex* (London, 1604), 35.

9 *Ibid.*, 34–5.

10 R. Grenewey, *The Annales of Cornelius Tacitus. The description of Germanie* (London, 1598), unpag. ded.

11 P. E. J. Hammer, *The Polarisation of Elizabethan Politics: the Political Career of Robert Devereux, Second Earl of Essex, 1585–1597* (Cambridge, 1999), especially 304–15; Hammer, 'The uses of scholarship: the secretariat of Robert Devereux, second earl of Essex, *c.* 1585–1601', *English Historical Review* 109 (1994), 26–51; Hammer, 'Essex and Europe: evidence from confidential instructions by the earl of Essex, 1595–1596', *English Historical Review* 111 (1996), 357–81.

12 Lambeth Palace Library (hereafter LPL), 658, fol. 136r: Essex to Edward Reynoldes, 28 July 1596 (copy).

13 It has long been claimed that Francis Bacon composed this letter as a 'hired pen' for Essex. While Bacon may have played a part in producing the version which we know today (which was clearly revised for circulation), Essex himself clearly wrote a letter to Rutland dated 16 October (1595) and claimed to have penned previous letters to him, although these do not survive in their original form: Hammer, *Polarisation*, 149.

14 Historical Manuscripts Commission, *A Calendar of the Manuscripts of the most Hon. the Marquis of Salisbury* (24 vols, London, 1883–1976) (hereafter *HMCS*) VIII, 141–2, X, 141–2, XIV, 129; PRO, SP 12/261/53 (the latter has been misdated to 1596 by the compilers of the SP 12 class).

15 P. E. J. Hammer, 'Fulke Greville, the earl of Essex, and the employment of scholars', *Studies in Philology* 91 (1994), 169–73; J. Spedding (ed.), *The Letters and the Life of Francis Bacon* (7 vols, London, 1861–74) II, 197–201.

16 R. Doleman, *A Conference about the next Succession to the Crowne of Ingland* ('N.' [probably Antwerp], 1594), sig. *3r; A. Collins (ed.), *Letters and Memorials of State in the Reigns of Queen Mary, Queen Elizabeth, King James ...* (2 vols, London, 1746) I, 357.

17 LPL, Ms 658, fol. 88r–v: Cuffe to Reynoldes, July 1596. For the 'True relacion' affair, see P. E. J. Hammer, 'Myth-making: politics, propaganda and the capture of Cadiz in 1596', *Historical Journal* 40 (1997), 621–42.

18 Bodleian Library, Oxford, Tanner Ms 77, fol. 93v: [?] to Sir Thomas Kitson, 23 July 1596.

19 While some copies of Essex's 'Apologie' circulated in the later 1590s (e.g. Folger Shakespeare Library, Washington DC (hereafter FSL), V.b.142, fols 32r–40v), many others seem to date from the 1610s or 1620s. The cachet attached to manuscripts meant that some works were apparently copied out of printed books and circulated in manuscript form. On 'manuscript culture', see H. Love, *The Culture and Commerce of Texts: Scribal Publication in Seventeenth-Century England* (Amherst MA, 1998).

20 For all this, see Hammer, *Polarisation*, especially chapters 1–2.

21 This point is dramatized, for example, in Shakespeare's *Troilus and Cressida*, which has strong allusions to Essex and his behaviour: as Ulysses reminds the Essex-like figure of Achilles, 'no man is lord of anything,/Though in him and of him there be much consisting,/Till he communicate his parts to others ... Till he behold them formed in th' applause' (3.3.116–20). For Troilus and Essex, see D. Bevington (ed.), *Troilus and Cressida* (London, 1998), 11–18.

22 Hammer, 'Essex and Europe', 379.

23 A. Young, *Tudor and Jacobean Tournaments* (London, 1987); P. E. J. Hammer, 'Upstaging the queen: the earl of Essex, Francis Bacon and the Accession Day celebrations of 1595', in D. Bevington and P. Holbrook (eds), *The Politics of the Stuart Court Masque* (Cambridge, 1998), 41–66.

24 FSL, V.b.214, fol. 109r: Raleigh to [Arthur Gorges?], 21 June 1596.

25 Hammer, *Polarisation*, 70, 299 ff.; Hammer, 'Greville', 174–80; G. W. Groos (ed.), *The Diary of Baron Waldstein, a Traveller in Elizabethan England* (London, 1981), 104–7.

26 William Hubbocke, *An Apologie of Infants in a Sermon* (London, 1595), sig. A4r; *HMCS* VI, 317, XI, 154; Nicholas Bownde, *The Doctrine of the Sabbath, plainely Layde forth and soundly Proved* ... (London, 1595), sig. A1v; G. L. Bird, 'The Earl of Essex, Patron of Letters' (unpublished Ph.D. thesis, University of Utah, 1969); A. Fox, 'The complaint of poetry for the death of liberality: the decline of literary patronage in the 1590s', in J. Guy (ed.), *The Reign of Elizabeth I: Court and Culture in the last Decade* (Cambridge, 1995), 231.

27 Hammer, *Polarisation*, 175 ff.

28 PRO, SP 12/275/28. Publications intended as commercial 'tie-ins' with Essex's departure included Thomas Churchyard, *The fortunate Farewel to the most forward and noble Earle of Essex* ... (London, 1599) and John Norden, *A Prayer for the prosperous Proceedings and good Successe of the Earle of Essex* ... (London, 1599). A pamphlet entitled *London's loathe to departe: to the noble Erle of Essex* ... , of unknown authorship, was also registered for publication on 31 March 1599 (Arber, *Transcript* III, fol. 49r). Famously, the Chorus at the beginning of Act V in Shakespeare's *Henry V* also alludes to Essex's expected triumph in Ireland.

29 George Peele, *An Eglogue gratulatorie. To the right honorable, and renowmed Shepheard of Albions Arcadia: Robert Earle of Essex and Ewe for his Welcome into England from Portugall* (London, 1589). Peele's subsequent publications included *Polyhymnia* (1590), in which Essex's prowess at the tilts of 17 November 1590 features prominently.

30 According to Thomas Nashe, there was desperate 'gaping' among the printers for copy after news arrived of the victory at Cadiz: R. B. McKerrow (ed.), *The Works of Thomas Nashe* (5 vols, 1904–10, Oxford, 1958 edn) V, 194.

31 *HMCS* X, 143; PRO, SP 12/274/150; Collins, *Letters and Memorials* II, 193, 194–5.

32 The equestrian engraving of Essex by Thomas Cockson was one of a series of three images, the others being of the earls of Cumberland and Nottingham. The privy council ordered Archbishop Whitgift to ban all engravings of noblemen on 30 August 1600: A. M. Hind *et al.*, *Engraving in England in the Sixteenth and Seventeenth Centuries* (3 vols, Cambridge, 1952–56) I, 243–6, 249; *APC* XXX, 619–20.

33 E. Guilpin, *Skialetheia or A Shadowe of Truth, in certaine Epigrams and Satyres*, ed. D. A. Carroll (Chapel Hill NC, 1974), 65.

34 *Ibid.*, 157–8; *Richard II*, 1.4.23–36; PRO, SP 12/264/10. Shakespeare's play was first performed in 1595–96 and the first quarto edition was entered in the Stationers' Register on 29 August 1597. Given the nature of the character of Richard II (especially in this part of the play), it is arguable whether or not this description of Bolingbroke's 'popularity' should be interpreted in a negative light. (I owe this point to Heather Hirschfeld). However, the satirists who allude to this passage in *Richard II* clearly wished to attack Essex.

35 LPL, Ms 657, fol. 140r: Essex to Reynoldes, 10 May 1596 (copy). It seems likely that an earlier publicity campaign to publicize Essex's credentials to succeed Burghley as Elizabeth's next chief councillor, based around Essex's performance at the Accession Day tournament in November 1595 and the creation of a version of Essex's letter of travel advice to the earl of Rutland for semi-public circulation, was overtaken by military developments in early 1596 and abandoned in favour of Essex's plan to capitalize on what became the Cadiz expedition: Hammer, *Polarisation*, 144–51, 247 ff.

36 LPL, Ms 658, fol. 136r; Hammer, *Polarisation*, 208–11, 252–5.

37 Spedding, *Bacon* II, 41, 43.

38 Guilpin, *Skialethia*, ed. Carroll, 65 (Satire I, ll. 71–2).

39 E.g. Manning, *First and Second Parts*, 69. Hayward was specifically questioned about his description of Bolingbroke's willingness 'to uncover the heade, to bowe the body, to stretch forth the necke & arme, &c' and admitted that he largely invented such details: he read that Bolingbroke 'was of popular behavior, but for the particulers he tooke the libertie of the best wrighters of histories of that kynd' (PRO, SP 12/278/17). Hayward's account of Bolingbroke was therefore directly inspired by Elizabethan notions of 'courteous' behaviour and almost certainly by references to Essex himself.

40 *Richard II*, 1.4.35–6.

41 Henry E. Huntington Library, San Marino CA (hereafter HEH), HM 41952, fol. 37r.

42 LPL, Ms 659, fol. 196r: Essex to Lord Burghley, September 1596 (copy).

43 D. B. Quinn (ed.), *The Hakluyt Handbook*, 2 vols, Hakluyt Society, 2nd ser., Nos 144–5 (1974), I, 312, II, 382–3, 490–1. The prolonged period during which the first volume remained on sale in its original format presumably explains why 'a surprising number' of surviving copies contain the offending pages on Cadiz (*ibid.* II, 494).

44 FSL, V.b.142, fols 49r–51v. A different account of these speeches is HEH, HM 41952, fols 68r–75r.

45 Collins, *Letters and Memorials* II, 148.

46 HEH, HM 46714, fol. 27v.

47 For Barlow's sermon, see LPL, Ms 2872, fols 51r–58r. It was printed as *A Sermon preached at Paules Crosse, on the first Sunday in Lent: Martii 1. 1600* (London, 1603). Francis Bacon, *A Declaration of the Practises & Treasons attempted and committed by Robert late Earle of Essex and his Complices, against her Majestie and her Kingdoms* (London, 1603). The extracts of testimony are printed on sigs G3r–Q5v.

48 For Elizabeth's reviling of Barlow, see R. P. Sorlien (ed.), *The Diary of John Manningham of the Middle Temple, 1602–1603* (Hanover NH, 1976), 87.

49 HMCS IX, 405–6. In a touch reminiscent of his former employer, Bacon's letter was couched as a letter to Lord Henry Howard (a friend of Essex) and circulated as a matched set with Howard's reply (*ibid.*, 406–7). Copies include those in Chetham's Library, Manchester, Ms 8012 (I am grateful to David Como and Peter Lake for access to

a microfilm of this manuscript) and Bodleian Library Ms e.Mus.55.

50 Bacon, Francis, *Sir Francis Bacon his Apologie, in certaine Imputations concerning the late Earle of Essex* (London, 1604). There were two printings of this work in 1604 and two in 1605. Essex's 'Apologie', of course, had been addressed to Bacon's brother, while Devonshire was effectively Essex's brother-in-law, finally transforming his long-term relationship with Essex's sister Penelope (since *c.* 1589) into marriage in 1605.

51 P. Croft, 'The reputation of Robert Cecil: libels, political opinion and popular awareness in the early seventeenth century', *Transactions of the Royal Historical Society*, 6th ser., 1 (1991), 47–8, 69; A. Beer, 'Textual politics: the execution of Sir Walter Ralegh', *Modern Philology* 94 (1996), 29–30.

52 Cited in Manning, *First and Second Parts*, 1–2.

53 J. Habermas, *The Structural Tranformation of the Public Sphere: an Inquiry into a Category of Bourgeois Society*, trans. T. Burger (Cambridge MA, 1992), 5 ff., 51.

54 P. Lake and M. Questier, 'Puritans, papists and the "public sphere" in early modern England: the Edmund Campion affair in context', *Journal of Modern History* 72 (2000), 587–627; P. Lake with M. Questier, *The Antichrist's lewd Hat: Protestants, Papists and Players in post-Reformation England* (New Haven CT, 2002), especially 255–62.

55 Lake, *Hat*, 261.

56 P. Collinson, 'The monarchical republic of Queen Elizabeth I', in Collinson, *Elizabethan Essays* (London, 1994), 31–57; J. Guy, 'The 1590s: the second reign of Elizabeth I?', in Guy, *Reign*, 1–19.

57 Cited in Hammer, *Polarisation*, 81.

58 J. Guy, 'The Elizabethan establishment and the ecclesiastical polity', in Guy, *Reign*, 126–49; P. Collinson, 'Ecclesiastical vitriol: religious satire in the 1590s and the invention of puritanism', in *ibid.*, 150–70. See also P. Collinson, *The Elizabethan Puritan Movement* (Oxford, 1967), 403 ff.

59 J. Hurstfield, 'The succession struggle in late Elizabethan England', in Hurstfield, *Freedom, Corruption and Government in Elizabethan England* (London, 1973), 123 ff. See also A. Pritchard, *Catholic Loyalism in Elizabethan England* (Chapel Hill NC, 1979) and Lake, *Hat*, 285 ff.

60 Although space does not permit discussion here, an important earlier high-profile airing of notions of political economy was the discourse(s) surrounding the so-called 'commonwealth men' in the mid-sixteenth century, whose writings not only reflected the impact of the Reformation and humanism but also notably coincided with the failure and abandonment (in 1549) of the pursuit of *gloire* – and recognition of the critical importance of trade – as the basis for English foreign policy. See, for example, N. Wood, *Foundations of Political Economy: some early Tudor Views on State and Society* (Berkeley CA, 1994).

61 A. Halascz, *The Marketplace of Printing: Pamphlets and the Public Sphere in early modern England* (Cambridge, 1997), 162.

62 *Ibid.*, 30 ff., 97–8, 178.

63 Manning, *First and Second Parts*, 42 ff.

64 E.g. Thomas Scott, *Robert Earle of Essex his Ghost, sent from Elizian* (London, 1624); Scott, *Sir Walter Rawleighs Ghost, or Englands Forewarner* (London, 1626); Hammer, 'Mythmaking', 640–2.

Chapter 5

The 'public man' in late Tudor and early Stuart England

Richard Cust

I

Peter Lake's chapter 'The politics of popularity and the public sphere' analyses the main features of a new style of politics which emerged in the 'monarchical republic' of Elizabethan England. It was a politics which opened up the political arena, encouraged involvement by a range of different 'publics' and exposed to discussion issues about which the subject was not normally supposed to have an opinion. It depended on, and helped to bring into being, an active citizenry, both in London and in the localities, who could be appealed to, mobilized and activated, in order to influence decision making and the formulation of government policy. And it created a space for a new type of politician who could connect the decision makers with the broader publics they were seeking to address, and by whom they were being addressed in turn.

Some of these politicians we know a good deal about. The 'men of business' and 'parliament men' of Elizabethan England, such as Thomas Norton and William Fleetwood, Robert Beale and Thomas Digges, have been studied extensively by Michael Graves and Patrick Collinson.[1] Their roles as spokesmen and drafters of position papers, managers and parliamentary committeemen, and intermediaries between the privy council, the House of Commons and the City of London were all essential to facilitating this new style of politics. But they were a distinct breed of politician, working in close proximity to the establishment and at home in the rarefied atmosphere of the royal court and Westminster. The new politics also gave rise to another type of politician who has received rather less attention. These were the 'good commonwealthmen', 'honest patriots' or 'public men'. They had many of the same skills as the 'men of business'. (They were often accomplished orators, adept at drafting legislation and experienced operators in parliamentary committees.) But, whereas the latter prided themselves on being in the political loop, they invariably presented themselves as outsiders. They were 'the simple men of the country'[2] (as Job Throckmorton characterized them in 1587), untainted and uncompromised by association with the 'court' and therefore qualified to speak for the cluster of interests and concerns associated with the 'public' or 'common weal'. They were also the natural representatives of the concerned and active citizenry in the provinces, politicians who in the words on the epitaph of one of their number, Sir William Skipwith, of Cotes, in Leicestershire,

> can when need requires with courage bold,
> To publike eares his neighbour's griefes unfold.[3]

The aim of this chapter is to investigate the genus of the 'public man'; explore the construction and composition of this political type; look at how it developed and adapted to political circumstances in England between the 1580s and the 1620s; and finally assess its significance and impact.

II

The best place to start is with the classical authors and their humanist interpreters from whom the language of the 'public', and the associated terminology of 'commonwealth', 'country' and 'patriot', derived. Foremost among these, for Elizabethan Englishmen, were the Stoics: Quintilian, Plutarch, Sallust, Seneca and, above all, Cicero. The latter's *De Officiis* was virtually a handbook for the conscientious magistrate. It was familiar to every schoolboy as the principal text for learning Latin in the grammar schools and it was revered as a source of moral instruction.[4] As John Brinsley explained in the preface to the standard early Stuart translation of the work, 'it doth so divinely point out the true pathway to all vertue and guide us into a right course of life as if it had received direction from the sacred Scriptures themselves'. He then went on to remind readers of the 'many learned men' – most famously, Lord Burghley – who had laid it 'under their pillows' and made it 'their companion which way soever they have gone'.[5]

The principal message of the *De Officiis* was that man's highest earthly duty and aspiration was the active service of his *respublica* (literally meaning 'public thing', but most commonly translated in the sixteenth century as 'commonwealth' or 'country'). Such service demanded certain basic qualities, largely defined by the four 'cardinal virtues' of wisdom, justice, temperance and fortitude. Only if a man succeeded in developing these, as part of a life of active political service, could he be regarded as truly noble.[6]

The issues raised by the Stoics' message were endlessly publicized and debated by humanist commentators during the Renaissance. Much of this discussion revolved around two stock themes: firstly, whether a life of action and political involvement (*vita activa* or *negotium*) was more worthy of honour than the life of philosophical contemplation and learning (*vita contemplativa* or *otium*); and secondly, what constituted true nobility (*vera nobilitas*) and, by implication, who was best qualified to hold public office.

The answer given to the first of these questions was variable. During the mid-Tudor period – from about the 1530s to the 1580s – Cicero's influence was very much in the ascendant among English humanists and they tended to argue more or less unequivocally in favour of the *vita activa*. This was based on the notion that man was a social animal who had been taught by reason to organize himself into societies or 'commonwealths'. His principal obligation, therefore, was the pursuit of the common good and any attempt to evade this, and withdraw into solitary contemplation, could be regarded as 'an uncivile kind of life', essentially brutish and inhuman. Cicero's maxim that 'we are not born for ourselves, but for our country' was endlessly reiterated.[7] John Barston, town clerk of Tewkesbury, who wrote a civic humanist treatise on the role of the local magistracy entitled *The Safeguard of Societie* (1576), insisted that 'our native country is the universall parente of us all, for which no good man will refuse his life'; whilst Thomas North, in the preface to his translation of Plutarch's *Lives* (1579), explained that the whole point of the gentry reading this work was to 'be animated to the better service' of their country and their queen.[8]

Like the Stoics, these authors accepted that there was a place for *otium*. It was a necessary part of the life of the good citizen that he should develop wisdom and virtue in order to learn how to subject his passions to reason and equip himself for public service. But it was the public service which really mattered, and without this he could never attain lasting honour and renown. Thus Haly Heron, in a more philosophical discussion of magistracy couched in the form of advice to a young student, *A new Discourse of Morall Philosophie, entituled the Kayes of Counsaile* (1579), warned of the hazards of 'too muche contemplation and desyre of knowledge'. 'Say with Tully that it is better to practise and doe advisedly then to thinke and imagine never so wysely.' The ultimate end of learning was its virtuous application, and it was this alone which could raise man to 'the toppe and type of honour'.[9]

By the 1590s, however, the stress on the merits of political engagement was having to compete with a new emphasis on the validity of the *vita contemplativa*. Ciceronian optimism about the possibilities of promoting the common welfare was tempered by a more sceptical approach to politics. This coincided with the first appearance in English of the main works of Tacitus and his neo-Stoic commentators, such as Justus Lipsius. Tacitus's penetrating analysis of the treachery and uncertainty of the imperial Roman courts, together with the responses of Lipsius and others to the turmoil of the Dutch Revolt and the French wars of religion, encouraged many Englishmen to adopt a fatalistic view of the whole political process. Ben Jonson's *Sejanus* (1604), for example, suggested that princely courts were places where the 'good patriot' bent on virtuous reform invariably went to the wall, whilst deceit, manipulation and corruption prospered. In these circumstances, self-preservation and survival had much more appeal than active engagement. It came to be argued that the virtuous man should no longer struggle to change his political situation but accept things as they were and concentrate on the one area that he could control, his own mind. There was renewed emphasis on the value of detachment, to enable one to remain steadfast to one's principles. The highest virtue came to be seen as constancy; and Stoic authors, like Seneca, were now read for the instruction they could provide on how to subdue the unruly passions rather than how to engage with the world of affairs.[10] Thus Thomas Lodge, in his translation of Seneca's *Workes ... both Morall and Naturall* (1614), insisted that 'no time is better spent' than in studying 'how to live well and die well': 'to subdue passion is to be truly a man ... to live well is to be vertuous and to die well is the way to eternitie'.[11] And this point was emphasized by John Ford in an extended discussion of the role of the 'publique man' in his treatise on nobility entitled *A Line of Life* (1620). Such a man, he insisted, 'hath not more need to be *bonus vir*, a good statist, then *bonus vir*, good in himself'. He must heed Seneca's counsel :

> Let a public man rejoyce in the true pleasures of a constant resolution, not in deceivable pleasures of vanitie and fondnesse. By a good conscience, honest counsells and just actions, the true good is acquired.[12]

All this led to a certain ambivalence on the part of the late Elizabethan and Jacobean governing classes when it came to assessing the relative merits of *otium* and *negotium*. This can be picked up in their advices to their sons. Advices constitute one of the principal literary and rhetorical genres through which the notion of the 'public man' was constructed, interpreted and disseminated. Others included conduct books, godly lives and, as we shall see, assize sermons, election addresses and jury charges.[13] For the generation which grew up in the 1580s and 1590s advices became a favourite means of passing on a sense of proper ethical standards as well as the fruits of their own wisdom and experience. The genre itself owed a good deal to the *De Officiis*, which was written in the form of advice to Cicero's son Marcus.[14] But that did not preclude them from offering a somewhat equivocal assessment of the benefits of the *vita activa*.

For Sir Christopher Wandesford, a Yorkshire magistrate and MP, it was very much an open question whether his son should 'content' himself

> with the comforts of a private life such as your owne fortune and the quiet of the country may abundantly minister unto you, or whether you apply yourself to the observation of the court and to more publick employments.

In support of the former, he urged the happiness and peace of mind which would come from retirement and contemplation, and, more pertinently, the hazards of the court, where 'flattery' and 'dependency' were the order of the day and it was 'difficult not to be transported with that unbridled passion of ambition'.[15] Others shared his concern. The fifth earl of Huntingdon, the leading local governor in Leicestershire, urged his son to remember that 'by birth thou art a publique person', but then went on to present a devastating critique of service at court, describing it as 'this glittering miserie' compounded of vice, expense, frustration and insecurity. He, therefore, urged his son to 'spend the greatest part of thy life in the country where thou shalt receive more pleasure, better contentment, be respected and do greater good to others'.[16] In spite of misgivings about involvement with the royal court, however, almost all the advice writers acknowledged that a gentleman's first duty still lay in public service. Sir John Oglander, an Isle of Wight justice, endorsed the view that 'there is no life to the honest country life and the more private the more happier', but nonetheless echoed Cicero in insisting that 'we are not born only for ourselves but for the public';[17] while the Cheshire magistrate and MP Sir Richard Grosvenor reminded his son that 'every man owes his country a tribute of action'.[18]

If early Stuart Englishmen gave out conflicting messages about *otium* and *negotium*, however, there was no such ambiguity on the topic of *vera nobilitas*. Here the argument came through loud and clear that virtue, and virtue alone, entitled a man to be regarded as truly noble. A favourite image was of the Roman temple of virtue through which the worthy had to pass before they could enter the temple of honour. There was widespread recognition that a distinguished pedigree had a part to play in acquiring virtue, because it offered examples of virtuous deeds amongst one's ancestors which one could readily emulate. But even as enthusiastic an exponent of this concept of 'mixed noblenes' as the Elizabethan heraldic writer John Ferne readily acknowledged that 'true nobility hath no other fountaine from whence to fetch her source then onely vertue'. And English humanists were quick to dismiss as unacceptable the 'vulgar' view that lineage and wealth were the principal qualifications for honour.[19] Thus John Barston condemned as 'bare bragges' the view that 'to bee a gentleman, to bee a riche man, to be an elder, without vertue, without wisedome, without experience or knowledge' was sufficient 'to bring a man to dignitie, estimation or credite'. The magistracy in a town like Tewkesbury, he argued, should be composed of 'suche as by wisedome, good moderation, vertuous endeavours and knowledge, deserved of the common weale'. Indeed, it was the hallmark of a well ordered civil society that such men should come to the fore. Rulers should always be willing to promote individuals on the basis of merit, even if this meant elevating 'very mean men'. In support of this Barston cited the example of Cicero himself, who had had none of the advantages of a distinguished pedigree, but had come to the fore in Roman politics entirely on the basis of his own virtues. Those who attained 'nobilitie by themselves' were, for Barston *'vere nobiles,* noble men indeede'.[20]

The view put forward in humanist treatises was again reflected in the gentry's advices to their sons. Although most of the writers boasted lengthy pedigrees, they endorsed the Ciceronian verdict that true nobility resided in virtuous conduct. Thus William Higford, a Gloucestershire magistrate, urged his grandson to remember that 'without virtue honour is but a false gloss ... titles of honour do not ennoble men, but worthy men ennoble their titles of honour',[21] while William Martyn, Recorder and MP for Exeter, reminded his son that 'much more is he to be admired that swayeth a kingdom by his vertues than hee that ruleth by the only priviledge of his ennobled and hero-icall descent. For honors are but servants and attendants of vertue.' At the same time, however, he insisted that honour resided not just in virtue itself, but in its practical application. 'It is not enough to boast the name of virtue without virtuous deeds and actions.' For his son to 'make himself the more famous' required 'the active distribution of his virtues'.[22]

But what of the qualities which constituted this 'active' virtue? Here again humanist commentators were in general agreement. The principles which were expected to guide the service of commonwealth and country could be summed up in the contrast between 'public' and 'private'. In the political vocabulary of the day these were highly charged terms with a moral force and potency which allowed them to stand for fundamentally opposed approaches to government and magistracy. They were an important example of the process of inversion, or arguing from opposites, which was a central feature of contemporary culture. 'Private gain' and 'private profit' were, of course, regarded as legitimate concerns for an individual acting in a personal capacity; but they could have no place when it came to the work of the magistrate. Here 'private' signified what was selfish, corrupt, even tyrannical, and was equated with vices such as 'covetousness', 'ambition', 'pride' and 'anger'. 'Public' was the antithesis of these, a concept which embraced the common good of the 'country' and the duty of every good citizen to serve it unselfishly.[23] The magistrate, according to Barston, 'must forget his private being so long as his office lasteth and should more esteem public utility than his own lucre'. Only if this was the case could a society enjoy liberty and stability.[24] In a similar vein, Lord Keeper Bacon reminded the MPs of Elizabeth's early parliaments that the commonwealth was an organic body which could function only if its various parts acted in a spirit of mutuality and co-operation. 'Private affection' and 'private wealth's devise' were 'the greatest adversaryes that can be to unitie and concorde, without which no common wealthe can longe endure or stande'. Members owed a duty to God, to the queen, 'to your countrie, whose weale it concerneth universallye' to act 'without respect of honour, rule or soveraigntie, profett, pleasure or ease ... and without regard of all other manner of private affection'.[25]

Gentleman magistrates again echoed these views. The Devonshire justice Sir John Strode used the same imagery as Bacon, urging his son to regard 'the weal public' as an organic whole. He must not only be faithful to the head, the monarch, but must seek to serve the interests of the 'country' as a whole, which meant specifically that he should dispense justice without fear or favour.[26] Sir Richard Grosvenor drew a clear distinction between 'such actions as concerne you as a private gentleman' and 'your publick deportment as you stand in relation to authority, being a justice in commission of the peace'. 'Every good magistrate should have his thoughts soe strongly possessed with zeale of the common good that he should have noe leasure to intertaine thoughts of private ends'. 'Proffitt, kindred, alliance, frendshipp, revenge and all by respects ought for that tyme to bee locked upp' and he should again follow the dictates of justice, 'without respect of persons'.[27]

The magistrate who displayed these qualities would earn the accolade of 'honest' – again a key word in the contemporary political lexicon (as it was for Cicero, for whom *vir honestus* described the man who possessed the four cardinal virtues and also the man who was worthy of honour). 'Honesty' implied virtue, integrity and above all courage and constancy in standing up for the 'public' interest. Appropriately enough it was often Cicero himself who was seen as the supreme example of the *vir honestus*. Described as *pater patriae*, 'the father of the commonwealth', he epitomized the man of virtue who had thrown himself into a life of active political engagement, fought courageously for liberties and the 'public' interest, and attained lasting honour and fame.[28]

This terminology and use of language were again picked up by the governing classes. The 'honest' magistrate, according to Grosvenor, was one who must 'ever ... bee more respective of the the publique interest of countrey then that more private of his nearest and dearest frends'. This often had different connotations in different public contexts. In the case of local justices and jurors it meant being vigilant and courageous in pursuing wrongdoers, incorruptible in the face of pressure or bribes and impartial in the exercise of judgement. For members of parliament, and those thrust on to a national stage, however, the list of qualities was even more demanding. The ideal knight of the shire, as Grosvenor described him to the Cheshire electors in 1624, should be 'quicke of capacitie, nimble of apprehension, ripe in judgment', but, above all, he must be 'such whose courage (uppon all occasions) dare commaund their tongues without feare to utter their countreyes just complaints and grievances'.[29]

As Grosvenor's list of requisite qualities implied, the 'honest patriot' played a critical role in safeguarding the 'public' weal. It was his readiness to stand up and be counted and set an example to others which provided the surest means of preventing corruption and tyranny. Humanist writers regularly cited examples of states which had collapsed in ruin when such men had been forced out of office, and 'clyming mindes and ambitious heds' had gained the upper hand.[30] Richard Brathwait, author of one of the most widely read conduct books for the magisterial classes, *The English Gentleman* (1630), compared the vocation of the 'honest patriot' to that of the orators of Athens and ancient Rome. They must be steadfast 'in their opposition to the greatest enemies of state ... constant for the liberty of their country', aiming 'neither at publique fame nor private safety', but gearing all their actions 'to the improvement and security of their countrey'.[31] As we shall, this role was regarded as an essential component in the make-up of 'the public man'.

Advices to sons demonstrate very clearly the extent to which the language and values of the civic humanists had become embedded in provincial political culture. They provided much of what Quentin Skinner calls the 'normative vocabulary' through which contemporaries sought to legitimate their actions and make sense of the political world around them.[32] Advices also illustrate how the mixed legacy of sixteenth-century humanism had filtered through to the localities. Some magistrates had clearly absorbed Tacitist rhetoric about the hazards of the *vita activa*, particularly as it applied to princely courts. But they had not been put off public service and remained wedded to the notion that it was an essential part of the honour and calling of a gentleman to engage with politics. However, whereas humanist commentators in Elizabeth's reign could still argue that service to the commonwealth meant first and foremost service at court, for the early Stuart gentleman, as we shall see, this was emphatically not the case.

III

Many of the same themes were highlighted in Calvinist readings of scripture. Calvinist ministers of the late sixteenth and early seventeenth centuries were generally well versed in the language and concepts of civic humanism, and sermons about magisterial office were full of references to honesty, the four cardinal virtues and putting the 'public' before the 'private'.[33] However, this rhetoric was overlaid with a language based on scripture which gave their vision of public service its own distinct character. They saw magistracy as a godly vocation. Magistrates, like princes, were little gods, called on by the almighty to fulfil the divine purposes of promoting justice and order, and fighting sin. If they failed to do this then the nation was liable to face God's providential wrath.[34]

These themes provided the subject matter for innumerable sermons and treatises by Calvinist ministers during the late Tudor and early Stuart period, but the message was particularly clear in the sermons delivered prior to assizes or elections. These were important set-piece occasions, addressed to audiences of local worthies and lesser officials, and frequently finding their way into print. Sometimes highly topical, they were an opportunity for ministers to preach about issues which they believed were of direct concern to an active godly citizenry, and to stir up this citizenry to action.[35] Minister after minister on such occasions emphasized that public service was a godly calling. At the Lincolnshire assizes, Robert Sanderson warned the gentlemen in his audience that they must not suppose that by dint of 'birth, lineage and estate' they were spared from 'labour in any vocation'. It was their duty to respond to divine expectation and fulfil their role as magistrates. Their 'greatest glory and delight' should be the administration of justice, which Sanderson described as 'that settled course of life wherein mainly to employ a man's gifts and his time for his own and the common good'.[36] Theirs was a role specifically ordained by God. Anthony Fawkner described 'the righteous judge' as 'a lay priest' and reminded the Northamptonshire justices that 'God hath said you are Gods, the protectors of his poor, the judges of his people'. It was only through conscientious discharge of these responsibilities that the godly gentleman could validate his personal claim to be numbered among God's elect saints.[37] In another series of assize sermons addressed to the Northamptonshire justices Robert Bolton repeatedly called on his audience to confront 'the crying sinnes of the country': blasphemy, usury, profaning 'God's holy and glorious sabbath', 'haunting' alehouses and, above all, 'that hydra of heresies', popery. These must be rooted out and scourged by the godly magistrate, lest his countrymen be subjected to the full force of God's judgements. 'Allowance, toleration, connivance' would 'pull down the vials of God's fiercest wrath upon our heads' and 'blast the beauty of the most fruitful nation and flourishing prosperity'.[38]

In carrying out this godly work the magistrate should be guided by reason and wisdom, but this alone was not enough. He must also ground his actions in faith and conscience. At the Oxford assizes in 1628 Robert Harris imagined some of the decisions his audience of justices and jurors might face. In each case it was conscience which would provide the necessary guidance and direction.

> What? Shall I indict my friend. – No, nor foe neither unless conscience binds thee; if [so] present him whatever he be. – What, a neighbour? – A Neighbour. – A kinsman? – A kinsman. – A justice? – A justice. – My landlord? – Thy landlord.[39]

Robert Bolton drew an explicit contrast between the dictates of 'carnal reason' and of the godly conscience. Without what he called this 'lode star', 'men of publike imployment' cannot be 'universally thorough and unshaken'. Mere 'civil honest men' might achieve fame and honour in the eyes of others, but their virtue was all too likely to 'degenerate' when put to the test. 'Some strong affection, feare, favour, or some thing will make them flie out and faile in some particular.' But with it 'you are won for ever to an invincible constancy and conscionablenesse in an uniforme, regular and religious discharge of your publike duties'. In the final analysis, it was only the man who had planted in him 'the right roote, faith in Christ' who could be relied on to 'take to heart the good of the country'.[40]

This emphasis on faith and conscience gave an added twist to the debate over *vera nobilitas*. In his sermon *The Holy Choice*, delivered prior to the mayoral election at the Guildhall in London, Thomas Adams presented the conventional humanist view that wealth and lineage were never enough to qualify a candidate for office, but then insisted that godliness as well as 'wise government ... shows an able man'. 'It is not birth but new birth that makes men truly noble.'[41] Bolton advanced similar claims for what he called the 'divine and supernaturall' nobility. Those who were 'truly and the onely noble indeed' were those for whom 'God is top of the kin and religion is the root'.[42]

The natural ally of such men was, of course, the godly minister. In the eyes of these ministers, the two must fight alongside each other to promote reformation and suppress sin. Thus, in a sermon to the Suffolk justices on the theme of those whom Jethro had urged Moses to choose as rulers of God's people, Samuel Ward could insist that 'the principall scope of magistracy in God's intention', was 'to promote his glory, countenancing the gospel and the professors of it'. 'Magistracy and ministry' must join together and, 'as guardians and tutors of the rest, should either prevent or reform their aberrations'.[43] A striking example of the teamwork this called for was provided by the 'eminently religious' Suffolk magistrate, Sir Nathaniel Barnardiston, and his local minister, Samuel Fairclough. The two men were said to have conferred at least twice about how to discharge their responsibilities and after Barnardiston's death Fairclough depicted their partnership as a prime example of how 'Magistry and Ministry joined both together and concurred in all things for the promoting of true piety and godliness'.[44] For the Calvinist minister, then, 'the public man' was not simply a virtuous bulwark against corruption and tyranny; he was also the spearhead of a godly crusade. Much of this rhetoric was picked up by the gentry themselves and recycled in their own addresses before the local courts. [45] Sir John Newdigate, a staunchly Calvinist north Warwickshire justice, reminded his fellows on the bench that 'God would have none idle, but he which is a judge should do the work of a judge ... he that is a magistrate the work of a magistrate'. 'You are the champion of justis, the patron of peace, the father of thy cuntry and as it were another God on earth.'[46] Sir Richard Grosvenor urged the Cheshire grand jurors to keep in the forefront of their minds the need to follow conscience. 'By keeping a good conscience you shalbe armed against all opposition'; it would help them to put aside 'fear to offend great men' and act with utter impartiality. 'God is greater than the mightiest and looks first to be served, first to be feared.'[47] And both men urged the partnership of magistracy and ministry, with Newdigate averting on several occasions to the image of Jethro advising Moses to appoint magistrates to assist in the work of promoting godliness.[48]

The origins of the image of 'the public man' can be found, then, in the blending of zealous Calvinism and classical republicanism. It was this same confluence which, as Peter Lake demonstrates, gave rise to this new-style politics in the first place. Now they furnished the vocabulary, role models and agendas which defined how 'the public man' should conduct himself and how he was perceived by others. But against whom were his energies to be directed?

IV

At the local level the enemy of 'the public man' was straightforward enough. It was those 'vices' castigated by the humanists, such as 'greed', 'pride', 'covetousness' and 'idleness', or those 'crying sins' against which Bolton inveighed. At a national level, however, the target was often less clear. Most Protestants could agree that the main enemy was 'popery'; and, as Lake has pointed out, 'popery could do duty as a symbol for all sorts of corruption, all sorts of threats to the commonweal'. It loomed large in the assize sermons of Robert Bolton and the jury charges of Grosvenor and Newdigate, where it manifested itself in everything from the 'sinful vanities, lewd sports [and] profanation of the sabath' denounced by Bolton to the 'extreame hazard' of the Gunpowder Plot, against which, Newdigate insisted, 'no good countriman ought to withold his tongue or hand according to his calling or facultie'.[49] But beyond this there were the more elusive forces of 'privacie' which encapsulated all manner of other evils and threats to liberty. By the latter part of Elizabeth's reign many of these threats were becoming associated with the royal court.

The changing image of the royal court and those who inhabited it at this time is a topic badly in need of investigation. It appears that in the early part of Elizabeth's reign it enjoyed an unusually positive image. Traditional depictions of the court as a source of vice and iniquity had been tempered by the reception of an Italian humanist literature which stressed the superior wisdom and sophistication of cities and courts when compared with the country. Castiglione's *The Courtier* demonstrated that it was possible to blend humanist learning with courtly accomplishments to produce the Tudor ideal of the 'man of parts', capable of turning his hand to anything from composing romantic verse to counselling his prince. This text was widely read by Elizabethans and its impact was reinforced by Ciceronian humanist works suggesting that the most appropriate setting for the *vita activa* was the court, because it was here that one could do most to influence the government of the common weal.[50] By the middle of Elizabeth's reign the courtier/counsellor was well on the way to being established as the model of the wise and virtuous 'public man'. Richard Robinson, for example, in his 1576 translation of Francesco Patrizi's *A Moral Methode of Civil Policie*, depicted Elizabeth's councillors as 'so many christal starres of stately light under her, garnishing and saveguarding the good government of this her majestie's realme'. They upheld the 'most holsome, godly and politique lawes and constitutions, for the continual conservation of the publique weale ... free from all private prejudice and publique perturbation'.[51] A seminal image in this respect was Roger Ascham's famous depiction of Lord Burghley, *The Schoolmaster* (1570) – taking time out from affairs of state to discuss the education of youth round his dinner table.[52]

Ascham's portrayal of Burghley had considerable resonance for the early Stuart gentry. They frequently harked back to him as a model of the wise and moderate councillor and copied his advice to his son into their commonplace books, sometimes trying to pass it off as their own.[53] No early Stuart statesman was able to establish a similar reputation. The third earl of Pembroke was sometimes hailed as 'a noble patriot' and 'a good commonwealthsman'. But his appeal was never as comprehensive as Cecil's and it was the oppositionist figure of Sir Walter Raleigh who was seen as laying the most convincing claim to these titles during James's reign.[54] This was an indication that the court was no longer seen as the obvious setting for the 'public man'.

The rot appears to have set in in the 1580s and 1590s. As Peter Lake's chapter shows, it seems to have had a good deal to do, initially, with the publication of *The Treatise of Treasons* (1572), which cast men like Burghley and Bacon as 'Machiavel Catilines', conspiring to deceive the queen about the loyalty of her Catholic subjects, overthrow the ancient nobility and promote their private agendas of self-enrichment and political dominance. This resurrection of the traditional stereotype of the 'evil counsellor' whose natural habitat was the household of the prince did much to poison the image of the court. For a Protestant audience, however, the work which probably had the greatest impact in this respect was John Stubbes's *Discoverie of a Gaping Gulf*. Published in 1579 as part of the campaign of opposition to the Anjou match, it set out to explain that, in spite of the obvious dangers in the queen marrying a foreign Catholic, the whole project had got off the ground because of the existence of 'evil counsellors'. 'Flatterers' and 'politics' whose natural home was the court of France, 'where Machiavelli is their New Testament and atheism is their religion', their plotting to serve their 'private' ends was threatening to destroy English Protestantism. In such circumstances, the clearest remedy was the willingness of 'Christian commonwealthsmen', like Stubbes himself, to speak out and alert the queen to the dangers of what was going on. The wide circulation of the *Gaping Gulf,* and the fuss made about its suppression and Stubbes's punishment, ensured that the whole episode had a profound impact on the psyche of the political nation. From this point onwards the image of the outsider, willing to speak out where the compromises and corruptions of the court prevented professional councillors from doing so, appears to have become firmly established.

One politician who keyed into this image during the 1580s was Job Throck-morton. One of the prototypes of the 'patriots' or 'public men', and a skilled and aggressive exponent of the new style of politics, in the 1586–87 parliament he spoke out with considerable effect in support of the execution of Mary Queen of Scots and the adoption of Cope's Bill and Book. He was also the probable author of the Marprelate tracts, which deployed the new methods of political pamphleteering to deliver a scurrilous and highly damaging exposé of the hypocrisy and corruption of bishops. Whether Throckmorton received support for his actions from more senior figures within the Protestant establishment is unclear. (The suspicion is that he did.) But in public he presented himself as an outsider, the simple, 'honest', mouthpiece of the 'country'.[55] This stance was skilfully worked into his speech in support of the Bill and Book, which began as a defence of parliament's right to freedom of speech, but quickly turned into an attack on councillors who failed to discharge their duty of counselling the queen on the dangers she faced. 'It is wondered at above,' he acknowledged, that 'the simple men of the country should be so forward.' But 'it doeth amate [sic] us in the countrey that wise men of the courte should be so backward ... can it be excused in a councellor to be to sleepye'.[56]

The image of the court deteriorated rapidly during the 1590s and then declined further still in James's reign. The damage done by the vicious, and well publicized, in-fighting between Essex and Cecil factions, and the series of court scandals culminating in the Overbury murder and the trial of Somerset, was compounded by the vogue for Tacitist readings of the nature of court politics and revelations about the activities of the earl of Northampton and Spanish pensions, which made it appear that the court was also a centre of popish plotting.[57] The associations with vice, corruption and self-interest which the court had acquired by the 1620s were summed up in the assize sermons and broadsides of the Norfolk minister turned pamphleteer Thomas Scott. At one level, he depicted it as the source of the 'spirit of privacie' which 'ever forerunnes and effects the ruine of the commonwealth'. It was home to 'the courtly theefe', the projector and monopolist whose selfishness and greed threatened to infect everyone and 'undo the publique for their private and inordinate desires'.[58] At another level, and even more alarmingly, it was also the natural habitat of the sinister figure of the evil counsellor who sought to turn the prince against his people. According to Scott, he was the direct agent of Satan who, knowing that princes needed to be told the truth, therefore

> labours to banish it from their presence; and to this end entertaines and armes his pensioners (flatterers those tame beastes, toothlesse traytours) to stave it off with many pretie pretences colourable enough being dyed deepe in hypocrisie, policie and court craft.

The principal aim of such counsellors was to 'use all their art and industrie' to persuade the king that 'he may rule by his absolute prerogative without a parliament'. This would 'open a dore to all manner of evil' and

> make that greate bodie of sovereigntie unproportionable, uncomely and ... altogether unserviceable to move itselfe, either for the restraint of vice, the encouragement of virtue, the execution of lawes or the uniting of the inward power against foreigne force and invasion which are the ends of royall institution.[59]

The court, then, had become not just a centre of corruption and self-seeking, but a means of striking to the heart of England's laws, liberties, religion and security.

For Scott and other contemporaries, the chief antidote to this threat was the purifying influence of 'the country'. As the court's reputation declined, that of 'the country' became purer and more pristine. Late Tudor and early Stuart literature was full of pastoral imagery culled from the likes of Horace and Ovid. The 'country' was presented as the setting for innocence and virtue, the place where traditional pastimes and hospitality were still practised and where a man could retreat from the cares of office and commune with nature. Gradually this imagery came to be appropriated by those with more overtly political agendas. For puritan ministers, such as Scott, 'the country' was taken to represent a vision of a godly nation, such as might exist if popery and sinfulness were overcome and England reformed along Calvinist lines. For those with a more secular outlook, it tended to mean a commonwealth freed from projectors, evil counsellors and threats to liberties. By the 1620s, if not before, 'court' and 'country' were widely perceived as representing two ideological poles. 'The court' stood for corruption, 'privacy' and popery, 'the country' was its direct antithesis, an image of a healthy, balanced and purified common weal.[60]

But how was the influence of the latter to be brought to bear on the former? Here again the main onus fell on the virtuous 'public man'. This was discussed in an essay 'Of a country life' published in 1620 by Sir William Cavendish who later on, as second earl of Devonshire, acquired a considerable reputation as a 'patriot peer'.[61] Cavendish carefully weighed the pros and cons of a life of retirement. The 'country' offered a calmer, more reflective, altogether more virtuous environment in which one could contemplate the higher things in life and help one's neighbours. In contrast, 'the court' was beset with ambition, rivalry and self-seeking; however, it was also a place where one generally encountered 'refined and judicious men' and which offered the best prospect of honour and recognition of one's accomplishments. What counted for most, however, as far as Cavendish was concerned, was the Ciceronian principle that 'we are not born for ourselves and to please only our own fancies, but to serve the publike in that kinde and in those places we be thought most fit for'. This he interpreted to mean that, although the majority of one's time should be devoted to local duties as a magistrate, one should also be prepared to engage with politics at Westminster. It was, after all, at court and in parliament that most matters were decided which related to the 'the good of the country'.[62] Exactly what this engagement should entail he did not spell out. But his own political career – in which he sat as knight of the shire for Derbyshire in every parliament from 1614 to 1626, as well as maintaining close contacts with 'patriot' councillors such as Pembroke and taking a stand against any repetition of the forced loan in 1628[63] – perhaps indicates what he had in mind.

At the centre of the processes by which the 'public man' applied the purifying influence of the 'country' to the ills of the commonwealth was, of course, parliament. As Lake's chapter emphasizes, parliament was at the centre of the new politics of the public sphere, in its various roles as debating chamber, legislative assembly and 'representative of the people'. Parliament's prominence in this respect owed a good deal to its status as an institution and its traditional position as counsellor to the monarch which meant that things unsayable elsewhere could – in the context of bills and petitions addressing the grievances of the commonweal – be openly enunciated. But it was also a consequence of the quasi-republican ideas about consent which were gaining ground. Civic humanists argued that the best safeguard against corruption and 'privacie' in the state was the principle of obtaining 'popular consent', both in the election of officials and the approval of laws and policies.[64] In an English context, parliament was generally regarded as the supreme embodiment of this principle. A 'free' parliament, with 'free speech' and 'freedom of voyce' for electors, was the surest guarantee of preserving the common weal.

The impact of these ideas was becoming apparent, both inside and outside parliament, from the 1580s onwards. In the early part of Elizabeth's reign 'counsel' was seen as almost entirely the responsibility of the queen's councillors; but as the image of the court became tarnished, the House of Commons became increasingly vociferous in its claims to be regarded as the fount of wisdom in such matters.[65] When Throckmorton made his speech in 1587 the general presumption appears to have been that the 'wise men of the courte' were still the guiding lights. But by 1602, when Nicholas Fuller spoke in the playing cards case of Darcy v. Allen, the onus had shifted to parliament. It was the Commons, he claimed, who now possessed the monopoly of understanding.

> Amongst the assembly of such wise men some will consider the inconvenience, some the damage, some the profit, some the mischief; some what is meete for this place, some for that place; therefore it is well said of Plato, Except wise men be made governors, or governors made wise men, mankind shall never have quiet rest, nor virtue be able to defend itself. [66]

This helped to bolster the notion that it was parliament's function to provide the prince with advice not only on legislation, but on all other matters of policy which affected the well-being of the commonwealth.[67] Thomas Scott articulated this view in a 1624 pamphlet:

> A parliament therefore, where Prince and People meet and joyne in consultation is fit only for that weightie and important worke in whose even ballancing the weale of a state doth consist. And without this councel the greatest peere or officer, yea the greatest profest enginere in state stratagems, may easily erre upon either hand many degrees from good government and so fall into an anarchy or tyrannie. [68]

Parliament's role as the safest and surest source of 'good counsel' was, of course, closely tied in with the recognition that it embodied the principle of consent. There were two aspects of this which had specific implications for the 'public man'. Firstly, an increasing stress on parliament's status as 'the representative of the people' gave him a much more prominent role as a link between the centre and the localities. George Carleton, speaking in the Commons in 1571, described an MP as 'not a private man' but someone 'especially chosen and ... sent', with a duty 'to supply the roome, person and place of the multitude'.[69] As Derek Hirst and Hassell Smith have shown, this was a function which came to be emphasized more and more from the 1590s onwards, with greater involvement by freeholders in the electoral process and improved facilities for reporting back to constituents on what was happening in parliament.[70] MPs were seen as having both the capacity and the responsibility to speak out on behalf of those who had elected them and to seek remedies for their grievances. Sometimes this involved pursuing an exclusively local agenda, but more often it required the blending together of local and national in the pursuit of measures which would contribute to 'the preservacon of the common weal'.[71] A good example was the outcry against projectors and purveyors in the 1590s and early 1600s, in which MPs like Sir William Skipwith or Sir Nathaniel Bacon presented instances of the damage being inflicted on local people and sought to enact legislation which would prevent it in the future.[72] The 'public man', sitting in parliament, then, was increasingly seen as protecting liberties and advancing public welfare through his role in promoting a series of ongoing dialogues between the localities and the centre.

It was recognized, however, that this role – as well as parliament's counselling function – could be sustained only as long as there were 'free elections'. This was the second aspect of 'consent' which had particular implications for the 'public man', and also for the ordinary citizen. Concern about it was being voiced in the context of parliamentary elections as early as the Warwick contest of 1586. The prime mover in this was, again, Job Throckmorton, who sought to unseat the regular MP, the town clerk, Thomas Fisher. His main tactic was to play on disquiet among 'the Commons' of Warwick over the principal burgesses' handling of town revenues and local elections. He presented himself as the candidate who backed openness and participation as the best means of curbing municipal corruption, insisting that he 'would not have the matter [of the election] huddled upp in a corner as the most of your matters be amongst yourselfs, & all in public'. He also took steps to ensure that if there was a parliamentary election the time and venue were announced two days in advance and threatened that if 'the Commons' were denied the opportunity to participate he would appeal to parliament. Finally to allay any doubts about his own commitment to public service he took an oath that in the coming parliament he would devote himself to working for 'good government and benefiting of the same borough, liberties, franchises and the people of the same'. [73] Throckmorton, then, was drawing on some of the key themes of the language of consent, and coupling them with a rhetoric of faithful service to town and commonwealth. The success of his campaign – in spite of Fisher's efforts to smear him as a 'popular spirit' – suggests that they already had considerable resonance amongst the active citizenry, well beyond the confines of Westminster.

During the early Stuart period much of the concern about 'free elections' focused on the threat from 'undertaking' and other forms of corruption which could again be traced back to the court. The remedy was seen as lying partly with 'public men' legislating to prevent such abuses in the future, but also with active citizens guaranteeing a 'free' electoral system by making an open and informed choice.[74] Again it was Thomas Scott who provided one of the clearest articulations of this, in an address to the Norfolk freeholders prior to the election of 1620. 'Let none amongst you,' he exhorted, 'bee seene to sit idely at home whilst these things are doing in the full countrey, as if it did not concerne you; but ride, runne and deale seriously herein as for your lives and liberties which depend heerupon.' They must take the initiative, 'conferre together and (neglecting both ... landlords, or great neighbours, or the Lord Liftenants themselves) looke upon the wisest, stoutest and most religious persons'. This would ensure the choice of such as have 'no dependencie upon greatnes, nor seeke change of state, lawes and religion, nor hunt ambitiously for place, honour and preferment for there is danger in these; but he that is religious will stand for his countries' good'. 'In choosing such you shall please God and the king, and profit yourselves and your posterity.'[75]

One of the consequences of Scott's call for robust activism on the part of the freeholders was to lift them above their normal station and impress on them that they too were 'public men'.[76] This had important implications for the political process as a whole, reinforcing the message of Elizabethan advocates of the new style of politics that it was something which involved every citizen and about which they should be kept fully informed, even if this meant encroaching on the *arcana imperii*.[77] Indeed, according to Scott, such encroachments were essential to conquering the 'spirit of privacie'.

Publique persons should do publique actions in publique, in the gates of the city, in the kings highway, in the eye of all. For chamber workes are suspicious and carry a shew of privacy and parciality.[78]

The practical implications of these various ideas for the role of the 'public man' were summed up in the address by Sir Richard Grosvenor to the Cheshire freeholders, prior to the county election of 1624. He explained parliament's mission to remedy the ills of the nation through its counselling and law-making functions. This had happened in the previous parliament when the issue of monopolies was raised:

His Majestie takinge notice from the parliament of the damage susteyned by many of his graunts (which otherwise had still bene kept from his knowledge) was pleased by his proclamation to decry many of them and shewed himselfe (like a true father of his countrey) as willinge to call them in as wee were to complaine of them.

If this was to work, though, a good deal depended on choosing the right sort of men to represent 'the country' – and this was where Grosvenor expounded the need for 'parliament men' who were wise, courageous, godly and 'honest'. Such men, however, were unlikely to be forthcoming unless the freeholders also took their 'public' role seriously. It was no use sitting back and allowing others to make their decisions for them. They must engage fully with the electoral process and make an informed and independent choice. It was their willingness to participate which guaranteed the integrity and effectiveness of a parliament. 'Freedom of voice,' he proclaimed, is 'your inheritance, and one of the greatest prerogatives of the subject which ought be all means to be kept inviolate and cannot be taken from you by any command whatsoever.' However, choosing the right representatives, on its own, was not enough. Electors must go further and give them a specific mandate to uphold the fundamental interests of the common weal. Thus Grosvenor concluded by urging them,

Commaund your knights that if there bee occasion offered they shall in the name of the countrey, and as by speciall commaund of the countrey, make publique protestation against a tolleracion of religion or the repealinge of laws formerly made against recusants.[79]

Grosvenor's address, then, presented a vision of how the voice of the people could be channelled through a 'free' parliament to remedy the grievances of the commonwealth. It envisaged an integrated political system in which the localities were linked to the centre through parliament's representative function and in which informed and responsible citizens had the power to shape events in the arena of national politics. Holding this system together, and enabling it to function effectively, were 'public men', like himself, distinguished for their godliness, courage and commitment to 'country' values. It was they who transmitted information backwards and forwards, who used their rhetorical skills to persuade and influence others and who, as 'parliament men', had the contacts and opportunities to effect reform.

By the 1620s the attitudes and ideas articulated by Grosvenor – and, indeed by Thomas Scott or Job Throckmorton, even though they were more unusual and avant-garde politicians – were widespread and commonplace. It is significant that Sir Richard's remarks were made before an uncontested election of the sort which Mark Kishlansky has reminded us was the norm during the early Stuart period.[80] The freeholders' apparent readiness to accept his recommendations suggests that suitability for election to parliament was coming to be judged, at least partially, in terms of whether or not one possessed the attributes of a 'public man'. Grosvenor himself was a beneficiary of this process. He took considerable pains to present himself to his Cheshire neighbours as a person ideally equipped to fulfil this role, and it paid dividends in that he was chosen to represent the county more regularly than any other local gentleman during the 1620s.[81] There were equivalents of Grosvenor in many other counties. Northamptonshire, for example, could boast Sir Edward Montague, who was applauded in the dedication of one of Bolton's sermons for his 'publicke deportment in the face of our country' and his 'true honesty, grave moderation and noblenes of spirit'. This reputation was said, by another local puritan, to have 'won and wedded to him such honour and esteem that what he said ordinarily went for current and that he was always chosen by the better sort to be one of the knights of parliament'.[82] A similar status appears to have been accorded to Sir Francis Barrington in Essex, Sir Francis Goodwin in Buckinghamshire, Sir Thomas Lucy in Warwickshire and Richard Knightley, again in Northamptonshire.[83] Their electoral success provides further evidence that the language and ideas associated with the 'public man' resonated deeply and widely among the active citizenry.

V

What broader conclusions can be drawn from this study of the construction and character of the 'public man'? On one level it provides a study in the formation of the political culture of the governing classes, illustrating how some of the central themes of Renaissance political thought – discussed at a relatively rarefied level by historians like John Pocock and Quentin Skinner – came to be applied to politics on the ground. Ideas about civic humanism, virtue and the *vita activa* were communicated to local elites and became part of their 'normative vocabulary'. They played an important part in daily decision making about how order should be maintained and who should be accorded status and respect, and were then fed back, via the processes I have described, into the debates and decisions of national politics.

It is worth emphasizing that, in this context, 'local elites' and 'provincial governing classes' meant more than just the gentry. It also embraced those of the middling sort who were cast in the role of active citizens. In the early part of Elizabeth's reign it was generally accepted that 'public' service was the preserve of those whose social eminence enabled them to acquire the skills and virtues needed to act as counsellors and magistrates. The freeholder classes had an important theoretical role – in guaranteeing the integrity of the magistrates and preserving liberties – but they were rarely seen as exercising political responsibility independently. Sir Thomas Smith's vision in the *De Republica Anglorum*, written in the 1560s, was of a group who were, for the most part, 'obedient to the gentlemen and rulers' and who 'come not to meddle in publike matters and judgments but when they are called, and gladde when they are delivered of it'.[84] Twenty years later this view was changing. Throckmorton's vision of 'the Commons' of Warwick was of a group who needed to be kept informed and encouraged to act on their own initiative in order to stave off corruption in the common weal. A similar vision can be seen in the articles of the Swallowfield town meeting in 1596, where, as Patrick Collinson has shown, a group of principal inhabitants formed themselves into 'a society or common doing of a multitude of free men' so that they could deal with pressing social problems without reference to the justices of the peace.[85] It was also visible in the quarter sessions charges of Sir John Newdigate, from the late 1590s and early 1600s, which called on jurors and constables to act as 'good' men, 'honest' men and 'the eyes of the country', following their consciences and conducting themselves without fear or favour towards their social superiors.[86] By the 1580s and 1590s, then, the middling sort were coming to be cast in the role of 'public men', with their own duties and obligations. It was a relatively short step from assuming these local responsibilities to being thrust into the role of informed pressure group for the House of Commons that Scott and Grosvenor envisaged in the 1620s.

Among the developments which gave these 'public men' their particular relevance and purchase in the political arena (which included growing alarm about evil counsellors, periodic threats from popery and the increase in prerogative taxation) perhaps the most significant was the perception of a growing divide between 'court' and 'country'. It was no coincidence that this was taking hold at the same time as the freeholder classes were being encouraged to adopt a more assertive role in politics.

The involvement and participation of those from outside and below was seen in some quarters as a vital corrective to the dangers of 'undertaking' and other forms of court-based corruption.[87] This perception led to a significant shift in ideas about the role of the 'public man'. The early Elizabethan version had found it relatively straightforward to keep a foot in both camps, brokering his connections at court for influence in the country and vice versa. But from the 1580s this intermediary role became more difficult to sustain. Links with the court, which might previously have been seen as advantageous in promoting the interests of one's neighbours, were coming to be regarded with suspicion. By the 1620s – certainly in the counties and larger borough seats – it had become very dangerous in electoral terms to be too closely identified with the court. Candidates almost invariably sought to present themselves as outsiders, spokesmen for 'the country', whose aim was to apply its curative powers to reforming the rottenness at the centre.[88] This transformation of the 'public man' from collaborator with the royal court to its sternest critic was assisted by a reaction against the openness which he embodied in his political persona.

This brings us back to the developments set in train by the emergence of 'the politics of the public sphere'. In another important paper, on 'Popularity, puritanism and anti-puritanism', Peter Lake has demonstrated that the new style of politics helped to trigger a growing sense of alarm at the threat from 'popularity'. As a term of current political usage, 'popularity' was virtually invented by John Whitgift during his confrontations with the Presbyterian Thomas Cartwright in the 1570s. He took Cartwright's vision of a church based on democratic principles and 'active godly citizenship' to be the clerical equivalent of the quasi-republican forms of secular politics which were being widely espoused at the time. He then proceeded to attack both of these approaches as dangerously 'popular', since they threatened to pull down existing hierarchies and undermine authority by stirring up a fickle and novelty-addicted populace. His assault was developed and intensified from the 1590s onwards, notably in Richard Bancroft's attacks on Presbyterians, and Robert Cecil and James I's diatribes against oppositionist MPs in the House of Commons. In the process contemporaries were provided with a language and a set of assumptions in which the politics of openness and participation was retyped as dangerous, subversive and potentially destructive of order. This offered an alternative, and very different, reading of those who sought to present themselves as 'public men'. Instead of selfless servants of the common weal, they could now be cast as ambitious, self-seeking demagogues, bent on stirring up the populace for their own ends and displaying precisely that spirit of 'privacie' which they were supposed to be standing out against. 'Patriots' were redescribed as 'popular spirits'. Whether this description could be made to stick became one of the rhetorical battlegrounds of the period, particularly at election time and during meetings of parliament. For the most part the 'public men' and 'patriots' succeeded in persuading their various audiences to accept their own valuation of their motives and actions. Those who took the contrary view tended to be confined to the court and local agents who identified with it. Nonetheless this retyping gave impetus to the construction and dissemination of a conspiracy theory in which the principal threats to order and security were seen as emanating no longer from 'popery' and the 'spirit of privacie' but from 'popularity' and 'popular spirits'.[89]

These developments helped to bring about an important change in the political landscape between the 1580s and the 1620s. In a political world in which most of the clichés and guiding assumptions were about unity and harmony, the fact that the 'natural' representatives of local societies were coming to be cast as 'oppositionist' contributed significantly to a process of polarization. It encouraged appeals to local audiences in terms of the highly charged language of the safeguarding of 'liberties' and the defence of 'the country', which served to politicize previously neutral issues relating to taxation or administration.[90] It also reduced the space for compromise and tolerance, which was especially significant in parliamentary proceedings, where successful outcomes often depended on a politics of bargaining and negotiation. Above all, it encouraged contemporaries to think in terms of a politics of 'them' and 'us', and to divide politicians into different camps.[91]

NOTES

1 M. A. R. Graves, 'Thomas Norton the parliament man: an Elizabethan MP', *Historical Journal* 23 (1980), 17–35; Graves, 'The management of the Elizabethan House of Commons: the council's "men of business"', *Parliamentary History* 2 (1983), 11–38; P. Collinson, *Elizabethan Essays* (London, 1994), 20–1, 59–86.

2 *Proceedings in the Parliaments of Elizabeth, 1558–1601*, ed. T. E. Hartley (3 vols, Leicester, 1981–95) II, 311–12. The context and implications of this speech are discussed more fully below, pp. 130–2.

3 J. Nichols, *The History and Antiquities of the County of Leicester* (4 vols, 1795–1811, repr. Hinckley, 1993) III, 359. The monument was erected at the behest of Skipwith's widow, Jane, in 1631 after her own death. However, it is likely that she planned the memorial at a date much closer to Sir William's death in 1610. The epitaph was written by Skipwith's friend and Leicestershire neighbour, Sir John Beaumont, brother to the playwright Francis and a distinguished court poet in his own right. Sir John died in 1627 and he had been composing elegiac memorials since the early 1600s: *The Poems of Sir John Beaumont*, ed. A. B. Grosart (London, 1869), introduction and 176–205. On Skipwith as 'a public man', see R. P. Cust, 'Purveyance and politics in Jacobean Leicestershire', in P. Fleming, A. Gross and J. R. Lander (eds), *Regionalism and Revision* (London, 1999), 145–62.

4 R. Tuck, 'Humanism and political thought', in A. Goodman and A. MacKay (eds), *The Impact of Humanism on Western Europe* (London, 1990), 43–9, 55–6; R. M. Smuts, *Culture and Power in England, 1585–1685* (Basingstoke, 1999), 33–5.

5 Cicero, *The First Book of Tullies Offices, translated grammatically* [by J. Brinsley] (1616), epistle dedicatorie; H. Peacham, *The Complete Gentleman*, ed. V. B. Heltzel (Folger Documents, Ithaca NY, 1962), 57.

6 Cicero, *On Duties*, ed. M. T. Griffin and E. M. Atkins (Cambridge, 1991), xliv–xlv, 9, 23–4, 28–9; Q. Skinner, 'Sir Thomas More's *Utopia* and the language of Renaissance humanism', in A. Pagden (ed.), *The Languages of Political Theory in Early Modern Europe* (Cambridge, 1987), 128–31.

7   M. Peltonen, *Classical Humanism and Republicanism in English political Thought, 1570–1640* (Cambridge, 1995), chapter 2; Skinner, 'More's *Utopia*', 126–8, 131–5.

8   Cited in Peltonen, *Classical Republicanism*, 62, 25.

9   Cited in *ibid.*, 21–2, 32–3, 38.

10 R. Tuck, *Philosophy and Government, 1575–1651* (Cambridge, 1993), 39–64; Smuts, *Culture and Power*, 38–9, 70–2; Peltonen, *Classical Republicanism*, 127–32.

11 Cited in Peltonen, *Classical Republicanism*, 130.

12 J. Ford, *A Line of Life, pointing at the Immortalitie of a vertuous Name* (1620), 57–8, 89.

13 For the role of godly lives, see P. Collinson, *Godly People* (London, 1983), 499–525; P. G. Lake, 'Feminine piety and personal potency: the "emancipation" of Mrs Jane Ratcliffe', *The Seventeeth Century* 2 (1987), 143–65; for conduct books, J. E. Mason, *Gentlefolk in the Making* (Philadelphia, 1935), 23–88.

14 For advices to sons as a genre, see *The Papers of Sir Richard Grosvenor, 1st Bart (1585–1645)*, ed. R. P. Cust, Lancashire and Cheshire Record Society CXXXIV (1996), xxiv; *Advice to a Son*, ed. L. B. Wright (Folger Documents, Ithaca NY, 1962), ix–xxvi.

15 *A Book of Instructions written by the right honourable Christopher Wandesforde ... to his Son and Heir, George Wandesforde, etc.*, ed. T. Comber (1777), 58–60.

16 Huntington Library, San Marco CA, HA Personal, Box 15, No. 8, fols 7–8 [*c.* 1614]; HA Correspondence, 5515.

17 Isle of Wight Record Office, OG 90/2, fol. 104; 90/6. Sir John Strode cited the same quotation: C. F. Aspinall-Oglander, *Nunwell Symphony* (London, 1945), 51 (Sir John Strode's advice, *c.* 1623) .

18 *Papers of Sir Richard Grosvenor*, 38.

19 Peltonen, *Classical Republicanism*, 35–9, 158–64; Skinner, 'More's *Utopia*', 135–40. For repeated use of the temple of virtue analogy, derived from his reading of Thomas Elyot's *Book Named the Governor*, see Sir John Newdigate's draft jury charges: Warwickshire Record Office, CR 136, B/695, B/719, B/633. Ferne is cited in Peltonen, *Classical Republicanism*, 37.

20 Cited in Peltonen, *Classical Republicanism*, 64.

21 'The Institution of a Gentleman. In three parts. By William Higford, esq.' (*c.* 1630), in *The Harleian Miscellany*, ed. T. Park (10 vols, 1808–13) IX, 585.

22 William Martyn, *Youth's Instruction* (1613), 20, 18–19.

23 Q. Skinner, *The Foundations of Modern Political Thought* (2 vols, Cambridge, 1978) I, 221–8; Peltonen, *Classical Republicanism*, 62–5, 147–8; S. Hindle, *The State and Social Change in Early Modern England, c. 1550–1640* (Basingstoke, 2000), 21–2. For the importance of binary oppositions, see S. Clark, 'Inversion, misrule and the meaning of witchcraft', *Past and Present* 87 (1980), 98–127; P. G. Lake, 'Anti-popery: the structure of a prejudice', in R. P. Cust and A. L. Hughes (eds), *Conflict in early Stuart England* (Harlow, 1989), 73, 89.

24 Peltonen, *Classical Republicanism*, 71; for increasing preoccupation with the notion of 'public service' from the 1580s onwards, see S. L. Adams, 'The patronage of the crown in Elizabethan politics: the 1590s in perspective', in J. Guy (ed.), *The Reign of Elizabeth I* (Cambridge, 1995), 42–3.

25 Cited in C. Holmes, 'Parliament, liberty, taxation and property', in J. H. Hexter (ed.),

Parliament and Liberty from the Reign of Elizabeth to the English Civil War (Stanford CA, 1992), 146–7.

26 *Nunwell Symphony*, 51.

27 *Papers of Sir Richard Grosvenor*, 36–8.

28 Peltonen, *Classical Republicanism*, 64, 248, 300.

29 *Papers of Sir Richard Grosvenor*, 1.

30 Cited in Peltonen, *Classical Republicanism*, 71, 58.

31 *Ibid.*, 299–300.

32 Skinner, *Foundations* I, xi–xiii.

33 Margo Todd has shown how the two traditions were blended together, particularly in the area of puritan social thought, where many of the central features constitutued a reworking of the ideas of the Christian humanists, notably Erasmus: M. Todd, *Christian Humanism and the Puritan Social Order* (Cambridge, 1987), particularly chapter 3. For a good example of the use of humanist language alongside biblical rhetoric in discussing the responsibilities of the magistrate, see the assize sermons of Anthony Fawkner: *Nicodemus for Christ, or The religious Moote of an honest Lawyer* (1627); *Eirenogonia, or The Pedegree of Peace* (1630) and *The Widowes Petition* (1635).

34 P. Collinson, 'Biblical rhetoric: the English nation and national sentiment in the prophetic mode', in C. McCeachern and D. Shuger (eds), *Religion and Culture in Renaissance England* (Cambridge, 1997), 18–20; M. Walzer, *The Revolution of the Saints* (New York, 1976), particularly chapter 7; P. Collinson, *The Religion of Protestants* (Oxford, 1982), particularly chapter 4; P. G. Lake, 'Defining puritanism – again?', in F. J. Bremer (ed.), *Puritanism: Transatlantic Perspectives on a Seventeenth Century Anglo-American Faith* (Boston MA, 1993), 10–17.

35 For the genre, see J. S. Cockburn, *A History of English Assizes, 1558–1714* (Cambridge, 1972), 65–6, and F. Heal and C. Holmes, *The Gentry in England and Wales, 1500–1700* (Basingstoke, 1994), 177–85. For examples of highly topical assize sermons, see Robert Wilkinson's sermon at Northampton following the Midland rising of 1607: *A Sermon preached at Northampton* (1607) and Thomas Scot's attack on projectors and monopolists: *The Highwayes of God and the King* (1623).

36 Robert Sanderson, *The Works of Robert Sanderson*, ed. W. Jacobson (6 vols, Oxford, 1854) II, 173–4, 178–80, 197–9, 202–4, 256–7, 274; C. Holmes, *Seventeenth Century Lincolnshire* (Lincoln, 1980), 81–3.

37 Fawkner, *The Widowes Petition*, p. 6; Collinson, *Religion of Protestants*, 181.

38 Robert Bolton, *Two Sermons preached at Northampton* (1635), 7–8, 28–9, 34, 38; *Mr Bolton's last and learned Worke of the four last Things* (1632), 165, 194–5, 263–4.

39 Robert Harris, *Two Sermons* (1628), 5, 13–14.

40 Bolton, *Last and learned Worke*, 212–13, 256–7; Bolton, *Two Sermons*, 51–3, 64–5; see also P. G. Lake, 'The godly and their enemies in the 1630s', in C. Durston and J. Eales (eds), *The Culture of English Puritanism, 1560–1700* (Basingstoke, 1996), 152–3. Thomas Adams made much the same point in *The Holy Choice* (1625), 64.

41 Adams, *Holy Choice*, 62–4.

42 Bolton, *Last and learned Worke*, 214.

43 Samuel Ward, *Jethro's Justice of Peace* (1618), 34, A3.

44 Cited in Collinson, *Religion of Protestants*, 164.

45 R. P. Cust and P. G. Lake, 'Sir Richard Grosvenor and the rhetoric of magistracy', *Bulletin of the Institute of Historical Research* 54 (1981), 40–53; R. P. Cust, 'Humanism and magistracy' (an unpublished study of the reading and writings of the Warwickshire magistrate Sir John Newdigate). Newdigate's jury charges provide an example of a local gentlemen drawing directly from the preaching of a Calvinist minister, in this case William Butterton, of Nuneaton: see Newdigate's notes on a sermon about the need for each man to serve God in his calling preached on 14 September 1606 which insisted, 'men must fight for their country. He is borne in vaine that thinketh he is borne to himself': CR 136, B632. For other examples of jury charges which incorporate a mix of humanist and biblical rhetorics, see the Elizabethan charges of Sir Francis Willoughby in Nottinghamshire and the Caroline charges of John Harington in Somerset: Nottingham University Library, Mi O, 15/12–13, 16/6, 12–14; *The Diary of John Harington, MP, 1646–1653*, ed. M. F. Stieg, Somerset Record Society LXXIV (Old Woking, 1977), 87–105.

46 Warwicks. RO, CR136, B/711; see also *Papers of Sir Richard Grosvenor*, 8.

47 *Papers of Sir Richard Grosvenor*, 17; see also Warwicks. RO, CR136, B/659, 696.

48 Warwicks. RO, B/683–700, unnumbered, 698, 700, 701; see also *Papers of Sir Richard Grosvenor*, 31.

49 Bolton, *Last and learned Worke*, 164–5; Warwicks. RO, CR136, B722. For Grosvenor on popery see Cust and Lake, 'Sir Richard Grosvenor', 43.

50 S. Anglo, 'The courtier: the Renaissance and changing ideals', in A. G. Dickens (ed.), *The Courts of Europe: Politics, Patronage and Royalty, 1400–1800* (London, 1977), 33–53; Smuts, *Culture and Power*, 36–9. There are echoes of Castiglione, for example, in Huntington's advice to his son, or in the funeral monument to John Farnham (d. 1587) at Quorn, Leicestershire: Huntington Library, HA Personal Box 15, No. 8, fos 8, 17–18; Nichols, *Leicester* III, 97–8.

51 Peltonen, *Classical Republicanism*, 51–2.

52 Roger Ascham, *The Schoolmaster* (1570), ed. L. V. Ryan (Folger Documents, Ithaca NY, 1967), 5–12. Burghley was also held up as as a model of virtuous wisdom in Henry Peacham's conduct book, *The Complete Gentleman*, first published in 1622: Peacham, *Complete Gentleman*, 55–7.

53 For depictions of Burghley in the 1620s, see J. Rushworth, *Historical Collections* (7 vols, 1659–1701) I, 467–72 (Sir Robert Cotten's advice to the privy council, *c.* 1628), and I. Atherton, *Ambition and Failure in Stuart England* (Manchester, 1999), 36 (Viscount Scudamore's reminiscences on his conduct at the time of the Spanish Armada). For Burghley's advice and the copying of it, see *Advice to a Son*, ix–xxvi, 9–13; Eaton Hall, Cheshire, Grosvenor personal and Misc., 2/3; Isle of Wight Record Office, OG 17/5; Historical Manuscripts Commission, *Report on the Mss of the Duke of Portland* IX (Norwich, 1923), 4–7. This image of Burghley was challenged from within the circles of Sidney and Essex, but it appears to have survived. Smuts in concentrating on the verse eulogies for Sidney is in danger of overlooking Burghley's posthumous repute as a more dependable, less exciting, embodiment of good government: *Culture and Power*, 45, 59, 62–5. Burghley escaped much of the vilification heaped on his son, Robert: P. Croft, 'The reputation of Robert Cecil: libels, political opinion and popular awareness in the early seventeenth century', *Transactions of the Royal Historical Society*, 6th ser., 1 (1991), 43–69.

54 For Pembroke, see Peltonen, *Classical Republicanism*, 276; D. Norbrook, 'Lucan, Thomas May and the creation of a republican literary culture', in K. Sharpe and P. G. Lake (eds), *Culture and Politics in early Stuart England* (Cambridge, 1994), 58–9; B. Worden, 'Ben Jonson among the historians', *ibid.*, 87–8. For Raleigh, see Smuts, *Culture and Power*, 65; A. Bellany, '"Rayling Rymes and Vaunting Verse": libellous politics in early Stuart England, 1603–1628', in Sharpe and Lake, *Culture and Politics*, 292, 300.

55 P. W. Hasler (ed.), *The House of Commons, 1558–1603* (3 vols, London, 1981) III, 492–4; P. Collinson, *The Elizabethan Puritan Movement* (London, 1967), 306–12, 391–6.

56 *Proceedings in the Parliaments of Elizabeth* II, 311–12.

57 Smuts, *Culture and Power*, 38–9, 66–70, 76–82; A. Bellany, *The Politics of Court Scandal in Early Modern England* (Cambridge, 2002); L. L. Peck, 'Corruption at the court of James I: the undermining of legitimacy', in B. C. Malament (ed.), *After the Reformation* (Manchester, 1980), 75–93; Peltonen, *Classical Republicanism*, 277–8, 280–1; Lake, 'Antipopery', 87–9.

58 P. G. Lake, 'Constitutional consensus and puritan opposition in the 1620s: Thomas Scott and the Spanish match', *Historical Journal* 25 (1982), 805–25; Thomas Scot, *The Highwayes of God and the King* (1623), p. 79; Peltonen, *Classical Republicanism*, 236.

59 Quotations from Lake, 'Thomas Scott', 817–20.

60 Smuts, *Culture and Power*, 78–84, 92–8; R. P. Cust and A. L. Hughes, 'Introduction: after revisionism', in *Conflict in early Stuart England*, 19–21.

61 Anon., *Horae Subsecivae* (1620), 135–75, 'Of a country life'; N. B. Reynolds and J. L. Hilton, 'Thomas Hobbes and the authority of *Horae Subsecivae*', *History of Political Thought* 14 (1993), 361–80; Norbrook, 'Thomas May', 58–9.

62 *Horae Subsecivae*, 135–75, quotations from 165–6, 172–3.

63 'Cavendish, William, second earl of Devonshire (1591?–1628)', *Dictionary of National Biography*; C. S. R. Russell, *Parliaments and English Politics, 1621–1629* (Oxford, 1979), 289 n.; R. P. Cust, *The Forced Loan and English Politics, 1626–1628* (Oxford, 1987), 84, 106

64 Peltonen, *Classical Republicanism*, 175–7, 181, 267; D. H. Sacks, 'Liberty and the commonweal', in *Parliament and Liberty*, 86–93.

65 J. A. Guy, 'The rhetoric of counsel in early modern England', in D. Hoak (ed.), *Tudor Political Culture* (Cambridge, 1995), 292–305.

66 Cited in Sacks, 'Liberty and the commonweal', 117–18.

67 Guy, 'Rhetoric of counsel', 303; Holmes, 'Parliament, liberty, taxation and property', 146–7.

68 Cited in Lake, 'Thomas Scott', 817.

69 *Proceedings in the Parliaments of Elizabeth* I, 238. On Carleton, see Collinson, *Elizabethans*, 84.

70 D. M. Hirst, *The Representative of the People?* (Cambridge, 1975), particularly chapter 9; A. Hassell Smith, *County and Court: Government and Politics in Norfolk, 1558–1603* (Oxford, 1974), particularly chapter 14.

71 Holmes, 'Parliament, liberty, taxation, property', 146–50.

72 Cust, 'Purveyance and politics', 145–62; Hassell Smith, *County and Court*, 314–32. A similar process can be discerned in the social legislation of the same period, much of

which originated in the specific concerns of local governors sitting in the Commons, but which was intended to bring order and prosperity to the commonwealth as a whole: J. Kent, 'Attitudes of members of the House of Commons to the regulation of "personal conduct" in late Elizabethan and early Stuart England', *Bulletin of the Institute of Historical Research* 46 (1973), 41–71.

73 For Throckmorton and the Warwick election of 1586, see T. Kemp (ed.), *The Black Book of Warwick* (Warwick, 1898), 385–97; J. E. Neale, *The Elizabethan House of Commons* (New Haven CT, 1976), 241–4; Hirst, *The Representative of the People*, 210–11; Hasler, *The Commons, 1558–1603* II, 122–3, III, 492–4.

74 Sacks, 'Liberty and the commonweal', 110–17; R. P. Cust, 'Politics and the electorate in the 1620s', in *Conflict in early Stuart England*, 152.

75 Scot, *Highwayes of God and the King*, 87. For comparable sentiments expressed by Robert Bolton and John Preston, see Bolton, *Two Sermons*, 81–2, and Sacks, 'Liberty and the commonweal', 111–12.

76 For the expression of similar ideas in the jury charges of Newdigate and Grosvenor, see Warwicks. RO, CR136, B659, 696; *Papers of Sir Richard Grosvenor*, 17.

77 Evidence that at least a section of the local electorate was responsive to this sort of plea is provided by the 1624 county election in Norfolk. This furnished precisely the scenario Scot had envisaged. The crypto-Catholic lord lieutenant, the earl of Arundel, and several leading justices were suspected of trying to foist on the freeholders Sir Thomas Holland, who was thought to be less than wholly sympathetic to the interests of 'the country'. Rather than accept this, a section of the electorate took the initiative and drafted in Sir Roger Townshend, about whose Protestant and 'country' credentials there seem to have been no doubts: *The Official Papers of Sir Nathaniel Bacon of Stiffkey, Norfolk*, ed. H. W. Saunders, Camden Soc., 3rd ser., XXVI (1915), 39; W. R. Prest, 'An Australian holding of Norfolk manuscripts: the Bacon–Townshend papers at the university of Adelaide', *Norfolk Archaeology* (1979), 121–3. On the day of the election, even though Townshend was absent, a group of freeholders put his name forward and fought hard to get him returned: Hirst, *The Representative of the People*, 144; *Papers of Sir Nathaniel Bacon*, 39–41.

78 Scot, *Highwayes of God and the King*, 69–70.

79 *Papers of Sir Richard Grosvenor*, 1–7.

80 M. Kishlansky, *Parliamentary Selection* (Cambridge, 1986), chapters 1–4.

81 Cust and Lake, 'Sir Richard Grosvenor', 51–2; *Journal of the Chester and North Wales Archaeological Society* 24 (1921–22), 99–100.

82 Robert Bolton, *Some Generall Directions for a Comfortable Walking with God* (1630), A2; Northamptonshire Record Office, Montague Mss, vol. 186, unpaginated.

83 Cust, 'Politics and the electorate', 155–6. The inscription on Lucy's funeral monument, probably composed by the Warwickshire minister Thomas Dugard, described him as 'a singular and much honoured patriot' who 'was frequently sent [to Parliament] by the unanimous and fervent suffrages of his endeared countrie': Thomas Dugard, *Death and the Grave* (1649), H2.

84 Sir Thomas Smith, *De Republica Anglorum*, ed. M. Dewar (Cambridge, 1982), 75.

85 Collinson, *Elizabethans*, 23–5. On Swallowfield, see also S. H. Hindle, 'Hierarchy and community in the Elizabethan parish: the Swallowfield articles of 1596', *Historical Journal* 42 (1999), 835–51.

86 Warwicks. RO, CR136, B/659, 696. For a similar rhetoric being deployed in the notes used by Sir Francis Willoughby for drawing up his charges to the Nottinghamshire bench in the late 1580s and early 1590s, see Nottingham University Library, Mi O, 16/6.

87 This applied especially to electoral politics, see Hirst, *The Representative of the People*, 8–12.

88 For a fuller discussion of the processes at work in electoral politics, Cust, 'Politics and the electorate', 143–56; R. P. Cust, 'Parliamentary elections in the 1620s: the case of Great Yarmouth', *Parliamentary History* 11 (1992), 179–91.

89 P. G. Lake, 'John Whitgift, puritanism and the invention of popularity'; see also my paper on '"Patriots" and "popular spirits": narratives of conflict in early Stuart politics', to be published in N. R. N. Tyacke (ed.), *The English Revolution c. 1590–1720*, Proceedings of the Neale Colloquium, London, 2004 (Manchester, 2007).

90 See, for example, the way in which the two Leicestershire 'patriots', Sir William Skipwith and Sir Thomas Beaumont, helped to transform purveyance into a highly sensitive political issue in the early part of James's reign: Cust, 'Purveyance and politics', 145–62.

91 For further reflections on this development, see R. P. Cust, 'News and politics in early seventeenth-century England', *Past and Present* 112 (1986), 79–90.

Chapter 6

——◆——

The embarrassment of libels: perceptions and representations of verse libelling in early Stuart England

Alastair Bellany

I

Rome, at night. Two gentlemen cross the Piazza Navona, heading for the 'Pasquino', 'the Idol of verity'. They carry copies of poems that, under cover of darkness, they pin upon the infamous mutilated statue. They will never acknowledge their work, but by fixing their verses to the statue the two gentlemen have made their poems public. They know that, with daylight, crowds will return to the square. Some will pass the Pasquino and pause to read the anonymous lines and absorb their political message. For these are no idle jottings, but blistering attacks on the corrupt rule of Pope Alexander VI and his son Cesare Borgia. These poems are 'libels'.

Perhaps we would expect this scene of political subversion to be coloured with an excited, fearful or even triumphant mood. Instead, the atmosphere is uneasy, embarrassed. As they complete the act of publication, pinning their verses to the Pasquino, the two gentlemen feel compelled to justify their actions. Part of their unease is aesthetic. As poets, they seek inspiration from only the highest muse, but to write these verses they perforce adopted a coarser style. One offers his muse an apology, explaining that 'we poets ... with pain' are now 'forc'd of men's impiety to plain;/And well thou wottest, wrought against our wills,/In rugged verse, vile matters to contain'. These gentlemen, then, are acting under compulsion – 'forc'd' – and so may have surrendered some of their gentility. Their lines are 'rugged', the content 'vile' – the adjectives are intriguing. The poets' aesthetic unease is clearly also a form of status anxiety. The 'rugged verse' and 'vile matters' of a libel are not fitting labour for a gentleman. When the aggrieved authorities discover these poems, they will assume they were written by 'beastly bards, and satirists,/Ribaldry rhymesters, and malicious curs', men who smear church and state with 'their ordure, and pollution'. Penning a libel, then, could implicate a gentleman in the behaviour of a cur – malicious, beastly, dirty. And so our gentlemen must justify their walk on the literary and social wild side. They blame the times. The 'malignity' of Borgia Rome is at fault. Good verse, they argue, is for praising virtues, virtues that Rome now conspicuously lacks. Libels are the poetry of political decay: evil times demand bad rhymes.[1]

This scene from Barnabe Barnes's 1607 play *The Divils Charter* compellingly dramatizes an important form of early modern English political expression. London may have had no 'Pasquino', but the writing and surreptitious publication of verse libels were as familiar to Barnes's English audiences as to the *habitués* of the Piazza Navona.[2] Recent research by political, social and literary historians has reconstructed the culture of verse libelling, uncovering libels' many forms – from crude couplets to sophisticated satires – and varied sites of publication – from the village alehouse to the aisles of St Paul's Cathedral. We have learned a great deal about how these poems were produced, circulated and collected and have made great strides towards situating them in contemporary social, political and literary contexts. By reading these verses as creations of oral culture, weapons of the weak, agents of popular politicization, or vehicles of scandalous political images, we have broadened our understanding of early Stuart society and politics. Unlike Barnes's discontented poets, we are no longer embarrassed by libels.

This chapter, however, is a study of embarrassment – of the queasy feelings that libels aroused. Instead of examining the content and circulation of verse libels, I explore how libels and libelling were perceived and represented in early Stuart England – by lawyers, kings, privy councillors, preachers and poets. I want to reconstruct the ambivalence that pervades Barnes's dramatization of the act of political libelling. Virtually no one had a good word for the practice: stylistically, socially, legally, politically and morally, libelling was seen as disreputable, dangerous, damned. Yet libels were written, read, circulated and collected in significant numbers. This paradox – an embarrassment at, yet an embarrassment of, libels – demands attention. These ambivalent perceptions of the libel may teach us, for instance, about the assumptions that shaped and constrained the production of these political media and the expectations and anxieties governing their reception. Furthermore, by reconstructing perceptions of this important form of political expression, we can explore how contemporaries imagined the operation, extent, limits and decorum of one form of public political speech. In other words, we can read these representations of libelling as evidence of early seventeenth-century understandings of some of the cultural phenomena that constituted the public sphere.

II

All verses attacking individuals, whether the village whore or the royal favourite, came within the scope of long-standing defamation laws, both

secular and ecclesiastical.[3] The legal understanding of political verse libels
– libels attacking royal councillors or courtiers, for instance – was, however,
fundamentally reformulated at the beginning of James I's reign. The key clar-
ificatory text is Edward Coke's report 'De Libellis Famosis', written in the wake
of the 1605 Star Chamber trial of the puritan Lewis Pickering for writing a
verse libel on the late archbishop of Canterbury, John Whitgift.[4] Coke's report
covered verbal and visual libels, of both private and public individuals, and
identified two forms of prosecution: by indictment in a common law court, or
by bill or *ore tenus* in Star Chamber.[5] Depending on the severity of the offence,
a libeller could face anything from a fine and imprisonment to 'pillory and
loss of his ears'.[6]

According to Coke, the law's concern with libels against private individuals
stemmed from the threat libels posed to the public peace in a society peculiarly concerned with honour and reputation. In a society where good name
mattered to gentleman and village housewife alike, any form of defamation
had serious *public* consequences. A libel threatened an individual's 'fame and
dignity'. It 'robs a man of his good name' – or, as one Star Chamber reporter
memorably noted, 'murdereth le bon fame de un homme' – which should be
'more precious to him than his life'.[7] In a society so tender of personal honour,
a libel was a provocation, compelling the insulted person, his friends and his
family to avenge the insult and thus breach the peace.[8] This emphasis on the
effect rather than the *content* of a libel made the truth of a libel's allegations
irrelevant to the legal determination of an offender's guilt or innocence. A true
libel could wound and provoke as much as a false one. Focusing on a libel's
effect also made it irrelevant if the victim were dead, for in a culture in which
honour was sustained through ties of blood and friendship the defamation of
a dead man could still sting surviving family and friends into action.

Coke extended the legal logic concerning the libelling of private individuals to the libelling of a magistrate or 'public person', including the ministers
of the crown, who were so often the butt of the libeller's art. Writing a libel
against a magistrate or privy councillor was a far greater offence than an attack
on a private individual, 'for it concerns not only the breach of the peace, but
also the scandal of Government'. A verse against a magistrate wounded not
only his honour but the honour of the king who appointed him, for 'what
greater scandal of Government can there be than to have corrupt or wicked
magistrates to be appointed and constituted by the King to govern his subjects
under him?'[9] These strictures applied to libels against all types and ranks of
royal officials. When a JP was libelled by a group of recusants who claimed
he would 'be put from the bench/For kissing Robert Taylor's wench', it was
argued in Star Chamber 'que contempt al Magistracie est contempt del roy:
For magistrates are honoured, for that they are apparelled with the royal robe
of authority, given to them from the King: and the honour given to them is

given to the King, and so the contempt'. To slander judges, noted Sir Thomas Lake in 1615, was to slander the king, for judges were 'part of the present active body of the King'.[10] Scandalizing the honour of the monarch or of government was a dangerous offence and could be interpreted as an act tending to sedition. 'De Libellis Famosis' did not explicitly take this last step from scandal to sedition, but that step was clearly implied: Lord Chancellor Ellesmere, for one, assumed that Coke's report had shown that libelling 'moveth to sedition'.[11] Thus, from the legal perspective, verse libels against ministers and courtiers were virtually equivalent to libels against the king's two bodies; libelling the king defamed royal honour, both personally and institutionally; the defamation of royal honour diminished respect and obedience for the monarch and monarchy; and diminished respect encouraged sedition. As with libels of private individuals, the offence remained even if the libel were true; and the offence did not die with the victim, for royal honour was immortal.

III

The most extensive royal commentary on verse libelling dwelt on another aspect of libelling's political illegitimacy. Early in 1623, James I took aim at a spate of verse libels criticizing his foreign policy by writing a poem of his own and allowing it to be scribally circulated.[12] The poem, entitled 'The Wiper of the Peoples Tears', portrayed verse libels – and all other forms of popular political expression – as unwarranted intrusions by the ignorant and vulgar into the *arcana imperii*, matters of state that they could not understand and had no right to discuss. Kings' actions, James argued, were beyond the people's ken, and the sovereign's only legitimate monitor was God:

> Kings walk the heavenly milky way,
> But you by bypaths gad astray.
> God and Kings do pace together,
> But vulgar[s] wander light as feather.

Kings, James claimed, should be obeyed, wondered at, and not discussed by their people:

> Hold you the public beaten way
> Wonder at Kings, and them obey.
> For under God they are to choose
> What rights to take, and what refuse;
> Whereto if you will not consent
> Yet hold your peace lest you repent
> And be corrected for your pride
> That Kings' designs dare thus deride
> By railing rhymes and vaunting verse
> Which your King's breast should never pierce.[13]

If the legal logic was clear – verse libels as defamatory acts could be vehicles of sedition – in the eyes of James I they were also unwarrantable intrusions upon the *arcana imperii*, violations of an oft-expressed norm of public silence and passivity in the face of the monarch's political activities. But did these views determine how the early Stuart authorities treated political verse libels? Coke's legal logic was certainly deployed in actual criminal cases. At the 1627 trial of three fiddlers for performing libellous songs against the royal favourite Buckingham, Chief Justice Richardson implied that libelling was so wicked that it might be taken as treason, for 'such a thing which alienateth the subject's affection from their sovereign is treason'. Libels – which, another royal official claimed, had grown to be 'the epidemical disease' of the day – deserved harsh punishment, for they 'nourish dissensions and jealousies between the King and his subjects'.[14] On at least two other occasions, we can observe the authorities strategically deploying the law's assumption that the libel of a minister necessarily implied a seditious attack on royal authority. Lewis Pickering, for instance, insisted that he had never intended to insult Queen Elizabeth or King James, but by seizing on the seditious implication of his verse libel, Star Chamber effectively tarnished not only Pickering but also, through him, the political legitimacy of a certain brand of puritan agitation. Three decades later, Archbishop Laud's preface to his published speech at the seditious libel trial of Burton, Bastwick and Prynne undercut the three puritans' insistence that their quarrel was with the bishops, not the king: '[']Tis not we only, that is, the Bishops, that are struck at, but through our sides, Your Majesty, Your Honour, Your Safety, Your Religion, is impeached.'[15]

The logic of 'De Libellis Famosis' and 'The Wiper of the People's Teares' suggests that the early Stuart authorities had good reason actively to police the circulation of verse libels. Yet evidence of active – rather than purely reactive – policing of libels is scarce. Indeed, it is one of the misfortunes of the historian – though clearly not of the libeller – that so few people were actually caught and prosecuted for writing political verse libels. A number of explanations are possible. Perhaps, despite their rhetoric, the authorities had no real will to prosecute this type of political expression; perhaps libels were even tolerated as a relatively harmless way of letting off political steam. A second argument, however, would contend that the authorities had the will but not the means to police the writing and circulation of verse libels. Coke insisted that individuals happening upon a libel of a magistrate should report it to the authorities, but only scattered evidence suggests this occurred. Political libelling was intrinsically difficult to police. In fact as well as in stereotype, libels were nearly always anonymous. For Coke, this anonymity was one symptom of libelling's baseness, but for the libeller it was a protective cloak. A libel posted in a public place could be removed by the authorities – halting the process of publication – but tracing its author, or even the person who posted it, was difficult. Policing coped even less well with other forms of circulation. Most verse libels surviving today were transcribed into poetry miscellanies and news-diaries by men who had received copies from friends and relatives, and who were unlikely to denounce their sources to the authorities. When the authorities did track down alleged authors, they relied more often than not on luck. Lewis Pickering came to the authorities' attention only because a friend with a copy of the poem had personally presented the king with a seditious puritan tract. Alexander Gill's stash of anti-Buckingham libels was discovered only after he indiscreetly offered a toast to the health of the assassin Felton at a mixed gathering in a semi-public place.[16]

A third explanation for the dearth of vigorous anti-libel policing shifts and complicates the discussion. Some powerful contemporaries felt the best policy towards libels might be to hold back, lest prosecution give a libel extra publicity. Sir Francis Bacon argued that libels and rumours were a 'sign of troubles', yet he doubted that 'suppressing of them with too much severity should be a remedy of troubles'. On many occasions, he thought, 'the despising of them … checks them best; and the going about to stop them doth but make a wonder long-lived'.[17] When the earl of Northampton took harsh action against libels circulating against him in 1613, some wondered whether his actions only drew attention to poems that might otherwise have sunk quickly into obscurity.[18] Thomas Wentworth's advice to William Laud, after the archbishop had been thoroughly scared by a series of bitter personal libels, is particularly inter-esting.[19] Though he considered these 'infamous and hellish libels' to be 'the diseases of a loose and remiss government', Wentworth considered that 'the best cure of them, in public, is contempt'. He recalled for Laud his own response to a spate of libels circulated against him in Yorkshire. He had refrained from a search for the authors, despite proffered information on their identities, and had weathered the assault in 'silence and patience'. Wentworth believed that by refraining from prosecution, he had stifled further publication. 'Thus did I quite spoil their jest, there was no noise of them at all went abroad. And … within a month the humour was spent.' In such cases, he concluded, 'I would bring them as little upon the stage as might be.' Yet Wentworth did draw a distinction between libels on 'particulars' – attacking the personal vices of an individual – and those 'insolencies' that 'trench upon the public'. According to the legal logic of 'De Libellis Famosis', of course, this distinction was invalid: a libel on the 'private' vices of the archbishop of Canterbury inevitably impinged upon the 'public', by scandalizing government. Wentworth, however, was willing to draw a line. A 'private' attack should be strategically ignored as far as public actions and statements were concerned – though the victim should make certain that the allegations would not damage the king's opinion of him. Yet a libel that directly engaged with public questions deserved more than just contempt: 'I would have them sought after,' Wentworth wrote, 'and driven to the uttermost of discovery and punishment.'[20]

'Invections,' opined Thomas Gainsford, 'are not accepted at all times alike.' In a 'settled state,' he thought, 'libels pass as pasquils; but in a time of innovation or confusion, they are dangerous in themselves, and perilous to the author.'[21] Here, then, is a fourth possible explanation: in times of political crisis, the authorities seized upon the seditious potential of libels, but during periods of calm laughed them off as 'pasquils'. This might explain the fact that some of the harshest official condemnations of libelling – and greatest concentration of recorded cases of prosecution – came during times of trouble: the ecclesiastical crises of 1604–05 and 1637, and the political crises of 1619–23 and 1626–28.[22]

Some of these deep and complex ambiguities in official responses to libelling are revealed further if we return to the case of James I's 'Wiper of the People's Teares'. As we have seen, the poem responded to libelling by demanding silence and reverence, and by insisting that the *arcana imperii* were the private province of the king. The poem concludes with a vague but explicit threat against those who fail to heed its warnings. James depicts himself as merciful by inclination, reluctant to inflict the punishments libellers deserve: 'slow I am revenge to take', he noted, adding a few lines later that 'I am slow/To give you your deserved woe'. Yet having insisted that his subjects cease their 'pratling' and 'spare your pen/Be honest, and obedient men', James warned them not to push him too far, not to 'Urge ... my Justice'. Alluding to two earlier attempts to silence criticism of royal foreign policy – his proclamations against 'Lavish and Licentious Speech of matters of State' issued in December 1620 and July 1621 – James warned that 'If proclamations will not serve' to silence dissent, then 'I must do more, Peace to preserve/To keep all in obedience/And drive such busy bodies hence'. What 'more' he might do remains vague, beyond the concluding allusion to expulsion and exile, but the threat is certainly there. Yet if James wanted to close down public political dissent and expression, he chose a curious way to go about expressing this desire. By writing a poem and by allowing it to circulate through the scribal networks that were simultaneously responsible for circulating the news and comment he found so distasteful James had in effect surrendered his own ideals of public silence and passivity. Indeed, as one might expect, James's poem ended up stimulating the kinds of activities it was dedicated to silencing – newsmongers discussed its appearance and provenance, and one poet saw fit to respond to the king's charges with a counter-verse of his own.[23] Furthermore, in the sections of James's poem where he was not demanding silence, he engaged in explicit criticism of the specific charges contained in the libels he wished to quiet. By engaging in this debate, James both amplified the audience for those charges and implicitly granted them a kind of legitimacy by deigning to argue with them in public.

IV

At the end of 'De Libellis Famosis', Coke insisted that libelling broke not only the laws of man, but also those of God: verse libels were unchristian and immoral as well as illegal.[24] 'There is no express word for libelling in the whole Bible,' Lord Chancellor Ellesmere commented, 'for that the Devil was not so cunning to invent such a sin until of late time.'[25] Many preachers and moralists also saw libelling as immoral and joined lawyers and privy councillors in linking libels with sedition. Personal insult, particularly of the dead, was a gross breach of charity, and the lewd content of many verse libels a pander to lust. Moral rebuke may have been a religious duty, but the personalized verse libel was not an acceptable vehicle.

Owen Felltham, perhaps with recent attacks on the disgraced Francis Bacon in mind, thought it 'inhumane' and 'diabolical' that men would libel those who had fallen from power. 'If they were heavenly, then would they with him condole his disasters, and drop some tears in pity of his folly, and wretchedness.' To libel someone 'that already is openly tainted' was like adding 'stripes with an iron rod to one that is flayed with whipping'.[26] A number of commentators reacted to the masses of libellous epitaphs by repeating the ancient proverbial injunction to speak no ill of the dead – at Pickering's trial one councillor commented, 'Nefas super mortuos gloriari, it is a poison.'[27]

Thomas Adams alleged that 'every guest of the Devil is continually sipping' from the 'vial' of defamation. Slanderers were like flies that 'leap over a man's good parts and virtues to light upon his sores'. Reputation is fragile, reasoned the preacher, and a good name 'is like a glass, if it be once cracked it is soon broken'. Depriving a man of his good name had direct spiritual consequences, for it removed his power to do good in the world. Adams even found biblical sanction for the law's rulings on true libels. Though it was undoubtedly morally worse to speak a false evil, speaking true evils was also sinful – Ham, after all, was cursed for declaring Noah's nakedness, even though he was telling the truth.[28] In another sermon, Adams compared libels – which he imagines primarily as an oral medium – to poisons that corrupted the soul through the ear. Each of the body's five senses was a source of great spiritual danger, and ears, Adams feared, were 'set wide open to receive in the poison of scurrilous songs, obscene jests, seditious libels'.[29] Thus the audience, as well as the author, was implicated in the libel's immorality. Adams's poison metaphor was common to legal discourse on libel. Coke, for instance, twinned libelling with poisoning – both were notoriously anonymous, surreptitious, underhand crimes against which men had great difficulty defending themselves. 'Libellers,' noted Attorney General Heath in Star Chamber, 'have been always most odious, being as bad as poisoners against whom there is no defence they so secretly annoy us'.[30]

In an Accession Day sermon at Paul's Cross, John White combined many of these legal, political and moral strands of anti-libel discourse into a sustained denunciation of political libelling. Like 'The Wiper of the People's Tears', White began with the divinity of kings. Not only was the king, whether he acted well or ill, of divine ordinance, White argued, but so too were 'all the eminency and distinction of authority that is under him' – nobles, councillors, judges and magistrates. It was 'a savage and popular humour' to 'backbite' any of this divinely sanctioned 'eminency'. 'The practise of libelling against magistrates and great persons, at this day', White continued, 'that neither the living can walk, nor the dead sleep, cannot be justified.' Even if great persons were actually doing wrong, libelling was not an appropriate response. Bad deeds by those in authority should be a 'cause rather of sorrow than laughter'. It was better that in such circumstances the people should pray, rather than 'lay our heads together at a scurrilous pasquil'. But libels were not simply an inappropriate or immoral response, they were also highly dangerous. Laughing at a pasquil threatened to bring proper authority into 'contempt and disgrace', a situation which would inevitably culminate in the 'overthrow of all at last'. 'Nothing,' White argued, 'is more dangerous in a State, then for Statesmen to lose their reputation.' In ancient Greece the 'best men', like Socrates, had been ruined by the 'rude people' who had seen their betters mocked in theatrical comedies. Drawing on an example from English history designed to send shivers down every respectable gentleman's spine, White also opined that 'those rhymes, *When Adam delved and Eve Span*, &c. were more like to be made in Wat Tyler's camp than anywhere else'.[31]

V

White's vocabulary is revealing. Repeatedly the preacher connected libelling with the lower orders – to the 'rude' people of 'savage and popular humour', to the Wat Tylers of the world. This is a standard feature of contemporary attacks on libels, and a crucial link in the perceived chain of connection between libelling and sedition. James I's attack on 'railing rhymes' focused on the 'vulgar' and the ignorant, men he considered mere 'babes', men who 'gad astray'. Barnes's play dramatized two gentlemen's anxieties about the link between libelling and 'malicious curs'. 'De Libellis Famosis' noted that 'increase of lewdness' and 'decrease of money' were two characteristics of a libeller.[32] And if libelling were like poisoning, then like poisoning it was a crime associated with the low-born and the cowardly.[33]

The social baseness of libelling was also ritually expressed in two of the prescribed punishments for the worst forms of the crime, pillorying and aural mutilation. Public exhibition in the pillory and physical mutilation were explicitly degrading punishments usually meted out to lower-class offenders. In libel cases they could be, and occasionally were, administered to gentlemen. Lewis Pickering, an upwardly mobile gentleman and sometime confidant of the king, was sentenced in 1605 to be pilloried in the three places where his degradation would cause the maximum personal shame. One privy councillor even suggested that, since Pickering's libel had called upon the Croydon colliers to sing a mock dirge round Archbishop Whitgift's hearse, Pickering should be forced to wear a collier's sack in the pillory. With a fine sense of the theatrical, this sartorial suggestion imposed on the upwardly mobile Pickering the new, lower-class status of seditious libeller.[34]

This social profiling of the libeller also had biblical sanction. The image of the base libeller is built into one of the biblical texts cited in 'De Libellis Famosis'. Job 30:7–10 recorded how even the epitome of godly patience was moved to anger at becoming the song of the 'children of fools ... children of base men ... viler than the earth'.[35] Coke's report also cited Psalm 69, in which David lamented, 'They that sit in the gate speak against me; and I was the song of the drunkards.' Here libel is figured as a crime of the drunkard, a man without the self-government that supposedly characterized the elite, and whose words were stigmatized by his inebriation. Yet Coke's allusions to the psalms actually complicate the libeller's social profile. As Anne Lake Prescott has noted, the psalms are full of evocations of slander.[36] David is a persistent victim of malicious speech, the moral, religious man in an immoral world of backbiting and envy. The primary early modern interpretation of David's suffering was, of course, spiritual. In the countess of Pembroke's translation of Psalm 69, the victim of this 'public prating' and 'songs of winy taste' was the godly person suffering the malice of the ungodly for his service to the Lord.[37] In this form, David could be a comforting prototype for William Laud, a libel victim, in 1637.[38] Coke's use of the psalm in 'De Libellis Famosis' clearly implies a socially base origin for slander and libel, and there were others, like Alexander Top, who glossed the psalms in a similar manner, imagining the unidentified slanderers of the Psalms as churls and slaves.[39] But other writers, including most significantly the annotators of the Geneva Bible, located the slander of the psalms in the world of Saul's court.[40] In these glosses, David was the victim of the malicious tongues of courtiers who compete for royal favour and attention and, if successful, inspire hatred and envy. The Geneva Bible's gloss on Psalm 69 does not specify the court as the locale, but it does suggest that 'The more [David] sought to win them to God, the more they were against him both poor and rich'.[41]

The connection between libel and the deadly sin of envy was a resonant one. Contemporary moralists assumed that the ascent of any individual to a position of eminence would provoke the demonic, monstrous sin of envy: as George Wither noted, 'Thus fares the man, whom Virtue, Beacon-like,/Hath fixt upon the Hills of Eminence,/At him, the Tempests of mad Envy strike,/

And, rage against his Piles of Innocence'. And the 'Tempests of mad Envy' were expected to take the form of verbal attacks: 'Let them snarl and bite,' noted Wither, 'Pursue thee, with Detraction, Slanders, Mocks.'[42] This identification of criticism as the child of envy could become part of early Stuart courtiers' self-fashioning, a way to delegitimate personal attacks by yoking them to a sin that was in effect recognition of the victim's true virtue. On at least three occasions in the mid and late 1620s, for instance, his artistic clients depicted the royal favourite Buckingham – the target of numerous libellous critiques – as a man of virtue plagued by envy. In Peter Paul Rubens's equestrian portrait of the duke, the goddess Charity repels a demonic figure lurking on the edge of the canvas: the snake on the figure's head identifies her as Envy. In a second Rubens portrait, Minerva and Mercury carry Buckingham away from Envy's grasp. And, in a now lost masque performed at York House, the duke took the stage pursued by 'Envy, with divers open-mouthed dogs' heads representing the people's barking'.[43]

VI

The image of libellers and libelling as socially problematic is replicated in literary discourse on libel, in which legal, political and moral hostility towards the genre is allied with sharp aesthetic disgust.[44] Some poets worked to differentiate libel from legitimate satire. Thomas Bastard – who, in his Oxford days, had himself been accused of penning libels – once satirized 'libel', thus drawing distinctions between it and his own craft. Libel was 'raw with indigested spite', full of 'envenomed injury' and 'spiteful infamy'. 'Why dost thou boast for [as] if thou hadst done well?' the satirist sneered. 'In naughty things 'twere easy to excel.'[45] In this and other cases, the image of the libeller provided an imagined Other against which poets could contrast their own poetic, artistic, social and intellectual ambitions. In 'An Epistle answering to One that asked to be Sealed of the Tribe of Ben', Ben Jonson linked libelling with drunkenness and lechery and represented the fad for libels as part of the news-crazy culture he so despised. He attacked those

> that will jest
> On all souls that are absent: even the dead;
> Like flies, or worms, which man's corrupt parts fed.

He declared to his poetic followers that 'I have no portion' in those

> That censure all the town, and all the affairs,
> And know whose ignorance is more than theirs;
> Let these men have their ways, and take their times
> To vent their libels, and to issue rhymes
> ...
> I study other friendships.[46]

Abraham Holland's riposte to one who had accused him of writing a libel was less subtle, yet Holland too used the allegation to fashion his own social and poetic identity. Annoyed that anyone could have charged him with fathering 'this vile brat/A stinking libel', Holland identified more plausible culprits among those who were social or artistic upstarts. The 'itching scrivener that doth make/Verses by an almanac'; the 'lazy leaden-witted ass/Professing poetry (alas)'; the 'Latin'd merchant, whose fine clothes/Scorn that he should write in prose'; the 'busy lawyer's clerk, that still/Will usurp poetic skill': these were the cloth from which libellers were cut. Holland's art, by contrast, was governed by the 'gentler muse' and honed in the quiet refuge of the country-side, 'Where sweet damsels did infuse/Flame into me, and to my Muse'.[47]

Perhaps the most striking literary image of the libeller, however, appears in Book 5 canto 9 of Edmund Spenser's *The Faerie Queene*. As we follow Spenser's protagonists into the court of Queen Mercilla we encounter, 'at the Scriene', a man 'whose tongue was for his trespasse vyle/Nayl'd to a post, adiudged so by law'. Among this man's offences was the composition of verse libels:

> he falsely did revyle,
> And foule blaspheme that Queene for forged guyle,
> Both with bold speaches, which he blazed had,
> And with lewd poems, which he did compyle;
> For the bold title of a Poet bad
> He on himselfe had ta'en, and rayling rymes had sprad.

Above the perpetrator's head the word 'Bon Fons' had been written but then altered to read 'Malfont'. This labelling indicates something of Spenser's purpose. The good poet (and good poetry) – as defined in the humanist tradition and defended by Spenser's contemporary Sidney – could have a positive moral effect. (It could operate on a public readership to produce public benefits.) The good poet then was Bon Fons, the Fountain of Good. But political libelling – here importantly assumed to be the spreading of untruths – had the opposite effect, becoming a fountain of evil spreading corruption through publication. The libeller was dubbed 'Malfont', Spenser noted, 'Eyther for th'evill, which he did therein,/Or that he likened was to a welhead/Of evill words, and wicked sclaunders by him shed'. Like Jonson and Holland, Spenser invoked the poetic Other, the libeller, to legitimate his own practice. Indeed, some critics have stressed that Malfont appears just as Spenser himself is about to venture on the most nakedly political allegory of his whole poem: the repudiated, muti-lated libeller thus served as a kind of guarantee that the daring poetry that followed was the work of a poetical 'Bonfons'.[48]

VII

Few positive *explicit* images counterbalance the great weight of legal, moral and literary censure of verse libels, but these few are instructive, revealing vestiges of a moral and political defence of the composition, circulation and collection of these poems. Barnabe Barnes's idea that political vice forces the poet to become a libeller is developed in other literary defences, which treat libelling as a legitimate form of moralizing satire. George Wither explicitly defended – while claiming that he himself would not write – satire that taxed the powerful by name, satire that others might call libels. 'What?' Wither asks the 'Satyro-mastix',

> you would fain have all the great ones freed;
> They must not for their vices be controll'd.
> Beware; that were a sauciness indeed:
> But if the great ones to offend be bold,
> I see no reason but they should be told.
> Yea and they shall; their faults most hurtful be,
> And (though I will not put them to that shame)
> No great injustice in it I did see,
> If they were taxed by their proper name.
> For, no sin can on earth have her full blame.[49]

Perhaps the most interesting brief for the moral efficacy – and literary potential – of libels came from a far greater poet than Wither. In a letter reflecting on the deluge of bitter verse that greeted Robert Cecil's death in 1612 John Donne drew an aesthetic distinction between 'coarse and railing' libels and those 'witty and sharp libels ... which not only for the liberty of speaking, but for the elegancy, and composition, would take deep root, and make durable impressions in the memory'. Donne argued that coarse libels were such poor poetry that they would have a negligible effect on the reader. It was thus 'better for the honour of the person traduced', reasoned Donne, 'that some blunt downright railings be vented, of which everybody is soon weary, than other pieces, which entertain us long with a delight, and love to the things themselves'. The best way for a courtier to dispel the negative effects of a poetically powerful libel, therefore, was to encourage the circulation of cruder verses on the same theme; the libels against Cecil, Donne opined, were so 'tasteless and flat' that 'I think they were made by his friends'. Donne argued further that poetically sophisticated libels had moral as well as artistic utility. Ignoring the logic of the libel laws, Donne argued that 'there may be cases, where one may do his Country good service, by libelling against a live man', the libel acting as a check to the vices of those who cannot be brought 'under a judiciary accusation'. The duke of Lerma, favourite of the king of Spain, had, according to Donne, been kept from extreme behaviour only by the checks that the periodic assaults of the libellers had imposed on his vicious tendencies. Personalized libel can thus, in Donne's view, serve a moral, reformist purpose. Donne's emphasis on moral reformation meant, however, that libels against the dead could not be justified. The posthumous attacks on Cecil, even if they had been gems of the poet's art, were 'ignoble, and useless' because the libellers clearly had no intention to 'mend him'. Donne also drew the line at libels against the monarch, which, he believed, now back in agreement with conventional legal thinking, would occasion dangerous 'tumult, and contempt'.[50]

Donne's letter is worth lingering over further as a particularly rich example of the ways in which analyses of libelling could contain implicit ideas about the nature of the public sphere and public opinion. If aesthetically pleasing libels can function as checks on corruption, as agents of moral reform, and indeed as substitutes for judicial censure, how exactly does Donne think this would work? One might contend that Donne imagined the subject of the libel reading the criticism and taking it to heart, his moral reform thus ensuing from an essentially private communication. On the other hand, Donne may be implying a corrective power in libels that depends on the existence of a *critical public* that would obtain the poem, assess its literary merits, and then in some unspecified fashion – perhaps through the formation of 'opinion' – act as a kind of check on the behaviour of the libelled subject.

VIII

The image of the libeller, and the arguments surrounding the nature of his art, also inflected the writings of libellers themselves, and were in turn deployed by those poets – anti-libellers we might term them – who felt compelled to compose poems in direct response to verse libels. On occasion we can find libellers deliberately alluding to and playing with the negative images associated with their work. One libellous epitaph on Robert Cecil, that dwelled both on his fiscal oppressions and his alleged role in the destruction of the earl of Essex in 1601, began by embracing the literary stereotype of the rude, unpolished libeller: 'Advance, advance, my ill-disposed Muse,' the poem opens, 'With uncouth style and ill-disposed verse.'[51] Two other libels on Cecil play with the stereotype of the libeller as socially base, noting that allegations against the late lord treasurer had come from 'base Detractors' or from the 'Vulgar', but then proceeded not only to summarize the charges the vulgar had made but also to pile on extra ones.[52] In these poems, it seems, the image of the libeller as social and poetic Other is playfully embraced, or perhaps worn as a mask, all to the end of sharpening the force of the poet's serious allegations.

Other libellers could cleverly engage with and thus disrupt the force of negative stereotypes. In a bitter libellous epitaph on the duke of Buckingham, the mysterious 'E.K.' – to whom several libels in the collection of the Cheshire gentleman William Davenport are attributed – inverted the intention of the moralist's command to speak no ill of the dead while asserting, against the lawyers, that the truth of an allegation mattered. 'I will not slander one that's dead,' he wrote. But having declared it, he used it to justify the attack on Buckingham that followed. For 'E.K.' quite explicitly defined slander not as the articulation of harmful accusation, but as the articulation of a falsehood. Thus he will not lie and

> say that Buckingham is fled
> to any place of rest,
> Or that he's in celestial sleep
> Or Christians true for him do weep
> or holy cross him blessed'.[53]

On the other hand, poets eager to defend Buckingham's memory against the libellous taunts that proliferated after his 1628 assassination deployed negative stereotypes of the libeller in order to sustain their contention that Buckingham's critics were a source of social and political danger. Poets depicted the libellous celebration of Buckingham's murder as the workings of 'the envious breath/Of foul detraction', as 'venom', as 'poison'. One poem fired back at the 'horrid yells' of 'snarling Satyrs', depicting them as 'base' breaches of charity to the dead, as 'ill tun'd organs' spouting 'sooty language' drawn from unreliable 'banks of common credit'. Libellers spoke from 'popular lungs', and cast their libels against the duke in socially marginal public spaces, 'the burse, or stews'.[54] The stereotype of the socially base libeller helped these poets forge a politically resonant connection between attacks on Buckingham and the perceived threat – so important to Caroline political consciousness – from the forces of seditious popularity.[55]

IX

What do these images of libellers and libelling tell us about the impact of verse libels on early Stuart readers? Widespread opinion held that libels were base, immoral, illegal, sinful, uncharitable, dangerous, seditious. The stereotypical libeller was a lower-class hack, addled by drink, pricked by malicious envy, whose verse was raw and leaden-witted. Did these stereotypes condition the reading, collection and impact of verse libels? Were readers nervous of, embarrassed by, libels? Did libels' dubious reputation undercut their credibility as political expression? And if so, how then to explain the fact that contemporaries continued to write, circulate, read, transcribe and preserve them? Most of the historians – myself included – who have rediscovered the political importance of libels have tended to make the reception and appropriation of these texts unproblematic, arguing that the circulation of verse libels not only reveals contemporary perceptions of Cecil or Buckingham but may also have shaped them. Without abandoning this claim, we must admit that the process of appropriation was, in fact, a little more complicated.[56]

Like all exercises in the history of reading, answering this question requires facing serious, though not insurmountable, difficulties of evidence.[57] We can note, for instance, that many of the representations of libelling we have encountered thus far in this chapter contained assumptions about the ways in which libels could be read and about the effects they could produce on the reader. We might recall, for instance, Coke's assumption that reading a libel could generate contempt for an individual or a monarch, and could lead to seditious activity; or John White's assumption that reading or hearing a libel would generate laughter where tears were more appropriate; or Thomas Adams's argument that hearing a libel would create sinful activity; or John Donne's evocation of readers morally engaged by aesthetically accomplished libels and driven to weariness and boredom by the clunky rhymes and metres of the typical railing rhyme. Other approaches to the modes of reception are also available. A few surviving libels carry revealing marginal comments from readers, including explicit statements explaining why they have copied such dubious stuff. Rich, though mostly implicit, evidence can be deduced from the positioning of libels in miscellanies and news-diaries, the juxtapositions perhaps revealing how readers appropriated and evaluated libels.[58] The texts themselves sometimes hold clues – some libels were designed to elicit laughter, others tears of rage. Some poems were designed as games that demanded an active reader to decode them – verses could incorporate visual tricks, acrostics or anagrams, or be written in such a way that slight rearrangement of the punctuation could reverse their meaning. Some libellous verse also aimed, as Donne acknowledged, to induce aesthetic pleasure. Yet, above all, the sheer quantity of libels suggests that, despite the prevailing image of the genre, contemporaries were fascinated and politically engaged by them, and could probably distinguish between bad and good verse, between uncharitable attacks and serious interventions, between patently false charges and legitimate accusations of corruption.

We should thus assume a range of reader responses to verse libels. Some contemporaries, even those embarrassed by the genre, collected verse libels as evidence of the temper of the times. Sir Simonds D'Ewes may have thought it socially inappropriate for the author of a libellous anagram to dub the countess of Somerset a 'whore', but he admired the deviser's wit and inserted the anagram, along with other libels, into the history of his life and times.[59] John Chamberlain was uneasy that 'when men are down the very drunkards make rhymes and songs upon them', but as a good newsmonger he nevertheless circulated the 'pretty epigram' on the fall of Edward Coke that had inspired his disparaging remark.[60] John Holles considered a Latin poem on

Coke's fall to be 'the ravings of an obsolete faded poet' and asked his friend Mr Bond not to pass it on to others 'lest they mock me', but he was not too embarrassed to send it to Bond in the first place.[61] Sir Peter Manwood thought Pickering's libel on Whitgift appalling, but as a man of antiquarian bent he copied and preserved it anyway.[62] A particularly rich example of hostile appropriation occurs in a collection from the later 1620s, whose compiler inserted a couple of libels among his transcripts of news and parliamentary reports. The collector copied a libel on Buckingham's journey to Dover in December 1626, noting in the preface that 'one libel (the author whereof was justly punished) I have set down, which the judicious reader may smile at'. Before transcribing the popular anti-Buckingham libel on the failed Ré expedition of 1627, 'And Art Return'd Again With All Thy Faults', the collector attributed the poem to 'some perplexed soul envying the happy return of the Duke', and described the libel as 'a most bitter verse which savours more of an envious and detracting wit, and violent passion, than of a sound and settled judgment'. The poem embodied 'vulgar' opinion, and vulgar opinion was always wrong: 'He is not wise who is vulgarly supposed wise; nor he an ill subject whom the people affect not, when the Prince knowing his worth, advanceth him to dignity.'[63]

Perhaps the most explicitly ambivalent relationship to verse libels is found in the newsbooks and diaries of John Rous, the Suffolk parson who has become something of a paradigmatic figure in the study of early Stuart news culture. In his news-diary Rous added bitter comments to his libel transcriptions, comments that echo contemporary stereotypes about libels and libellers. After transcribing a widely circulated poem attacking Buckingham's conduct on the Ile de Ré, Rous wondered whether the poem was merely 'vulgar rumour, which is often lying'; kings' favourites, he asserted, assuming with the moralists the omnipresence of envy, 'are most subject to slander of tongues, the vulgar delighting herein, who judge of all things by events, not by discretion'. One libel prophesying Buckingham's death Rous glossed as a 'dangerous rhyme, fruit of an after wit'. 'Light scoffing wits, not apt to deeper reach,' Rous noted about a libellous epitaph on the murdered duke, 'can rhyme upon any the most vulgar surmises, and will not fail to show themselves, though charity and true wisdom forbid.' Another couplet on the duke he dismissed, 'Thus foully will the vulgar disgrace him whose greatness they hate.'[64] Despite Rous's unease, his friends kept giving him libels and he kept transcribing them. In the end, the parson came clean with some wretched verse of his own: 'I hate these following railing rhymes,' he noted in 1640 at the head of some libel transcriptions, 'yet keep them for precedent of the times.'[65]

But clearly more was at stake than antiquarian interest, even if we do not read Rous's desire to collect and record political news as an inherently assertive political act. Verse libels unsettled Rous. He could not simply dismiss them. He was especially nervous, for instance, about an elaborate and widely circulated poem called 'The King's Five Senses', which depicted James I at the height of the Spanish match crisis surrounded by interlinked popish, Spanish and homosexual temptations. In this instance, Rous used another 'report' to gloss and defuse the poem's charges. He noted that the poem – couched as a prayer to preserve the king's senses from corruption – had 'been showed to the King' who 'made light of them ... saying (as it is reported the King's majesty said) this fellow wished good things for him'.[66] But sometimes reports failed to neutralize a libel's charge. Commenting on Buckingham, Rous noted that despite all the libellous allegations – which he assumed were 'vulgar' in origin – he 'should have been free from all harder censure' of the duke if parliament had not been so adamant in its opposition to him. 'The wise,' Rous noted – meaning parliament – 'will never be rashly uncharitable.'[67] Reports of parliamentary attacks on Buckingham gave 'vulgar' libels against the duke added credibility. Truth – here guaranteed by the social status of MPs – may not have mattered to the law, but it did matter to readers. When the earl of Northampton sent the royal favourite Carr a copy of a libel on Robert Cecil, he was quick to note the poem's literary shortcomings – 'I have seldom seen the traces of a more unhappy pen' – but added that 'if I should die in this instant, I know not what one point to tax of untruth or fiction'.[68]

The Rous case reminds us that libels did not circulate – and were not read and appropriated – in isolation. Verse libels were only one element of a rich and highly varied manuscript and oral news culture; they were often written and appropriated in the context of other news material. In news-diary collections, like the one compiled by William Davenport of Bramhall, Cheshire, copies of libels intermingled with copies of newsletters and separates, each type of news information commenting upon and potentially reinforcing the credibility and legitimacy of the others.[69] Similar clues to the complexity of appropriation can be found in the collections of verse libels in manuscript poetry miscellanies. Andrew McRae suggests that the transcription of libels in miscellanies alongside works by 'legitimate' poets, like Donne, Jonson or Herrick, indicates that miscellany compilers with a claim to literary discrimination agreed with Donne and, despite all the stereotypes of rugged verse, accorded some libels real literary worth.[70]

Thus some collectors of libels might organize them not according to the political personalities or scandals they attack, nor in a chronological sequence that recorded political change or simply the rhythms of the news, but according to 'aesthetic' or 'literary' categories like genre (libellous epitaphs collected alongside other epitaphs, libellous epigrams next to other epigrams, etc.) or rhetorical form, or according to general subject matter (the vices of women, for instance).[71]

Verse libels *were* a stigmatized genre of political and literary expression. In principle, they breached legal, political, social and artistic decorum. Clearly this must have had some effect on their political impact, if only to generate embarrassment, unease or doubt about their credibility. Yet unease could be circumvented. Poets asserted that libels were not good poems, but some collectors (and some poets) begged to differ. The unreliability of a libel's charges could be remedied by the circulation of other forms of news in less disreputable and untrustworthy forms. Ultimately we can never be certain how most individuals read a libel and what they took from it. Yet the prevalence of libels, libellers and libel readers does, at the very least, reveal the gap between the aspiration of a king to be an object of wonder, to be gazed upon and obeyed, and the reality of a nation of scribblers and readers, poking fun at courtiers, railing at royal policies, sifting through separates, compiling newsbooks and miscellanies, and, perhaps, in the process, constructing and engaging in a nascent public sphere and thus transforming themselves from subjects into citizens.

NOTES

1 Barnabe Barnes, *The Divils Charter: A Tragaedie Conteining the Life and Death of Pope Alexander the sixt* (London, 1607), Act 1, scenes 2 and 3, sigs A4, B2r.

2 See, e.g., Alastair Bellany, '"Raylinge Rymes and Vaunting Verse": libellous politics in early Stuart England, 1603–1628', in Kevin Sharpe and Peter Lake (eds), *Culture and Politics in Early Stuart England* (Basingstoke, 1994), 285–310; Bellany, 'A poem on the archbishop's hearse: puritanism, libel, and sedition after the Hampton Court conference', *Journal of British Studies* 34:2 (1995), 137–64; Bellany, 'Libels in action: ritual, subversion and the English literary underground, 1603–1642', in Tim Harris (ed.), *The Politics of the Excluded, c. 1500–1850* (Basingstoke, 2001), 99–124; Bellany, *The Politics of Court Scandal in Early Modern England: News Culture and the Overbury Affair, 1603–1660* (Cambridge, 2002); Thomas Cogswell, 'Underground verse and the transformation of early Stuart political culture', in Mark Kishlansky and Susan Amussen (eds), *Political Culture and Cultural Politics in Early Modern England* (Manchester, 1995), 277–300; David Colclough, *Freedom of Speech in Early Stuart England* (Cambridge, 2005), chapter 4; Pauline Croft, 'The reputation of Robert Cecil: libels, political opinion and popular awareness in the early seventeenth century', *Transactions of the Royal Historical Society*, 6th ser., 1 (1991), 43; Croft, 'Libels, popular literacy and public opinion in early modern England', *Historical Research* 68 (1995), 266–85; Richard Cust, 'News and politics in early seventeenth century England', *Past and Present* 112 (1986), 60–90; Adam Fox, 'Ballads, libels and popular ridicule in Jacobean England', *Past and Present* 145 (1994), 47–83; Arthur F. Marotti, *Manuscript, Print, and the English Renaissance Lyric* (Ithaca NY, 1995), chapter 2; Andrew McRae, 'Renaissance satire and the popular voice', in Geoffrey Little (ed.), *Imperfect Apprehensions: Essays in English Literature in Honour of G. A. Wilkes* (Sydney, 1996), 217–28; McRae, 'The literary culture of early Stuart libelling', *Modern Philology* 97:3 (2000), 364–92; *Literature, Satire and the Early Stuart State* (Cambridge, 2004). For an internet-based annotated edition of over 300 early seventeenth-century libels, see now Alastair Bellany and Andrew McRae (eds), 'Early Stuart libels: an edition of poetry from manuscript sources', *Early Modern Literary Studies*, text ser., I (2005) (http://purl. oclc.org/emls/texts/libels/).

3 See J. A. Sharpe, *Defamation and Sexual Slander in Early Modern England* (Borthwick Papers LVIII, York, 1982), 4–5; and Martin Ingram, *Church Courts, Sex and Marriage in England, 1570–1640* (Cambridge, 1987), 292–9, for useful overviews.

4 'The Case De Libellis Famosis', reprinted in *The English Reports* 77 (Edinburgh and London, 1907), 250–2; for the religio-political and legal contexts shaping the report see Bellany, 'Poem on the archbishop's hearse'; Roger B. Manning, 'The origins of the doctrine of sedition', *Albion* 12:2 (1980), 99–121; and Philip Hamburger, 'The development of the law of seditious libel and the control of the press', *Stanford Law Review* 37 (1985), 691–97.

5 'Ore tenus' means 'by word of mouth'.

6 'De Libellis Famosis', 251.

7 Inner Temple Library Ms Barrington 16, fol. 30v; 'De Libellis Famosis', 251.

8 'De Libellis Famosis', 251.

9 *Ibid.*

10 Inner Temple Ms Barrington 16, fol. 30v; Huntington Ms HM 41952, fol. 97r.

11 BL, Stowe Ms 422, fol. 118v.

12 The timing of the poem's appearance can be reconstructed from contemporary news reports: see Thomas Birch (comp.), *The Court and Times of James I* (London, 1849) II, 355, 364–5, and Norman E. McLure (ed.), *The Letters of John Chamberlain* (Philadelphia, 1939) II, 473, 478. One copy of the poem – in BL, Harley Ms 367, fol. 151r – suggests James was responding in particular to a (now lost) libel called 'the Comons teares'.

13 Bodleian Ms Malone 23, 49–56. At least sixteen other copies survive in manuscript. For an important reading of James's late political poetry, see Curtis Perry, '"If proclamations will not serve": the late manuscript poetry of James I and the culture of libel', in Daniel Fischlin and Mark Fortier (eds), *Royal Subjects: Essays on the Writings of James VI and I* (Detroit MI, 2002), 205–32.

14 BL, Landsdowne Ms 620, fol. 50.

15 Bellany, 'Poem on the archbishop's hearse'; William Laud, *A Speech delivered in the Starr-Chamber* (London, 1637), sig. A4r.

16 Bellany, 'Poem on the archbishop's hearse', 140–1; PRO, SP 16/116/56, 95; 16/117/10, 73; 16/118/77.

17 Francis Bacon, *Essays* (London, 1906), 42–3. For more on Bacon's attitude to libels, see Colclough, *Freedom of Speech*, 210–11.

18 See, e.g., *Letters of John Chamberlain* I, 453.

19 Laud knew from Suetonius that some great men had suffered 'the tearing and rending of their credit and reputation, with a gentle, nay, a generous mind': *A Speech*, 1–2.

20 Sheffield City Library Archives, WWM Strafford Papers, Str P7, fols 55v–56r.

21 Thomas Gainsford, *The Rich Cabinet* (London, 1616), sig. 68v.

22 For another exploration of some of these issues, focusing on manuscript news in general, see Sabrina Baron, 'The guises of dissemination in early seventeenth-century England', in Brendan Dooley and Sabrina A. Baron (eds), *The Politics of Information in Early Modern Europe* (London and New York, 2001), 41–56. For the most sophisticated recent discussion of government print censorship in this period, see Cyndia Susan Clegg, *Press Censorship in Jacobean England* (Cambridge, 2001).

23 Bodleian Ms Ashmole 36–7, fol. 59r, 'An Answeare to the Wiper away of the Peoples Teares'.

24 'De Libellis Famosis', 252; Bellany, 'Poem on the archbishop's hearse', 159. Debora Shuger has argued forcefully that the dictates of charity not only induced widespread reluctance among writers to dwell on others' faults but also undergirded royal defamation laws and other attempts to restrict speech in this period: see Debora Shuger, 'Civility and censorship in early modern England', in Robert C. Post (ed.), *Censorship and Silencing: Practices of Cultural Regulation* (Los Angeles, 1998), 89–110.

25 BL, Stowe Ms 422, fol. 118v.

26 Owen Felltham, *Resolves Divine, Morall, Politicall* (London, 1623), 181–2.

27 William Paley Baildon (ed.), *Les Reportes del Cases in Camera Stellata, 1593–1609* (London, 1894), 224.

28 Thomas Adams, 'The fatal banquet: the second service', in Joseph Angus (ed.), *The Works of Thomas Adams* (Edinburgh, 1861) I, 187–8.

29 'A Generation of Serpents' in *The Workes of Tho: Adams. Being the Summe of his Sermons, Meditations, and other Divine and Moral Discourses* (London, 1629), 889.

30 'De Libellis Famosis', 251; BL, Landsdowne Ms 620, fol. 50. On early Stuart images of poisoning and poisoners, see Bellany, *Politics of Court Scandal*, 144–8.

31 John White, *Two Sermons* (London, 1615), 19–20.

32 'De Libellis Famosis', 252.

33 Bellany, *Politics of Court Scandal*, 144–5.

34 Bellany, 'Poem on the archbishop's hearse', 159–60.

35 'De Libellis Famosis', 252; the social status of the offenders is reinforced by the Geneva Bible gloss, see Lloyd E. Berry (intro.), *The Geneva Bible: a Facsimile of the 1560 Edition* (Madison WI, 1969), 230v.

36 Anne Lake Prescott, 'Evil tongues at the court of Saul: the Renaissance David as a slandered courtier', *Journal of Medieval and Renaissance Studies* 21:2 (1991), 163–86.

37 J. C. A. Rathmell (ed.), *The Psalms of Sir Philip Sidney and the Countess of Pembroke* (New York, 1963), 157–60.

38 Laud, *A Speech*, 3.

39 Prescott, 'Evil tongues', 181–2.

40 Prescott, 'Evil tongues'.

41 *Geneva Bible*, 249r.

42 George Wither, *A Collection of Emblemes, Ancient and Moderne* II (London, 1634/5), 97. See too the depiction of the paired hags of Envy and Detraction in Book 5 of Edmund Spenser, *The Faerie Queene*, ed. Thomas P. Roche, Jr (Penguin Classics edn, Harmondsworth, 1987), 871 ff. A useful sketch of the Christian and classical understandings of envy that underpin Spenser's description can be found in Ronald B. Bond, 'Envy', in A. C. Hamilton (ed.), *The Spenser Encyclopedia* (Toronto, 1990).

43 Gregory Martin, 'Rubens and Buckingham's "fayrie ile"', *Burlington Magazine* 108:765 (1966), 613–18; Thomas Birch (comp.), *The Court and Times of Charles I* (London, 1849) I, 226.

44 For some brief reflections on this literary strategy, see McRae, 'Renaissance satire and the popular voice', especially 11–14; McRae, 'Literary culture of early Stuart libelling', 369.

45 Thomas Bastard, *Chrestoleros: Seven Bookes of Epigrames written by T.B.* (London, 1598), 70–1.

46 George Parfitt (ed.), *Ben Jonson: the Complete Poems* (Harmondsworth, 1978), 192.

47 Abraham Holland, 'Holland his hornet to sting a varlet', in *Hollandi Post-huma* (Cambridge, 1626), sigs G3r–G4v.

48 Spenser, *Faerie Queene*, 830. Recent critical opinion on the passage is conveniently summarized in A. Leigh DeNeef, 'Bonfont, malfont', in Hamilton, *The Spenser Encyclopedia*.

49 George Wither, 'To the Satyro-mastix', from 'Abuses Stript, and Whipt' in *Iuvenilia: a Collection of those Poemes which were heretofore imprinted, and written by George Wither* (2nd edn, London, 1633), sig. B1v. For a brilliant reading of Wither's wrestlings with the blurred distinctions between 'satire' and 'libel', convincingly linked to his and others' conceptions of the character of the 'public sphere', see Michelle O'Callaghan, '"Now thou may'st speak freely": entering the public sphere in 1614', in Stephen Clucas and Rosalind Davies (eds), *The Crisis of 1614 and the Addled Parliament: Literary and Historical Perspectives* (Aldershot, 2003), 70–2.

50 Charles Merrill (ed.), *John Donne: Letters to Severall Persons of Honour* (New York, 1910), 77–9; on the Cecil libels, see Croft, 'Reputation of Robert Cecil'. On Donne's letter, see too the reading in Colclough, *Freedom of Speech*, 209–10.

51 'Poems from a seventeenth-century manuscript', *Texas Quarterly* 16:4 (1973), supplement, 44.

52 BL, Harley Ms 6947, fol. 211r; Bodleian Ms Malone 23, 65–6.

53 Cheshire County Record Office, Ms CR 63/2/19, fol. 69r.

54 Bodleian Ms Malone 23, p. 123; J. A. Taylor, 'Two unpublished poems on the duke of Buckingham', *Review of English Studies* 40:158 (1989), 1–4; Bodleian Ms Malone 23, 128–30.

55 For a survey of the concept of 'popularity', see Richard Cust, 'Charles I and popularity', in Thomas Cogswell, Richard Cust and Peter Lake (eds), *Politics, Religion and Popularity: Early Stuart Essays in Honour of Conrad Russell* (Cambridge, 2002), 325–58.

56 For some bracing general comments on the hermeneutic problems that accrue when cultural historians fail to study reception and modes of reading, see Jonathan Rose, *The Intellectual Life of the British Working Classes* (New Haven CT and London, 2001), 'A preface to a history of audiences'; and see too the critical comments on earlier studies of libels in Kevin Sharpe, *Remapping Early Modern England: the Culture of Seventeenth Century Politics* (Cambridge, 2000), 402. Several important studies have begun the overdue work of problematizing the reception of news in early modern England: see, e.g., Andrew Mousley, 'Self, state, and seventeenth century news', *The Seventeenth Century* 6:2 (1991), 149–68; Ian Atherton, '"The Itch grown a Disease": manuscript transmission of news in early modern England', in Joad Raymond (ed.), *News, Newspapers, and Society in Early Modern Britain* (London, 1999), 39–65; Daniel Woolf, 'News, history and the construction of the present in early modern England', in Dooley and Baron (eds), *Politics of Information*, 80–118, especially 100 ff. on 'News, rumour, distrust, and anxiety'; and David Randall, 'Sovereign Intelligence and Sovereign Intelligencers:

Transforming Standards of Credibility in English Military News from ca. 1570 to 1637', unpublished Ph.D. thesis, Rutgers University, 2005. These investigations are all linked with a broader historiography on the problem of credibility and trust in early modern culture. See, e.g., Steven Shapin, *A Social History of Truth: Civility and Science in Seventeenth-Century England* (Chicago, 1994); Adrian Johns, *The Nature of the Book: Print and Knowledge in the Making* (Chicago, 1998); and, with important reflections on news, Brendan Dooley, *The Social History of Skepticism: Experience and Doubt in Early Modern Culture* (Baltimore MD, 1999).

57 On these issues, see the 'Introduction' to James Raven, Helen Small and Naomi Tadmor (eds), *The Practice and Representation of Reading in England* (Cambridge, 1996), and Kevin Sharpe, *Reading Revolutions: The Politics of Reading in Early Modern England* (New Haven CT and London, 2000).

58 For a forceful statement about the necessity of reading libels within the contexts of the miscellanies into which they were transcribed, see Colclough, *Freedom of Speech*, 203. Colclough's provocative chapter on libels argues that they 'acted as an unofficial means of counsel to which individuals might have recourse when more acknowledged fora ... appeared to have failed' (205), and that libel collectors were motivated by anxieties about 'the counsel that was allowed to reach the king and the range of information that was allowed to reach his people' (203). The making of news miscellanies – including the incorporation of verse libels – was thus a form of political agency and an assertion of a right to that agency in the face of royal prohibitions and legal limits on 'free speech'.

59 J. O. Halliwell (ed.), *The Autobiography and Correspondence of Sir Simonds D'Ewes* (London, 1845) I, 87; BL, Harley Ms 646, fol. 26r.

60 *Letters of John Chamberlain* II, 40.

61 P. R. Seddon (ed.), *Letters of John Holles, 1587–1637*, Thoroton Record Society 31 (Nottingham, 1975) I, 146–7.

62 BL, Additional Ms 38139, fol. 58r.

63 BL, Sloane Ms 826, fols 28r, 31v–32r. A possible candidate for the compiler of this news collection is one 'R. Wrighte' of Kingston, whose name is inscribed at fol. 151v. The Ms contains (fol. 153r ff.) in a different hand one of the richest collections of libels on Buckingham's assassination.

64 Mary Anne Everett Green (ed.), *Diary of John Rous*, Camden Society LXVI (London, 1856), pp. 22, 26, 30, 31. For a brief assessment of Rous as a reader, see Sharpe, *Reading Revolutions*, 296–7.

65 *Diary of John Rous*, 109; see, too, John Selden, *Table Talk* (London, 1898), 76.

66 BL, Additional Ms 28640, fol. 105v.

67 *Diary of John Rous*, 30.

68 PRO, SP 14/70/21.

69 Cheshire County RO, Ms 63/2/19.

70 McRae, 'Literary culture of early Stuart libelling', 382–5.

71 David Colclough, '"The Muses Recreation": John Hoskyns and the manuscript culture of the seventeenth century', *Huntington Library Quarterly* 61:3–4 (1998), 375 ff. I am especially indebted here to a number of papers by literary scholars delivered at the 2004 'Rayling Rymes' conference at the University of Exeter, especially those by James

Doelman on epigrams, David Colclough on rhetoric and Joshua Eckhardt on poetical miscellanies. Many of the essays from this conference will appear in a forthcoming special issue of the *Huntington Library Quarterly*. For a brief version of Colclough's arguments on rhetoric, see *Freedom of Speech*, 249.

Chapter 7

Marketing a massacre: Amboyna, the East India Company and the public sphere in early Stuart England

Anthony Milton

I

On 27 February 1623, Gabriel Towerson, the chief factor or merchant of the East India Company (EIC) in Amboyna, was beheaded after torture by command of the local Dutch governor, Herman van Speult. Nine other Englishmen, ten Japanese and one Portugese shared the same fate, all charged with having plotted to kill van Speult and overwhelm the Dutch garrison on Amboyna. The events have become notorious and English outrage has echoed down the centuries. One author writing in 1945 called it 'one of the blackest crimes in all history'.[1] The fact that someone could write this at the time of the Holocaust, and after so many countless massacres in the intervening centuries, suggests perhaps just how effectively the event has been glossed by later English historians. Some of the extraordinary later resonance of these events was the result of their exploitation in later propaganda – the so-called Amboyna massacre was dredged up endlessly whenever anti-Dutch sentiment was required. This was true in the Anglo-Dutch wars of the seventeenth century, and also in the extraordinarily detailed account given by Beckles Willson in his two-volume history of the East India Company published in 1903 – where the vicious Dutch character displayed in the massacre was imputed dexterously to their South African descendants, the Boers.[2] But the immediate English public response to the events in Amboyna in 1624 and 1625 was also dramatic. The government felt impelled to order an extra 800 men to stand watch in London on Shrove Tuesday in 1625 for fear of anti-Dutch riots.

It is the initial response to the Amboyna incident which will be the principal concern of this chapter. This is partly because a number of historians, briefly noting the fuss, have remarked that the East India Company seems to have launched a sustained propaganda campaign, using a range of media, including plays, pamphlets, woodcuts and ballads, in order to whip up anti-Dutch and pro-Company sentiment, and to force the government to bring diplomatic pressure to bear on the Dutch States General to avenge the massacre.[3]

Since in recent years the political history of the period has started to focus on the questions of the spread of news and the role of public opinion, it seems appropriate to take a closer look at this apparent attempt to manipulate public opinion. This would appear to be a classic example of that process of the taking of politics out of doors, of the appeal to notions of public interest and public opinion, which has so interested those recent historians interested in deploying (in suitably adapted form) the notion of a developing 'public sphere' first delineated by Jürgen Habermas in the 1960s. But the Amboyna affair allows us to explore a number of specific aspects of this phenomenon. How far was a public sphere really being invoked, what was its perceived extent? How far was the East India Company truly in control of the public discussion of its misfortunes? How did the varying arenas, of printed pamphlet literature, plays, privately circulated manuscripts, privately viewed pictures, operate, and what do they reveal of the changing perceptions and construals of what was deemed to be appropriate to 'public' and 'private' discourse? What role did parliament play? In ideological terms, how far was it possible for the Company to mount a hostile campaign against the Dutch without seeming to undermine Protestant unity at precisely the time when it was most needed in the wake of the Thirty Years War? How did the Company negotiate the Amboyna agenda through the muddy and treacherous waters of the political and religious divisions of the 1620s? Was the East India Company consciously involved in an appeal to a broad swathe of public opinion? And what were these publications and activities actually intended to achieve? Were they seeking to coerce the government into action? Was this an attack on government inaction by an 'opposition'? How did they seek to explain and defend their position?

II

On the face of it, the East India Company seems an unlikely subject for any study of the role of public opinion (or indeed of the emergence of a public sphere which Habermas depicted as emerging in antagonism with the state). For in many ways the EIC was a department of state. Not only did it owe its existence to the monopolistic charter which the crown had granted it, but for the high-risk and politically volatile trading in which it was involved the Company was inevitably dependent on the support of the crown. Even in its first voyage of 1601, the Company had had to seek repeated injunctions from the privy council in order to compel subscribers to pay their share.[4] Its fractious dealings with the Dutch and Portugese impelled the Company into military manoeuvres and frequent crossing of the thin line between aggressive trade and diplomatic transgression. The export of bullion required continued exemption from the restrictive laws on the practice. Constant dealings with the crown were inevitable, and even assumed in the *Laws or Standing Orders* of the Company, which specified among the duties of the Governor that of attending on the king and privy council (and the Court Minutes leave one to wonder whether he had time for anything else besides this).[5]

This is not to say, of course, that crown/Company relations were those of harmonious symbiosis. On the contrary, they were often fraught with tension. The crown showed a persistent tendency to grant licences to other adventurers which violated the Company charter, and then to require the Company to pay substantial sums to buy their rivals off (and in one case also provide the king with a loan of £20,000 in gratitude).[6] The Company regularly provided enormous New Year's gifts to people at court, and felt obliged to accept on damaging terms any courtiers who wished to gain a share of the profits.[7] A major crisis occurred in relation to Ormuz, a Portugese port on the Persian Gulf, which fell to a joint Anglo-Persian force in 1622. The duke of Buckingham demanded the sum of £10,000 as his prize money as lord admiral, and the Company was required to pay another £10,000 to James as punishment for its involvement in the Ormuz affair. The Court Minutes are notably laconic in this period, and make it plain that the loathing being expressed towards Buckingham was so profound that they dared not commit it to paper.[8]

Anger at crown policies did not, however, provide the EIC with a welcome entry into the ranks of the 'country' 'patriots'. On the contrary, the Company was occasionally the target of the 'country's' fury. Part of the Company's problem arose from the fact that it was a private monopoly – and was therefore immediately among the targets of parliamentary wrath, and acutely vulnerable to the charge of pursuing private interest at the expense of the commonweal. The Company's chief propagandist, Thomas Mun, complained of how the Company's opponents used 'the gilded tearmes of the Common-wealth', but it was imperative for the Company to defeat its negative associations as a monopoly by mastering the same terminology as its opponents, claiming that the Company was acting in the public interest, and preserving the commonweal.[9] Accounts of Company voyages such as that of Edmund Scott depicted the Company factors as brave defenders of the honour and interests of their country in far-off lands, and the EIC followed the Virginia Company in having its deeds and forts represented in lord mayor's pageants.[10] The Company never lost an opportunity to invoke their status as upholders and representatives of 'the honour and reputation of the English nation', particularly when they were losing out in their dealings with the Dutch or the Spanish.[11]

The first sustained attack on the Company came in 1615 in the form of a pamphlet by one Robert Kayll, and Kayll's charges provide a useful summary of the objections that would continually be made against the EIC. Kayll argued that the Company ruinously exported bullion into heathen hands; that it spent lavishly on its trade; that it wasted ships (which were therefore unavailable for the navy and the defence of the kingdom); that it depleted timber stocks (conducting 'a parricide of woods'); that it took the best ships out of other trades; that it depleted the number of mariners (there was a high fatality rate on Company voyages); that it then neglected to look after the dead mariners' widows and families; and that it inhibited free trade – and all this for luxury commodities that were unnecessary. Many of the same charges were levelled against the Company in Thomas Scot's famous *Vox Populi* of 1622, where the Spaniards were depicted as applauding the English voyages to the East Indies as wasting the English state – removing bullion from the country, and killing off the mariners that the English would need to defend themselves against the Spanish fleet.[12] The anonymous pamphlet *The Interpreter* – published in the same year – attacked those lukewarm Protestants who were acquiescing in the Spanish match, and associated them with those merchants who clashed with the Dutch in the East Indies. It attacks

> ....   he, that fain would take
> Occasion from the East or West, to shake
> Our League with the United Provinces:
> To which end, he hath many fair pretences.
> Our Honour first, for in the Greeneland, they
> And the East Indies, beat our ships away.
> Our Profit likewise, for in both those places
> We do great loss sustain, besides disgraces.[13]

In response, the East India Company did its best to defend itself against the charges, and to present its own version of events. Dudley Digges mounted a robust defence against Kayll's pamphlet in a pamphlet of his own. Not only did Digges dispute the figures provided by Kayll, but he also emphasized the benefits that the Company bestowed on Londoners through its charitable enterprises. On this point, it is notable that in 1623 the Company specifically ordered that the distribution of money and victuals to the poor of Stepney should *not* to be left to churchwardens, but should be performed by the Company's own servants.[14] The obvious importance that was attached by the Company to such charity helps to remind us of the degree to which public charity not only reinforced bonds of deference between giver and receiver, but also vindicated the public honour of the charitable, whether individual or corporate.

Another recurring charge that had to be tackled was the claim that the Company essentially worked against the national interest by shipping specie out of the kingdom. This was a charge that was difficult to repulse – in a simple sense, because it was true: there was no obvious market for English goods in the East Indies, and this meant that the Company was obliged to purchase its East Indies goods with bullion. The point, however, was that this did not necessarily undermine the currency reserves of England, since the outlay was more than recompensed by the other forms of trade which the Company embarked upon, both between the islands of the East Indies and also by selling East Indian wares in Europe.[15] The Company's task, however, was to reassure potential investors that they were not assisting in depleting the reserves of the country. This ultimately required a re-education in economic ideology, and the Company not surprisingly concluded that this would be best achieved by means of a popular pamphlet, and a leading member of the Company, Thomas Mun, responded with his short tract, *A Discourse of Trade*, which provided a further response to Kayll's charges.[16] Incidentally, it is emblematic of the EIC's approach that, as well as publishing refutations of Kayll's anonymous pamphlet, they also secured a privy council order to track down and imprison the offending author.

The Company also did its best to play up its religious orthodoxy. Digges had highlighted the 'good summes of money yearely to releeve poore painfull preachers of the Gospell' which the Company continually disbursed. Indeed, only the previous year Sir Thomas Smith had persuaded the Company to make an annual payment of £100 to 'poore preachers', and by 1623 the Company was complaining that its charity to poor ministers had brought down upon it a multitude of suitors.[17] This need for clear public signs of Protestant zeal was all the more important for the Company as its constant clashes with the Protestant Dutch made it vulnerable to charges of undermining Protestant unity.

Parliaments were, of course, the potential flashpoints for these discontents and hostile charges against the EIC. Parliaments could always spell danger for monopolies such as the EIC. The Company managed in its early years to be the one privileged exporting agency which found favour in parliament (partly by its very open policy towards investors, who included many MPs). But by 1621 this was no longer the case. With economic depression came renewed complaints about the Company's export of bullion.

The Company was acutely aware of the danger of seeming in any way to be acting against the public interest at times when parliament was sitting, and usually made sure that it orchestrated a vigorous defence of its interests. The speeches and pamphlets orchestrated by the Company in 1621 seem to have been effective.[18] But the 1624 parliament was notable for its attacks on the chartered companies, and the EIC faced calls for its fleet to be stopped and its books searched – especially because of renewed concern over the export of bullion.[19] These were calls which Buckingham was happy to encourage, as he wanted to seize Company ships to use them in his planned naval campaign.[20] The EIC thus ran the risk of ending up on the wrong side of this government populism.

The Company showed sensitivity not just to arguments over bullion exports. The Governor, Maurice Abbot, warned of the bad public impression that was created by people who hung around parliament with personal petitions against the Company. The cries of these petitioners threatened to undermine the Company's efforts to present itself as a defender of the country's interests.[21] In 1624, at least, MPs needed little encouragement to support anyone with a grievance against the East India Company. The Company noted how a Commons subcommittee gave the EIC 'very coarse usage, and not without some words of reproach and scandal' after hearing the complaints of Lady Dale (the widow of Sir Thomas Dale, who claimed that Dale had seized a large prize which should have come to her).[22]

One further complicating factor here was the fact that the Company itself was not united, and that some of the attacks were led by a faction within the Company itself. This is not to suggest that this was *just* a factional quarrel – more was clearly at stake. Nevertheless, it is notable that when one faction (in this case that of Sir Edwin Sandys) sought to discredit their opponents in the Company, they had recourse to precisely the charges of the pursuit of private interest that opponents of the EIC had habitually deployed.[23] The accusations against the Company had thus acquired such common currency that even members of the EIC themselves were not averse to using them.

Squeezed between crown and parliament, and attacked by both, the EIC clearly had a substantial 'public relations problem' on its hands by June 1624, when news of the Amboyna massacre finally leaked out. If a 'public sphere' were to be appealed to, it could not be guaranteed that it would not be a hostile one.

III

Initial Company discussions of the Amboyna massacre were bleak, coming as it did on the back of the attacks in the 1624 parliament. At the June 1624 meeting of the Court of Committees, discussion focused on how the Company suffered from false friends, the Dutch, and 'common obloquy at home', where everyone cried out against the trade. The Governor, Maurice Abbot, cut such negative thoughts short, however, and while admitting that the EIC 'hath mighty enemies'[24] he urged them to await the actions of the state in the business.

The Company's original intention was indeed to work through the government. The initial exchanges with James were tense, however, and unpromising, being still dominated by Ormuz and the king's demands for payment.[25] These initially discouraging signs from James prompted the Company to contemplate another means of getting their concerns across – namely through a written narrative of the events. The same Court meeting that listened to Abbot's discouraging account of his initial exchanges with James ordered the writing up of a narrative of the events at Amboyna. Ostensibly, this was to counteract the accounts of the events that were already being spread by the

Dutch, and which presented the EIC and their factors in the worst possible light. (The fact that such rumours were reported as 'spreading among the vulgar' perhaps demonstrates just how great the popular hostility towards the EIC was.)[26] But this narrative was to be the first weapon in the Company's response. Although Abbot reported to the General Court that the written account would be published 'as farr as may',[27] the initial preferred move was via this written narrative, which was discreetly but cunningly circulated in manuscript (to Carleton and other influential ministers).[28]

The narrative played its first important role when it accompanied a petition of July 1624 to the king. The petition threatened to abandon the trade in the East Indies altogether (and this was no mere bluff – the General Court, in its debate on Amboyna, had stated an intention to cease trading unless a major resolution of the Anglo-Dutch clashes was achieved).[29] The threat to withdraw from trade certainly rattled the privy council, who responded that they were anxious that the trade should be continued 'insomuch as it is become a business of state' (a revealing remark in itself).[30] But the most effective part of the petition was the fact that it was accompanied by the narrative of the events at Amboyna. This narrative was read out at the Council Table, and at last had the desired effect. It reportedly 'mooved passion in their lordships': some councillors wept, some urged an alliance with the Portugese to 'roote the bloody Dutch out of the Indies', and an order was given that if any Dutch people in England defended the proceedings in Amboyna then their names should be given to the privy council for punishment.[31]

Clearly, the narrative was a powerful piece of writing, and even though printing was not initially attempted, Abbot reported to Dudley Carleton in August that the Company had dispersed 'very many written Coppies', which were in great demand, especially (he said) from MPs, 'and they in the next session hearinge of no Justice done will Certainely bee much alienated in harte upon the readinge of so bloudy a tragedy'.[32] There was no parliament in session, but Abbot's remark was clearly intended to demonstrate the Company's readiness to target the political elite, and most of all the next parliament, in pursuance of their preferred policies against the Dutch.[33] Dudley Carleton, the English ambassador in the Netherlands, certainly warned the Dutch, and the Prince of Orange, of the powerful impact that the EIC might have when parliament reconvened in November.[34]

The next move was clearly to get the narrative into print. Robert Barlow, the English agent in Amsterdam, was voicing the report in London as early as July that the Company's relation of the 'butchery' and 'devilish proceedings' at Amboyna would come out in print.[35] Even if the distribution of manuscript copies was the initial strategy, the continuing production of VOC pamphlets on the issue may have decided the matter, and certainly provided the EIC with the perfect pretext to publish their own account without appearing simply to be courting a popular audience.[36] Off to see the king at Woodstock in August 1624, the Company included among its petitions the specific request that the Company's narration be printed, delivering for the king's gaze copies of the Dutch version, translated into English.[37]

There was certainly nothing new in the Company resorting to the press to publicize their preferred reading of events. We have already noted the pamphlets written by Mun and Digges. But just two years before, in 1622, the Company had also been involved in a very similar pamphlet war with the Dutch East India Company (VOC) to that which was now contemplated over Amboyna. Several English trading stations had been seized by the Dutch in 1622, on the islands of Lontar and Pulu Run, but while the EIC had published two accounts of the events, they were then confronted by a rival account written by the Dutch company, which the VOC had translated into English and circulated in England.[38] They had published their own 'Answer to the Hollanders Declaration' in 1622, but with little success.[39]

With their Amboyna pamphlet, however, the EIC adopted a more wide-ranging and sophisticated approach. This pamphlet – *A True Relation of the Unjust, Cruel and Barbarous Proceedings against the English at Amboyna* – displays a great leap forward in the EIC's grasp of the potential of printed propaganda. Their earlier *Courant of Newes* of 1622 described the Dutch atrocities in Pulu Run and Lontar in a straightforward and unembellished narrative (and these really were massacres, even if the English endured only disgrace, humiliation and physical violence rather than actual death). The account of Amboyna, however, was dramatically different. The first point is not related to the text at all, and that is the fact that the work contains a woodcut representing the tortures at Amboyna. This was a new departure for the EIC, and shows a good sense of how powerful visual images could be. Certainly Archbishop Abbot appears to have been anxious about the damage that such a graphic picture might cause to Anglo-Dutch relations, and urgently sought out his brother Maurice on the matter.[40] The same picture was used on a ballad broadsheet. This was presumably also the work of the EIC itself, as after the verses the reader (or singer) is advised: 'You may read more of this bloody tragedy in a book printed by authority, 1624' (i.e. the *True Relation*).[41] The woodcut is particularly notable as at least one of the figures represented seems to have been lifted from a depiction of a martyr in the 1570 edition of Foxe's *Book of Martyrs*.[42]

The echo is hardly a coincidence, because in fact a good deal of the *True Relation* is in essence an imitation of martyrological works like those of Foxe. The narrative makes explicit attempts to invoke martyrologies: the Englishmen are described as having been 'martyred by the torture'.[43] The English victims are paragons of godly virtue – their leader Towerson is described as 'that honest and godly man', all the English factors ask to receive the sacrament, and they spend the night before their execution praying, singing psalms and refusing Dutch offers of wine.[44] A biblical tone is adopted in the narrative as it reaches the execution of the English factors: 'at the instant of the execution' a sudden darkness falls over the land with 'a sudden and violent gust of winde and tempest'. Strange providences continue to occur after the evil deed: a fatal sickness afflicts the island, a Dutchman goes mad and dies after falling into the Englishmen's grave.[45]

It is this use of providential, martyrological tropes which enabled the EIC to get their message across without seeming to be striving irreligiously to destroy the alliance with the Dutch which godly opinion desired for the war with Spain. Indeed, Maurice Abbot himself expressed to Dudley Carleton his concern that the Amboyna issue was repugnant to the 'agitations of our State', and that he would procure the ill opinions of many of his honourable friends by venturing in the business. Mindful both of the need to appear uninflammatory and of the charges of pro-Spanish sentiment made in popular pamphlets by Scot and others, the introduction to the *True Relation* therefore emphasized that the Company was anxious not to endanger the 'ancient amity' between the English and Dutch nations.[46]

Nevertheless, the Company was all too well aware of how far their cause could be strengthened by appealing to anti-Dutch prejudice. The Company minutes make it crystal-clear that they considered the massacre to represent much more than the activities of an unrepresentative number of individual Dutchmen acting on their own initiative. It was central to the EIC's case that the 'massacre' was a carefully planned plot by the VOC to drive the English out of the East Indies. In discussions, Company members emphasized that the events at Amboyna demonstrated why it was pointless for them to seek to make any treaties with the Dutch – they could not be trusted as a nation.[47] Not only therefore does the *True Relation* seek to maximize the implications of the Dutch actions by emphasizing that the Dutch had executed inhumanity 'upon the English Nation'.[48] It also paints the Dutchmen at Amboyna in the worst possible light: they taunt the English before their execution, they blasphemously conduct their torture on the sabbath day, and they refuse the sacrament to the condemned men.[49] These were all details that could be included in the hope that they could build upon the sort of popular anti-Dutch sentiment of which the Dutch regularly complained. In treaty discussions in 1622 the Dutch representatives had formally complained about 'songs against the States'. Plays such as John Marston's *The Dutch Courtezan* had even provided its villain with expressions in pidgin Dutch, which must have struck a familiar note with its London audience.[50]

While the EIC's *True Relation* was playing to the crowd in one sense, however, it was also very careful to insist that it was doing no such thing. The Company took pains to ensure that the work could not be dismissed (like its

Dutch counterpart) as an anonymous 'libel'. They sought out the king's prior approval, and made sure that the Company arms were prominently displayed on the pamphlet, which it was claimed was published 'by authority' (unlike their earlier pamphlets on the Pulu Run and Lontar massacres, which had been published in Amsterdam).[51]

The pamphlet also paid particular attention to defending itself from the charge that the Company was being deliberately populist and seeking to excite public opinion. Rather, the introduction to the pamphlet emphasized that the Company had taken every care to pursue their grievances in a private way – they were deliberately not seeking to bring in the public. It was the Dutch company that had sought to do that.[52]

This was not entirely disingenuous. The EIC were not of course averse to creating a random 'public opinion' in their favour: 2,000 copies of *A True Relation* were printed and 'dispersed into all parts of England', and these must have reached a diverse readership. [53] But the Company were also seeking to address another 'public sphere' that was socially and politically very specific and limited. Circulation began with the nobility: it was resolved by the Company to distribute copies of the book 'to some principall Persons of the Nobility, and if they bee well taken then to adventure to putt abroad the rest, which if they shall doe, the benefit will pay for the rest'. Three weeks later the Company gave even more explicit directions, emphasizing that 'principall Care' should be had that a copy of the book 'of the fairest binding' should be presented to each member of the privy council, and also 'the principall Nobility residing in and about London'.[54] The EIC knew whose opinions they really needed to swing: the nobility, courtiers and gentry parliamentarians who were best placed to sway policy, and whom they were usually happy to have as members of the Company

The EIC did not confine their campaign simply to the publication of the *True Relation*, however. They also commissioned an enormous painting. The Company were clearly determined to create a large depiction of the Amboyna massacre, and in the floating of the possible commission there was a suggestion that it be 'cutt out in brasse'. In the event, the commission went to a painter, one Richard Greenbury. Greenbury's work was later described as 'a verie lardge picture' in which the tortures and executions inflicted at Amboyna were 'lively, largely and artificially' painted, telling ·'the whole manner', 'describing the whole action', 'done to the life', apparently on cloth.[55] It seems likely that it was a life-size picture, and we can safely assume that, unlike the woodcuts, it was lavishly coloured, with a good deal of red paint. The painting also included the text of the petition delivered by the Netherlanders to Queen Elizabeth to succour them in their distress – presumably the more to emphasize the Dutchmen's perfidy. We can get some idea of the extraordinary size of this painting from the fact that Greenbury demanded the collosal sum of £100 for it. Clearly this was no small portrait but a major canvas that might have covered an entire wall.

Clearly, such an enormous picture was not intended simply for Company members to contemplate in their house, for all that they protested (after Dutch complaints) that they had commissioned the picture 'not with intent to stir up the people to tumult, but thereby to keep in their owne house a perpetuall memory of that most bloudy and treacherous villany'.[56] The Dutch, it was reported, were afraid that the picture had been made with the intention that the members of the impending parliament should see it, and there seems little reason to doubt that it was intended to be on public display, and that it would have coincided exactly with the meeting of the 1625 parliament. Indeed, in February Greenbury was ordered 'not too much to hasten the finishing of that picture' – surely one of the very few times in history when a painter has been instructed to move more slowly.[57] After a meeting with the privy council the Company had to agree that they would refuse to show the picture to 'divers knights and other people of worth who have pressed much to see the same because it should not provoake them as it hath incensed many who heretofore have taken view thereof'.[58] So inflammatory was it that the Council gave order that the door of the Company's house in which the picture stood should be kept locked.[59] Here we can observe a different sort of 'publishing' (and it is interesting to note that this precise term was used by the privy council), but one which required no publishing licence; a very public artefact which the Company could still claim (however unconvincingly) was for their purely private use.

In the event, Buckingham expressed his pleasure that the picture of the Amboyna massacre should be sent to him, and there it seems to have remained (or, more likely, been destroyed).[60] Greenbury certainly never got his £100, being given a mere £40, along with the complaint that he had permitted 'such a multitude' to have sight of the picture in his house 'for by the viewe thereof not onely that picture was taken away but divers other Conceipts upon the same subiect was quashed'.[61] It is perhaps worth noting here, not just the Company's frustration that the premature exhibition of the painting had prevented its effective use, but also their concern that by allowing a 'multitude' to view it Greenbury had courted too popular an audience.

But what were these 'divers other Conceipts upon the same subject' which, to the EIC's frustration, had been stopped as a result of Greenbury's indiscretion? The first was a sermon entitled *The Stripping of Joseph*, republished by one Dr Myriell, with a dedication to Maurice Abbot and the EIC. The sermon was the work of the deceased Robert Wilkinson, and had been delivered back in 1618 before King James. It was Myriell's contention that in this sermon 'the present cruelty of the Dutch is reproved, and deciphered some years since, though not in their persons, or the particular case of Amboyna'. In fact, the sermon, on the theme of fraternal betrayal, looks far more like a condemnation of Englishmen's failure to aid their co-religionists. Myriell's preface wrenched the text completely out of this context, and instead provided an intemperate critique of the Dutch. Their actions showed 'more than Scythian barbarisme' which made the Dutch 'stink before other Nations'. If they did not make reparation for 'this execrable Villainy', he warned them, 'none of your Cities and Territories shall drink in our blood without just revenge'. The religious problem for pro-Company pamphleteers (of how to excuse an attack on fellow Protestants) was dealt with in an ingenious fashion: the Dutch behaviour was compared throughout with the savagery of Roman Catholics (there is a strong anti-papal tone throughout Myriell's lengthy preface), and in a final note by the printer it was suggested that the Dutch who committed the deed were in fact 'either Atheisticall or Arminian'. In theory, there was nothing here that would directly upset anti-Catholic Calvinists.[62] Indeed, it henceforth became common for Englishmen to associate the 'massacre' and the VOC leadership with the Arminians.[63]

The Company denied before the privy council that they had had any involvement in Myriell's production, and it seems reasonable to assume that the initial inspiration was Myriell's own. Nevertheless, the Company was happy to accept Myriell's dedication and his gift of twenty-four 'fair bound' copies of the book, and gave him a reward of £10 for his pains.[64] The other 'Conceipts' were a play and a broadsheet, for both of which the Company denied responsibility. The play was apparently blocked by the privy council just before it was due to be performed. While it does not seem to survive, it apparently covered 'not only the tragedy of Amboyna, but also such other wrongs as the English suffer by the Dutch, in England, Groenland, New England, and ellswhere'.[65] The other piece was a work variously described as 'a printed piece of the several tortures in effigy of our men at Amboyna' or 'a pamphlett expressinge in Effigie the severall tortures' or 'a picture in the quallity of a libell wherein is described in effigie the tortures executed upon the English at Amboyna, togeather with a writing casting the fault generally upon the Dutch Nation', allegedly printed in the Spanish Netherlands. This may well refer to the reprinting of the narrative section of the *True Relation* by the English Catholic press at St Omer, which (it has been suggested) may have sought to use the Company's pamphlet as recusant propaganda to dissuade English troops from fighting on the side of the Dutch.[66]

The Company denied involvement in all three of these works,[67] but they provide striking examples of how, once a patriotic audience had been primed, a company could then in part sit back and watch a series of initiatives from independent authors, printers and playwrights. These independent contributors may have been enraged by what they had read and heard, or alert to the commercial possibilities of feeding popular anger (or presumably both), or possibly (in the Catholic case) seizing on the value of the Amboyna incident for feeding into different confessional battles altogether.[68] In Myriell's case, too, there was clearly the hope that the commercial opportunity would also involve patronage from the Company itself. Indeed, Myriell would not be the last author for whom a tirade upon the evils of the Amboyna massacre would seem to provide the easiest and most obvious route to winning the East India Company's favour (or at least placating their anger). In the 1630s one of their erring employees, Walter Montford, wrote a whole play extolling the virtues of the EIC and deploring the events at Amboyna in the hope of having Company charges against him dropped.[69]

The danger, of course, was that these inflammatory marginal works might excite government fears of a disorderly 'popularity'. That is indeed what happened in this case, as the Company found itself carpeted before the privy council, and had to endure the suppression of all four 'Conceipts'. Maurice Abbot had noted with delight that people's horror at the Dutch cruelties on Amboyna was proving a great help to righting wrongs – the only danger was when this started to appear in government eyes as a threat to public order. After 1625 the Company's pressure for a resolution of the Amboyna affair continued, but they seem to have become slightly more circumspect about the means employed.[70]

IV

What, then, did the EIC gain from this combination of commissioned and uncommissioned reflections on Amboyna? One thing we can note from the outset is that there were fewer attacks on the EIC in parliament (although there were still plenty of private petitions to parliament against the Company in 1626, including another one from the indefatigable Lady Dale).[71]

As for government dealings with the Dutch, the preferred EIC solution all along was the seizure of ships of the VOC.[72] As Dutch prevarication increased, so this increasingly became the solution threatened by the government. James was certainly happy to encourage it. He had commented to the Dutch ambassador Caron in 1621 that his subjects would not give him any rest until he had granted them letters of marque for reprisals against Dutch shipping as an answer to Dutch exactions against the English in the East Indies.[73] In 1625, while letters of marque supposedly went out to stop Dutch ships, the English captains who were in a position to execute them always seemed confused and unsure as to their orders, and the Dutch vessels sailed on undisturbed. The East India Company, which provided a regular stream of information concerning Dutch shipping that could be stopped, complained furiously at these failures.[74] For all the Company's urgings, however, they were more than ready to deny any direct responsibility. When Secretary Conway demanded of the EIC in exasperation what on earth the English ships were meant to do if the VOC ships were well armed and ready to fight, he was met with the response that this was 'State business', and therefore nothing to do with the EIC.[75]

Once the EIC finally thought that they had had strong orders sent out to arrest Dutch shipping, it was only to discover that the letters ordering reprisals had been suspended for eighteen months by Charles as part of the Treaty of Southampton of September 1625, agreed with the Dutch in order to support the war against the Habsburgs. This was the real rock on which the EIC's hopes of revenge for Amboyna were wrecked – the demands of Charles and Buckingham's war policy.

EIC resentment was obvious (although it would be fair to say that Charles had been dealt a very poor hand by James, who had saddled him with an EIC furious over the money extorted from it because of Ormuz, and bought off with the promise of reprisals against the Dutch). Charles did not help matters, however, by the extraordinarily high-handed manner that he adopted in discussions. While the text of royal letters dictated to Conway and Coke displays genuine concern on Charles's part, the king's body language always sent the wrong signals. One description by Company officials of the delivery of yet another EIC petition to Charles in June 1625 noted how Charles 'looked upon it and found it long. He demanded what the matter was ... to which remonstrance he signified three several times that he would take care of it, and folded up the petition and put it in his pocket.'[76]

The EIC did not accept with good grace the eighteen-month suspension of hostilities. In fact, they kept up constant demands to Charles for the seizure of VOC ships.[77] Nevertheless, whatever their frustration, the Company were prepared to wait on Charles, and there was no attempt made to publish a new account of Amboyna (although they had one ready), or to inflame public opinion in order to press the king further. It was only when the ending of the eighteen-month suspension approached in January 1627, and when Buckingham asked for a statement in writing of the Company's grievances against the Dutch, that the Company looked into the printing of a further tract on Amboyna.[78] Again, there was a sense that there was no point in publishing tracts on Amboyna unless the government was already implying some positive support. In the event, the new publication ended up being called in in record time: the Company complained in June 1627 that the printer, Nicholas Bourne, had dispersed copies of the pamphlet in advance – even selling one to the Dutch ambassador, whose inevitable complaint to the privy council led to the book's suppression even before the EIC itself had managed to receive copies.[79] Foreign ambassadors could usually be reasonably sure of securing the suppression of hostile books, as they had been able to suppress the 'Conceipts' on Amboyna of 1625, but this was only further evidence of why the East India Company had to tread so carefully when they brought their complaints over

Amboyna into the public domain. In this case, the Company seem to have found a partial compromise by apparently providing the privy council with handwritten copies of the pamphlet just two weeks after they were informed that the book had been stayed at the press. The fact that the privy council drew up a memorial the next day to the Dutch ambassadors requiring action on Amboyna and noting that the eighteen months' suspension of hostilities had expired may reflect that the text of the intended pamphlet had had an effect, even if its print publication had been prevented.[80]

The EIC's patience was rewarded in September 1627, when, as promised, Charles did indeed have three VOC ships stayed in Portsmouth, and they were kept hostage for the best part of a year, despite the dire situation of the crown at war simultaneously with France and Spain.[81] Three months after the seizure, the EIC duly lent the crown £30,000. The problem, however, was that the VOC was happy to carry on regardless. By April 1628, with a new parliament and EIC frustration building up again, the Company made its appeal for alternative support. But this was not an appeal to the public masses through plays and pamphlets. Rather, it took the form of a lengthy petition to parliament, composed by Thomas Mun, asking for 'some public declaration' supporting and countenancing the trade, and even in this case the EIC had been careful to gain the prior approval of Secretary Coke before they submitted the petition, so that it could not be construed as hostile to the crown.[82] The *Petition and Remonstrance* was in fact a response to the 'causelesse Complaints in the mouths of many of his Majesties Subjects of all degrees and in all places of the Realme' against the EIC. In just a single brief allusion to Amboyna the Company simply remarked that it waited patiently for a solution, 'wherein we doubt not of his Majesties most gracious favours and resolutions so well begun'.[83] When Charles did finally resolve to release the Dutch ships, he attempted to sugar the pill by sending no fewer than seven privy councillors, including Buckingham and Pembroke, to attend the Company to explain the rationale behind his decision.[84]

That being said, while the petition to parliament was in no way an attempt to court its support against the crown, 1628 did see a notable decline in relations between the Company and the crown. One Thomas Smethwicke launched a violent attack on the policies of the directors of the Company with the clear support of Charles, being closely associated with a simultaneous proposal that the king should be admitted as an adventurer into the Company; and the Company refused to lend the crown £10,000 – a decision based on unimpeachable commercial reasoning, but also doubtless sharpened by resentment at Charles's sponsoring of Smethwicke.[85] In December 1628 there were also reports of 'certain printed papers' going from hand to hand which set down the Amboyna events 'in such manner as may breed much disaffection between the King's subjects and those of the Low Countries', which prompted a proclamation to suppress them. It is not clear what these 'certain printed papers' were – perhaps illegal copies of the second book on Amboyna that had been stopped at the press in April. It is certainly not clear that the EIC was behind the dispersal of these papers.[86] Even if relations with the crown were in decline, however, Maurice Abbot successfully persuaded the Company not to join the customs boycott launched by other companies in 1629, urging that this was unwise for the EIC, 'considering the many occasions they have now with the king, from whom the company cannot expect any favour if herein they show themselves refractory'.[87]

With England suing for peace with France and Spain in 1629–30, however, Charles's leverage on the Dutch was essentially non-existent, and Amboyna was effectively a dead issue. The EIC tried to raise the issue again in pamphleteering in 1632 (although their reprints of the *True Relation* and the *Remonstrance* in that year were suppressed by order of the privy council).[88] This renewed interest of the EIC in lobbying again inspired independent efforts to capitalize on it, in the shape of Walter Mountfort's suppressed play. Pamphleteering was resumed again in 1641, when the political atmosphere seemed conducive, but it was not until the Anglo-Dutch wars of the 1650s and 1660s that Amboyna really captured the public imagination again.

V

What conclusions can we draw from these early years of debate and lobbying over the Amboyna incident? First of all, perhaps, they suggest a caveat for those historians enthusiastically uncovering evidence of a nascent 'public sphere', that we cannot assume the existence of an orchestrated propaganda campaign simply from the fact that there is a collection of pamphlets in the Short Title Catalogue. Parts of the public response to Amboyna do not seem to have been under the EIC's direct control – and there do seem to have been cases of individuals seizing on the Amboyna incident either as a means of gaining Company patronage or in order to exploit commercial opportunities. As I have argued with relation to Laudian propaganda, defences of Laudian policies were not necessarily simply being commissioned by the authorities, but could represent initiatives being seized upon by different individuals for a variety of purposes (and thereby often changing the message that the authorities wanted to hear).[89] Similarly, the violently anti-Dutch tone of Myriell's preface (and presumably of the intended play) may have fitted the Company's sentiments, but not the carefully balanced nature of the message that they were seeking to convey, and left the whole Amboyna issue vulnerable to complaint from the Dutch ambassador, and hence a government crackdown.

This leads us to a second point – and that is the problematic nature of 'popularity', the bringing of matters into an unrestricted domain of public discourse. As other historians have noted, this was an enterprise fraught with potential dangers in this period, as it could easily be branded as potentially subversive. It was vital for the EIC's purposes that it should not be viewed as stirring up trouble or appealing to unruly popular sentiment, and the Company went to some trouble to avoid this impression. That said, it was not a mere matter of tactical rhetoric. There is little evidence that the Company were really seeking to address some broader form of 'public opinion'. They were certainly acutely conscious of a degree of public hostility to their trading activities, and that private petitions at parliament time could create an unfavourable climate. But ultimately it was only the opinion of the political elite, in parliament and at court, whose opinions the EIC were worried about, as it was only here that their charter could ever be seriously endangered. Thus it was parliament time when anxieties about public opinion arose; it was MPs who were to be shown the picture, it was the nobility around London to whom copies of the pamphlet were sent.

Nor was this an attempt to prime parliament, MPs and courtiers to coerce an unwilling government which had not been persuaded by normal petitioning. Rather, the intention seems usually to have been to keep the issue on the boil, building up momentum (and perhaps using this partly to head off any other potential attacks on the EIC), and often the real spur was the fact that the Dutch were spreading contrary ideas – there was clearly a sense that it was important to make sure that the correct account was in the public domain. The Company were acutely conscious that they simply could not afford to burn their boats with the crown. They clearly did not trust Charles or Buckingham, and were quite prepared at times to reject their demands, but they challenged the government most clearly only in a negative sense. Moreover, while Robert Brenner has explained the link between chartered companies and the crown in terms of the traditional exchange of commerical privileges for merchant political and financial support, it must be emphasized that for the EIC *diplomatic* support was also indispensable. The fact that the government *failed* to secure reparations for the EIC means that historians have missed the extent to which (within limits) the government *was* trying to secure redress, and that it was very much in the Company's interest to continue to wait for government action.

At the heart of the Company's strategy, at the heart of its very existence, was the fact that it was not simply a private trading venture but was also, as the Privy Council put it, involved in 'State business'. Moreover, the dichotomies of 'public' and 'private', 'government' and 'opposition', 'State business' and 'private trade' are not necessarily terms that we can use to describe different sides – these are the terms of debate, and the distinctions which are the rhetorical tools of the different protagonists. It is these very terms which are, in a sense, the battleground.

And the EIC provides a useful reminder that this was a battleground that was not just about economic ideology. It is common for the pamphlets of Mun, Digges, Kayll and others to be read only by historians of economic thought, as contributions to the development of a concept of the balance of trade. But they are also tackling political and religious issues too. The battle over the legitimacy of the EIC could not be won simply on economic terms – its political, religious and social legitimacy was also crucial, and the Company's responses to the Amboyna incident were attempts to boost the Company's legitimacy in all these areas.

And this is perhaps also the point at which a case could be made for putting all trading companies (and not just the puritan colonial ventures) squarely into the cultural and ideological history of this period (as well as the political and economic). Not only do the EIC's activities present us with wonderfully rich material for analysing the personality and behaviour of Charles, and of court and city politics, but they also show how some of the contemporary rhetoric of honour, reputation and commonwealth could be deployed in corporate and commercial form.

In particular, if early modern historians are now more attuned to studying how far institutions sought to prime and track an inchoate 'public opinion', it is trading companies, but most of all the joint-stock companies like the EIC, which invite study. For these were organizations which relied on investor confidence for their survival. Hostile rumour can undermine a commercial venture much more rapidly than it can a political career. All foreign trading companies were, in a sense, institutions which were dependent on public support, in the shape of the investors who would provide the capital to keep the company solvent. To keep those investors sweet, the Company needed to ensure that the popular perception of their trade was that it was lucrative. As Andrew Fitzmaurice has shown in his study of the Virginia Company, this was a necessity that could oblige companies to resort to a whole series of measures to stimulate support, by tuning popular pulpits and so on.[90] And commercial monopolies needed to convince people not only of their profitability, but also that they acted throughout in the public interest.[91]

In this chapter I have not looked in the most obvious or richest place for a pre-modern 'public sphere'. But the campaigns over Amboyna can demonstrate the degree to which public opinion and common interest could be invoked and addressed in a manner that was not built on a simple confrontation between a state built on 'representational authority' and a bourgeois public sphere. It can show that the EIC was caught awkwardly between the two – that mercantile interest could seek to exploit elements of a conceived public sphere without using it in simply oppositional mode to a state on which they were ultimately dependent. The EIC seem to have been addressing a very episodic, contingent form of 'public sphere', with a very delimited sense of accessibility. Moreover, given the ambiguous relationship of the EIC with the crown, we could argue that, like the examples being cited more recently in the work of Peter Lake, the Company's attempts to take politics into the political nation were undertaken by what were to some extent members of the establishment.

NOTES

1 M. E. Wilbur, *The East India Company* (Stanford CA, 1945), 101–2.

2 B. Willson, *Ledger and Sword or the Honourable Company* (2 vols, London, etc., 1903) I, 148–78.

3 K. Chaney, 'The Amboyna massacre in English politics, 1624–1632', *Albion* 30 (1999), 588; M. A. Breslow, *A Mirror of England* (Cambridge MA, 1970), 86.

4 K. N. Chaudhuri, *The English East India Company: the Study of an Early Joint-Stock Company, 1600–1640* (London, 1965), 3 n.; cf. *The First Letter-Book of the East India Company, 1600–1619*, ed. G. Birdwood and W. Foster (London, 1892), 12.

5 Chaudhuri, *East India Company*, 29.

6 E.g. the cases of Michleborne and Penkewell (R. Ashton, *The City and the Court, 1603–1643*, Cambridge, 1979, 89–90), Sir James Cunningham (103) and Sir William Courteen (140).

7 E.g. BL, India Office Records [IOR], B/7 (Ct Min. Bk V), 299–301.

8 IOR, B/8 (Ct Min. Bk VI), 449, 450, 450–4.

9 Thomas Mun, *A Discourse of Trade* (1621), 10.

10 Edmund Scott, *An exact Discourse of the Subtilties, Fashions, Policies, Religion, and Ceremonies of the East Indians* (London, 1606), reprinted in Samuel Purchas, *Purchas his Pilgrimes* (4 vols, London, 1625) I, 164–85; L. Manley, *Literature and Culture in Early Modern London* (Cambridge, 1995), 286, 290–1.

11 E.g. *Calendar of State Papers Colonial, East Indies* [CSPC], *1622–1624*, 82. Cf. *ibid.*, 236–7.

12 Robert Kayll, *The Trades Increase* (1615), 13–32, 53–5; Thomas Scot, *Vox Populi* (London, 1622).

13 [Alexander Leighton?], *The Interpreter* (1622).

14 Dudley Digges, *The Defence of Trade* (London, 1615); IOR, B/8 (Ct Min. Bk VI), 316–20. (They do grudgingly allow the churchwardens to be present at the distribution if they want to.) The EIC seems to have become less insistent on this point in later years: see *Court Minutes of the East India Company, 1635–1640*, ed. E. B. Sainsbury (Oxford, 1907), 133.

15 Chaudhuri, *East India Company*, 14–22 and *passim*.

16 See also *CSPC 1622–24*, 68–9. Mun's work prompted further contributions from Edward Misselden and Gerald de Malynes. For a useful summary of their debate see David Wootton, 'The study of society', in P. Burke and H. Inalcik (eds), *History of Humanity* V (London, 1999), 98–9.

17 Digges, *Defence of Trade*, 38–9; *CSPC 1622–24*, 179 (cf. 189). Such payments may have been the particular inspiration of the godly Smith, even if others were aware of the practical value of such public charity. Nicholas Tyacke has suggested that it was Smith

who initiated the scheme as Governor, and largely chose the recipients, who included the lecturers of the notoriously puritan St Antholin's. Payment of St Antholin's lecturers (at least) seems to have been discontinued with Smith's death in 1621: N. Tyacke, *Aspects of English Protestantism, c. 1530–1700* (Manchester, 2001), 19–20

18 Conrad Russell, *Parliaments and English Politics, 1621–1629* (Oxford, 1979), p. 97; K. N. Chaudhuri, 'The East India Company and the export of treasure in the early seventeenth century', *Economic History Review* 16 (1963–64), 23–38.

19 IOR, B/8 (Ct Min. Bk VI), 449–50; Russell, *Parliaments*, 183.

20 R. Lockyer, *Buckingham* (1981), 184, 230; CJ, 846, 847.

21 IOR, B/8 (Ct Min. Bk VI), 490–97; *CSPC 1622–24*, 295.

22 IOR, B/8 (Ct Min. Bk VI), 218–48, 523–36, 536–40.

23 Ashton, *City and Court*, 114–16. *Pace* Ashton, however, Sandys's *bête noire* Sir Thomas Smythe was *not* Governor of the Company by 1624: there were broader issues at work, and certainly the EIC did not see itself as merely being targeted by a small faction, although it did complain of 'false friends'.

24 IOR, B/8 (Ct Min. Bk VI), 544–7.

25 *Ibid.*, 550–7.

26 *Ibid.*

27 IOR, B/9 (Ct Min. Bk VII), 1–2.

28 This was presumably the *Narration* – for a copy of this see *CSPC 1622–24*, 303–20 (which notes the variants from the printed version). Carleton was not immediately convinced: writing to Sir William Trumbull in July, he commented noncommittally, 'where the truth lies [between the Dutch and English accounts], we are searching as neere as we can at such distance': BL, Trumbull Ms XVII/102.

29 IOR, B/9 (Ct Min. Bk VII), 16.

30 Chaudhuri, *East India Company*, 30; IOR, B/9 (Ct Min. Bk VII), 23.

31 IOR, B/9 (Ct Min. Bk VII), 31, 33. It is not entirely clear from this account whether it was the councillors or the EIC representatives who urged the alliance with the Portuguese.

32 PRO, SP 84/119, fol. 47r: Maurice Abbot to Dudley Carleton, 7 August 1624.

33 *Ibid.*

34 PRO, SP 84/120, fol. 81r: Dudley Carleton to Prince of Orange, 14/24 September 1624 (*CSPC 1622–24*, 400, 402).

35 *CSPC 1622–24*, 328.

36 IOR, B/9 (Ct Min. Bk VII), 62. Cf. PRO, SP 84/119, fols 60–1 (Carleton to Barlow, 8/18 August 1624); 84/119, fol. 85r (Barlow to D.C., 10 August 1624). The anonymous tract had been published in Amsterdam, first in Dutch, and then translated into English and circulated in England under the title *A True Declaration of the News that came out of the East Indies*. The VOC denied having publishing the work, but it was claimed that their stockholders had helped to distribute it (*CSPC 1622–24*, 339), and they issued a similar work soon afterwards giving account of the confessions: *An Authentick Copy of the Confessions and Sentences against M. Towerson and Complices, concerning the Bloudy Conspiracy enterprised against the Castle at Amboyna*. It was rumoured that Boreel, one of the directors of the VOC, had written *A True Declaration*.

37 IOR, B/9 (Ct Min. Bk VII), 79.

38 *A Courant of Newes from the East India: A True Relation of the Taking of the Islands of Lantore and Polaroone* (Amsterdam, 1622); *A Second Courant of Newes from the East India in Two Letters* (Amsterdam, 1622). These were in response to the Dutch company publishing pamphlets on the matter – one of which was translated into English and circulated in England, entitled *The Hollanders Declaration of the Affairs of the East Indies or A True Relation of that which passed in the Islands of Banda in the East Indies: in the Yeare of our Lord God, 1622* (Amsterdam, 1622).

39 *An Answer to the Hollanders Declaration, concerning the Occurrents of the East India* (Amsterdam, 1622).

40 IOR, B/9 (Ct Min. Bk VII), 329.

41 *Newes out of East India: of the cruell and bloody Usage of our English Merchants and others at Amboyna, by the Netherlandish Governour and Councell there. To the tune of Braggendary* (1624) (STC547).

42 John Foxe, *Actes and Monuments* (London, 1583), 780. I am grateful to Dr Thomas Freeman for this reference. Further significance may be attached to a different woodcut image used in the Dutch translation of the EIC pamphlet, representing the use of candles for torture but not the use of water: *Een waer verhael vande onlancksche ongerechte, wreede, ende onmenschelycke procedure teghen de Enghelsche tot Amboyna* (1624) (STC 7455). The image has presumably been taken from another work, although I have not yet been able to identify the source. The halberds and ruffs on the soldiers make it possible that the woodcut was lifted from a representation of the tortures inflicted by Alva's Spanish troops on the Dutch. If this were the case, it would have been deliberately chosen to increase the impact on a Dutch readership.

43 *A True Relation*, 28.

44 *Ibid.*, 19, 24, 26, 27, 28, 37.

45 *Ibid.*, 29, 30.

46 *Ibid.*, sigs Ar–A4v.

47 E.g. IOR, B/9 (Ct Min. Bk VII), 31.

48 *A True Relation*, 38.

49 *Ibid.*, 12, 37.

50 *CSPC 1622–24*, 28; John Marston, *The Dutch Courtezan*. On anti-Dutch attitudes see also Breslow, *Mirror*, 94–5; O. P. Grell, *Dutch Calvinists in early Stuart London* (Leiden, 1989), 16–26.

51 The Company formally instructed that the arms of the Company should be set on the front of the book 'in token that they avowe them to bee true', and 'that it may not bee taken for a libell' IOR, B/9 (Ct Min. Bk VII), 151.

52 *A True Relation*, sigs A2r–A3r.

53 IOR, B/9 (Ct Min. Bk VII), 239–58. I am grateful to Jason Peacey for emphasizing this point to me.

54 IOR, B/9 (Ct Min. Bk VII), 149 (6 October 1624), 151 (8 October 1624), 178 (29 October 1624).

55 IOR, B/9 (Ct Min. Bk VII), 359, 418; PRO, SP 84/122, fol. 165r

56 PRO, SP 84/122, fol. 165r (EIC to Carleton, 19 February 1624/5).

57 *Ibid.*, fol. 165v; IOR, B/9 (Ct Min. Bk VII), 346.

58 PRO, SP 84/122, fol. 176 (EIC to Carleton, 26 February 1624/5).

59 IOR, B/9 (Ct Min. Bk VII), 351.

60 *Ibid.*, 359.

61 *Ibid.*, 418. Cf. IOR, B/10 (Ct Min. Bk VIII), 20, 31–2.

62 Robert Wilkinson, *The Stripping of Joseph: or The Crueltie of Brethren* (London, 1625).

63 Thomas Scot, *Symmachia*, 34; *CSPC 1625–29*, 406, 492.

64 IOR, B/9 (Ct Min. Bk VII), 343, 346.

65 PRO, SP 84/122, fol. 165r.

66 *Ibid.*; IOR, B/9 (Ct Min. Bk VII), 350–1; *The Purchas Handbook*, ed. L. E. Pennington (2 vols, Hakluyt Society, London, 1997) II, 525 n.

67 PRO, SP 84/122, fol. 165r. Breslow (*Mirror*, 86) repeats the charge that the play was 'commissioned' (implying by the Company) but provides no evidence to support it.

68 A slightly different case is that of the publication of the theological geographer Samuel Purchas's four-volume *Pilgrimes* (1625): see A. Milton, *Catholic and Reformed* (Cambridge, 1995), 505.

69 F. S. Boas, *Shakespeare and the Universities* (Oxford, 1923), chapters 8–10.

70 *CSPC 1622–24*, 417.

71 *CSPC 1625–29*, 192–3, 195, 200.

72 IOR, B/9 (Ct Min. Bk VII), 31.

73 Chaudhuri, *East India Company*, 30 (*CSPC 1617–21*, 434).

74 IOR, B/9 (Ct Min. Bk VII), 385–9, 415–19, 419–26; B/10 (Ct Min. Bk VIII), 45–54, 78–88, 103–9, 131–7.

75 *CSPC 1625–29*, 22–3. Similarly, back in July 1624, when the privy council had asked the Company how the government should respond to the massacre, the EIC representatives had excused themselves 'as a thing ill becoming them to Direct the State' (IOR, B/9 (Ct Min. Bk VII), 31).

76 IOR, B/9 (Ct Min. Bk VII), 78–88.

77 *CSPC 1625–29*, 113, 188, 122, 126, 246.

78 *Ibid.*, 300. It is worth noting the EIC's link with Buckingham. It is entirely true that the Company provided the necessary information for one of the articles in the impeachment of Buckingham in 1626 (relating to the Ormuz affair), but this was not a straightforward working-out of Company resentment. In fact, the Court of Committees had anxious discussions about whether or not to comply with the Commons' request for the information. And it is striking that when Buckingham returned to England in 1627 it was he whom the Company repeatedly sought out as a mediator with the king (e.g. *CSPC 1625–29*, 303–4, 308, 309–10).

79 IOR, B/11 (Ct Min. Bk IX), pp. 348, 362, 376, 386, 484; B/12 (Ct Min. Bk X), 420–4.

80 *CSPC 1625–29*, 342–3.

81 *Ibid.*, 390, 395.

82 *Ibid.*, 489, 490.

83 *The Petition and Remonstrance of the Governor and Company of Merchants of London trading to the East Indies* (London, 1628), sig. A2v, 24.

84 *CSPC 1625–29*, 528.

85 Ashton, *City and Court*, 127–8; Chaudhuri, *East India Company*, 221.

86 PRO, SP 16/122/2.

87 Brenner, *Merchants and Revolution*, 236.

88 PRO, PC 2/41, 166, 217.

89 A. Milton, 'The creation of Laudianism: a new approach', in T. Cogswell, R. Cust and P. Lake (eds), *Politics, Religion and Popularity* (Cambridge, 2001), 162–84.

90 A. Fitzmaurice, '"Every man, that prints, adventures": the rhetoric of the Virginia Company sermons', in L. A. Ferrell and P. McCullough (eds), *The English Sermon Revised* (Manchester, 2000).

91 See Wright, *Middle-Class Culture in Elizabethan England*, 452–3; G. B. Hotchkiss (ed.), *A Treatise of Commerce, by John Wheeler* (New York, 1931).

Chapter 8

Men, the 'public' and the 'private' in the English Revolution

Ann Hughes

In July 1647 Ann Overton wrote to the Yorkshire parliamentarian Ferdinando, Lord Fairfax seeking his help for her husband, Robert. She wanted Fairfax to intervene with his son Sir Thomas, commander of parliament's New Model Army, to obtain a post in the northern army for Robert Overton, in place of his service far from home in the south of England. Ann Overton's arguments were marked by a clear contrast between public and private interests, with pious hopes that 'private intrists obstructe not publick concernments'. In this case, Ann Overton was able to argue that the public good coincided with her own personal desire to have her husband close at hand:

> if he wear as like to promote the service of this country in the other as he is heer, I should cheerfully as formerly, so now resine him up to the publike and forgett al privat intrists and relations, but when I consider the malignity of these parts, the paucitie of publick spirited men, the necessity ther is that such should be intrusted, whoe have by their meritt intrissted themselves in the countries' afections ...

The public interest demanded Overton's appointment although the 'fraternity of agitators' who had prompted a mutiny against the Presbyterian northern commander, Sydenham Poyntz, favoured the appointment of Robert Lilburne under Poyntz's likely replacement, John Lambert.

The contrasts between the public and the private were combined in Overton's letter with vivid images of manly loyalty underpinning parliament's godly cause:

> When I consider what ingratitude ther is in almost al men of this present age I am strouke into a silent admiration that God should do such great things for so ungratful a people as we are and wish that present mercies abused prepare not future unavoidable iudgments for this land. To be plaine Sir, 'tis not unknown how my husband in the worst of times hath stood like Hercules his piller, enduring all shockes, yet ferme to his principles of promoting the public good, to the great damage of his person and estat in outward things.

He had ever been 'taken up with love to honest and honorable action'.[1]

The Pillars of Hercules are the two peaked rocks on either side of the straits of Gibralter where the hero broke apart the mountains separating the Mediterranean Sea from the ocean. Both Hercules himself and, very obviously, the pillars were symbols of steadfast manliness. Hercules, associated in the early modern period with Christian fortitude, and the establishing of peace through military strength, was subsequently used to represent fraternal solidarity during the French Revolution.[2] Praising loyalty to the public good in strongly masculine terms is common during the English Revolution of the 1640s and 1650s. Lucy Hutchinson, a better known parliamentarian woman, who wrote about her republican husband at length in prose and verse, is an obvious example:

> Religious, Good, Wise, Honorable, Just
> Constant to God and to his Publick trust
> ... Him selfe cheife Pillar of his house, They all
> He taken up, did unsupported fall[3]

Decisively masculine visual imagery was also used to present Oliver Cromwell in 1653 as an active, effective godly ruler in a print – 'Cromwell between the Pillars' – that seems to have presented a deliberate contrast with the frontispiece of *Eikon Basilike* (1649), which showed the passive, feminized suffering of the martyred Charles I.[4]

These examples highlight the themes of this chapter: the centrality of a concept of the 'public' to parliamentarian debates and parliamentarian political identities in the mid-seventeenth century, and the gendering of this concept as robustly masculine. The meanings of 'public' most often deployed in this period and their gendered character need some initial clarification. A rhetorical or theoretical distinction between the 'public' and the 'private' is of long standing, being indeed one of the most 'influential, structuring myths of western culture'.[5] Richard Cust's chapter in this volume reveals the classical, humanist and religious influences on the 'public man' of Tudor and early Stuart England – a man devoted to public service in the public interest and for the public good. In classical and modern formulations alike private is connected with the domestic or familial, but in late medieval and early modern usage it more commonly and simply meant the individual or the particular as opposed to the common or collective: 'This private–public distinction is a way of thinking about the human person in relation to his or her fellows, in which the collective is more highly valued than the individual.'[6]

This conventional and enduring contrast underwent a transformation in the mid-seventeenth century when parliament – a representative institution – took up arms against a personal monarchy. Geoff Baldwin suggests that 'public' became used as a noun as much as an adjective, to describe an entity or community, referring to the political nation rather than to the public interest or service.[7] Baldwin points to the importance of Henry Parker's stress on parliament (properly the House of Commons) as a representative institution, acquiring its legitimacy from representing the 'public'. It is not necessary to posit such a clear contrast; many different understandings of 'public' tended to overlap when Parker and others argued in the early 1640s that parliament was better placed to govern in the public interest or to attract true public servants. Parliament was the representative of the people and also, quite simply, a formal, collective, institution, part of an impersonal state, whereas monarchs and their courtiers were irredeemably private. In the more developed republican framework of the 1650s such ideas were expressed particularly clearly, as Marchamont Nedham argued against the monarchical tendencies of the Protectorate: 'it being usual in Free-States to be more tender of the Publick in all their Decrees, than of particular Interests: whereas the case is otherwise in a Monarchy'.[8]

Imprecise, overlapping uses of the 'public' are ever-present in parliamentarian discourse, found in propaganda, more developed political theorizing and personal lobbying. More complex implications might lurk in an apparently straightforward request for a personal or 'private' favour. In June 1646 Sir Thomas Fairfax recommended the petition of a 'poore widdow', Bridget Powell of Pembroke, to the Speaker of the House of Commons. He was 'very loath to trouble you with a private business when your tyme is soe much taken upp with the Publiq' but her sufferings (in the siege of Pembroke) 'have been greate' and her 'affections to the publique' well known. Her dead husband 'stood all waies well affected to the proceedings of both the Honourable Houses of Parliament' and two sons still served in parliament's army.[9] The Powells' loyal adherence to the 'public' (a noun that might mean parliament, or the state or the community of the well affected) made her private suit a valid concern of parliament, a matter of public interest. A more obviously politicized deployment of very similar language is found in a late work of the Leveller John Lilburne, arguing against his banishment and imprisonment: 'it is said mine is but a private business and the Publique takes up all your time … To which I answer: Can there be a more publike businesse in the world; then the doing of justice and relieving the oppressed.'[10] It was the crucial political tactic of the Levellers, and of Lilburne in particular, to make their own individual 'private' oppression the basis for a generalized, public critique of parliamentary tyranny. An initially neutral contrast between private and public, one and many, almost always hinted at the normative or political argument that the general or collective was to be valued above the specific or individual. The private then had inevitable connotations of selfishness or even corruption. In parliament's *Souldiers Catechisme* answers to the question of 'What do you think of those Protestants which sit still' and do not join parliament's military struggle included 'they are of base and private spirits' or 'faint-hearted cowards'. The catechism was optimistic about parliament's success because 'the most of our Commanders are men of dis-ingaged and Publique spirits' and their soldiers deserved respect because they were 'men of publike spirits, and true lovers of their countrey'.[11]

The bitter divisions of the 1640s and 1650s thus in themselves provided a vital context for a pervasive rhetoric of the public and the private.[12] It was not at all clear what the public interest was or through what allegiance an honourable public service was to be found. Strongly held, and widely divergent, views of where proper public authority lay and how it should be exercised complicated the justifications of individual political stances or trajectories. Contrasts between the public and the private were mobilized in debates between royalists and parliamentarians: for parliamentarians 'The ideal state was one where public interests prevailed over private concerns; monarchy tended inexorably towards the private interests of the prince and his favourites, subsuming the whole nation under a single household'. The 1649 act abolishing the office of king declared that to have power in 'any single person' was 'unnecessary, burdensome, and dangerous to the liberty, safety and public interest of the people'.[13] But the same rhetoric was used in the intimate but very bitter conflicts surrounding rival understandings of the parliamentary cause. Even in the relatively trivial, intra-parliamentarian matter of commissions in a provincial army, all claimants attached their personal ambitions to particular versions of the public interest. – as an associate of Poyntz's rival Lambert had it, 'I confess I think the taking of the Major General [Lambert] out of the North will do a great disservice to this nation, and feare this rather a designe to advance and satisfie particular interests then the publique service'.[14]

How do these understandings of 'public' relate to the 'public sphere'? As this volume testifies, the Habermasian concept has been pushed back from the end of the seventeenth century, where Habermas himself located its emergence. It has been detached or set free by many scholars from its bourgeois connections. Nonetheless, rather than adopting a vague version of the 'public sphere', it is worth being precise about how far Habermas's term is relevant to this discussion. Habermas's 'public sphere' (a realm of communicative practices and associations) is located somewhere between the state and the intimate sphere of the family:

> The bourgeois public sphere may be conceived above all as the sphere of private people come together as a public; they soon claimed the public sphere regulated from above against the public authorities themselves, to engage them in a debate over the general rules governing relations in the basically privatized but publicly relevant sphere of commodity exchange and social labor. The medium of this political confrontation was peculiar and without historical precedent: people's public use of their reason.[15]

The public sphere thus brought together 'private people' whose greatest fulfilment was to be found in the private or 'intimate sphere of the conjugal family'.[16] They adopted a critical or oppositional stance towards the state or public authority. The men and women who are discussed in this chapter were very different. It was within the public, the world of politics, that they sought fulfilment, and family life might well be an unwelcome diversion or distraction. Discussions of the public versus the private reflected the dilemmas of men who were or sought to become part of public authority. This concern with public service in the public interest is connected with a more recognizable version of the 'public sphere' because in the 1640s and 1650s there were so many conflicting versions of that public interest. Rival claimants to honest public service had to appeal for validation and support from divided communities. Participants in disputes over the public good evoked common principles and could be seen as engaged in rational or at least ordered debate. Nonetheless a 'public sphere' on the Habermas model is somewhat distant from my concerns. More relevant is the preference for the public life found in classical and then civic humanist views of politics, akin to Habermas's ancient or classical public sphere or to Hannah Arendt's rehabilitation of classical republican models.[17]

For several reasons the public interest was usually gendered male within parliamentarian discourse. In the first place gender operated as an influential symbolic system; it was 'a primary way of signifying relations of power'. Hierarchical contrasts in general, and political divisions in particular, could be vividly portrayed in gendered terms, with a male label attached to the positive pole of any binary. Because male superiority and male authority within the household were taken for granted, this was a most effective way of indicating approval.[18] In Norwich, for example, both sides in a 1646 petitioning dispute between Independents and Presbyterians adopted gendered imagery to denigrate their opponents. The Independents accused the Norwich Presbyterians of aping a London Presbyterian remonstrance: the 'London Remonstrance ... proves Generative, and hath begotten a Norwich Remonstrance ... but abortion hath been its doome'. The Presbyterians responded to this smear of a feminized, monstrous birth with an assertion of their rational masculinity: 'Sir you are mistaken, London Remonstrance was a masculine Remonstrance, Judicious discreet men that had a hand in it. They are your Female Petitions of the Independents that are the engenderers, such as are filled with maids and girles hands.'[19] Imagery of male strength and female weakness was deployed in another dispute over parliamentarian aims when the prophetess Elizabeth Poole interrupted the Army Council debating the trial of the king in December–January 1648–49. Poole recounted a vision wherein she saw a man, who represented the army and who expressed 'his respect unto his Country, to its liberty and freedome which he should gladly been a sacrifice for'. A woman signified 'the weake and imperfect distressed state of the land ... This woman was full of imperfection, crooked, weake, sickly, imperfect.'[20]

Gendered imagery endorsed or undermined general political positions, but it had a particular force within the public–private polarity. The association of women with 'secrecy, intrigue and deception' was common within parliamentarian thinking, as it was in the French political culture of the eighteenth century. The royalist intriguer Lady Aubigny was described affectionately by Edward Hyde as 'a woman of a very great wit, and most trusted and conversant in those intrigues which at that time could be best managed and carried on by ladies', but a parliamentarian broadside put her at the centre of a group portrait of 'forraigne and homebred treacherous Enemies'.[21] In her verse epic of Genesis, the republican Lucy Hutchinson showed how the fall of Eve revealed the dangers of secrecy:

> But so the Devil then, so lewd men now
> Prevail, when women privacies allow.[22]

Furthermore, characteristically early modern modes of thinking about politics through analogies between the household and the kingdom, and thus between fatherly and kingly power, or between marriage and consensual political subordination made gendered understandings of politics inevitable. To some extent such analogies chimed more easily with royalist allegiance, for, as Herrup has written, 'the household was the emulative structure that at once illustrated and legitimated the benefits of monarchy'.[23] Although Elizabeth Poole used marital analogies to criticize the army's plans to try the king, most parliamentarians rejected for obvious reasons the royalist stress in the 1630s on royal marriage as an embodiment of right order and harmony in the kingdom.[24] Henry Parker is often but effectively quoted: 'the wife is inferior in nature, and was created for the assistance of man' but 'it is otherwise in the state betwixt man and man' for that 'civil difference ... is for civil ends';[25] the republican John Hall made a similar point in 1650: 'As for the antiquity from Adam it is true, before his fall his dominion was large and wide but it was ... oeconomically, not despotically over his wife and children, But what is this to Civil Government?'[26] Whether or not they were fully committed republicans, parliamentarians tended towards a classically derived conception of politics which, following Aristotle, regarded the household and the formal political realm as distinct or parallel (in the literal sense) rather than analogical worlds. A citizen's capacity to engage freely in public life depended on his private autonomy as master of a household; the public world of office-holding and assemblies was confined to men. Practical parliamentarian politics, played out within formal male collectivities – armies, committees and council chambers – bolstered this theoretical position. Royalism, in contrast, was based essentially on personal relations within a household – the royal court.[27]

It is important to stress the manliness of politics, particularly parliamentarian politics, for this has too often been taken for granted in historical analysis. While political theorists explain that a 'construction of masculinity undoubtedly underpinned the ideology of civic humanism', it is still common for scholars to write of how human beings or 'people' are understood within republican thought when men specifically are clearly intended.[28] Equally, early modern discussions of masculinity have focused on sexuality and culture with a more recent attention to men's 'self-sufficient mastery' and economic responsibility within the household.[29] Much less attention has been paid to the fact that 'public life has been constructed as a key element in masculinity' and that the right to bear arms was a marker of elite male authority.[30] Parliament regarded its cause as the more 'public', and the more manly; the two characteristics indeed reinforced each other. Yet parliamentarians were increasingly divided and so the questions of how best to serve the public, how best to act politically as a man were very troubling. Anxieties were intensified because of the traumatic political divisions of civil war, involving armed resistance of a monarch who on some readings of the political held patriarchal authority analogous to fatherly power in the household. Finally armed conflict in itself, especially civil war, inevitably challenged ideas of manliness. When Ann Overton praised her husband's 'honest and honorable action' she was making a political and martial judgement with an implicit contrast with less honourable men.

The parliamentarian uneasiness about political manliness manifested itself in a variety of ways. Frequent contrasts were drawn with servile, effeminate royalists, commanded by an overly uxorious king. The publication of Charles's correspondence captured at Naseby offered ample opportunities for editorializing:

> It is plaine here, first, that the Kings Counsels are wholly governed by the Queen; though she be of the weaker sexe, borne an Alien, bred up in a contrary Religion, yet nothing great or small is transacted without her privity & consent ... The Queens Counsels are as powerfull as commands. The King professes to preserve her health before the exigence and importance of his owne publick affaires.[31]

George Wither wrote that royal tyranny had turned 'his Lords and Courtiers' into 'slaves', the 'king's mere creations', who showed a sad decline from the 'bold Barons' who had previously defended England's liberties. They had been 'Lords over, not Apes unto the French, and he was counted the bravest Lord, who conquered most of their Men, not the finest, that followed most of their fashions, scarres were the ornaments of a noble face, not blacke patches, and hair powdered with dust and dewed with sweat, and bloud, not with perfum'd powders and Gesmin butter, was the dress wherein England's Nobles courted their Mistresse, Heroick fame'.[32]

Descriptions of honourable parliamentarian masculinity stressed their public commitment. Political honesty was underlined in the life of Sir Henry Vane, written by his friend and fellow republican Algernon Sidney, through a sharply drawn public/private distinction: 'He was as sollicitous for the public good as he was negligent of his own private interest, leaving the care of his domestic affairs intirely to his wife.' Vane's wife indeed is never named. One vivid story in the life, however, illustrates Vane's qualities of self-mastery, moderation and rationality in a domestic setting. Shortly after Vane had played a prominent part in reforming parliament's army, he 'was awakt about midnight by a terrible knocking at the doors, which greivously frighted his Lady' and his servants, who suspected a robbery. Vane calmly opened the door to discover messengers bringing news of parliament's decisive victory at Naseby – a triumph ensuring 'immortal glory' for Vane himself as well as security for parliament. Vane remained calm: 'very well, says he, I'm glad to hear the news, so turning away, went again to bed'. Vane, claimed Sidney, 'always preserved the same steady resolution of mind', immune to anger, joy or danger, and 'all kind of unbecoming passions and affections', instead 'obeying reason' and characterized by magnanimity and self-control.[33] But, of course, this story shows that households could not be banished from accounts of male political integrity, because it was Vane's restraint, magnanimity and rationality, revealed in a domestic setting, which showed his fitness for public service. As Mary Beth Norton has shown for early America, attention to the boundaries between public and private worlds had most meaning for men rather than women, for it was men who tried to straddle both worlds.[34]

Consequently, parliamentarian discussions of how to be truly manly, truly public-spirited, frequently involved meditations on men's personal qualities or domestic lives. *The Souldiers Catechisme* described a military camp as a 'Schoole of Vertue' wherein qualities such as continence, temperance and humility as well as the more obviously warlike virtues of hardness and obedience were fostered.[35] In one of his divorce tracts Milton argued that an unhappy marriage rendered a man 'unactive to all public service, dead to the Commonwealth'; and Edmund Waller claimed Cromwell's domestic qualities before the Civil War fitted him for public office:

> Your private life did a just Pattern give
> How Fathers, Husbands, Pious Sons should live.
> Born to command, your princely vertues slept,
> Like humble David's, while the flock he kept.[36]

Many prominent parliamentarian men defined their own political honesty, their dedication to the public, through writing about their wives and families. Sometimes male political commitment was contrasted with less securely public-spirited females; sometimes it was bolstered by the support of good women and their own appropriate uxoriousness. They were, in other words, 'thinking with women', as a way of exploring painful dilemmas of loyalty and commitment during civil war and revolution.[37] The voluminous writings of the parliamentarian lawyer Bulstrode Whitelocke provide a variety of illustrations. Whitelocke is sometimes seen as a moderate parliamentarian, but, although not an obvious zealot, he was a committed religious Independent who served both the Rump and the Protectorate energetically after initial hesitation. A distinction between the public and the private was fundamental to Whitelocke's self-representation. He tried to distinguish between his annals, a 'public history', and a 'private history' (recently edited as a 'diary'). The distinction was initially between national events and an account of his own life but it sometimes overlapped with a contrast between 'public business' and 'private family'.[38] The numerous manuscripts, written in the form we have after 1660, but based on detailed contemporary notes, diaries and pamphlets, were themselves partly private attempts to make sense of political defeat, but also intended for a public audience of his children and a broader godly network. The public–private distinction was always breaking down, however. The 'public' annals in fact included both domestic and general affairs, divided between two columns on each page, while the 'diary' summed up both public and private life:

> Thus was ended the 44 year of Whitelockes age, a year of huge perplexity & daunger to the Parlement party, wherin he was so deeply inngaged, & a year of the greatest sorrow & tribulation to him in his private family, wherin he laboured not a little & suffered very much, & hath left the remembrance of these passages to his children, that they have some advantage by them; when he was preferred to a place of high honor & power, to checke this & any pride of corrupt nature by it, presently divers of his children fell sicke of the smalle poxe, his eldest son went from him into the daunger of the war, & his deare wife was taken from him by death, & himselfe afterwards hardly escaped.[39]

The distinction in the end became unmanageable and the 'Annals' were abandoned in 1656. This was partly because Whitelocke's own career was so tied up with general developments that in the 'Annals of my own life', the 'public story' was 'necessarily intertwined' with 'private transactions'; and partly because the annals, composed first, were in a larger book and so had more space for 'personal' material.[40] Above all, notions of family were crucial to Whitelocke's own sense of his public duty; public life and private affairs were distinct but connected aspects of his identity as a man. Whitelocke's happy family, properly governed, guaranteed his standing as a man, and his political integrity.

Two examples from Whitelocke's many discussions of his private life are instructive. The first is the account of the death of his second wife, Frances, more extended in the 'Annals' than in the 'diary'.[41] One of the columns in the 'Annals' for April and May 1649 was preoccupied with Frances's illness and death, while in the other Whitelocke described public events – army mutinies and his service as a Keeper of the Great Seal. The entry for 16 May, when she died, 'the saddest day of all the dayes of my life hitherto', gave a very brief account of Frances Whitelocke's behaviour and appearance, followed by a much longer discussion of her role in Whitelocke's public life.[42] Whitelocke adopted the common rhetorical procedure of praising some women by denigrating most in stressing Frances's rationality and public spirit: 'In the most perplexed & difficult matters, which befell me, in my publique imployments, I received sound & wise counsell from her, beyond imagination to come from a woman's braine, unexperienced in such affayrres.'[43]

In this account Whitelocke's far from straightforward political trajectory is made possible and validated by his more steadfast wife, who listens to but overcomes his doubts and hesitancies:

> She was constantly & in all the time of the war, whilest she lived, most firme to the parlemts interest, and to the Army, and uppon any doubts in my selfe in the carriage of business she would still confirm me to go on and join with them, in the cause of God, which she tooke to be the parlemts cause ... she was much unsatisfied with the kings proceedings, butt more with the finall proceedings agt him.

> In all companies she would maintain the justness of the Parlaments cause & would show more than ordinary passion agst those who did traduce or censure them & ever perswaded me to continue my affections and assistance to them ...

> She could have no private end or interest to sway her judgement, butt it must proceed meerly out of conscience & the dictate of Gods spirit, ... this caused me much to depend upon her counsel which was always backed with solid reason.

This passage culminated in an unflamboyant but moving tribute to his 'good Angell':

> I injoyed the blessing of her society 14 years, 6 moneths & 6 dayes, in all which time I never heard an ill worde from her to me or any other nor an unworthy or ill-action done by her. [44]

Whitelocke's idealized picture of his lamented wife, as a staunch, rational and public-spirited woman, may or may not be an accurate description of Frances; it is clearly a means by which Bulstrode justified and underlined his own political loyalties.

The second example is a most knowing and consciously crafted volume among Whitelocke's papers where he stressed his unselfish commitment to the public service through extended contemplation of the pure delights of his private life: 'Whitelocks History of the fourty eight year of his Age ... dedicated to his Children, For their instruction in private and publique duetyes, and in the Governement of their Countrey'.[45] This covered August 1653, a crucial month in Whitelocke's life when he was out of favour during the upheavals following the forced dissolution of the Rump and the calling of the radical Barebones parliament. The distinction between public and private here is the classical one between *otium* and *negotium*, the delights of family and rural life contrasted with the ambiguous duties of public office at a time of drastic and alarming change. To quote Whitelocke's own translation of Horace:

> The man is blest who free from publique toyle
> With his own oxen ploughs his native soyle.[46]

Someone like Whitelocke who clearly enjoyed being at the centre of affairs, or felt it his duty to serve the public, faced a real dilemma here which he dealt with by pretending to himself he preferred a country life. This is not quite the same as the notion of retreat common in royalist writing in the 1640s and 1650s – where the private serves as a consolation for and a criticism of a public world from which royalists were forcibly excluded.[47] In Whitelocke's retrospective version he could console himself for a loss of public office he in fact knew to be temporary. During this month Lord Lisle was nominated as ambassador to Sweden, but (as Whitelocke of course knew by the time of writing) Lisle ultimately refused the post, so Whitelocke could reluctantly abandon his rural idyll for the tougher compromises of the political life. For each day of the month Whitelocke provided details of council proceedings about the Swedish expedition, followed by extended accounts of his own idyllic private life. On 4 August, for example, 'the Lord Viscount L'Isle went on in his preparations for his journey to Sweden ... and thereby Wh had the more injoyment of his privacy and the comforts of his wife and children'. There followed long conventional musings on the importance of marriage from biblical and classical sources.[48]

The next day Whitelocke remained at Chelsea (not the remotest of rural retreats) 'in the contentment of his privacy and retirement ... contemplating the wonderfull power and goodnes of God appearing in the grasse, herbs, plants, trees'. A week later he

> continued in his privacy and retirement with his wife and family injoying the comforts of them, his wife a true helper to him, in his household affayres and in all matters, pertaining to a discreete affectionate wife, his children, many of them now about him, performing the duety of loveing children to loving parents & hee was blest in having his quiverfull of them.[49]

Even on 17 August 'Nothing was said in the Councell for naming another person to go to Sweden and Wh not interrupted in his recreation in the country and in his divine meditations.' This was the cue for further praise of hawking, hunting, and the natural authority of simple herdsmen and silly shepherds. On 22 August he rejoiced that his life was more 'private' than ever, 'having now lesse trouble of visits & company then hearetofore, because Wh.

was looked uppon as lesse in Cromwell's favour'. By 30 August Whitelocke acknowledged the end of 'liberty' was at hand, but he was in no hurry to hasten proceedings and continued to enjoy 'observing the shepheards with their flocks of sheep & the husbandmen at their Labour, innocent, industrious & necessary occupations for the good & substance of mankind'.[50] These were conventional meditations, mobilizing all the sources available to a well educated man of the mid-seventeenth century: the classics, including Horace and Virgil, of course, Pliny, Herodotus, Aristotle and Cicero; the Bible and the church fathers (Augustine in particular); and early modern works by Sidney, Calvin, Purchas, Grotius, Erasmus, Bacon.[51]

The conventional nature of Whitelocke's writing does not detract from the interest in seeing how anxieties about the risks and validity of political office when public authority was in turmoil were smoothed over by a focus on a tranquil family life and the pleasures of private recreation. It was Whitelocke's reluctant willingness to abandon this pure existence that guaranteed his public integrity. Again there is an instructive contrast with royalist 'domestic' writing. Whitelocke used 'private' meditations to work through the dilemmas of his public service, whereas John Evelyn in the 1640s and 1650s had to make a 'virtue of necessity' by praising a life of retirement. A man could avoid idleness by active regulation of a family and so a 'Publiq Calling' was unnecessary: 'Private Families, the Husband & Wife, being the first Politiq & society in the World, are the seminaries both of Church and State.'[52]

For Whitelocke public service took priority over his private fulfilment in his happy family. The need to sacrifice private happiness for the public good was a parliamentarian commonplace. George Wither praised 'those who have ventured their lives and fortunes in their Country's defence, who have thought nothing too dear to part with for Religion and Liberty, who with the hazard of their private, have sav'd the publike'.[53] From this polarity it was a short step to a darker view of private life than that constructed by the uxorious Whitelocke, one that saw the domestic sphere as an enervating trap where selfish women distracted men from their public duty. Such arguments surface frequently in the writings of the Leveller John Lilburne. In 1647 John and his wife Elizabeth were both called for examination before a committee of the House of Commons, when, according to John's pamphlet, Elizabeth 'burst out with a loud voice and said, I told thee often enough long since, that thou would serve the Parliament and venture thy life so long for them, till they would hang thee for thy paines'. As parliament was 'a company of unjust and unrighteous judges, that more sought themselves and their owne ends, than the publique good of the Kingdome', it was time Lilburne too looked to his own interests. John himself, though, insisted his conscience bound him to his public duty despite his love for his wife and children.[54] In 1647 Elizabeth Lilburne could at least recognize where the public interest lay. By the early 1650s, during his banishment, John had stronger condemnations of his wife's 'irrationall perswations' for him 'to be quiet and silent' and submit to Cromwell. His 'poor simple wife' was contrasted with his own self-image as 'a manly and a faire adversarie', 'a single-hearted, honest, just plaine-spoken Englishman, that hath bin valiant and couragious'.[55] Women here serve as counterpoint rather than reinforcement to manly political commitment; Lilburne's political zeal is demonstrated by his willingness to sacrifice his private relationships in favour of the public good; his rationality is revealed in his rejection of his wife's irrational cowardice.

Anxieties about how personal ties might tempt men from their public service were not confined to male writing about women. Lucy Hutchinson always regretted she had persuaded her republican husband to save his life by repudiating the regicide at the Restoration. She was glad that before John's death 'God had remooved me ... that I might not tempt him [to?] looke back upon this world as a flaming Sodom'.[56] Lucy Hutchinson's distinctive praise for Rebecca (and indeed for 'Rebecca's spies') in her verse epic focused on her renunciation of such temptations in the interests of preventing her son Jacob from harm:

> His dearest mother's farewell, who at last,
> Conquering her passions with a virtuous force,
> Chased from her soul all womanish remorse,
>   ... Heaven forbid I should
> For my own pleasure thus oppose thy good. [57]

Parliamentarian manliness was debated amid divisions over the fruits of victory and ultimately had to come to terms with defeat. Whitelocke's thinking with women, like Hutchinson's biographical and religious writing, circulated within godly, ex-parliamentarian circles after the Restoration. It may be that the intersections of private and public in the form and content of these manuscripts had a particular purchase in encouraging hope and perseverance in communities that had lost a public role.[58] A final example of 'thinking with women', as a way of dealing with personal and public disaster, returns us to the Overtons, but this time to Robert's accounts of Ann. Robert Overton was an opponent of Cromwell's assumption of personal power, associated with the millenarian political ideas of the Fifth Monarchists. Consequently he spent many of the years 1655–71 in prison (with a brief respite in 1659–60). Overton compiled a lengthy manuscript towards the end of this imprisonment, mostly after his wife's death in 1665. Ann's death was the main theme of the manuscript, which copied long letters from his daughters on her deathbed; letters of condolence to and from Robert; prose meditations and many elegies adapted mainly from Phillips, Donne and Herbert: 'the blushing tribute of a borrowed muse'.[59] Personal matters were interwoven with general and political reflections, which connected Overton's political eclipse with his personal calamity. Defeated politically, Overton had also to practise godly resignation in the face of the grievous loss of a much loved wife: a 'faithfull yokefellowe', 'my best half Adam, my rare Rose Garden of delight' – one who 'layde not soe longe in my Armes as she did and will doe in my heart'.[60] Overton's steadfastness was revealed both in his acceptance of God's will in taking his wife, and in his enduring, if passive, commitment to the broader godly cause: thus three friends wrote that the Lord 'hath caused you to suffer soe many thinges for his Name both now and heretofore and hath favoured you (as Psal. 41.11.12) in upholdinge your Integrity under soe longe various and tedious tryalls'. As Overton stressed, his passive obedience in the face of public and private trials was 'not performed without great paine' – but followed 'our heavenly father's patterne'.[61]

Political defeat had made Overton more disillusioned than Whitelocke about public life. Overton urged a cynical adherence to private life. In a long treatise within this manuscript, *Government's Gaine and Goodnesse*, he cautioned, 'Upon an uncertaine publick pursewance of power postpone not thy owne private preservation.' The very first line insisted: 'Itch not after any untried government, chainge is often a cheat.' Governments inevitably compromised manliness: they were 'God's plagues' on us and our 'primitive parents', making 'our wills (like Eves) subject to others'. Manliness had been betrayed, and the valour of parliament's soldiers was a sham: they had become 'common soldiers resembling cocks that feighte for the benefit and ambition of others more then theire owne. Theirfore rather stay within doores then step into the distempers of superior plannets.' 'Let nobody begg to be buried in the ruines of publicke liberty, but yet hees brave who that way sinkes where sicophants swim.'[62] This despairing advocacy of a private life is the precise opposite of Sidney's optimistic dismissal of the domestic in his life of Vane.

But, in contrast to her husband's resigned pessimism, Ann Overton is constructed as staunch, determined and optimistic, advising her daughter to 'labour to walke closely with God, in a strict and holy life, for though ye wayes of holynesse are now scoft and scorned, yet keep in them and thou wilt finde much comfort'. Her deathbed revealed her own steadfastness, her membership of a godly community and her faith in God's goodness: 'I reioyce to thinke that any of mine may be Instruments to bringe glory to God when I am gone,' she declared, and Robert immediately repeated this passage almost word for word. Ann's deathbed was attended by the radical Independent John Bacheler and the prophetess Sarah Wight, and she asked to be buried 'as neare ye olde Prophet Mr Jesse as could be'. Crucially, 'she had her strong reason to her last breath'.[63] Robert Overton presented himself as Job, whose sufferings made him part of God's 'little remnant ... a sufferinge seed whoe have not bowed their knees to Baall'.[64] But his wife's loyalty to the good old cause was more positive and rational, bolstered by a godly network. She was Robert's 'best half Adam', retaining her zeal in times of trouble, and Robert's representation can be seen as contributing to a sense of defiant community among nonconformists.

I have argued that parliamentarian men faced difficulties in demonstrating their commitment to the public good in a period where definitions of that good were profoundly divided. These dilemmas had particular implications for male identity and were reflected in a range of writing, propagandist, reflective and personal. While parliamentarian rhetoric insisted that public service took precedence over private ease, men also found it useful to think with women, to define their identities through descriptions of their public-spirited (or irrational) wives, and their tranquil or enervating homes. Such accounts reveal male dilemmas as much as women's experiences. This is of course a partial account. Wendy Wall's criticism of how 'the category of "woman"' is often used 'solely as a metaphor for the insecurities of a patriarchal order' is echoed by many others.[65] Effacing women's agency in an account of men's dilemmas may be particularly partial for the English Revolution, when women were clearly active: as petitioners, preachers, prophets, plotters, lobbyists and counsellors in what on any definition is a public – or political – world. Exploring the place of gender in constructions of meaning should not be taken as a denial of the agency of 'real' women. Indeed, in the 1640s and 1650s the activism of women (even women on the 'same side') may well have reinforced male anxieties about their own political roles, and driven men to comment on their wives and their households.[66] But it is important to note that men were thinking with 'real' women, women they knew intimately and others were acquainted with. These accounts – even if quasi-private (and they were clearly to be shared with family and with ideologically defined communities) had to be recognizable or plausible descriptions, not merely abstractions or stereotypes. Ann Overton's letter to Lord Fairfax, with which this chapter began, was of course an attempt to influence the public world. Robert's account of Ann Overton is supported by much contemporary comment, and her career sabotages any attempt to consider her only as a means by which Robert came to terms with political defeat. Contemporaries considered her an assertive woman with a profound (and to many malign) influence on her more passive, mystical husband. The minister at Hull claimed in 1658 (when he was trying to get Robert Overton freed from prison) that he would not have 'continued so obstinate if it had not been for the imperious spirit of his wife'.[67] Similarly Lucy Hutchinson's literary endeavours have been rehabilitated by David Norbrook as a public service, preserving a republican tradition within her family and within dissenting circles.[68]

It is hardly necessary to insist that the contrasts drawn between the public and the private were not a straightforward reflection of 'reality'; Hutchinson's acceptance of the division in her poetry and prose is contradicted by her own semi-public role in defiant Restoration networks. It is no longer possible to argue that the 'public' and the 'private' realms became increasingly separate and increasingly gendered in the modern world. The frontiers are 'ragged' (Davidoff) and continually contested.[69] We know also that, in practice, women have been present in a range of public contexts in most periods. But neither was the conventional rhetorical contrast between public and private, particularly emphasized during the English Revolution, irrelevant to actual political practice. Periods of intensified political conflict and change seem to prompt a special concern with the boundaries between public good and private life and, consequently, with the proper roles of men and women. Until very recent times this has involved a reinforcement of the enduring construction of high politics as that realm from which women are excluded. This has never meant that women were absent from political activities, but it did mean that their presence in male social and political spaces was precarious, open to ridicule and challenge. Women's political activities were 'freighted with suspicion'.[70]

If parliamentarian discourse during the English Revolution stressed the 'public' it also contributed to a transformation of private life. The overwhelming pressure of public events in the mid-seventeenth century drove many men and women to a kind of politicized introspection, where they sought to understand their own personal dilemmas within providential and historical frameworks. Overton, Whitelocke and Hutchinson are but a few of the many examples of royalists and parliamentarians, civilians, soldiers and clerics, who constructed personal narratives or collected, annotated and ordered printed and manuscript material on the conflicts of the 1640s and 1650s.[71] Private identities as well as a stronger sense of 'the political' were forged through an engagement with public dilemmas.

NOTES

Versions of this chapter have been presented to seminars at the Universities of Hull, London and Keele and at the twelfth Berkshire Conference on the History of Women, June 2002. I am particularly grateful to Amanda Capern, Sue Wiseman and Peter Lake for their comments.

1 British Library [BL], Additional Ms 18979, fols 251–2. For the mutiny against Poyntz, Robert Ashton, *Counter-revolution: the Second Civil War and its Origins, 1646–1648* (New Haven CT and London, 1994), 390–92, and for Lambert's (successful) claims to the overall command, David Farr, *John Lambert, Parliamentary Soldier and Cromwellian Major General, 1619–1684* (Woodbridge, 2003), 63–6.

2 Stephen B. Baxter, 'William III as Hercules: the political implications of court culture', in Lois G. Schwoerer (ed.), *The Revolution of 1688–1689: Changing Perspectives* (Cambridge, 1992), 94–106. Henry IV of France as well as William III was associated with Hercules. Hercules was proposed as an alternative to Marianne as a symbol of the revolution in the 1790s: Joan B. Landes, *Women and the Public Sphere in the Age of the French Revolu-*

tion (Ithaca NY and London, 1988), 163–4, drawing on the work of Lynn Hunt.

3 Hutchinson, in David Norbrook, 'Lucy Hutchinson's "Elegies" and the situation of the republican woman writer', *English Literary Renaissance* 27 (1997), 518. Cf. 515, 'Him selfe The Pillar wch his whole house bore.' In an elegy on her husband's 'Picture in Armour', Lucy Hutchinson wrote how 'He like a rock of Vertuious Courage Stood/And brooke ye force of ye Prevauling flood': *ibid.*, 496.

4 Lois Potter, *Secret Rites and Secret Writing: Royalist Literature, 1641–1660* (Cambridge, 1989), 194–5. In contrast royalist satire attacked Cromwell (and his nose) as excessively and oppressively masculine: Laura Lunger Knoppers, 'Noll's nose, or Body politics in Cromwellian England', in Amy Boesky and Mary Thomas Crane (eds), *Form and Reform in Renaissance England: Essays in Honor of Barbara Kiefer Lewalski* (Newark NJ and London, 2000).

5 Paula R. Backscheider, 'Introduction', in Backscheider and Timothy Dykstal (eds), *The Intersections of the Public and the Private Spheres in Early Modern England*, special issue of *Prose Studies* 18:3 (1995), 1.

6 Felicity Riddy, '"Publication" before print: the case of Julian of Norwich', in Julia Crick and Alexandra Walsham (eds), *The Uses of Script and Print, 1300–1700* (Cambridge, 2004), 29–49, at 45.

7 Geoff Baldwin, 'The "public" as a rhetorical community in early modern England', in Alexandra Shepard and Phil Withington (eds), *Communities in Early Modern England* (Manchester, 2000), 199–215. Baldwin stresses the emergence of a notion of the 'active public' which he defines as a community but it is clear that parliamentarians also used 'public' as a noun meaning something like state (or public authority).

8 *The Excellencie of a free State*, quoted in Baldwin, 'The "public" as a rhetorical community', 208.

9 Bodleian Library, Tanner Ms 59, fols 335–8. Fairfax's arguments are matched by Mrs Powell's own petition.

10 John Lilburne, *The Upright Mans Vindication* (London, 1653), 17.

11 *The Souldiers Catechisme* (London, 1644), 6–7, 11, 28.

12 Elizabeth Clarke, 'The garrisoned muse: women's use of the religious lyric in the Civil War period', in Claude J. Summers and Ted-Larry Pebworth (eds), *The English Civil War in the Literary Imagination* (Columbia MO and London, 1999), 130–43, at 132–3, points out that the public–private split had an impact on literary genres, with a 'number of private writing enterprises made public for political reasons'.

13 Lucy Hutchinson, *Order and Disorder*, ed. David Norbrook (Oxford, 2001), introduction, xlvii.

14 BL, Additional Ms 21417, fol. 9, quoted in Farr, *John Lambert*, 64.

15 Jürgen Habermas, *The Structural Transformation of the Public Sphere: an Inquiry into a Category of Bourgeois Society*, trans. Tomas Burger and Frederick Lawrence (Oxford, 1992), 27. There are very useful discussions of Habermas's relevance to seventeenth-century England in Craig Calhoun (ed.), *Habermas and the Public Sphere* (Cambridge MA and London, 1992), David Zaret, *Origins of Democratic Culture: Printing, Petitions, and the Public Sphere in Early Modern England* (Princeton NJ, 2000), and Brian Cowan, 'What was masculine about the public sphere? Gender and the coffee house milieu in post-Restoration England', *History Workshop* 51 (2001), 127–50.

16 Habermas, *Structural Transformation*, 48. In practice Habermas recognized more fully than his critics allow that the family was influenced by the public world

17 *Ibid.*, 3–4, 46–8; cf. Timothy Dykstal, 'Introduction', in Backscheider and Dykstal, *The Intersections of the Public and the Private Spheres*, 22–40, especially 27–9; Judith A. Vega, 'Feminist republicanism and the political perception of gender', in Martin van Gelderen and Quentin Skinner (eds), *Republicanism: a Shared European Heritage* II, *The Values of Republicanism in Early Modern Europe* (Cambridge, 2002), 157–74; Jonathan Barry, 'Communicating with authority: the uses of script, print and speech in Bristol, 1640–1714', in Crick and Walsham, *The Uses of Script and Print*, 191–208, at 206–8.

18 Joan Scott, 'Gender: a useful category of historical analysis', in her *Gender and the Politics of History* (New York, 1988); Rachel Weil, *Political Passions: Gender, the Family and Political Argument in Enland, 1680–1714* (Manchester, 1999).

19 *Vox Populi, or The People's Rage against the Clergy* (London, 1646), 10; *An Hue-and-Cry after Vox Populi, or An Answer to Vox Diaboli* (Norwich, 1646), 25. As with much slander there is some connection with 'reality', for the membership of the Norwich Independent church was largely female: Dr William's Library Harmer Ms 76/1 (Norwich Church Book), fol. 13r, for membership in November 1645.

20 C. H. Firth (ed.), *The Clarke Papers* II, Camden Society, new ser., XLIX (1894), 151; E. Poole, *An Alarum of War given to the Army* (London, 1649).

21 Dena Goodman, 'Public sphere and private life: toward a synthesis of current historiographical approaches to the old regime', *History and Theory* 31 (1992), 17. Edward, Earl of Clarendon, *The History of the Rebellion and Civil Wars in England*, ed. W. Dunn Macray (Oxford, 1888) XII, 20; *England's Monument of Mercies in her miraculous Preservations from manifold Plots ... against the Parliament* (London, 1646), BL 669 fol. 10 (85).

22 Hutchinson, *Order and Disorder*, 58.

23 Cynthia B. Herrup, *A House in Gross Disorder: Sex, Law and the Second Earl of Castlehaven* (Oxford and New York, 1999), 70.

24 Ann Baynes Coiro, '"A ball of strife": Caroline poetry and royal marriage', in Thomas Corns (ed.), *The Royal Image: Representations of Charles I* (Cambridge, 1999), 26–46.

25 Henry Parker, *Observations upon some of his Majesties late Answers and Expresses* (1642), here quoted from William Haller (ed.), *Tracts on Liberty in the Puritan Revolution* (New York, 1965) II, 185. This passage is quoted by Susan Wiseman, '"Adam, the Father of all Flesh": porno-political rhetoric and political theory in and after the English Civil War', *Prose Studies* 14 (1991), 134–57, also published as a separate volume, James Holstun (ed.), *Pamphlet Wars* (London, 1992), and Hilda L. Smith (ed.) *Women Writers and the early modern British Political Tradition* (Cambridge, 1998), 8.

26 John Hall, *The Grounds and Reasons of Monarchy Considered* (London, 1650), 22–3. Like Milton, Hall included 'obedience to his wife' among the crimes of Charles I: 125.

27 The role of women in royalist politics was, of course, more controversial than parliamentarian propaganda allowed. One of the factors encouraging Sir John Hotham to defect from the parliament's side in spring 1643 was the prospect of an alliance with the Marquess of Newcastle against female dominance at court: Andrew Hopper, 'The Extent of Support for Parliament in Yorkshire during the early Stages of the first Civil War', D.Phil. thesis, University of York (1999), 172–4.

28 Van Gelderen and Skinner, *Republicanism* II, 5; Markku Peltonen, *Classical Humanism and Republicanism in English Political Thought* (Cambridge, 1995). Feminists have

similarly criticized Habermas for his disregard of the hierarchies within the private realm that disadvantaged or even disqualified women from qualifying as rational citizen participants in the public realm: Nancy Fraser, *Unruly Practices: Power, Discourse and Gender in Contemporary Social Theory* (Oxford, 1989), 126–9.

29 Anthony Fletcher, *Gender, Sex and Subordination in England, 1500–1800* (New Haven CT and London, 1995), especially chapter 5; Elizabeth A. Foyster, *Manhood in Early Modern England: Honour, Sex and Marriage* (Harlow, 1999); Alexandra Shepard, 'Manhood, credit and patriarchy in early modern England', *Past and Present* 167 (2000), 75–106, at 82.

30 Leonore Davidoff, 'Regarding some "old husbands' tales": public and private in feminist history', in Davidoff, *Worlds Between: Historical Perspectives on Gender and Class* (Oxford, 1995), 227–76, at 241–2; see also John Tosh, 'The old Adam and the new man: emerging themes in the history of English masculinities, 1750–1850', in Tim Hitchcock and Michele Cohen (eds), *English Masculinities, 1660–1800* (Harlow, 1999), 217–38. Literary scholars have been more interested in male political dilemmas: Wiseman, '"Adam, the Father of all Flesh"'; Diane Purkiss, 'Dismembering and remembering: the English Civil War and male identity', in Summers and Pebworth, *The English Civil War*, 220–41.

31 *The Kings Cabinet opened: or, Certain Packets of Secret Letters & Papers* (London, 1645), 43. For hints at a failure of masculinity here see Joad Raymond, 'Popular representation of Charles I', in Corns, *The Royal Image*, 58. Examples could be multiplied: Lucy Hutchinson's attack on Charles's effeminate subservience to Henrietta Maria (*Memoirs of the Life of Colonel John Hutchinson*, ed. N. H. Keeble (London, 1995), 70) and Milton's assaults on the royalist defender Salmasius as a 'filthy pig' of Circe (*Milton: Political Writings*, ed. Martin Dzelzainis (Cambridge, 1991), 11, 193, 238) are amongst the best known.

32 George Wither, *Respublica Anglicana, or The Historie of the Parliament in their late Proceedings* (London, 1650), 39–40. The ancient barons, according to Wither, also let their land at 'easie rates' so their tenants could function as 'able men' – independent and determined. See Anna Bryson, *From Courtesy to Civility: Changing Codes of Conduct in Early Modern England* (Oxford, 1998), 270–5, for a general discussion of courtiers and effeminacy.

33 Reprinted in Violet A. Rowe, *Sir Henry Vane the Younger* (London, 1970), 278–9; cf. Christopher Durston, *The Family and the English Revolution* (Oxford, 1989), 92. Among respectable society the wives of Athenian citizens were not named in public: Paul Cartledge, *The Greeks: a Portrait of Self and Others* (Oxford, 2002), 89.

34 Mary Beth Norton, *Founding Mothers and Fathers: Gendered Power and the Forming of American Society* (New York, 1996), 8–11; cf. Tosh, 'The old Adam', 217, on the importance of straddling the public and the private worlds in discussing masculinity. On the other hand Foyster has suggested (*Manhood in Early Modern England*, 4) that there was 'no separation of spheres for men'. But although men operated within both the household (if that could be seen as a private sphere) and the formal public world, distinctions were clearly made between the two.

35 *The Souldiers Catechisme*, 18–19.

36 *Tetrachordon* (1645), quoted in Martin Dzelzainis, 'Milton's classical republicanism', in David Armitage, Armand Himy and Quentin Skinner (eds), *Milton and Republicanism* (Cambridge, 1995), 11. David Norbrook, 'Lucy Hutchinson versus Edmund Waller: an unpublished reply to Waller's *A Pangyrick to my Lord Protector*', *The Seventeenth Century* 11 (1996), 80. Hutchinson's response attacked Cromwell's 'private' role as a provider for his family: 'Who lavisht out his wiue's Inheritance/Ruynd the Children that he should

advance/And Gam'd away his little thriftles stock/Slept not like David for he kept his Flock.'

37 The term is drawn from Levi-Strauss via Peter Brown, *The Body and Society: Men, Women and Sexual Renunciation in early Christianity* (New York, 1988), 152–4. Compare Diane Purkiss's point: 'it was routine to establish masculine identity in war in relation to a displaced femininity': 'Dismembering and remembering', 233.

38 Blair Worden, 'The "Diary" of Bulstrode Whitelocke', *English Historical Review* 108 (1993), 122–34, is crucial to these points. Worden has noted the value of Whitelocke's manuscripts for the history of the family, but the 1681–82 edition of his *Memorials* (based mainly on the 'Annals') consistently removed all family references; the British Library manuscripts still show the pencil marks indicating deletions. Whitelocke is used as a source for politics, not for the family, yet both aspects of his life were, for him, inextricably connected.

39 *The Diary of Bulstrode Whitelocke 1605–1675*, ed. Ruth Spalding, British Academy, Records of Social and Economic History, new ser., XIII (Oxford, 1990), 244, end of July 1649; also quoted in Worden, 'Diary', 127.

40 Worden, 'Diary', 126–7, quoting BL, Additional Ms 53726.

41 The diary version is: 'The saddest day of Whitelockes life when his deare wife dyed, then whom never wife was a truer comfort & helper then she was. Her birth, her beauty, her disposition, her wisdom, her cheerfullnes, her entire affection to her husband, he cannot now relate for tears, they are in pl[enty] exprest in his larger booke. so are her orders of housekeeping, of breeding her children, of governing her family, & her incomparable love of her husband & desire to please him, who can say no more of this subject' (*Diary of Bulstrode Whitelocke*, ed. Spalding, 238).

42 BL Additional Ms 37344, fol. 296r.

43 *Ibid.*, fol. 296v. For a briefer but similar comment on a dead wife see Anthony Ashley Cooper's comment in his diary for 10–11 July 1649, kept in the leaves of John Woodhouse, *A New Almanac*: 'a lovely beautifull faire woman, a Religious devout Christian, of admirable witt and wisdome beyond any I ever knew, yett the most sweet affectionate and observant wife in the world ... in discourse and counsell farr beyond any woman' (National Archives, PRO 30/24/8/2). Cooper's brief diaries, like Whitelocke's wordy productions, cover both his public service and his family affairs.

44 BL Additional Ms 37344, fol. 296v.

45 BL Additional Ms 31984.

46 *Ibid.*, fol. 220v.

47 Potter, *Secret Rites and Secret Writing*; Tom Cain, 'A "Sad Intestine Warr": Mildmay Fane and the poetry of civil strife', in Summers and Pebworth, *The English Civil War*, 27–51.

48 BL, Additional Ms 31984, fols 33v–34r.

49 *Ibid.*, fols 42r–v, 78r. The next day he complacently noted how his thirteen children by three different mothers were all united (fol. 88v). The wife praised here is Mary, the widow of the republican Alderman Rowland Wilson who died in February 1650. She and Bulstrode were married privately on 5 August 1650 after a fairly rapid courtship. Mary's first child Samuel, 'a childe of prayers' was born on 30 May 1651 after fourteen years' childlessness in her first marriage, as Bulstrode complacently noted: *Diary of Bulstrode Whitelocke*, ed. Spalding, 253–68.

50 BL, Additional Ms 31984, fols 127v, 161v, 214v–215r.

51 BL, Additional Ms 31984, *passim*. Samuel Purchas (died 1626) compiled a series of works, *Purchas his Pilgrimage* (or similar titles), covering the history of mankind, or world religions, and England's explorations by sea. They provided Whitelocke with many examples of miscellaneous natural and social phenomena.

52 Frances Harris, *Transformations of Love: the Friendship of John Evelyn and Margaret Godolphin* (Oxford, 2002), 19, 44–5.

53 Wither, *Respublica Anglican*, 20.

54 John Lilburne, *The Resolved Mans Resolution* (London, 1647), 8, 23. Households are more complex in Leveller writing than this example suggests: see Ann Hughes, 'Gender and politics in Leveller literature', in Susan Amussen and Mark Kishlansky (eds), *Political Culture and Cultural Politics in Early Modern England* (Manchester, 1995).

55 John Lilburne, *L. Colonel John Lilburne Revived* (London, 1653), 8; *L. Colonel John Lilburne his Apologetical Narration* (London, 1652), 42–3; John Lilburne, *As You Were* (London, 1652), 9.

56 From an addendum to her memoirs of her husband: Lucy Hutchinson, *Memoirs of the Life of Colonel Hutchinson*, ed. N. H. Keeble (London, 1995), 337, also quoted in Norbrook, 'Lucy Hutchinson's "Elegies"', 481.

57 Hutchinson, *Order and Disorder*, ed. Norbrook, 237; 235 for Rebecca's spies.

58 The work of Elizabeth Clarke and Sue Wiseman is revealing how the circulation of godly manuscripts such as Mary Love's life of her martyred husband Christopher helped maintain solidarity in dissenting communities.

59 David Norbrook, '"This blushing tribute of a borrowed muse": Robert Overton and his overturning of the poetic canon', *English Manuscript Studies* 4 (1993), 220–66. I owe my knowledge of this manuscript to Norbrook's work. The manuscript, 'Gospell Observations and Religious Manifestations', is Princeton University Library MS CO 199. I am grateful to Peter Lake for help in acquiring a microfilm. Whitelocke also printed letters of condolence and composed a verse elegy for his wife, Frances (in the form of a dialogue with his daughter), in BL, Additional Ms 37344. Overton's poetry is also discussed in Andrew Shifflett, '"A Most Humane Foe": Colonel Robert Overton's war with the Muses', in Summers and Pebworth, *The English Civil War*, 159–73.

60 Princeton University Library Ms CO 199, pp. 93, 142, 97.

61 *Ibid.*, pp. 93, 109. The connections between public and private are illustrated by Overton's inclusion of a meditation on passive obedience in the midst of letters about his wife's death.

62 This section of the Princeton Ms has been edited by Barbara Taft, ' "They that pursew perfaction on earth ...": the political progress of Robert Overton', in Ian Gentles, J. S. Morrill and Blair Worden (eds), *Soldiers, Writers and Statesmen of the English Revolution* (Cambridge, 1998), and references are to her chapter, 301, 299, 300.

63 Princeton MS CO 199, pp. 80–1, 85, 89–90.

64 *Ibid.*, p. 119.

65 Wendy Wall, *The Imprint of Gender: Authorship and Publication in the English Renaissance* (Ithaca NY and London, 1993), 7.

66 Kate Peters has shown how Quaker men privately fretted over the assertiveness of

Quaker women even as they publicly defended their movement for the opportunities it gave women: '"Women's Speaking Justified": women and discipline in the early Quaker movement, 1652–1656', *Studies in Church History* 34 (1998), 130–1.

67 C. H. Firth, 'Two letters addressed to Cromwell', *English Historical Review* 22 (1907), 313; cf. the comments of a ship's carpenter in 1656 about Ann Overton's opposition to the Protectorate: SP18/129/91.

68 Norbrook, 'Lucy Hutchinson's "Elegies"', 477–8.

69 Davidoff, 'Some "Old husbands' tales"', 258; important cautions include Lawrence E. Klein, 'Gender and the public/private distinction in the eighteenth century: some questions about evidence and analytic procedure', *Eighteenth Century Studies* 29 (1995), 97–109; Amanda Vickery, 'Golden Age to separate spheres? A review of the categories and chronology of English women's history', *Historical Journal* 36 (1993), 383–414.

70 Cowan, 'What was masculine about the public sphere?', 133; Natalie Z. Davis, in Davis and Arlette Farge (eds), *A History of Women in the West* III (Cambridge MA, 1993), 175; Scott, 'Gender and the politics of history', 173.

71 The range of potential reference is enormous, but see, for example, *The Journal of Thomas Juxon*, ed. Keith Lindley and David Scott, Camden Society, 5th ser., XIII (1999); *The Diary of Ralph Josselin, 1616–1683*, ed. Alan Macfarlane, British Academy, Records of Social and Economic History, new ser., III (London, 1976); John Loftis (ed.), *The Memoirs of Anne, Lady Halkett and Ann, Lady Fanshawe* (Oxford, 1979); Michael Mendle, 'Preserving the ephemeral: reading, collecting and the pamphlet culture of seventeenth century England', in E. Sauer and J. Andersen (eds), *Books and Readers in Early Modern England* (Philadelphia, 2001).

Chapter 9

The state and civil society in early modern England: capitalism, causation and Habermas's bourgeois public sphere

Steven Pincus

I

'Phrases involving the resurrection, reemergence, rebirth, reconstruction, or renaissance of civil society are heard repeatedly today,' observe Jean Cohen and Andrew Arato in their *Civil Society and Political Theory*. They hasten to add that this society which is being resurrected was based originally on the 'early modern concept of civil society'.[1] Robert Putnam attributes his own transformation from 'an obscure academic' into a celebrity 'invited to Camp David, lionized by talk-show hosts' and pictured 'on the pages of *People*' to the publication of his essay *Bowling Alone* that lamented the demise of a civil society that had early modern roots. Putnam blames his newfound pop-star status not on the 'scholarly elegance' of his essay but on the articulation of a widely felt 'unease'.[2]

In early modern British historical and literary circles, and indeed among early modernists more generally, the interest in civil society has become focused on the more particular claims advanced by Jürgen Habermas in *The Structural Transformation of the Public Sphere*. In particular, early modern British scholars have been intrigued by Habermas's claim that 'a public sphere that functioned in the political realm rose first in Great Britain at the turn of the eighteenth century'.[3]

Historians and literary critics, I suggest, have fundamentally misunderstood the nature of Habermas's argument about the emergence of the bourgeois public sphere. That sphere was not a realm for general discussion but a much more specific realm in which discussion about political economy was added to the ancient public sphere, a sphere in which arguments about politics and religion were already present. Political economy was the characteristic subject of the modern bourgeois public sphere. Understood this way, Habermas's arguments need to be taken more seriously than scholars have hitherto allowed. However, his claims are marred by a misunderstanding of the early modern state and a misdiagnosis of the issue that generated the bourgeois public sphere. Although Habermas is right to posit 1688–89 as a turning point, the key development was not so much a crisis of capitalism as the replacement of an agrarian modern state with a manufacturing one. A state committed to the development of the manufacturing sector was compelled to allow free flow of information about markets and state activity in a way that an agrarian state was not.

II

What does Habermas mean by the bourgeois public sphere and why did he think that it emerged first in England?[4] These questions, I think, are harder to answer than they appear at first glance.

For Habermas the emergence of the bourgeois public sphere was simultaneous with the development of the modern state. 'A public sphere in the sense of a separate realm distinguished from the private sphere cannot be shown to have existed in the feudal society of the High Middle Ages,' Habermas argues.[5] Only the emergence of 'a depersonalized state authority' brought civil society into existence.[6] Habermas makes it clear that the public sphere is that realm which mediates between the private on the one hand and the sphere of public authority on the other.[7] 'The bourgeois public sphere may be conceived above all as the sphere of private people come together as a public,' he insists. 'They soon claimed the public sphere regulated from above against the public authorities themselves.'[8] Eventually the political public sphere, Habermas suggests, would take on its primary function of 'criticism of public authority'.[9] Significantly, 'early capitalist commercial relations' were able to manifest 'their revolutionary power only in the mercantilist phase in which, simultaneously with the modern state, the national and territorial economies assumed their shapes'.[10] Habermas, however, has a very specific understanding of the mercantilist state. As 'the basis of the bourgeois public sphere' it had to be capable of recognizing 'the separation of state and society'.[11] When Habermas comes to describe the structural transformation of the public sphere he makes clear the limited nature of the early modern state. Until the late nineteenth century the state only acted 'domestically by means of the police and the judicial system, and a very cautiously handled tax policy, and internationally based on military forces'. Until the late nineteenth century the state assumed no 'formative functions'.[12] When the state came to intervene 'in the social order through advance planning, distribution and administration' the bourgeois public sphere 'could no longer be maintained as a principle'.[13] It was at this moment 'that the public sphere in the world of letters was replaced by the pseudo-scientific or sham-private world of culture consumption'.[14] Large capitalist corporations sought to control simultaneously portions of the state and the organs of information dissemination. The genesis of the bourgeois public sphere was necessarily inseparable from a story of state formation. The state to which the public sphere was juxtaposed was a severely limited one. It was a state that did not pursue socially transformative tax policies, which took on as its prime functions the defence of the realm and the maintenance of order. It was a state committed, in short, to a Berlinian negative liberty.[15]

What then was the nature of the bourgeois public sphere that emerged in a dialectical relationship with the modern state? Habermas's concept can best be understood in the twofold distinction he draws between publicity in the medieval period and the bourgeois situation on the one hand, and between the bourgeois public sphere and the ancient public sphere on the other. What distinguishes the modern public sphere from pre-modern 'representative publicness', as Harold Mah has carefully detailed, is 'the particular modern form of the public subject'.[16] The modern public sphere 'preserved a kind of social intercourse that, far from presupposing the equality of status, disregarded status altogether'. 'The celebration of rank' that gave authority in the pre-modern situation was replaced by a situation in which the quality of the arguments advanced rather than the status of the speaker determined the significance of the utterance.[17] The modern public sphere claimed to be all-inclusive, and all-inclusive irrespective of one's participation in a group. Habermas was well aware that the bourgeois public sphere was an ideal, not a concrete reality. 'Not that this idea of the public was actually realized in earnest in the coffee houses, the salons and the societies,' he admits, 'but as an idea it had become institutionalized and thereby stated as an objective claim.'[18] In fact, Habermas later shows that the bourgeois public sphere proved incapable of incorporating 'the unpropertied masses'.[19] So it is no criticism of Habermas to highlight exclusions in the historical bourgeois public sphere, nor is it worth pointing to inclusions unappreciated by Habermas. The bourgeois public sphere was not a tangible material space; it was an ideal.

It is worth pointing out in passing that the critical rationality so central to the bourgeois public sphere was generated in this idealized realm. Habermas does not suggest that all utterances in the bourgeois public sphere are rational. Instead, he makes clear, that 'the 'truth' of the laws' was 'only guaranteed as long as a public sphere, elevated in Parliament to an organ of the state, made it possible to discover, through public discussion, what was practically necessary in the general interest'.[20] Many irrational things might and would be said, but their ultimate irrationality would be discovered through public discussion.

Habermas not only distinguishes the modern bourgeois public sphere from the medieval world celebrating status and rank, but he also distinguishes it from the ancient public sphere. The theme of the modern (in contrast to the ancient) public sphere,' he clarifies, 'shifted from the properly political tasks of a citizenry acting in common (i.e. administration of law as regards internal affairs and military survival as regards external affairs) to the more properly civic tasks of a society engaged in critical public debate (i.e. the protection of a commercial economy).'[21] Habermas knew full well that the concept of the public came from the classical tradition. His schema is compatible with a Renaissance revival of the ancient public sphere, which was in turn distinct from medieval public performance . 'The political task of the bourgeois public sphere was the regulation of civil society,' he says, 'in contradistinction to the *res publica.*'[22] Prior to the emergence of the bourgeois public sphere there may well have been very public debates about things of narrowly political or religious concern. It is no criticism of Habermas to demonstrate that there were public religious debates, or public debates about the nature of absolutism, prior to the genesis of the bourgeois public sphere. The new focus of the bourgeois public sphere was 'the sphere of commodity exchange and social labor'.[23] The economy of antiquity, belonging to the realm of private discussion, was transformed into 'political economy'.[24] Habermas specifies that the subject that distinguishes the modern bourgeois public from the ancient public sphere is the discussion of commercial affairs.

For Habermas the genesis of the public sphere and its ultimate structural transformation were both the results of crises in capitalism. Although Habermas suggests that the explanation for the early genesis of England's bourgeois pubic sphere 'is a problem not yet resolved', he does offer some very pointed hints.[25] In general it was 'the emergence of early finance and trade capitalism' that fomented the creation 'of a new social order'.[26] In particular the dynamic of change was spurred on by 'the traffic in commodities and news created by early capitalist long-distance trade'.[27] It was because this 'capitalist mode of production' had reached such an advanced stage in England that the bourgeois public sphere emerged there first. Habermas, however, is more precise about this causality. In England, Habermas claims, there was ' a new conflict of interest between the restrictive interests of commercial and finance capital on one side and the expansive interests of manufacturing and industrial capital on the other'. 'At the start of the eighteenth century,' Habermas posits, 'it was an obvious step for the weaker party to carry this conflict into the public sphere.'[28] It was the development of capitalism beyond the stage of 'horizontal exchange relationship[s] among individual commodity owners' that ultimately and necessarily led to the demise of this public sphere.[29]

Habermas's story, then, is much more and in many ways less than a story about the rise and fall of public opinion. It is an account of the emergence of a specific type of bourgeois discussion in the face of a specific kind of state. It is an explanation for the development of civic discussion, by which he means political economy. That discussion could occur only when the modern state was weak and refrained from extending its tendrils more than minimally into the private sphere. Habermas argues that the cause of the early appearance

of the public sphere in England was a conflict between financial and manufacturing capitalism. This chapter will first examine the nature of the English
state in the era of the genesis of the bourgeois public sphere, then test his
hypothesis about the cause of that genesis. Finally, I will speculate about the
broader implications of my historical analysis for the broader normative issues
raised in Habermas's analysis.

III

The 1640s and 1650s were a pivotal era for the development of English political,
religious and economic debate. Literary scholars, in particular, have done much
to demonstrate the efflorescence of a public sphere in this epoch.[30] Indeed, in
the 1640s and 1650s there was an extensive discussion of political economy.
Benjamin Worsley, who was secretary of the Rump Parliament's council of
trade, explained that 'it is by trade, and the due ordering and governing of it,
and by no other means, that wealth and shipping can either be increased or
upheld; and consequently by no other, that the power of any nation can be
sustained by land or by sea'.[31] 'If we have any desire to be more formidable
to our enemies, or more aidful to our friends, or more gainful to ourselves,'
advised Henry Parker, traffic 'may be held sufficient.'[32] In fact, much of the
criticism of the Cromwellian state centred on concerns about its commercial
efficacy.[33]

The restoration of the monarchy in 1660 did not put an end to the public
discussion of civic issues. Indeed, the state did much to facilitate the expansion
of the discussion of political economy. It licensed the new coffee houses which
increasingly became the place where business transactions and economic
discussion took place.[34] The postmaster general, Roger Whitley, transformed
the post office from an institution carrying the correspondence of the court
into the primary vehicle of commercial interaction.[35] In the 1670s Whitley
proudly proclaimed that 'the commerce of the nation is maintained by the
ministration of this office'.[36] The vast expansion of the post office combined
with the remarkably rapid penny post in Greater London transformed the
English into a letter-writing people. 'Though the number of letters missive in
England were not at all considerable in our ancestors' days,' commented one
pamphleteer, they were now 'prodigiously great'.[37] In 1663 parliament passed
the first turnpike act, which greatly improved the economic infrastructure of
the country. By the last decade of the seventeenth century Guy Miege, who had
travelled widely throughout Europe, could confirm that 'the English nation is
the best provided of any for land-travel'.[38] Despite Charles II's ambivalent attitude to public discussion, the Exclusion crisis revealed that many had accepted
the normative value of the public sphere.[39]

The late seventeenth century was not, however, always so tolerant of the bourgeois public sphere. James II's activities demonstrate that England had already developed a strong and interventionist state. From 1681 onwards the government used the powers of the state to suppress public discussion of all civic matters – political, religious and political economic. James II's modern regime was hostile not only to the bourgeois public sphere but to the ancient public sphere as well. James II and his advisers rejected the principle of the rationality of public discussion. 'Since men, when they differ, are so wedded to their own sentiments, that few are so wise as to see their own mistakes, or so ingenious as to confess them, when they see them,' argued Sir George Mackenzie, who was one of James II's Scottish advisers. 'Prudence and necessity have obliged men to end all debates by making laws.'[40]

In the event, James II did much more than make laws. The Post Office was transformed from a facilitator of commercial intercourse into an engine of state surveillance. While still duke of York James consolidated his control over the Post Office with the explicit intent of preventing 'false and seditious news'.[41] When he became king the opening of letters became routine. Sir Nicholas Butler had 'all letters for or from Holland ... for the most part opened'.[42] Sir William Trumbull, James's ambassador to France, was warned to be circumspect, because 'all pacquets are opened'.[43] The government was not only worried about foreign correspondence. 'There is nothing more frequently practised at the post office than inspection of letters,' reported one concerned writer.[44] 'All letters are opened,' agreed Lady Sunderland, who was in a position to know.[45] 'Writing [letters] has been unfortunate to several,' warned the East India merchant Nathaniel Cholmley.[46] The tactic achieved its desired result. The West India merchant Christopher Jeafferson informed one of his trading partners 'that it is imprudent as well as dangerous to write any news'.[47] The marquess of Halifax had taken to burning his letters for fear they would be seized.[48] Even the son of the archbishop of York, Gilbert Dolben, claimed a letter 'must serve now to light my pipe for I dare not trust it by the post'.[49] The Post Office ceased to be an avenue through which the English could conduct activities characteristic of either the ancient or the modern public sphere.

The coffee houses so celebrated by Habermas also could no longer assert the ideal of the bourgeois public sphere. In order to maintain their licences, coffee house owners were compelled to billet soldiers throughout the country.[50] In early 1686 James II announced that he was 'justly offended at the licentious practice of daily exposing diverse newsletters and other papers in coffee houses and other public houses'.[51] The government acted quickly, decisively and frequently to suppress coffee houses that were known to continue to host public political discussions despite the presence of troops.[52]

The military were a ubiquitous presence in James II's England. Army atrocities were a commonplace. Englishmen and women complained of a climate of fear in London, Leicester, Exeter, York, Cambridge, Bristol, Aylesbury and elsewhere.[53] Despite James II's Declaration of Indulgence many dissenters shared in the terror.[54] Townspeople rose up against the troops quartered upon them in Hull, Oxford, Salisbury, Yarmouth, York and London, only to be brutally suppressed in each case.[55] Sir David Nairne was therefore guilty of Scottish understatement when he noted that 'the army since Monmouth's business kept up in England, became a grievance'.[56]

James II created an extensive, modern and intrusive state. He also intervened actively in the economy, promoting the expansion and rationalization of a colonial regime in India, the West Indies and North America. He conducted the first known systematic political survey. He used his new army to guarantee liberty of conscience at the same time that he suppressed public discussion. Every effort was made to compel the clergy, both Nonconformist and Anglican, 'to avoid matters of dispute and controversy in their sermons'.[57] Guy Fawkes Day celebrations were suppressed.[58] Not only were unlicensed presses sought out and destroyed, but bookshops and chapmen were routinely searched for controversial pamphlets, broadsides and ballads.[59] James II vastly expanded the secret service. Spies visited all sorts of churches and secular gatherings, many of them reporting directly to the king.[60] So pervasive was James II's surveillance that one Chichester prebend was tried for praising a book at a dinner party.[61] John Lauder was so afraid that his papers would be searched that he was necessitated to 'hide' his historical notes 'and intermit my Historical Remarks till the Revolution in the end of 1688'.[62] Not only was there no bourgeois public sphere, remarked one Englishman, 'we have almost lost our liberty of thinking freely'.[63]

Habermas clearly underestimated the extent of the Restoration English state. James II's state created in the aftermath of commercialization was certainly modern. It was not, however, the English liberal state described by Habermas. But perhaps he was right to suggest that *after* the Glorious Revolution England created a non-interventionist 'liberal' state. Perhaps after the experience of James II's reign Englishmen and women banded together to create a state committed to negative liberty.

There was certainly an explosion of public discussion after the Glorious Revolution. Although 'news was as scarce as rosemary after the great frost' in James II's time, immediately after his flight the English reasserted their 'liberty of tongue, as well as their liberty of conscience'.[64] Foreigners extolled the revived public sphere in England. The minister of Aberfoyle, Robert Kirk, thought it was 'a great advantage in England, that whatever be the changes continually occurring in the Church or state, there be so many learned men who immediately publish their advice pro and con that each may see and quickly choose what is safest and best to do without much study'.[65] The Huguenot exile Henri Misson, who had lamented the restrictions on public discussion under James II, thought that post-revolutionary 'England is a country abounding in printed papers, which they call pamphlets, wherein every author makes bold to talk freely upon affairs of state, and to publish all manners of news'. Coffee houses, in particular, he found 'very convenient' to 'meet your friends for the transaction of business'.[66]

Post-revolutionary England not only revived the ancient public sphere but it also became home to the modern bourgeois public sphere. There was a flood of pamphlets, broadsides and position papers on political economy.[67] Parliament was overwhelmed by an unprecedented number of petitions on economic matters.[68] Perhaps most important, John Houghton revived his weekly periodical *A Collection for Improvement of Husbandry and Trade*. The journal, like the *Athenian Gazette*, encouraged its readers to send in enquiries and initiate debates, seeking to enhance the commercial knowledge of Englishmen and women.[69] Houghton, as well as his competitor James Whiston, provided the entire nation with weekly price lists for major commodities and stock quotes.[70] Houghton was a remarkable entrepreneur, always recommending new ways to improve the distribution of his periodical. By the summer of 1693 he was convinced that his *Collection* was second only to the official *Gazette* in national readership.[71] Certainly Misson reported that 'the paper is to be found in all the coffee houses and could be read there for free'.[72]

William and Mary's England was not devoid of informers, spies or political trials. Jacobites and Nonjurors, though under less frequent surveillance than the suspected enemies of James II in the 1680s, were subjects of government enquiries. But the regime now accepted the principle that public discussion was valuable, and indeed essential, for a commercial society.[73] Coffee houses bustled again with political and commercial gossip, largely free from paid government informers. Almost immediately after the arrival of William in England one postmaster in Edinburgh remarked, 'I can hardly think that now while all things are reforming that that ugly custom of breaking up and keeping of letters will yet be practised.'[74] It is true that, when the possibility of Jacobite invasion seemed most imminent, some floated the notion of returning to James II's postal policies. But William Aglionby was typical of the new regime's servants when he exclaimed that 'I do not know how far opening of letters can be justified.'[75]

Nevertheless, Habermas was wrong to assume that the English state after the Glorious Revolution was weak, or that it refrained from intervening in the private sphere. The financial revolution of the 1690s was not confined to servicing the war debt and financing forces that fought overseas. The Williamite state was massive and socially interventionist.[76] Excisemen and customs officers proliferated. The quantitative growth of the state may well have been an unintended consequence of the massive wars against France, but the new direction of social policy was no accident. Charles II and James II had consciously used tax policies to support state-run monopolies and improving landowners. These policies were immediately reversed after the Revolution. The hearth tax that disproportionately fell upon England's emerging manufacturing sector was repealed in 1689.[77] The first Williamite parliament instead shifted the tax burden on to landowners, reprising the taxation strategy of the 1650s.[78] Perhaps more important, the Bank of England, created in 1694, was much more than the debt servicing institution that Habermas imagined.[79] The bank was designed to redistribute money from comparatively moribund sectors of the economy, like agriculture, into the newly dynamic manufacturing sector. John Cary declared banks 'to be so many shops to let out money, for which they receive such security and for such time, as stands most for the conveniency of trade, and therefore the more the better'.[80] 'The most visible means to preserve these kingdoms in their trade and navigation,' advised Sir Francis Brewster, 'is the setting up a national bank.' So obvious was this point that Brewster presumed 'the usefulness of banks in England is not now controverted'.[81] 'Money in a nation of trade, is like blood in the veins, if it circulates in all parts, the body is healthy; if it be wanting in any parts, it languisheth,' noted H.M., one of the earliest proponents of the bank. Banks guaranteed the circulation of money, which will 'beget trade and people, and they will beget riches …. Riches are the conveniencies of a nation: but trade and people are the glory and strength of the kingdom.'[82] H.M. was sure that a bank would initiate a series of knock-on effects, because with a bank 'people will increase, for trade will bring in people as well as riches to the nation: where trade is, there will be employment; where employment is, there will people resort; where people are, there will be consumption of all commodities'.[83] This was why, as John Brewer has pointed out, 'for more than a generation the state was seen as one of the major agents of social and economic change'.[84]

Because England had a strong and interventionist state in the late seventeenth century, because the English state at the supposed moment of genesis of the bourgeois public sphere was engaged in activities characteristic of the state at the moment of the structural transformation, Habermas's question needs to be reformulated. The question is not why did England generate the ideal of the bourgeois public sphere capable of restraining state intervention into society before other Europeans. That ideal was never promoted in England. The right question is, why was Britain 'able to enjoy the fruits of military prowess without the misfortunes of a *dirigiste* or despotic regime'?[85] Why was the post-revolutionary English state able to be simultaneously powerful and protective of public discussion of political economy?

IV

Habermas may have described the symptom imprecisely, but perhaps he understood the cause of the disease. Was the simultaneous emergence of bourgeois public discourse and England's strong state the result of a crisis of capitalism? Was it the consequence of a struggle between the financial and manufacturing sectors?

Again, empirical research suggests that Habermas is on to something, but he is too analytically imprecise. There was no crisis of capitalism in the late seventeenth century pitting the manufacturing against the financial sector. Instead there was a great political struggle between the defenders of an agrarian and the defenders of a manufacturing political economy. There was a struggle between those who understood property as potentially infinitely expansive because of the productive capacity of human labour and those who understood property to be finite and commerce a zero-sum game.

The overseas trading monopolies, in particular the Royal African Company and the East India Company, so favoured by James II, developed a coherent and consistent economic philosophy in the 1680s. Company correspondence, court briefs and political position papers all enunciated commitment to the notion that the basis of property was land and that therefore international commerce was a fierce competitive game to capture that necessarily finite resource. 'The principal advantage and foundation of trade in England is raised from the wealth which is gained out of the produce of the earth,' contended Sir Josiah Child, the long-time director of the East India Company.[86] This implied a finite economy totally 'derived out of this principal stock of good husbandry'.[87] Since no wealth was created by human labour, international trade was necessarily a zero-sum game: 'whatever weakens' Italy, France or Holland 'enriches and strengthens England'.[88] In Child's view the government should intervene in the economy to support the landed gentleman as against the manufacturing capitalist. The government, he thought, was responsible 'for promoting the credit, and securing those privileges which the land is justly entitled to' and should therefore replace 'public taxes that are laid on the land' with an 'excise', thereby 'easing those few that are the proprietors of land, to lay it on those many that raise their estates out of the produce of the land'.[89]

Josiah Child, Benjamin Bathurst and a whole range of merchants had long worked with James in the committee rooms of the African and East India companies. In 1685 the King's Bench ruling on the case of the East India Company v. Sandys made their economic views official English policy. 'As to manufactures', the creation of goods by human labour, argued Chief Justice Jefferies in his most expansive opinion, 'the public weal is little concerned therein.'[90] Land, not manufactures or exchange, was what mattered for Jefferies. 'The King is the only person truly concerned in this question' of the East India Company, Jefferies reasoned, 'for this island supported its inhabitants in many ages without any foreign trade at all, having in it all things necessary for the life of man.'[91] Property and livelihood depended on land. Trade was clearly a luxury, not a necessary, and therefore it was well within the king's prerogative to regulate all foreign trade as he saw fit. Justice Holloway asserted that the king 'hath the sole right and power of trade'.[92]

The opponents of this view suggested instead that England was a relatively small country that could not hope to compete economically with the great European powers in agrarian wealth. Instead, these polemicists argued, England's economic future lay with manufacturing. They argued, with more than a passing nod to the economic miracle occurring in the Netherlands, that no country was absolutely limited by its raw materials. Human ingenuity and human labour could turn even the least well endowed country into an economic powerhouse. 'It is the manufacturers of a commodity that is in general sale, that employs people and produces the great profit,' Carew Reynell argued, 'although the original materials are not in the country.'[93] 'It is manufactures must do the work,' he enthused, 'which will not only increase people, but also trade and advance it. It saves likewise money in our purses by lessening importation, and brings money in by exportation.'[94] Manufacturing set in motion a process which rendered property infinite; trade was no longer a zero-sum game.

> Where abundance of manufacturing people are, they consume and sweep away all country commodities, and the wares of ordinary retail trades, with all sorts of victuals, wearing apparel, and other necessaries, and employ abundance of handicraftsmen, in wooden and iron work for tools, and instruments that belong to their trades, and so maintain and increase abundance of husbandmen, retailers and artificers of all sorts, and they again increasing, take up more manufactures, and so they thrive one by another, ad infinitum.[95]

'Though we are a nation already pretty substantial,' Reynell concluded, 'yet it is easy for us to be ten times richer.'[96]

Many opponents of James II's economic policies, many critics of the East India and African companies, expressed similar views. 'It is manifest by experience,' claimed William James, 'that where a manufacture and much people are settled in any part of the nation, there the lands are not only occupied, but yield the greatest rents, and the fruits thereof the greatest price.'[97] James Whiston, who sought to compete with John Houghton in the market place for economic information, thought that 'industrious inhabitants', not land, were the 'original riches, as well as strength of the nation'.[98] John Locke was sure that 'if we rightly estimate things as they come to our use, and cast up the several expenses about them, what in them is purely owing to nature, and what to labour, we shall find that in most of them 99/100 are wholly to be put on the account of labour'. No wonder he was convinced that for states 'the honest industry of mankind' and 'numbers of men are to be preferred to largeness of dominions'.[99]

In late seventeenth-century England there was a fierce and wide-ranging debate about England's economic future. There was no crisis of capitalism. Both James II and his opponents defended modernizing economic policies. This was not a conflict between manufacturers and financiers. Manufacturers came to detest the East India Company and the African Company because the two commercial monopolies preferred to import finished goods from the East and West Indies rather than export English textiles and other manufactured goods. When James II was overthrown, they sought to reverse the state's economic priorities. The post-revolutionary state intervened in the economy by promoting the Bank of England, an institution that from the first helped English manufactures.[100]

The debate over political economy that took place in the public sphere in late seventeenth-century England was eerily similar to the debate that took place in France.[101] But that debate took place at Versailles, not in city streets, urban coffee houses, or in the press. Political economy was debated in France only in government memoranda, and at times through the back-room intrigues of an intensely competitive court. Francois de Salignac de la Mothe Fénelon, one of the most articulate critics of Louis XIV's economic policies, was able to express his views in print only in the form of a novel.[102] Indeed, his criticism of French political economic practice resulted ultimately in his exile in August 1697.[103]

The different histories of the bourgeois public sphere in England and France in the late seventeenth century had much to do with the countries' relative economic positions. France, as contemporaries knew, had three times more arable land than England.[104] France had perhaps four times the population of England.[105] Although Louis XIV's finance minister Jean-Baptiste Colbert attempted to create a vibrant French manufacturing sector to compete with the English and the Dutch in the late seventeenth century, modern historians agree that he failed.[106] Louis XIV was able to build up his tremendous armies, to cow the majority of Europe, by extracting the wealth amassed on the large estates of the French nobility.[107] England, by contrast, could become a major player on the European scene only by combining land revenue with taxes on manufactures and foreign trade.[108] The English state, unlike its French counterpart, could not afford to shut down the bourgeois public sphere. It needed merchants and tradesmen to have information about markets, overseas developments and government policies. However much it did not like to open the floodgates to political and economic criticism, the post-revolutionary regime realized that it needed to do so. The creation of the Bank of England depended on the existence of a public confident that its money would be safe. That is why contemporaries often pointed out that 'all national banks have hitherto been peculiar to commonwealths'.[109] In the 1660s Colbert had considered and rejected a public solution to Louis XIV's early financial troubles precisely because it would have required some form of public oversight of governmental financial policies.[110] Only with the exigencies of war on a global scale hitherto unknown did it become clear that France's rich land could no longer support the state's insatiable appetite. Only then did the French state turn to new methods of public finance, only then did the French initiate a very public debate about political economy.[111]

The bourgeois public sphere in a Habermasian sense emerged in England in the late seventeenth century as the result of crisis. Because Habermas was imprecise about both the nature of the early modern state and the tenor of the debate about capitalism he was not able to describe the causes or consequences of that crisis with the necessary precision. There was no crisis of capitalism in late seventeenth-century England. There was instead a crisis in the state. Both James II and William III pursued modernizing state policies. Both rejected the notion of a weak, non-interfering state. James II sought to follow policies not unlike those of Colbert, favouring agriculture at home and colonies abroad. William III and his advisers, however, determined that England could not hope to compete with France by employing an agrarian policy. Instead they promoted domestic manufacturing, supported by an integrated colonial system in which the colonies would provide raw materials, not finished goods.

V

Much of the attraction of Habermas's *Structural Transformation* has been that it spoke to current normative concerns. Just as Robert Putnam became the darling of American talk shows, so Jürgen Habermas has become the social theoretical pop star of early modernists. Both scholars spoke to contemporary concerns about the impoverishment of our own political culture. Concerns about the inability of the public sphere to act as a check on the state have become only more urgent with revelations about British and American governmental reports about Middle Eastern politics. Perhaps the implication of this engagement with Habermas's work speaks to the present lament. England developed a bourgeois public sphere before France, before the Holy Roman Empire and before Spain because the English state became committed to the notion that wealth was potentially infinite. Only by allowing public discussion could it harness that wealth. The English government needed to persuade the manufacturing sector to invest in the state. It needed to persuade English men and women to purchase stock in the Bank of England. Compulsion and repression, experience had shown, would result in the flight of manufacturers and their capital. Similarly, I suggest, contemporary states committed to more Keynesian economic policies may have more of an interest in free and unregulated discussion of economic issues. States that are more pessimistic about human potential may be more willing to allow Rupert Murdoch, Silvio Berlusconi and others to monopolize and transform the bourgeois public sphere.

NOTES

I am grateful for the comments and suggestions of Don Herzog, Emilio Kouri, Peter Lake, Claudio Lomnitz, Patchen Markell, Bill Novak, Susan Stokes, and Rachel Weil.

1 Jean L. Cohen and Andrew Arato, *Civil Society and Political Theory* (Cambridge, 1992), 15, 29.

2 Robert D. Putnam, *Bowling Alone* (New York, 2000), 506. Putnam outlines the early modern origins of civil society in *Making Democracy Work* (Princeton NJ, 1993), 86–91; 121–32.

3 Jürgen Habermas, *The Structural Transformation of the Public Sphere*, trans. Thomas Burger (Cambridge, 1989), 57.

4 Habermas says Great Britain but refers in the early modern period exclusively to England.

5 Habermas, *Structural Transformation*, 7.

6 *Ibid.*, 19. It is important to note that, for Habermas, civil society, 'the realm of commodity exchange and social labor', lay not in the public sphere but in the private sphere (30).

7 *Ibid.*, 30–1.

8 *Ibid.*, 27.

9 *Ibid.*, 51.

10 *Ibid.*, 17.

11 *Ibid.*, 142.

12 *Ibid.*, 146.

13 *Ibid.*, 178.

14 *Ibid.*, 160.

15 It is possible to posit that Habermas saw the bourgeois public sphere emergeing in dialectic with the mercantlist state which it later trimmed. But, given Habermas's reliance on Heckscher, who emphasized the failure of the mercantilists to intervene successfully in the economy, either reading seems to me to be plausible.

16 Harold Mah, 'Phantasies of the public sphere: rethinking the Habermas of historians', *Journal of Modern History* 72 (March 2000), 167. I am grateful to Rachel Weil for calling my attention to this stimulating article.

17 Habermas, *Structural Transformation*, 36.

18 *Ibid.*, 36–7.

19 *Ibid.*, 177.

20 *Ibid.*, 178.

21 *Ibid.*, 52.

22 *Ibid.*, 52.

23 *Ibid.*, 27.

24 *Ibid.*, 19–20.

25 *Ibid.*, 57.

26 *Ibid.*, 14.

27 *Ibid.*, 15.

28 *Ibid.*, 57–8.

29 *Ibid.*, 144.

30 Sharon Achinstein, *Milton and the Revolutionary Reader* (Princeton NJ, 1994), 24–5, 34–7; Joad Raymond, *Pamphlets and Pamphleteering in Early Modern England* (Cambridge, 2003), 264–75; David Norbrook, *Writing the English Republic* (Cambridge, 1999), 13 and *passim*.

31 Benjamin Worsley, *The Advocate* (London, 1651), 12.

32 Henry Parker, *Of a Free Trade.* (London, 1648), 5.

33 Steve Pincus, 'Neither Machiavellian moment nor possessive individualism', *American Historical Review* 103:3 (1998), 711–36. For a particular local example in which economic discussion played a significant role, see Andy Wood, *The Politics of Social Conflict* (Cambridge, 1999), 267–94.

34 Steve Pincus, '"Coffee politicians does create": coffeeehouses and Restoration political culture', *Journal of Modern History* 67 (1995), 807–34. I emphasize the coffee house as a site of commercial transaction in chapter 3 of *The First Modern Revolution* (Cambridge, forthcoming)

35 G. R. Robinson, *The British Post Office* (Princeton NJ, 1948), 48. Robinson discusses the transformation of the Post Office. Whitley's significant role is based on my own research in the Post Office archives.

36 Roger Whitley (London) to Mr Cale, 18 March 1673, Consignia, POST 94/12, unfoliated.

37 J.P., *The Merchant's Daily Companion* (London, 1684), 388. This qualitative assessment was confirmed by quantitative analysis: 'Lords of the Treasury's Order for the Increase of Salaries in the Post Office', 5 April 1688, Consignia, POST 1/1, fol. 51r.

38 Guy Miege, *The New State of England under their Majesties K. William and Q. Mary* (London, 1691), Part II, 46. Miege's estimation is based on his travels in the 1680s. See also John Chartres, 'Road carrying in England in the seventeenth century: myth and reality', *Economic History Review*, new ser., 30:1 (1977), 74; William Albert, *The Turnpike Road System in England* (Cambridge, 1972), 14–20.

39 These developments are best followed in Mark Knights, *Politics and Opinion in Crisis* (Cambridge 1994), especially 154–92.

40 Sir George Mackenzie (HM Advocate in Scotland), *Jus Regium* (London, 1684), 55.

41 John Lauder, 'Historicall Observes', 1683, National Library of Scotland, Adv. 24.4.6, fol. 165r.

42 Earl Rivers (London) to Sindey, 17 November 1687, Nottingham University Library, PwA 2097a.

43 Owen Wynne to Sir William Trumbull, 19 November 1685, BL, Trumbull Misc. XXIII, unfoliated.

44 R.D. (London) to ?, 3 November 1688, BL, Egerton Ms 2717, fol. 411r.

45 Lady Sunderland to Henry Sidney, 11 September 1688, BL, Additional Ms 32681, fol. 309v.

46 Nathaniel Cholmley (Whitby) to ?, 20 January 1686, North Yorkshire Record Office, ZCG, unfoliated.

47 Christopher Jeafferson (London) to ?, 29 January 1686, in John Cordy Jeafferson (ed.), *A Young Squire of the Sevententh Century: from the Papers (AD 1676–1686) of Christopher Jeaffreson of Dullingham House, Cambridgeshire* II (London, 1878), 269.

48 Marquess of Halifax to Sir William Trumbull, 22 March 1686, BL, Trumbull Misc. XXIV, unfoliated.

49 Gilbert Dolben (London) to Sir William Trumbull, 28 January 1686, BL, Trumbull Ms 54. The examples of this could be multiplied almost indefinitely.

50 Barillon (Windsor) to Louis XIV, 27 August/6 September 1685, PRO, PRO 31/3/161, fols 36–7. Petition of Marmaduke Ayscough, Barber Surgeon, of York [1686/7], West York-shire Record Office, MX 46/21. I have located the extensive list of coffee houses, taverns, and inns throughout the country forced to host James II's new standing army among the War Office papers in the Public Record Office – in another context I will present the findings from my analysis of those papers.

51 Proclamation of the Mayor of London, 19 January 1686, Corporation of London Record Office, Journal of the Common Council, No. 50, fol. 151v; Ham de Pay (Whitehall) to John Ellis, 19 January 1686, BL, Additional Ms 4194, fol. 14r.

52 The examples are numerous. Here are some: Roger Morrice, Entering Book, 14 August 1686, Doctor William's Library, 31 P, 599; London Newsletter, 9 October 1688, BL, Additional Ms 4194, fol. 366r; Newsletter (Whitehall), 12 October 1688, Beinecke, Osb Mss 1, Box 2/Folder 90; William Westby, Memoirs, 25 October 1688, Folger Shakespeare Library, V.a. 469, fol. 41r.

53 Evelyn, *Diary*, ed. E. S. De Beer (6 vols, Oxford, 1955–59), 24 August 1688, IV, 596–7; William Hamilton (Whitehall) to earl of Arran, 5 October 1686, National Archives of Scotland, GD 406/1/3307; Memoire de M. Robert, 27 December/6 January 1685/6, PRO, PRO 31/3/163, fol. 82r; Information of William Martyn of Exeter, 18 February 1686, PRO, SP 31/3. fol. 77r; Petition of Thomas Woodhouse, Serjeant at Mace, City of York, December 1686, West Yorks. RO, MX 45/13; C. Reresby (Cambridge) to Sir John Reresby, 9 November 1686, West Yorks. RO, MX 49/14; Sir Ralph Verney (Claydon) to John Verney, 2 August 1685, Buckinghamshire Record Office, Verney Mss; Roger Morrice, Entering Book, 23 January 1685/6, Dr William's Library, 31 P, 517.

54 Richard Parkinson (ed.), *The Autobiography of Henry Newcome* II (Manchester, Chetham Society, 1852), Chetham Society XXVII (15 March 1686), 262; K. W. H. Howard (ed.), *The Axminster Ecclesiastica, 1660–1698* (Sheffield, 1976), 27 December 1685, 110; Thomas Story, *A Journal of the Life of Thomas Story* (Newcastle upon Tyne, 1747), 3. These examples could be multiplied.

55 Charles Morgan (Hull) to earl of Huntingdon, 26 September 1685, HEH, HA 9383; Dr Parman (London) to Sir Ralph Verney, 17 August 1687, Bucks. RO, Verney Mss; Sir Nicholas Slarning (Salisbury) to William Blathwayt, 2 November 1686, Beinecke, Osb Mss 2, Box 8/Folder 172; William Blathwayt (London) to Sir Robert Douglas, 16 October 1686, PRO, WO 4/1, fol. 18v; George Balle (York) to Sir John Reresby, 15 January 1686, West Yorks. RO, MX 43/29; William Hamilton (Whitehall) to earl of Arran, 26 April 1687, NAS, GD 406/1/3467; James Vernon (London) to d'Albeville, 20 January 1688, Indiana University, Albeville Mss.

56 Sir David Nairne, Journal, April 1686, National Library of Scotland, Ms 14226, fol. 7v.

57 Newsletter to Richard Bulstrode, 15 March 1686, University of Texas, Henry Ransome

Library, Bulstrode Newsletters; Barillon (Windsor) to Louis XIV, 8/18 July 1686, PRO, PRO 31/3/166, fol. 39r. Both Nonconformists and Anglicans were placed under severe pressure when they ignored James II's warnings: H. Thynne (London) to earl of Weymouth, 18 March 1686, Longleat House, Thynne Mss 14, fol. 109r; London Newsletter, 15 January 1687, FSL, Lc 1761; Roger Morrice, Entering Book, 23 October 1686, Dr William's Library, 31 P, 640; Privy Council Minutes, 17 July 1686, PRO, PC 2/71, fol. 153v; Jonthana Trelawney (bishop of Bristol) to Sunderland, 21 May 1686, PRO, SP 31/3, fols 70–1; James II to William Sancroft, 5 March 1686, CSPD, p. 57; Robert Yard (Whitehall) to d'Albeville, 14 January 1686, Indiana University, Albeville Mss; Bonrepaus (London) to Marquis de Seignelay, 11/21 March 1686, PRO, PRO 31/3/165, fol. 79r.

58 Evelyn, *Diary*, 5 November 1685, De Beer IV, 487; John Lauder, 'Historicall Observes', 5–6 November 1685, NLS, Adv. 24.4.6, fol. 133r; Owen Wynne (London) to John Ellis, 13 November 1686, BL, Additional Ms 4194, fol. 197r; Van Citters (London) to States General, 28 October/7 November 1687, BL, Additional Ms 34510, fol. 58v; Roger Morrice, Entering Book, 10 December 1686, Dr William's Library, 31 Q, 33; John Verney (London) to Sir Ralph Verney, 6 December 1687, Bucks. RO, Verney Mss.

59 Proclamation of the mayor, 2 June 1687, Journal of the Common Council, CLRO, 50, fol. 318r; *A Letter to the Author of the Dutch Design Anatomized*, 8 November 1688 [1688], 1; London Newsletter, 24 September 1687, FSL, Lc 1861; London Newsletter, 19 January 1688, FSL, Lc 1910; London Newsletter, 14 February 1688, FSL, Lc 1919; Examination of Richard Lambert, Bookseller, in York, 14 September 1687, BL, Additional Ms 41804, fol. 315r; Roger Morrice, Entering Book, 30 October 1686, Dr William's Library, 31P, 646; Instructions for Sir Edmund Andros, 12 September 1686, PRO, CO 5/904, fol. 148r; Richard Bentley to John Evelyn, 4 September 1686, BL, Evelyn In-letters 2, No. 155; *A Proclamation Inhibiting all Persons after the Four and Twentieth Day of June next to use the Trade of a Pedlar or Petty Chapman, unless they be Licensed ...*, 7 May 1686 (London, 1686); Robert Yard (Whitehall) to d'Albeville, 15 May 1688, Indiana University, Albeville Mss.

60 Ailebury, *Memoirs*, Buckley, p. 161; *The Late Revolution: or, the Happy Change*. (London, 1690), 12; Hudson (London) to Gilbert Burnet, 25 April 1687, BL, Additional Ms 41804, fol. 278r; Christopher Jeafferson (London) to Capt. J. Phipps, 8 September 1686, in *Young Squire* II, 316; Barillon (Windsor) to Louis XIV, 20/30 September 1686, PRO, PRO 31/3/167, fol. 20.

61 Robert Harley to Sir Edward Harley, 9 February 1686, BL, Additional Ms 70013, fol. 322r; London Newsletter, 27 November 1686, FSL, Lc 1739.

62 John Lauder, 'Historicall Observes', April 1686, NLS, Adv. 24.4.6, fol. 127r. For similar trepidation, see earl of Chesterfield to marquess of Halifax, 30 January 1687, BL, Althorp C3.

63 Samuel Masters (Preacher to Bridewell Hospital), *The Case of Allegiance in our Present Circumstances Consider'd* (London, 1689). Licensed: 21 March 1689, 2–3. He was referring to James II's reign.

64 *A Dialogue between Dick and Tom* (London, 1689). Licensed: 18 January 1689, 4.

65 Robert Kirk, Minister, of Aberfoyle, 'Sermons, Occurrences ...', 1690, Edinburgh University Library, La. III. 545, fol. 101v.

66 Henri Misson, *M. Misson's Memoirs and Observations in his Travels over England*, trans. John Ozell (London, 1719), 39–40, 203–4. One could multiply examples from English men and women, but both Kirk and Misson highlight that England was a comparatively talkative place.

67 The average year in the 1690s had twenty times more publications on economic matters than in the 1620s, six and a half times more such publications than in the 1650s, and fifteen times more such publications than in the 1680s. This survey has been based on Goldsmiths–Kress listed titles, excluding those listed in the 'political' category. The yearly averages were 4.3 a year in the 1620s; 12.2 a year in the 1650s, 85.8 a year in the 1690s. I am grateful to my research assistant Jessica Hanser for completing this survey.

68 Perry Gauci, *The Politics of Trade* (Oxford, 2001), 209–20.

69 Houghton, *A Collection*, 1 June 1692, 20 January, 3 February, 17 March 1693; Margaret Hunt, *The Middling Sort* (Berkeley CA, 1996), 175–6.

70 Houghton, *A Collection*, 6 April 1692, 17 March 1693.

71 *Ibid.*, 28 July 1693.

72 Henri Misson, *Memoires d'Angleterre* (The Hague, 1698), 12 September 1697, 62 (my translation). This is one passage that was left out of the eighteenth-century English translation.

73 These points I advance with a good deal of documentation in *The First Modern Revolution*.

74 ? (Edinburgh) to William Dunlop, 18 November 1689, NLS, 9250, fol. 110r.

75 William Aglionby (The Hague) to Mr Warre, 17/27 June 1690, PRO, SP 84/221, fol. 151r.

76 Thomas Ertman, *The Birth of the Leviathan* (Cambridge, 1997), 208–17; John Brewer, *The Sinews of Power* (London, 1989), 88–9 and *passim*.

77 David Hey, *The Fiery Blades of Hallamshire* (Leicester, 1991), 136–8.

78 Brewer, *Sinews of Power*, 95; Henry Roseveare, *The Treasury* (New York, 1969), 70.

79 Habermas, *Structural Transformation*, 58.

80 John Cary, *An Essay on the State of England in Relation to its Trade* (London, 1695), 32.

81 Sir Francis Brewster, *Essays on Trade and Navigation* (London, 1695). Licensed: 3 January 1695, 6, 109.

82 H. M., *England's Glory; or, the Great Improvement of Trade in General by a Royal Bank* (London, 1694). Licensed: 23 June 1694, sig. A3r, 11–12.

83 *Ibid.*, 23 June 1694, 18–19.

84 Brewer, *Sinews of Power*, xxi.

85 *Ibid.*, xviii. For the purposes of this chapter I have assumed that there was a more vibrant discussion of economic issues in England than in France. This will need to be proved.

86 Josiah Child, *A Discourse of the Nature, Use and Advantages of Trade* (London, 1694). Licensed: 23 December 1693, 7.

87 Child, *A Discourse* (1694), 8.

88 Child, *A Discourse concerning Trade and that in Particular of the East Indies*, published with *A Supplement* (London, 1689), 25 June 1689, 3.

89 Child, *A Discourse* (1694), 17.

90 Chief Justice Jefferies opinion, 31 January 1685, EIC v. Sandys, in T. B. Howell (ed.), *A*

Complete Collection of State Trials X (London, 1811), 523.

91   Jefferies opinion, 31 January 1685, EIC v. Sandys, in Howell, *State Trials* X, 534.

92   Holloway's opinion, 31 January 1685, EIC v. Sandys, Bodleian Ms Rawl C130, fol. 223v.

93   Carew Reynell, *A Necessary Companion, or, The English Interest Discovered and Promoted* (London, 1685), 17–18.

94   Reynell, *Necessary Companion* (1685), sigs (A1)v–(A2)r.

95   *Ibid.*, 48.

96   *Ibid.*, sigs A5v–A6r.

97   William James, *Englands Interest* (London, 1689). Licensed 9 July 1689, 2.

98   James Whiston, *A Discourse of the Decay of Trade* (London, 1693), 3.

99   John Locke, 'Second Treatise of Government', in David Wootton (ed.), *Political Writings of John Locke* (New York, 1993), 281–2.

100 I have outlined this case elsewhere. The evidence that the East India Company's opponents were behind the creation of the Bank of England is presented by D. W. Jones, *War and Economy* (Oxford, 1988), 12–13.

101 Lionel Rothkrug, *Opposition to Louis XIV* (Princeton NJ, 1965), 373–419.

102 *Les Aventures de Télémaque*, which was published in 1699.

103 Rothkrug, *Opposition to Louis XIV*, 286, 373.

104 Miege, *New State of England*, 1691, part I, 2.

105 François Crouzet, *A History of the European Economy* (Charlottesville VA, 2001), 73.

106 James B. Collins, *The State in Early Modern France* (Cambridge, 1995), 112; Crouzet, *History of the European Economy*, 86.

107 Ertman, *Birth of the Leviathan*, 130.

108 Brewer, *Sinews of Power*, 95–9.

109 *Some Considerations offered against the Continuance of the Bank of England* [1694], 2; John Briscoe, *A Discourse of the late Funds of the Million-Act, Lottery-Act, and Bank of England* (2nd edn, London, 1694), 4. This was probably why John Toland was so enthusiastic about the creation of the bank: *The Oceana of James Harrington and his other Works* (London, 1700), iii.

110 Ertman, *Birth of the Leviathan*, 129.

111 *Ibid.*, 133–55; Rothkrug, *Opposition to Louis XIV*, 392–457; Collins, *State in Early Modern France*, 140–75.

Chapter 10

◆

Matthew Smith versus the 'great men': plot talk, the public sphere and the problem of credibility in the 1690s

Rachel Weil

I

Much talk about politics in the late seventeenth century revolved around stories about plots, counter-plots and sham plots. Arguably, talk about plots was the most important form of critical political discourse in the period.[1] In the absence of a concept of loyal opposition, disagreement with government policies was often expressed as an accusation of treason against members of the government. Thus, Whigs in the Exclusion crisis used Titus Oates's revelations of a popish plot to criticize royal policies and advisers.[2] Likewise, in the 1690s members of parliament like Jack Arnold and Sir Henry Dutton Colt energetically promoted the discovery of conspiracies in order to enhance their own reputations for patriotic zeal and embarrass political rivals at the centre of power.[3] A person's belief or disbelief in the existence of the Rye House Plot, Popish Plot, Mealtub Plot or Lancashire Plot came to be a defining marker of his or her party loyalty.

An examination of 'plot talk' invites us to reflect critically upon two influential claims that scholars have made about late seventeenth-century England. The first, that of Jürgen Habermas, is that the period witnessed the emergence of a 'public sphere'. Because discussion of plots took place in print and in coffee houses, because it interested a wide range of persons, and because it focused on matters of public importance and the public good, it can and should be studied for what it can tell us about that emergent public sphere. At the same time, plot talk was centrally concerned with deciding which stories and witnesses should be believed. It therefore calls to mind the important work of Steven Shapin, in *The Social History of Truth*, on the construction of credibility in this period. Although Shapin's research was confined to the problem of credibility in the realm of natural philosophy, it has been fruitfully extended into other arenas – most notably by Adrian Johns with respect to print culture[4] – and it is certainly tempting to test its applicability in the context of politics. It is important to note that neither Habermas nor Shapin addresses the phenomenon of plot talk. Nor do they seem to address one another's arguments, which are, as we shall see, in tension. It is precisely for these reasons that plot talk may be a valuable way to evaluate both of their theoretical frameworks, and to put them into dialogue with one another.

Let me first briefly introduce each of these frameworks, as they seem relevant to the phenomenon of late seventeenth-century plot talk, and then bring up some of the difficulties that arise when they are applied.

Talk about plots seems to stand as a compelling instance of the public sphere in action. It is a striking feature of the period that political informers turned to the public by publishing their discoveries, petitioning parliament or starting rumours. Talk about plots inherently threatened to penetrate the *arcana imperii*, to expose precisely what governments claimed needed to be kept secret. Moreover, the public talk about plots ranged over precisely those areas that Habermas has identified as the typical objects of scrutiny in a nascent public sphere. The common good, especially the common *economic* good, was widely canvassed in these discussions. For example, a printed petition of London citizens demanding an investigation of plot allegations identified the suspected 'horrid conspiracy' and a threat to the nation's trade and credit, which could be restored only by a thorough inquiry.[5] Investigations of plots in the 1690s were closely connected with investigations of smuggling, excise fraud, coining, and counterfeiting, involving not only the same personnel but also the same concerns about the 'credit of the government'.

Moreover, if a Habermasian public sphere is defined as 'a social space of critical debate available to all, regardless of social position',[6] then the plot talk of the period stands as a shining example of an arena in which people of all ranks and both sexes could claim a licence to speak in the interests of the nation. The Association oath of 1696, to which vast numbers of people subscribed in the aftermath of the Assassination Plot, explicitly committed its adherents to doing everything in their power to protect the government. Informing was thus a legitimate, necessary expression of citizenship. Lack of social status was not a bar to participation in discussions of plots. Indeed, the lowly and down-and-out were thought to know more about plots than respectable people; informers were able to inform accurately about crimes and plots precisely because they had taken part in them. James Vernon, the secretary of state and therefore the chief official charged with investigating alleged conspiracies, remarked that 'the witnesses may be pitiful fellows and such as have assisted in the same crimes [as they are informing on], but may they not therefore be able to discover them ... the generality of informers are scoundrels, and yet their oaths must pass until they are disproved'.[7]

Nonetheless, the plot talk of the period fits rather uncomfortably into a narrative of an emergent public sphere. It was often fantastical and murderous.

Beyond that, in one important respect, plot talk defied the Habermasian model of the public sphere. For Habermas, arguments in the public sphere were disembodied, detached from persons. The 'best argument' was to win, no matter who made it.[8] But in debates about plots, the identity and motivation of the source were all-important. How else but by knowing the source could one distinguish true information about a plot from a plot to pretend there was a plot, and that in turn from a plot to pretend there was a plot to pretend there was a plot?[9] Plot talk thus tended to affix information to particular bodies, not let it float freely. It was about persons and their credibility, not disembodied facts.

This brings us to the question of how plot talk might fit into Steven Shapin's account of credibility in the *Social History of Truth*. Shapin argues that credibility in the late seventeenth century was thought to be the monopoly of the social elite. It was only these elites who were thought capable of 'free action', that is, of action (or speech) uncorrupted by their personal interest or dependence upon a superior; hence only their testimony was truly reliable.[10] As advice literature from the period routinely put it, 'we ought to give credit to a noble or gentleman before any of the inferior sort'.[11] 'The distribution of imputed credit and reliability,' Shapin argues, 'followed the contours of authority and power.'[12]

There is an interesting tension between Shapin's and Habermas's narratives. Whereas Habermas, as we noted, sees the space of the public sphere as being open to all, Shapin's work suggests that the ability to speak in public about matters of importance to that public *and to be believed* was dependent upon social position.

The perspectives of Shapin and Habermas might be brought closer into line, however, if we pursue the suggestion of Harold Mah that the 'public sphere' is best understood as a powerful fiction. In a very lucid gloss on Habermas and the uses to which historians have put his work, Mah suggests that we err in thinking the 'public sphere' was a literal reality. Rather, he suggests,

> construing the public sphere as a powerful political fiction would lead historians [try to] ... figure out why and how certain groups are able to render their social particularity invisible and therefore make viable claims to universality, while other groups are consigned to public performances that always undo themselves because those performances end up proclaiming their own identity, their social particularity.[13]

On this reading, then, Shapin's gentlemen are the social group most able to put on the mantle of universality, even though it is in fact their social position that allows them to do so.

My goal in this chapter is to empirically investigate the processes by which claims of public credibility – that is, claims to speak *believably* about matters of public importance – were constructed in the late seventeenth century; to determine exactly where, how, and whether it mattered that social identities were erased or invoked when a 'public' engaged in the practices of critical-rational debate. I will look at the contest over the credibility of one informer, Matthew Smith, whose activities posed a threat to the reputations of particular members of the ministry, above all the duke of Shrewsbury, and therefore more broadly to the 'credit of the government'. Exploring the strategies of legitimation used by each side, I will show that Habermasian ideals of what would constitute rational-critical public debate were in fact invoked on both sides. At the same time, social identities were hardly irrelevant in the tactics and outcomes of the debates. Smith's antagonists were the secretary of state, Charles Talbot, duke of Shrewsbury, his under-secretary, James Vernon, and their allies, the 'court whigs' (also known as the Junto), including Wharton, Somers, Sunderland, Admiral Russell, the earl of Portland and the king himself. Smith was significantly lower on the social scale. The son of a Coventry mercer who had held local and civic office, Smith had been a student in the Inner Temple and had served as captain of a garrison in the reign of James II. At the time of the events with which we are concerned, he had lost his army post and apparently earned a living as a writer and a spy.[14] The conflict with which we are concerned was understood by its participants as one between 'great' and 'little' men. The story raises questions about how to account for the significance of social relationships within the practices of public rationality: how to put together Habermas's public sphere and Shapin's *Social History of Truth*?

The conflict between Smith and Shrewsbury is an especially well documented instance of what I think was a fairly typical conflict between secretaries of state, the officials responsible for uncovering conspiracies against the government, and the informers who provided information about such plots in the expectation of a reward. Alan Marshall, in his study of intelligence in Charles II's reign, has described the relationship between these groups as one of mutual dependence and mutual contempt, and there is no reason to think this changed after 1688.[15] Indeed, the relationship may have gotten worse. There are a number of intriguing instances in the 1690s in which the secretaries of state apparently felt afraid that the informers with whom they dealt might, if insufficiently rewarded, turn around and accuse them of 'stifling plots'. The dangers that informers could pose was described in a letter from Richard Kingston (himself an informer) to Secretary of State William Trumbull. Kingston described the headaches that one Ormeston had given the earl of Nottingham, Trumbull's predecessor in office. Ormeston, said Kingston,

> always hung very heavy upon my Lord's [Nottingham's] purse strings, and for one truth told twenty stories. He would invent horrible plots and then exercise his faculties in telling how they were disappointed ... in these practices my Lord slighted him, and at last returned his letters whole by the same hand that brought them, for which he took this revenge. When he saw the current run strong against my

Lord, he [and others] drew up an information against my Lord for stifling plots and discouraging informers, which by means of the Scotch Secretary found access to the King.[16]

Kingston later told Trumbull that he would have to pay Ormeston two guineas for worthless information, but that it was worth it 'to prevent the hideous clamour that will otherwise be made against you for stifling plots'.[17] Trumbull and Nottingham's experience with Ormeston eerily foreshadowed that of Shrewsbury and his under-secretary, James Vernon, with Matthew Smith. As Vernon was to complain, 'I find I am over and over in his [Smith's] remarks for a concealer of the plot and a discourager of the discovery.'[18]

Given the readiness of at least part of the public to believe in just about any plot, the secretaries of state needed to worry about their own public image. They had to be seen to be active in the prevention of plots in order to avoid being accused of complicity in them. The vulnerability of secretaries was further compounded by the fact that there were almost always two of them, one for 'North' and one for 'South', who at times represented antagonistic parties or factions. The inbuilt politicized rivalry meant that an informer who didn't receive a hearing from one secretary of state could go to the other, who might gleefully embrace the idea that his rival was derelict in his duty. This is how Ormeston's accusations of Nottingham, described above, had come to the king by way of 'the Scotch Secretary'. This was likewise how Smith, finding Shrewsbury unresponsive, came to deal with Trumbull.

Finally, secretaries of state in the 1690s may have been unusually vulnerable because allegations of Jacobitism in high places were frequent and (to a degree) plausible. The Williamite political elite contained many people who had Jacobite relatives, may have briefly flirted with Jacobitism, or were at some point rumoured to be Jacobites. The earl of Marlborough was famously accused in 1692 of Jacobitism. Indeed, as our story takes place, the earl of Sunderland, the notorious henchman of James II, was remaking himself as a trusted counsellor to William III.[19] William's attitude (and the attitude of the political elite) seems to have been that past behaviour was not a reason to refuse the services of talented politicians. But this relatively tolerant standard of loyalty which members of the elite applied to one another must have come to look uncomfortably lax. This would have been especially the case after the Association oath of 1696, widely imposed not only on the elite but also on humbler subjects, demanded unwavering, unambiguous adherence to the new regime. In this context, informers who accused high-ranking ministers of being insufficiently zealous for the revolution would seem especially dangerous.

Secretaries of state in the 1690s, then, seem to have concerned themselves not just with the discovery of actual plots, but also with the management of informers in order to ensure that their self-serving allegations did not wreak havoc with the reputations of respectable men in the government.

This required in turn that they maintain a monopoly on the accreditation of informers, that is, retain the power to say who and what should be believed. The story of Matthew Smith is the story of Shrewsbury trying to defend his monopoly, and having a tough time of it. Smith took his case to other audiences: the other secretary of state (Trumbull), other officials with access to the king, the king himself, the parliament, the bystanders in a tavern, and the readers of the press.

II

The narrative that follows here is derived from Matthew Smith's published pamphlets, supplemented by correspondence between Shrewsbury and Vernon, and other members of the Junto. Interestingly, there is little conflict among these sources as to the basic events which occurred in the relationship between Smith and Shrewsbury. About the meanings of those events, of course, there was much conflict, which will be analysed in the following section.

Captain Matthew Smith was nephew to Sir William Parkyns, a Jacobite gentleman who was ultimately convicted and executed for his role in the Assassination Plot. Smith had held a commission in the duke of Norfolk's regiment, but his commission was taken from him after 1688, he said, because he had Catholic relatives. His resentment led him to the Jacobites, among whom 'my disgrace and other circumstances brought me into a confidence and greatness'. But, Smith continued, when he learned that his new friends were French-loving king killers, he resolved to 'to disappoint such damnable designs'.[20] So in November 1694 Smith began to provide intelligence about Jacobite doings to the secretary of state, the earl of Shrewsbury, and the under-secretary, James Vernon. Some of this was generalized political information that would have been available elsewhere, such as the fact that the Jacobites were split into Melfordian and Middletonian factions. Other 'discoveries' by Smith, such as information about the location of arms buried at William Parkyns's estate in Warwickshire, seems not to have been acted upon by Shrewsbury or Vernon. As Paul Hopkins notes, Shrewsbury and Vernon's slowness to take action may have been related to their recent experience in the Lancashire Plot trial of 1694, when over-hasty willingness to try men for treason on the word of an informer, John Lunt, had resulted in an acquittal of the defendants and an embarrassment for the government.[21]

Whatever the reason, Shrewsbury's response to Smith was lukewarm. Payments to Smith dribbled out in £20 chunks, but Shrewsbury was clearly holding back. In December of 1694, for example, he told Smith in a note that 'though I shall be willing to give all reasonable encouragement to your endeavours; yet it being the King's money I am to dispose of, I cannot think myself discharged, if I advance any money before I see some service performed'.[22] Indeed, Shrewsbury even made efforts to break off the relationship, telling Smith 'you will upon my account put yourself to no further charge or trouble'.[23] He did enclose £20 with this note, however, which gave Smith a chance to declare himself in Shrewsbury's debt, and hence to endeavour to repay him with more service. The relationship had its ups as well as downs. In December 1695 Shrewsbury seemed positively enthusiastic about the prospects of Smith cultivating an informant, Jack Hewett, who could find the private boats that carried letters to and from France.[24]

Smith soon had something even more interesting than letters from France. He began to tell Shrewsbury of a plot to seize and/or kill the king, involving among others Jack Hewett's uncle, Mr Holmes. The details of this plot were not yet clear to Smith, and so he began to request large cash advances from Shrewsbury in order to enhance his credit with the Jacobites and thus garner the information needed. To be allowed into the details of the plot, he explained, he needed to show himself ready to help out, and had to equip himself with a horse and weapons at the cost of £50. Moreover, he had already run up huge debts working himself into the plotters' confidence. As he explained to Shrewsbury, Jacobites liked to drink,

> so that my expenses are very considerable, by reason I am necessitated to excuse some of the company from paying; and a man is also obliged to appear well in clothes, otherwise he is slighted: and it prevails upon people to be the more open and free when they see he has the appearance of a gentleman.[25]

If Shrewsbury would pay his expenses (and not a farthing, he promised, would be spent but for the service of the king) he would soon be in a position to rout the plot.

As it turned out, there was a plot, but it was routed without Smith's help. Even as Smith pleaded for money, two conspirators, Prendergast and De la Rue, betrayed what has come to be known as the Assassination Plot to the authorities in February 1696.[26] This did have the effect of validating some of Smith's information, as people he had named (Holmes, William Parkyns, Robert Charnock and John Friend) were indeed among the plotters. But, to Smith's disgust, Prendergast and De la Rue got the credit for being the 'first discoverers' of the plot. Smith's services went unrewarded.

Smith expressed his frustration in public places like coffee houses and taverns, and also claimed to be preparing a petition to parliament.[27] He also sought alternative patrons. Smith took his complaints to his old commander, the duke of Norfolk, who in turn introduced him to William Trumbull, who was the other secretary of state and Shrewsbury's antagonist. Smith also met with Charles Mordaunt, earl of Monmouth, who was gentleman of the bedchamber to the king and the cousin of Norfolk's wife. Eventually Smith met with Portland, and with King William himself. According to Smith, all of these people showed, at least initially, appreciation for his services. For their benefit, Smith put together copies of all the letters he had exchanged with Shrewsbury and Vernon, as well as minutes of meetings he had with them. Copies of this manuscript were left with Trumbull and shown to the king. Other copies seem to have circulated. Smith's complaints in various circles were loud enough that in May of 1696 Vernon threatened Smith, saying he heard it discoursed that Smith intended to accuse Shrewsbury of negligence for having never acquainted the king with Smith's discoveries.[28]

The issue for Smith was money and glory, but the issue for Shrewsbury was the potential accusation that he and Vernon had deliberately ignored evidence of the Assassination Plot. I am not sure how much of a threat to Shrewsbury's reputation Smith's manuscript or his tavern brags would have been in and of themselves. But in September 1696 something else occurred to increase Shrewsbury's vulnerability. The captured Jacobite conspirator John Fenwick, in an effort to save his own neck, wrote a confidential letter to William offering 'a sincere and ingenious confession of all I know of men who correspond with France, employed by him [William] in places of trust in the government, fleet and army'. These men included Admiral Russell, Sidney Godolphin, Lord Marlborough and the duke of Shrewsbury.[29] This revelation in fact made very little impression on William, who complained that Fenwick 'only accuses those in my service, and not one of his own party'.[30] But rumours that Fenwick had implicated members of the political elite began to spread like wildfire, even though the precise contents of his confession remained a matter of speculation. 'I can't but take notice again,' wrote James Vernon, 'how the reports increase concerning persons, supposed to be accused by Sir John Fenwick, of all orders and degrees, friends and enemies to the Government, as if that were a contest of parties, who should name most of those they don't affect.' He also reported that 'some hot-headed citizens delivered in a strange paper at the meeting of the Common Hall on Tuesday last, in order to the bringing the examination of the plot in parliament'.[31] Shrewsbury kept offering to resign (admittedly his usual response to a crisis), and even the friends who urged him to stay acknowledged the seriousness of the situation. 'For although you are above suspicion,' wrote Portland, 'if it do not remain secret, everyone having enemies as well as friends, it will be impossible to prevent disagreeable conversation and reflections, as I know by experience.'[32] In the following weeks Shrewsbury's political allies decided that it was better to bring the matter before parliament than to ignore it. They hoped, moreover, that a rousing vote by parliament in vindication of Fenwick's victims might facilitate the subsequent business of getting a subsidy voted in.[33] Elaborate discussions of strategy ensued among Vernon, Somers, Portland, Wharton, Sunderland, Russell. Shrewsbury, who had fallen off his horse, remained in the country but corresponded with the group. They considered such questions as who should introduce Fenwick's papers, and when, what role the king should play, and whether they should try to use some of Fenwick's confession against political enemies like Godolphin.[34] The group carefully worked out a strategy for managing the discussion, and made sure to apprise the most important MPs in advance so as to gain their support. This gesture of inclusion no doubt smoothed the management of the affair, and the upshot was that the house not only voted to attaint Fenwick for treason but also resolved that his informations were 'false and scandalous, and a contrivance to undermine the government'.[35]

The Fenwick business matters to our story because it made Matthew Smith potentially more dangerous: his complaints, if known, would give more credibility to Fenwick. And so, as the bill to attaint Fenwick wound its way through the Commons, and then the Lords, Shrewsbury's allies paid Smith off to keep him silent. The money came from Shrewsbury and Vernon's office. Vernon, however, was careful to hide the genesis of the money from Smith, and arranged instead for it to be paid to Smith by the earl of Portland.[36]

Smith might well have been quiet, were it not for the intervention of the earl of Monmouth, to whom Smith had already appealed in his search for patrons. For reasons that have mystified both his contemporaries and historians, Monmouth tried to bring about a full investigation of Fenwick's allegations. Monmouth caused Smith to be questioned at the bar of the House of Lords, whereupon Smith reiterated his complaints about Shrewsbury's failure to reward him. This gave Shrewsbury and Vernon a chance to show Smith's worthlessness in public. Having been requested to provide copies of all his correspondence, Shrewsbury wrote a letter to the House of Lords explaining that he had failed to keep copies of Smith's letters because they had been so useless, except for the very oldest ones, which he kept when 'I had more value for his intelligence than I had afterwards'.[37] Smith was above all humiliated when John Hewett, his informant, was questioned and told the House that all the information he gave Smith had been taken by him out of printed copies of the *Post-Boy*![38] Somers put another nail in the coffin of Smith's reputation: having learned that Smith had once tried to trick a widow into marriage to get her property, Somers took 'care to acquaint such as I thought most proper' with that fact.[39] The House of Lords voted both that there was no ground for Smith's complaint against Shrewsbury and that Smith deserved no further reward.[40]

Smith, by his own account, intended to petition the House of Commons for redress, and found a member, Jack Arnold, willing to present his case. But he was distracted from this purpose by a mysterious benefactor who brought welcome news that King William wanted to employ Smith to keep an eye on Jacobites exiled to France. Smith went abroad, but the money supply dried up. He concluded he had been deceived and returned to England.[41] In 1699 he finally went into print. His timing may have been inspired by other political scandals which impinged upon the reputations of his opponents, such as recent revelations that Shrewsbury and other members of the Junto had invested in the now notorious pirate voyage of Captain William Kidd.[42] Darkly observing that 'notorious truths must prevail at this time in my favour',[43] Smith now gambled that the public was ready to believe the worst about the 'great men'.

The first book that Smith published in 1699, *Memoirs of Secret Service*, essentially reproduced the correspondence with Shrewsbury that he had already shown around in manuscript. He followed up *Memoirs* with a much more combative piece, *Remarks upon the D— of S——'s letter to the House of Lords.* Because the latter tract did in fact publish a copy of Shrewsbury's letter to the Lords, the house found him guilty of breach of their privilege. They ordered the book burnt by the common hangman, and once again voted that Smith didn't deserve any reward for his services. The task of cudgelling Smith was then taken up by Richard Kingston, another professional informer and pamphleteer, who attacked Smith in print. There is no time here to discuss the ensuing pamphlet war. Suffice it to say that both Smith and Kingston deployed a wide vocabulary of dishonour: Kingston charged Smith with cowardice, of not having written his own pamphlets, of being ignorant of Latin, and likened his writing to a horse's fart; Smith claimed Dr Kingston had faked his clerical credentials, and was a bigamist, adulterer, rapist and sodomite.[44]

It was very hard to get rid of Smith. How widely his books circulated is unknown, but Vernon did take notice in February 1700 that 'some poor refugee has been translating Smith's book, in hopes to get a penny by it'.[45] But if Smith continued to do battle in the press, he also tried to keep open the option of *not* using the press, of being once again paid to keep silent. We catch a glimpse of him writing to Vernon in June 1700, wanting (Vernon reported) to 'to make a composition, as he called it, to keep his other books from coming out in public'.[46] Smith returned some time after William's death with a petition to the House of Commons, again asking compensation for his services.[47] *Memoirs of Secret Service* was published again in 1718, for reasons I have yet to determine.

III

Let us now consider the terms in which the battle between Smith and his opponents was fought. In many ways, Shrewsbury and his allies played by the rules of critical-rational discourse, trusting to arguments rather than status as they willingly engaged in public debate. Vernon's comments on how to handle the rumours about Fenwick's confession show a preference for airing matters rather than for stifling them. It was inevitable that a parliamentary inquiry would be demanded, he argued, and 'keeping this matter in such a smothering condition, that serves only to augment jealousies, without giving any opportunity to refute them'.[48] 'Here is an impostume gathering,' he added a few days later, 'and I don't know it is best to bring it to a head, and when it breaks, one shall be the better for it.'[49] The one exception to this preference for openness was the condemnation of *Remarks upon the D— of S——'s letter* by the House of Lords for breach of privilege. Arguably, however, this exception proves the rule: to isolate the privilege of the house is to acknowledge the lack of privilege elsewhere. With the lapsing of the Licensing Act in 1694 censorship was not an option, and the 'great men' did not try to make use of it.

At the level of argument, too, the 'great men' seemed to apply rational-critical criteria to the evaluation of Smith as an informer. Three arguments stand out in Shrewsbury's and Vernon's explanations of why Smith was not better rewarded.

First, there was Smith's failure to come up with precise times and places for the assassination attempt, to provide information that was consistent and useful. Shrewsbury, in his letter to the House of Lords, recollected Smith was 'different in his accounts about the manner of seizing the King: sometimes Mr Latin's lodge near Richmond was to be attacked ... sometimes an attempt of the like nature was to be made on Kensington; and at other times the King was to be set upon going to, or coming from hunting'.[50] Similarly, Vernon complained of Smith's 'obscure and confounding way of telling his story'.[51]

Second, Vernon and Shrewsbury drew attention to Smith's 'perpetual craving for money'. Smith's 'sharping pretences of craving money' were cited by Vernon as one of the things 'which gave me such a jealousy and mean opinion of him, that I could never bring myself to believe one word he said of any kind'.[52] Somers confidently assured Shrewsbury that when Smith's letters were read to the house, 'the impertinence appeared to the last degree, and gave every one a proper character of the man, and that his whole design was to get money'.[53]

Finally, Shrewsbury and his allies took steps to make sure that what was said in their defence did not appear to come from themselves, but from disinterested parties. Thus Vernon encouraged Richard Kingston, the anti-Smith pampleteer, to 'make it understood that he does it [writes] of his own head' lest 'your Grace [Shrewsbury] should be charged with having solicited him to write on that subject, or that it was done by your means and procurement'.[54] Sure enough, Kingston presented himself in his book as 'a friend to truth and justice' who 'is so perfect a stranger to the D[uke] of S[hrewsbury] that he never had the honor of speaking to him but once in his life'.[55]

We could say, then, that the great men beat Smith in open debate: they showed he lacked reliable sources, demonstrated the low utility of his information, and exposed the private motives which rendered his information suspect. Of course, as the last example makes clear, these gestures at playing by the rules of critical-rational debate were just gestures. Richard Kingston was indeed a stranger to the duke of Shrewsbury, but he had received clear instructions from Vernon. There are strong connections between Vernon's research into Smith's background and Kingston's writing on the subject. For example, Vernon told Shrewsbury in January 1696/7 that he had learned from the conspirator Captain George Porter that Sir William Parkyns had held a 'very mean opinion' of his nephew Matthew Smith, and that 'Smith used sometime to thrust himself into their [the Jacobites'] company but they either went away or changed their discourse none of them trusting him'.[56] This information, which damned Smith as a person not even worthy of being credited by Jacobites, was repeated three years later (again with Porter named as the source) in Kingston's pamphlet, *A Modest Answer.*[57] Although Kingston claimed to have interviewed Captain Porter directly, it is probable that the information came from Vernon. Covering one's tracks, engineering events while maintaining the appearance of aloofness from them, paying people while having the money seem to come from somewhere else, were in the repertoire of techniques used by the 'great men'. These tactics served to preserve the illusion that information was flowing freely when in fact it was carefully managed.

Moreover, in reading the great men's reactions and responses to Smith, it is hard to escape the feeling that a strong sense of class solidarity was the foundation which made all the more 'rational' arguments seem rational. Shrewsbury's letter to the House of Lords explained that he had not kept copies of Smith's letters because he did not value them at the time. He offered instead his *recollections* of the letters, which were all the sharper because, he said, he was surprised that Smith had gotten some things right! Shrewsbury thus privileged his own feeling about the letters over the letters themselves. His own letter functioned more as a gesture of contempt than as an argument. His references to Smith as 'this man' who complained of him 'in an unhandsome manner' such that he, Shrewsbury, found it 'neither safe nor decent to have any more to do with him' all called attention to issues of decorum and propriety, and thus to the social gap between the informer and the duke.[58] Not surprisingly, it was Smith's 'impertinence' and 'impudence' that drew commentary from Shrewsbury and his friends. 'The malice, folly and insincerity that Smith showed yesterday at the committee turned almost everybody against him,' Vernon told Shrewsbury.[59] Somers likewise reported of Smith that the 'whole house was sensible of the falsehood and folly of his pretence'.[60] Both men spoke as if Smith's falsehood, malice and so on were utterly obvious, written on the man's skin or given off as a smell.

Moreover, perhaps no argument but contempt was necessary precisely because the discussion of the Smith/Fenwick accusations did not take place, until the very last stages, in the press but rather in parliament. In one sense, of course, parliament was a representative of society, of the 'public'. But it was also a club. It is striking how confident Shrewsbury's allies were that all of the Whigs and even most of the Tories would identify with the plight of one of their number whose reputation was threatened precisely because of his high place: Somers told Vernon, with reference to the Fenwick allegations, that he could not

> imagine there should be a prevailing party in the house to admit of such an accusa-tion from one under these circumstances. But rather, they will see of what conse-quence it is not to leave the friends of the government to be blasted and destroyed by the enemies of it, and be filled with indignation, that any guilty persons shall presume to make use of those methods to wound the innocent. In the so toler-ating whereof, they can't but see that the most faithful and useful subjects must be ravished from the service of the kingdom, whenever a plotter, to save himself, raises a lie on them, and because it can never be proved or disproved, further than it is confuted by all the other actions of one's life, it must with scorn be rejected, and declared a base calumny.[61]

The great men counted on the mutual interest that members of the elite had in protecting elites in general from impertinent attacks, their investment in one another's Teflon coating, and hence preferred the controlled 'public' space of parliament to the more anarchic public spaces of the street, taverns and coffee houses. After the event, those who helped protect Shrewsbury, even and especially political opponents, were praised not for their objectivity but for their civility. 'Everybody says my Lord Rochester hath behaved himself in this last act with great regards to your grace,' Vernon wrote to Shrewsbury.[62]

IV

Smith also made a number of appeals to established canons of credibility and publicity. Notably, he invoked the language of experimental procedure. He described his response to Shrewsbury's letter as a 'dissection' in which he would 'take it to pieces for nearer inspection'.[63] His pamphlets were filled with references to actual artefacts, letters and lists existing in the real world which would prove his case. These included arms that he had helped discover, dies which Jacobites would use to cast new coins, letters in the possession of the House of Lords, lists of exiled Jacobites with passes for England which had been given him by the benefactors who sent him abroad, testimonial letters from witnesses to conversations.[64] These were as far as possible produced within his text. Alternatively, their locations were specified to show that Smith (unlike Shrewsbury) could provide evidence. 'We live in an age,' he remarked, 'that takes very little upon trust, and is very apt to suspect the veracity of that man that refuses to produce such evidence as he has.'[65] His opponents, on the other hand, were shown to 'doubt after conviction, and argue against demon-stration'.[66] Shrewsbury had, after all, failed to produce copies of his letters to and from Smith, and 'letters could neither be bribed nor awed'.[67]

Whereas Shrewsbury had regarded the uncertain and changing nature of Smith's reports as a reason not to credit them, Smith turned the same quali-ties into a sign of his scrupulous accuracy. That each new report specified a different time and place for the intended assassination attempt was 'a demon-stration of their truth and exactness' which 'manifestly evinces that I was constantly acquainted with the most minute passages, and that I was nice and exact to a scruple'.[68] Similarly,

> I gave them daily an account; in which I was so early, and so particular ... nothing was offered amongst the conspirators, of which his Gr— had not an immediate and minute information. Of my care and exactness in this matter, this I think may be sufficient evidence, that nothing escaped me; and yet I was so far from amusing him with reports and conjectures, that all my informations have since been verified to a tittle.[69]

The preference for precision over dogmatic certainty was precisely the ideal espoused by Robert Boyle and the Royal Society for reporting on scientific experiments.[70]

Smith also denied that social status should in any way determine cred-ibility. That his informant Jack Hewett may have been a youth of low status was, he proclaimed, irrelevant. Such things, indeed, might make him a better informant. Indeed, Smith asserted, Truth was Truth, no matter where it came from. Shrewsbury, he said, 'finds the quality of my intelligencer to be such that it brings my intelligence into disesteem with him'[71] but 'I always thought in discoveries of this nature, the importance of the matter had been to be weighed more than the quality of the discoverer'.[72] The behaviour of King William was contrasted favourably with that of Shrewsbury. When Prender-gast the plotter, who was 'mean in both condition and figure', came to make his discoveries to the king, noted Smith, 'no vouchers are required for his credit, nor doubts or scruples started about the reality of his discovery, though a very obscure man.... his majesty in his wisdom considered the nature and importance of the thing, more than the quality of the discoverer'.[73]

Most spectacularly, Smith defended his expectation of reward in exchange for information. Although he repeatedly asserted his 'zeal for his majesties' service' as a 'dutiful and loyal subject',[74] he saw no conflict between patriotism and self-interest. Indeed, 'I do not pretend to so little self-interest, but that I own I was pleased with the hopes of making my fortune, when at the same time I was endeavouring to save my King and country'.[75] His philosophical defence of giving rewards to informers is worth quoting at length:

Men are undoubtedly bound in duty to contribute all that lies in their power to the public security. But the only natural reason that I can find for it, is, because as members of the public, they have their principal security and protection from it. But that consideration alone does not carry men very far; self-preservation is a principle of more caution than action, and renders men more careful to give no offence, than to do any service. It is Hope only that animates 'em for action, and makes 'em forward in its service. They expect that what they do for the public, should redound in some proportion to their own particular benefit, and that themselves should be considered as instruments, for the advantages that may accrue to the public, and the fatigue or hazard they expose themselves to. This is so universally true that I doubt some who pretend to have done the nation great service would abate of their zeal, if they did not find it as necessary and advantageous to their own private fortune. I say this not invidiously to lessen the services of any man, or to reproach him, for the just advantages he may make of 'em, but to obviate the objections of some of my unreasonable adversaries, who pretend my services lose their merit, when I appear to expect any reward.[76]

The fact that Shrewsbury had paid him, Smith argued, proved that his information was valuable. He thus reversed Shrewsbury's logic, whereby Smith's receipt of payment showed the base motives which invalidated his information. Moreover, by stingily not rewarding people who offered information, even punishing them, Shrewsbury had put the security of the state at risk: 'For if services of the highest importance, and of the greatest hazard, shall be rewarded with contempt, and those that do 'em exposed, such a prospect will cool men's zeal.'[77]

V

This chapter began by juxtaposing Habermas's account of an emerging public sphere and Shapin's account of the gentlemanly monopoly on truth as two different ways of predicting who in the late seventeenth century was allowed to say what about matters of common political concern, and with how much credibility. How do these two accounts stack up in the light of Matthew Smith's story?

Matthew Smith articulated a model of credibility that differs diametrically from the one proposed by Shapin in *The Social History of Truth*. Unashamed of taking money, Smith was the antithesis of the disinterested gentleman. Yet he insisted that he was none the less credible. Our story thus puts pressure on Shapin's contention that only gentlemen would be believed – clearly, one person did not agree. And yet the 'great men' in our story did invoke, in the political arena, criteria of assessing credibility which Shapin has described as prevailing in the Royal Society and the realm of natural philosophy. Despite making gestures in the direction of seeking an open debate without respect for persons, the great men implicitly relied upon social status and political position to establish their credibility against that of Matthew Smith.

Smith, by contrast, seems sincere in his embrace of an ideal of the public sphere, as Habermas described it. His emphasis on evidence and accuracy without respect to status do indeed seem to place him as a defender of the ideal of critical-rational public discourse. Moreover, Smith might be regarded as having widened the range of people who might count as legitimate participants in the making of public opinion. In a seventeenth-century context, the refusal to pit self-interest against patriotism was a profoundly anti-elitist move, since entirely disinterested virtue was, and was recognized as, a monopoly of the rich.

Smith's defence of taking money in return for information, however, fits less easily into a Habermasian model, since Habermas tells us that 'laws of the market were suspended' in the public sphere.[78] But arguably, for Smith (who had not read Marx), the laws of the market were not corrupters of truth but guarantors of it: to attempt to sell information was to submit it to a critical test.[79] Moreover, the notion of the market in information is what made it possible for Smith to expand the potential audience for his information, to legitimate his appeals to alternative publics. That is, if Shrewsbury was not buying his information, the king or other patrons might; if not them, the parliament; if not the parliament, then the readers of his books would be the purchasers. Smith might ultimately have preferred to be rewarded by the patronage of great men, but the market model he worked with implicitly put the parliament and the reading audience on the same par with kings and dukes: they were all consumers of information.

Yet Smith still remains problematic as an exemplar of a participant in a Habermasian public sphere. He did, after all, seek elite patrons and submit himself to their management. Moreover, he seems to have been willing *not* to publish whenever he thought he could be bribed to keep silent. Moreover, his books show an obsession with the defence of personal honour, functioning almost in themselves like thrusts in a duel, a mode of settling arguments antithetical to the ideals of the public sphere.[80] Arguably, Smith was more concerned with his own glory and reputation than with the common good.

An examination of plot talk, and of Matthew Smith's duel with the great men, allows us to both expand and show the limits of Habermas's claims for the existence of a public sphere. That the players in our story all paid homage to ideals of rational-critical public discourse is strong evidence that the public sphere existed *as an ideal*. And yet the social identities of the players, the social and economic framework in which knowledge was produced and evaluated, also seem to have made all the difference here. If the public rational debate was honoured as an ideal, that ideal was surely undercut or at least modified by the inescapable realities of privilege and power.

NOTES

1 For one of the few attempts to discuss the relationship of plots to politics, see Paul Hopkins, 'Sham plots and real plots in the 1690s', in Eveline Cruickshanks (ed.), *Ideology and Conspiracy: Aspects of Jacobitism, 1689–1759* (Edinburgh, 1982).

2 The best account of the Exclusion crisis is Mark Knights, *Politics and Opinion in Crisis, 1678–1681* (Cambridge, 1994). See also J. P. Kenyon, *The Popish Plot* (New York, 1972).

3 See D. W. Hayton, 'John Arnold', in Eveline Cruikshanks, Stuart Handley and D. W. Hayton (eds), *History of Parliament: the House of Commons, 1690–1715* (Cambridge, 2002); D. W. Hayton, 'Sir Henry Dutton Colt', in *ibid.*

4 Adrian Johns, *The Nature of the Book* (Chicago, 1998).

5 See single-sheet broadside beginning 'London, the 29th day of September. This day the citizens being met at Guildhall ...' [1696]. Also, *The Request of the Citizens of the City of London in the Common Hall assembled to their Representatives in Parliament*.

6 The phrase is from Harold Mah, 'Phantasies of the public sphere: rethinking the Habermas of historians', *Journal of Modern History* 72 (March 2000), 153–82. The quote is at 165. I have found this article to be an especially useful gloss on Habermas. For statements from Habermas himself on the erasure of social identity in the ideal public sphere, see Jürgen Habermas, *The Structural Transformation of the Public Sphere*, trans. T. Burger and F. Lawrence (Cambridge MA, 1993), especially 36, 54–6.

7 James Vernon to Mr Mountstevens, September 1698, BL Additional Ms 40772, fol. 135.

8 Habermas, *Structural Transformation*, 36, 54–6.

9 I have discussed this dilemma with respect to Elizabeth Cellier and the Mealtub Plot in '"If I did say so I lyed": the construction of credibility in the Popish Plot crisis', in S. Amussen and M. Kishlansky (eds), *Political Culture and Cultural Politics in Early Modern England* (Manchester, 1995).

10 Steven Shapin, *The Social History of Truth* (Chicago, 1994).

11 Henry Peachum, *The Complete Gentleman* [1622], quoted in Shapin, *Social History of Truth*, 69.

12 Shapin, *Social History of Truth*, 69.

13 Mah, 'Phantasies', 168.

14 Paul Hopkins, 'Matthew Smith', in *Oxford Dictionary of National Biography* (Oxford, 2004).

15 Alan Marshall, *Intelligence and Espionage in the Reign of Charles II, 1660–1685* (Cambridge, 1994).

16 Kingston to Trumbull, 10 August 1695, Trumbull papers, BL Additional Ms 72570, fol. 69.

17 *Ibid.*, fol. 78.

18 Vernon to Shrewsbury, 19 January 1696/7, in *Letters from James Vernon to the Duke of Shrewsbury, 1696–1708* [microform]: *from the Shrewsbury Papers in Boughton House, Northhamptonshire* (East Ardsley [1980]) II, letter No. 55. Hereafter cited as 'Vernon Ms'.

19 John P. Kenyon, *Robert Spencer, Earl of Sunderland, 1641–1702* (London, 1958), especially chapter 8.

20 Matthew Smith, *Memoirs of Secret Service* (London, 1699), viii.

21 Paul Hopkins, 'Matthew Smith', in *Oxford Dictionary of National Biography* (Oxford, 2004).

22 Shrewsbury to Smith, 15 December 1694, quoted in *Memoirs of Secret Service*, 44.

23 *Id.* to *id.*, 2 February 1694/5, quoted in *ibid.*, 57.

24 *Memoirs of Secret Service*, 67–9.

25 Smith to Shrewsbury, 23 December 1695, quoted in *ibid.*, 76.

26 On the Assassination Plot, see Jane Garrett, *The Triumphs of Providence: the Assassination Plot, 1696* (Cambridge, 1980).

27 Vernon to Shrewsbury, 24 September 1696, printed in G. P. R. James (ed.), *Letters Illustrative of the Reign of William III, from 1696 to 1708, addressed to the Duke of Shrewsbury, by James Vernon* (London, 1841) I, 2–3; Richard Kingston, *A Modest Answer to Captain Smith's immodest Memoirs of Secret Service* (London, 1700), 16; Matthew Smyth [Smith], *Remarks upon the D— of S——'s letter* ('Printed and sold by the booksellers of London and Westminster', 1700), xv.

28 *Memoirs of Secret Service*, 149.

29 'Fenwick's Information, first paper', printed in *Journals of the House of Commons* II, 577–8 (6 November, 8 William III [1696]).

30 William III to Shrewsbury, 10 September/30 August 1696, printed in William Coxe, *Private and Original Correspondence of Charles Talbot, Duke of Shrewsbury* (London, 1821), 145.

31 Vernon to Shrewsbury, 1 October 1696, in James, *Letters Illustrative* I, 12.

32 Portland to Shrewsbury, 10 September/30 August 1696, in Coxe, *Private and Original Correspondence*, 146.

33 Vernon to Shrewsbury, 24 October 1696, in James, *Letters Illustrative* I, 28.

34 For reports of these meetings, see letters from 12 October to 5 November 1696 printed by Coxe and James. Vernon to Shrewsbury, 12, 13, 15, 20, 24, 27, 30 October and 3 and 5 November 1696, in James, *Letters Illustrative* I, 15–45; Somers to Shrewsbury, 15 , 27 October 1696, Russell to Shrewsbury, 29 October 1696, Wharton to Shrewsbury, 29, 31 October 1696, Somers to Shrewsbury 31 October, 3 November 1696, in Coxe, *Private and Original Correspondence*, 408–10, 414–15, 416, 417, 417–18, 419–20, 420–2.

35 *Journals of the House of Commons*, 6 November 1696 (vol. II, 579).

36 See especially Vernon to Shrewsbury, 24 November 1696, in James, *Letters Illustrative* I, 70–1; 1 December 1696, in I, 90; 5 December 1696, in I, 103–5; 8 December 1696, in I, 108; 10 December 1696, in I, 114–15; 12 December 1696, in I, 117; 17 December 1696, in I, 138–29. Somers to Shrewsbury, 10 December 1696, in Coxe, *Private and Original Correspondence*, 439–41.

37 Printed in Matthew Smyth [Smith], *Remarks upon the D— of S——'s letter* ('Printed and sold by the booksellers of London and Westminster', 1700), xiii. The letter was sent from Shrewsbury to the house on 13 January 1696/7.

38 Somers to Shrewsbury, 12 January 1696/7, in Coxe, *Private and Original Correspondence*, 459.

39 *Id.* to *id.*, 16 January 1696/7, in *ibid.*, 463.

40 *Id.* to *id.*, 20 January 1696/7, in *ibid.* 463–5.

41 This story is told in *Remarks upon the D— of S——'s letter*, 21–5.

42 On the Kidd scandal, see Robert C. Ritchie, *Captain Kidd and the War against the Pirates* (Cambridge MA, 1986).

43 *Memoirs of Secret Service*, preface, vii.

44 The pamphlets are: Richard Kingston, *A Modest Answer to Captain Smith's immodest Memoirs of Secret Service* (London, 1700); Matthew Smith, *A Reply to an unjust and scandalous Libel, intituled A Modest Answer* (n.p., 1700); Richard Kingston, *Impudence, Lying and Forgery, detected and chastiz'd* (n.p., 1700). For Kingston's attacks on Smith, see especially *A Modest Answer*, 7, 14, 31, 32. For Smith's attacks on Kingston, see especially *A Reply*, 36–8.

45 Vernon to Shrewsbury, 27 February 1700, in James, *Letters Illustrative* II, 454.

46 *Id.* to *id.*, 22 June 1700, in *ibid.* III, 93.

47 'The case and petition of Matthew Smith', BL Harley Ms 6210, fols 138–47.

48 Vernon to Shrewsbury, 12 October 1696, in James, *Letters Illustrative* I, 15.

49 *Id.* to *id.*, 15 October 1696, in *ibid.* I, 19.

50 *Remarks upon the D— of S——'s Letter*, xiv–xv.

51 Vernon to Shrewsbury, 10 June 1697, in James, *Letters Illustrative* I, 261.

52 *Id.* to *id.*, 10 June 1697, in *ibid.* I, 261–2.

53 Somers to Shrewsbury, 12 January 1696/7, in Coxe, *Private and Original Correspondence*, 458.

54 Vernon to Shrewsbury, 25 January 1699/1700, Vernon Ms, vol. IV, letter No. 24.

55 *A Modest Answer*, 4.

56 Vernon to Shrewsbury, 18 January 1696/7, Vernon Ms, vol. II, letter No. 54.

57 Kingston, *A modest Answer*, 25–6.

58 *Remarks upon the D— of S——'s Letter*, xiii–xv.

59 Vernon to Shrewsbury, 20 January 1696/7, Vernon Ms, vol. II, letter No. 56.

60 Somers to Shrewsbury, 16 December 1699, in Coxe, *Private and Original Correspondence*, 597–8.

61 Vernon to Shrewsbury, 20 October 1696, in James, *Letters Illustrative* I, 23.

62 *Id.* to *id.*, 20 January 1696/7, Vernon Ms, vol. II, letter No. 56.

63 *Remarks upon the D— of S——'s Letter*, 1.

64 See, for example, *Memoirs of Secret Service*, x–xii, 21; Smith, *Remarks upon the D— of S——'s Letter*, 25–31; Smith, *Reply to an unjust and scandalous*, 13–14.

65 *Remarks upon the D— of S——'s Letter*, 1.

66 *Ibid.*, 6.

67 *Ibid.*, 1–2.

68 *Ibid.*, 8.

69 *Ibid.*, 13–14.

70 Simon Schaffer and Steven Shapin, *Leviathan and the Air Pump* (Princeton NJ, 1985), 61–9.

71 *Remarks upon the D— of S——'s Letter*, 6–7.

72 *Ibid.*, 4–5.

73 *Ibid.*, 12.

74 *Memoirs of Secret Service*, 32.

75 *Ibid.*, preface, viii.

76 *Remarks upon the D— of S——'s Letter*, ix–x.

77 *Ibid.*, x–xi.

78 Habermas, *Structural Transformation*, 36.

79 *Memoirs of Secret Service*, xi–xii.

80 *Remarks upon the D— of S——'s Letter*, v.

Chapter 11

◆

How rational was the later
Stuart public sphere?

Mark Knights

I

Habermas argues that reason was *the* characteristic of the first public sphere that he sees emerging in the late seventeenth and early eighteenth centuries.[1] It is the degradation of reason, he suggests, in favour of passive consumption of other men's ideas, that characterises the decayed modern public sphere. This chapter probes these ideas in several ways. First, by focusing on the period identified by Habermas as the key to the emergence of the public sphere, it challenges his 'structural transformation' from an era of rational, equal, active and vibrant debate to one of passive, consumed, stagnant and often irrational and manipulated debate. It argues that Habermas deliberately oversimplified and exaggerated the rationality of the first public sphere in order to emphasize this process of decay. Indeed, the period that Habermas saw as witnessing the emergence of the first public sphere was itself marked by contemporary fears of a highly *irrational* and manipulative form of public discourse. In other words, irrationality or the perceived degradation of critical-rational public debate was apparent at the very inception of the public sphere.

Second, and paradoxically despite these criticisms, Habermas was right to stress the importance of reason, because the idealization of reason marked late seventeenth and early eighteenth-century politico-religious discourse and helps explain not only the emergence of idealized concepts of a public sphere but also the rules of public discourse.[2] A glance at the contemporary debate about print libels suggests that older anxieties were both exacerbated and reformulated. What Habermas discerned, then, was the emergence (or perhaps the reshaping) of an idealized discourse of reason and politeness, a discourse that was indeed new to the later Stuart period.

This conclusion, then, will in turn necessitate comments about the extent of change and continuity over the early modern period. Whilst the discourse of the first Age of Party owed much to earlier usage and ideals there was also something novel that merits attention. Habermas has been much criticized for getting the timing of the emergent public sphere wrong and his paradigm wrong.[3] But this may in part result from a misunderstanding of his model. This chapter thus questions the reality of the ideal described by Habermas but also sees that idealization as one of the strengths of his definition of the emergent public and recognizes novelty as well as continuity over the early modern period.

II

First, I want to sketch Habermas's observations about reason as they apply to the emergence of the public sphere. He defined the bourgeois public sphere as 'the sphere of private people come together as a public' to engage the public authorities in debate, and 'the medium of this political confrontation was peculiar and without historical precedent: people's public use of their reason'.[4] It is useful here to relate Habermas's ideas to those of Kant, not only because Habermas himself acknowledges the debt, but also because doing so helps explain his distinction between public and private and his attempt to recover an Enlightenment ideal of rational free discourse.[5] In 1784 Kant wrote a short essay, 'What is the Enlightenment?', in which he suggested that enlightenment lay in breaking free from what he called self-incurred tutelage. Individuals could do so by daring to be free: that is, by thinking for themselves rather than being led by others.[6] Kant explained how the private individual (conceived of as masculine) could use his reason to benefit the state and society and hence contribute to the progress of mankind. Kant made a distinction that might seem odd to us, for he said that a cleric acting in his official public role was in fact acting as a private individual. The exercise of free reason was thus not, Kant said, to apply to the offices which individuals occupied in civil society. There are shades here of Kant's hero and patron, Frederick the Great, the archetypal enlightened despot who famously said that men could argue all they liked so long as they obeyed. Kant did not want the free exercise of reason to disturb those things that were the particular province and responsibility of an individual, for chaos in civil society would result. For Kant, then, the public meant the state and society outside one's own particular sphere of responsibility. And it was to improve this that private individuals came together to engage the authorities in rational debate. For Kant, reason was the tool by which private individuals might enter and participate in the public sphere.

From this very cursory analysis of Kant's ideas it is apparent that Habermas follows Kant very closely not only in the stress on reason but also in the way in which he defines public and private, with all its implications for gender and class.[7] Like Kant, then, Habermas distinguished between an intimate and private sphere, on the one hand, and a public sphere on the other. The conceptual debt to Kant is important because it suggests that Habermas was *deliberately* positing an Enlightenment confidence in the *ideal* of reason against a post-Enlightenment failure to reason for the public good.[8] He was thus drawing on what even in 1784 was an idealized view of the potential of reason, and then grafting on to this analysis a post-Marxist perspective. The development of capitalism, he suggests, brought the private and public together. It was for this reason that Habermas identified the public sphere as emerging only after the Glorious Revolution, when he felt that a truly capitalist economy first emerged. One further point about Kant is worth making. Kant argued that very few people exercised their reason in the public sphere, and that those who did so should argue as though they were (like him) scholars. In other words, Kant's rational public sphere was one restricted in the number of participants and in the type of discourse that should prevail.

The thrust of Kant's essay was, significantly enough, a plea for freedom of religious thought. Like so many other *philosophes*, he was attacking the restrictive and intolerant attitudes of institutionalized religion. Kant's musings on freedom of religious thought, reasonable religion and rational debate thus helped to shape Habermasian notions of the public sphere even though Habermas preferred not to refer to the spiritual dimension of the 1784 essay – a dimension which was so strong that Kant ended his work with an encomium to Frederick for being strong enough to maintain religious toleration in Prussia.

Having analysed the crucial role of reason and politico-religious debate in the construction of the Habermasian model, and hence in the emergence of the first public sphere, it is also necessary briefly to examine the way in which Habermas deliberately constructed his model in order to emphasize the degradation or transformation of the public sphere. In the second half of *The Structural Transformation* Habermas charts a shift towards what he calls consumed discussion. In order to highlight this he contrasts it sharply with an earlier form of critical discussion that took place in the coffee houses, salons, press and theatres. His comparisons of the first and modern public spheres are worth quoting. In acquiring a mass market, he said, 'the press that submitted issues to critical discussion in the long run lost its influence' to a consumer-oriented press that eliminated political news.[9] 'The rigorous distinction between fact and fiction is ever more frequently abandoned';[10] 'critical discussion of a reading public tends to give way to ... talk about what is consumed'.[11] Habermas thus explicitly argues that debate is back under the 'tutelage' castigated by Kant.[12] At the end of the path 'from a public critically reflecting on its culture to one that merely consumes it' lie propaganda and manipulation. Modern political debate is carried on without the public, between self-interested parties, and publicity is now designed to manipulate the public.[13] 'The consensus developed in rational-critical public debate has yielded to compromise fought out or simply imposed non-publicly.'[14] The press no longer amplifies and transmits the rational-critical public debate but shapes it from the start.[15] Modern consensus differs from that brought about by the 'rational agreement between publicly competing opinions', 'for the criteria of rationality are completely lacking in a consensus created by sophisticated opinion-moulding services under the aegis of a sham public interest'.[16]

Habermas's model thus implicitly or explicitly contains a number of assumptions about the character of the first public sphere. First, that it articulated a unified public opinion, which was the result of consensus after hard-fought rational debate revealed what was true. Second, that public debate was both rational and critical. Third, that public critical debate was not a form of manipulation. Fourth, that the critical debate clearly defined the boundaries of what was true and what was fictitious. Each of these assumptions needs to be tested. In order to do so I will examine one of the politico-religious controversies after the passage of the Toleration Act of 1689, useful because it coincides with the socio-economic changes that Habermas saw as vital for the emergence of the public sphere and because it revolved around the political and religious concerns discussed by Kant.[17] The same highly charged politico-religious debate exploring the boundaries between the state and the church, occurring in Britain in the later seventeenth and early eighteenth centuries rather than later eighteenth-century Prussia, produced similar calls for the exercise of reason and the legitimacy of public discourse about the authority of the state. Yet it also raises questions about the degree of rational printed debate, about the manipulation of the public as readers inherent in the first public sphere and about the tutelage that party allegiance imposed on free discussion.

The case thus touches on two related, extensive and important historiographical debates, one concerning civility and civil discourse in the early modern period, and another concerning the nature of seditious speech, libel and print. It is therefore briefly worth outlining the points of contention in order to highlight the significance of the discussion that follows and because they also impact on the acceptability of the Habermasian model. The discussion about civility and civil discourse turns on the degree and nature of transition over the early modern period. Norbert Elias long ago sought to relate the rise of civility to state formation in the sixteenth to eighteenth centuries as part of his study of modernization.[18] The increasing power of the state, he argued, facilitated but also manipulated a civil and gentle means of correcting behaviour. Anna Bryson refined this framework by suggesting another transition over the early modern period from 'courtesy', based around the court and its *mores*, to 'civility', based on a wider, more public code. John Pocock also identified the emergence of a polite discourse in the later seventeenth century, a point developed further by Larry Klein and others working on the later Stuart coffee houses, public opinion and press.[19] The suggestion that there was a significant shift towards a new way of talking is nevertheless coming under scrutiny, particularly from those who see politeness and civility as embedded in the civic culture, and hence present throughout early modernity, or who see the impact of print as exaggerated.[20] If the politeness and print culture of the later Stuart period were not really novel then this finding would further question Habermasian notions of the emergence of polite and rational debate in sites such as the coffee house that, he claimed, provided an interface between society and the state.[21] On the other hand, if the later Stuart debate did, as I suggest, stimulate a widespread demand for informal rules to public discourse, and thereby developed a powerful set of political tools that could be used to exclude some forms and types of argument, then the Habermasian model has more to offer.

The second cognate debate concerns the nature of early modern libel. Some innovative work on sixteenth and early seventeenth-century manuscript libels and on the vitality of the oral and scribal culture of the period has shown a vibrant public discussion of state affairs long before the Habermasian model would seem to allow.[22] What is less clear from this work is the impact of the seventeenth-century transition from manuscript to print libels and the capacity through print to spread slander on a far larger scale and to integrate it into national debates. Many of the earlier libels had also concerned courtiers; by the late seventeenth century, however, the realm of politics had broadened very considerably, so that partisans and political parties were routinely libelled, almost as a matter of course, in local and national election campaigns. *Ad hominem* attacks were part of everyday political life. In this culture, I suggest, the public became the key court or umpire and the press a principal tool to counter its own poison.

II

My case study concerns a print controversy that arose between the champion of the high church, Dr Henry Sacheverell, and one of his low-church clerical critics, Dr William Bisset. Sacheverell was condemned by parliament for libel in 1710 but found widespread, though far from unanimous, support in the country.[23] In a sermon delivered at Derby in August 1709, and subsequently printed, Sacheverell had attacked the Nonconformists for their 'extravagant opinions and bewitching false doctrines, the impudent clamours, the lying misrepresentations, the scandalous and false libels, upon both the king and the church'.[24] A few months later he had found himself impeached by parliament on very similar charges.[25] To many Whigs it appeared that he had attacked the principle of religious toleration and the intellectual rationale for the Revolution of 1688. In the aftermath of the trial there was a heated print exchange. Embroiled in this was fellow cleric William Bisset. The dispute is illuminating because for most observers it failed claims to be a rational debate and appeared more like a set of abusive, *ad hominem* attacks designed to fictionalize and mislead. Participants used a press that had been emancipated from pre-publication censorship to manipulate its readers by offering rival, even wildly diverging views about characters, events and politico-religious programmes. In other words, it fails the Habermasian tests of offering a single public opinion, of offering a critical but rational discussion of public issues, of rising above manipulation and of hammering out consensual truth. Yet, at the same time, it also sought to invoke ideals of the public and of critical-rational debate and hence contributed to the shaping of an *ideal* described by Habermas, an ideal nevertheless sometimes described by him as though it were the *practice* of the first public sphere.

Rather than tackle the substance of Sacheverell's claims about the dissenters, Bisset published an intemperate attack on Sacheverell himself, called *The Modern Fanatick*, which sought to turn the epithet usually reserved for dissenters back on the high-church Sacheverell, who had, of course, bitterly attacked the dissenters. Bisset claimed that, rather than there being a danger from dissenting fanaticism, 'an artificial hired Mobb' had been whipped up 'by swarms of libels' into a high-church frenzy in time for the 1710 general election – at which Whig candidates were abused and attacked. Bisset's pamphlet was thus a personalised and partisan counter-attack, though he began with ardent avowals of his own impartiality, protesting that he belonged 'to no party, that I know of; being sensible there are knaves and rakes among all'.[26] The core of the tract was a character assassination of Sacheverell. Bisset accused him of many things: using unbridled language that, he said, exceeded Martin Marprelate; of stringing along a lover who died broken-hearted when he dropped her; of Jacobitism; of being fond of the bottle; and of lying. He even suggested that a Sacheverellite high-church mob had thrown stones into the house of a dissenter, killing a woman in childbirth.[27]

Sacheverell's defenders duly rounded on Bisset, accusing him of defamation. Bisset was told that 'unless you bring better proofs for what slanders you lay on him, no man of sense can believe you'.[28] Another attack on Bisset placed him as part of a Whig conspiracy to misrepresent opponents by employing 'forgery, slander and barefac'd lying'.[29] This tract then went on, brazenly, to counter-claim that the dissenters had pulled down their own meeting houses during the Sacheverell riots in order to inspire pity.[30] The tract claimed that the female dissenter described by Bisset had died of natural causes, rather than stoning, and that, since she was seventy years old, could not possibly be with child. The author admitted that stones did break her windows but 'they hardly went into the room; the woman in bed was dying and no more heard or felt them at that time than she does me now'.[31] The tract then poured as much slander as possible on Bisset's own career. It was, for example, alleged that Bisset had been expelled from university for impudence, that he himself had misled a lover and then turned her out of *his* house, and that he was the liar.[32] A print depicting Bisset as the devil's scribe (Figure 11.1) drove the point home. Slander thus bred counter-slander and rival versions of what was 'true', and Bisset was made to appear the embodiment of Sacheverell's own caricature of the lying, hypocritical, malicious low-churchman.[33]

Bisset had accused Sacheverell of lying and Sacheverell's supporters had turned the charge back on Bisset. The theme of lying was taken up by a mock defence of the latter, *A General Apology for the Lies made Use of against Dr Sacheverell occasion'd by the Pretended Answer to Mr Bisset* (1711). The author set out, satirically, to justify lying *per se* by passing it off as irony:

> whether propagated by oral tradition or whis[t]led about the country in pamphlets and loose papers. To the first I plead that the said slanders are so contrived, as if they were never design'd to pass upon any man of common understanding; and the language they are generally convey'd in, is so very broad and artless, as makes it impossible they should ensnare one that has the least notion of good manners or common civility. Now in a polite nation, as ours is in the present age, there can be no reasonable suspicion that so shocking a sort of rhetorick can spread any mischief far or be very dangerous to the publick'.[34]

This pamphlet thus, through mockery, claimed that Bisset's contribution to the Sacheverell debate violated the boundaries of critical-rational discourse, and that Whig public discourse was deliberately misleading and manipulative. But, as part of a rhetorical strategy countering Bisset's polemic, its author also explicitly fostered a notion of a polite, rational nation capable of discerning, judging and discounting irrational public discourse.

Another tract in the series also sought to highlight the abusive nature of the quarrel between Bisset and Sacheverell. In a fictional dialogue between them, written explicitly as 'instruction' in 'Billingsgate', the language of railing fish-wives and hence deliberately gendered to emphasize irrationality, the two men greet each other with a stream of abusive epithets culled from the pamphlet exchanges. Bisset greets Sacheverell as

> thou Sybyl, thou Pythoness upon the tripod, bloody flag officer, gogler, mover of sedition, perverter of holy scriptures, papist in disguise, knight of the fire-brand, whifling novice, denyer of thy brethren, ingrate, unnatural, uncharitable, blaspheming, cursing, tricking, towzing, smuggling, drinking, gaming, non-residing, lying, forging, brazen idol of the modern fanatical party.[35]

Here, then, the public dialogue is characterized by defamation rather than rationality. And this was trial by the press as a sort of consumer sport. Thus one

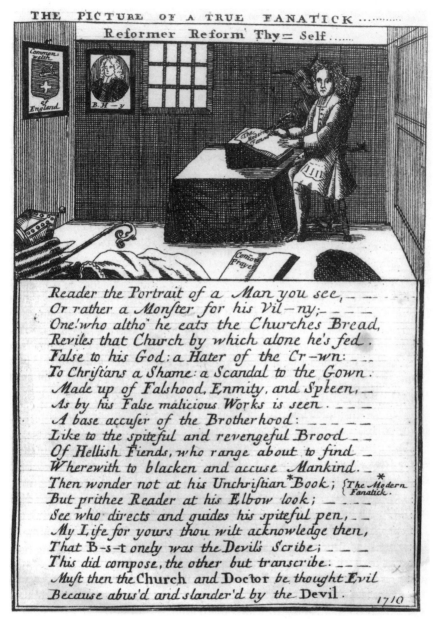

Figure 11.1 'The Picture of a True Fanatick'. This 1710 satire of Bisset depicts the devil whispering in his ear as he writes his 'unchristian' attack on Sacheverell. On the wall hang the arms of the mid-seventeenth-century commonwealth and a portrait of Benjamin Hoadly, whose low-church views Bisset was alleged to follow. The print questions the rational nature of later Stuart discourse but also appeals to the public judgement of the 'reader' to discern the 'falshood' of Bisset's slander. *BM, Sat. 1548, reproduced by courtesy of the Trustees of the British Museum.*

tract imagined the rival ranks of pamphleteers meeting to try their strengths: 'here are we pamphleteers met to decide the fate of the nation, to prove our innocence and loyalty to each other, to see which party must preside, which must govern, and which obey'.[36] Party or polemical pamphleteering was thus depicted as designed to manipulate the public for political purposes:

> it's the only aim and end of pamphleteers to gain credit with their readers, to asperse the party which they hate and save themselves harmless, while they are murdering others. Hence they have learned to shelter themselves under borrowed names, to screen their slander behind some malicious fable, to suit well-known characters to the persons at whom they aim, or else to leave out a vowel or two in their names, whose reputation they are going to stab with their envenomed stilleto's.[37]

Bisset prepared a response. In it he alleged he was at a loss to know when the vindication of Sacheverell was 'in jest and when in earnest; what he would have pass for romance and what for reality'. Bisset was thus able to dismiss the attacks on him as a patchwork of 'notorious falsehoods in fact' and 'mere fiction'.[38] Although Bisset was forced to clarify some details of fact (he now admitted that Sacheverell's lover had not died of a broken heart) the public debate had rather tended to produce *rival versions of the truth* rather than consensual agreement about a single truth, as Habermas would indicate was the norm. Partisanship destabilized truth claims, for each partisan thought he had truth on his side and everything could be reinterpreted according to partisan loyalty. Indeed, the tracts explicitly acknowledge an element of fiction in the partisan claims.

Bisset produced yet another response, in 1714, in which he made further slanderous allegations against Sacheverell, even down to suggesting that the doctor once had the misfortune on the way back from the playhouse 'to b[eshi] t his coatch'.[39] Here Bisset was revenging himself on an earlier printed spat with a high-churchman who had entitled a 1704 attack *B–ss–t B–sh–t or The foulness of more plain English*. This attacked two of Bisset's earlier sermons for containing little but foul language, 'pulpit buffonry ... fitter for the playhouses'. Yet such manipulative, passionate, abusive and partisan material sold well to a developing market of consumers. The three parts of Bisset's *Modern Fanatick* were published in 1715 in what claimed to be the twelfth edition. It was a best-selling dispute, in which the boundaries of public discourse were explored. Libel thus tackled libel; slander provoked counter-accusations of slander, which were in turn opposed with rehearsals of the slander, a slanging match in which each side increasingly asserted that the claims of their rival were mere fabrications and fictions. Libels were denied as lies which were in need of refutation. Print thus offered a public prosecution; but it also offered the *umpire* of the public. And here a Habermasian public sphere might be discerned. For at one point the dispute nearly entered the formal arbitration of the courts over an alleged assault made by Bisset on what he called a 'purse-proud clown (set on by the big Folk of the Neighbourhood)' who, ironically for a man who did not shrink from abuse, 'gave [him] the foulest language'.[40] Yet it is significant that the matter stayed out of the legal realm and entered the court of public opinion, with the pamphlet material deploying legal language to substantiate the proof of the allegation. Indeed, the legal procedures of libel and slander were aped in a mock recantation published in Bisset's name in which the fictional Bisset 'confessed' that 'every word in my book is false and scandalous'.[41] The parties thus acted like legal parties in a lawsuit, invoking rules of evidence but appealing not to a judge and twelve jurors, but to a jury of public opinion conjured up by the print exchange they were judging. This 'judge' had legitimacy as a result of the printed appeal. As one of the tracts in the dispute put it:

> every man that prints appeals to the people ... ought to be content to hear them pass their censures – nor is it unjust for any man to answer, censure, or animadvert upon a printed paper provided only that his answers, censures of animadversions are but themselves to be defended in the nature of them.[42]

As Hannah Arendt claimed, 'the public realm is constituted by the critics and the spectators and not by the actors or the makers'.[43]

One other aspect of the dispute is worthy of note. Habermas claimed that the political public sphere was an extension of the literary one, occurring only after the literary debates of the coffee houses and theatres had begun. The Sacheverell–Bisset controversy, however, suggests that the two spheres developed alongside one another. For response and counter-response, intrinsic to party polemic, necessitated careful attention to text and detailed criticism of text. Partisan authors necessarily engaged in textual appreciation. Political censure, then, often involved a process of extensive literary criticism, in which the style and language employed were carefully scrutinized. This was in part necessary because, as Defoe observed in his contribution to the Bisset–Sacheverell exchange, men in the later Stuart period habitually wore masks.

> This, Sir, is an age of plot and deceit, of contradiction and paradox; and the nation can hardly know her friends from her enemies ... it is very hard under all these masks, to see the true countenance of any man – there are more kinds of hypocrisie than that of occasional conformity – and the whole town seems to look one way and row another.[44]

Since actors habitually hid their motives, textual analysis was one way of trying to uncover their true designs and offered one guide to aid public judgement. Unusually, Defoe thought (with tongue in cheek), Sacheverell had actually used language *without* artifice and thus the age was 'infinitely oblig'd' to him because he had thrown off his 'mask' of language and 'fairly tells these impos'd upon gentlemen, what it is th[e high-churchmen] *really* mean rather than what they pretend'.[45] Literary style was thus scrutinized as a means of uncovering authenticity, veracity and intent. 'There have been always criticks,' remarked the earl of Mulgrave, 'but I believe there was never such an age and nation for that humour as ours is at present'.[46] Printed disputes thus appealed to the umpire of the public, who were asked to judge as though they were judges and literary critics. The role of 'censor' thus shifted from a prerogative court or licenser of the press to published authors in dialogue with their reading public. This shift raised new difficulties. Authors had to be careful how they attempted to fill the role of director of opinion. The modern censor had to be persuasive rather than dictatorial, had to use the press rather than seek to suppress it, and had to use language both as rhetoric and as a means to uncover the hidden motives of partisan participants.[47]

The Habermasian model thus has both weaknesses and strengths. On the one hand it overplays the reality of a rational-critical public sphere in the later Stuart period. As the Bisset–Sacheverell dispute makes clear, there was a public eager to consume debate that was intemperate, personalized, abusive, passionate, and which traded printed accusations of lying and manipulation. Language was implicated in the irrationality and duplicity of the public sphere, for its debasement reflected and facilitated degraded discourse. There was no single public opinion that arrived, by consensus, at a version of the truth. And yet, at the same time, the polemicists' attacks on each other invoked, implicitly or explicitly, the notion of a governing public opinion, of a rational nation capable of discerning truth amid the lies it was being told, and a set of rules by which judgement of public discourse could be made. And a notion of a single public opinion did emerge at the polls, when in 1710 the high-churchmen, on the back of the Sacheverell cause, achieved a landslide victory. Thus the very irrationality of the first public sphere, its capacity to mislead the public and abuse, its passion and distortions produced by allegiance to party, generated counteracting impulses. There was widely shared hostility to what one tract of 1711 described as the bitter language prevalent in coffee houses, taverns, private houses and the pulpits 'not manag'd (as formerly) with some sort of decency and good humour, but with meer scolding and the most scurrilous reflections; insomuch that (what I grieve to say) not only Christianity but civility and good manners seem to be laid aside and forgot'.[48] Appeals to reason, politeness and impartiality were thus part of the construction of an ideal form of public discourse in which rationality might flourish. And alongside this went notions of a public that could decide, whether at the polls or as the umpire over the press, matters that were debated. The revulsion against the excesses of the rage of party fostered ideals of new forms of public discourse. In true Frankfurt school tradition there *is* a dialectic at work here: the mutual conflict of two divergent ideologies that produced convergence on an ideal way of talking. Heightened party conflict – what contemporaries called the 'rage of party'

– fostered an ideal public discourse to which all parties subscribed.

This while to some extent later Stuart notions of politeness were merely restatements of older notions of civility we must recognize change as well as continuity.[49] There were good reasons why the political culture should have taken on a new aspect. After 1640 the press played a new role in facilitating a public sphere, undermining previously held notions and norms of secrecy and privacy as well as setting up a public dialogue without closure and invoking an engaged reading public.[50] And not only was there more print and print innovation (particularly after 1695, when the periodical market was transformed) but the ways in which the press could be used changed. Print interventions as a means of carrying on politics became more common. Print libels extended defamation and slander as far as the disseminators of the press could reach.[51] Ideological division and public partisanship offered occasion, motivation and a language for abuse as well as a lens through which the faults and failings of individuals and groups appeared magnified and significant. Yet a shared determination to avoid civil war and dangerous enthusiasm (of both civil and religious brands) necessitated formal and informal discursive rules to accommodate conflict. The public thus had to become critics of irrationality and a good deal of polemic had this explicitly pedagogic role. The press was both poison and its own antidote, a means not only to corrupt but also to correct error. Indeed, for this very reason the partisan polemic ironically needs to be considered as part of the early Enlightenment attack on unreasonableness and prejudice.

Frequent electioneering – there was a general election on average every two and a half years between 1679 and 1716 – provided numerous occasions for print warfare, and it heightened anxieties in every borough that the public might be misled and even corrupted by manipulative and dishonest discourse. But electioneering also offered a means by which the public came together and could cast a judgement about the claims and counter-claims of the candidates and their supporters, and stimulate a platform for public debate. Indeed, increasingly voters were being advised by a growing barrage of print that highlighted the errors of opponents but also constructed ideals of how candidates (and voters) ought to behave as models of rational umpires. Finally, the financial revolution did widen a public with an economic stake in the state, increase the value of news as a commodity and heighten awareness of the relationship between language and credit. In short, from the 1640s, and especially in the first Age of Party, the public acquired a new role as arbiter of a public discourse that had itself became a conscious concern and matter of debate. And that picture is not too far from the Habermasian model, after all.

NOTES

I am grateful for the support of the AHRB in funding the research for this chapter.

1   J. Habermas, *The Structural Transformation of the Public Sphere: an Inquiry into a Category of Bourgeois Society*, trans. T. Burger and F. Lawrence (Cambridge MA, 1989). The book was first written in German in 1962.

2   For an excellent overview of how Habermasian ideas have been treated more generally see H. Mah, 'Phantasies of the public sphere: rethinking the Habermas of historians', *Journal of Modern History* 72 (2000), 153–82.

3   See, for example, J. Raymond, 'The newspaper, public opinion and the public sphere in the seventeenth century', in Raymond (ed.), *News, Newspapers and Society in Early Modern Britain* (London, 1999); J. A. Downie, 'How useful to eighteenth-century English studies is the paradigm of the "bourgeois public sphere"?' *Literature Compass* 1 (2003), 1–18.

4   *Stuctural Transformation*, 27.

5   *Ibid.*, section 13.

6   A translation is available in P. Hyland with O. Gomez and F. Greensides (eds), *The Enlightenment: a Sourcebook and Reader* (London, 2003), 53–8.

7   Habermas, however, largely replaces Kant's stress on private offices with a Marxist stress on the private world of commodity exchange (*Structural Transformation*, 55). For a discussion of the private/public distinction see G. Schochet, 'Vices, benefits and civil society: Mandeville, Habermas and the distinction between public and private', in P. Backscheider and T. Dystal (eds), *The Intersections of the Public and Private Spheres in Early Modern England* (London, 1996).

8   For the public sphere as an idealized fiction see Mah, 'Phantasies'.

9   *Structural Transformation*, 169.

10   *Ibid.*, 170.

11   *Ibid.*, 171.

12   *Ibid.*

13   *Ibid.*, 176, 178.

14   *Ibid.*, 179.

15   *Ibid.*, 188.

16   *Ibid.*, 195.

17   For discussions of the relationship between religious discourse, reason and the public sphere in the later Stuart period see T. Claydon, 'The sermon, the "public sphere" and the political culture of late seventeenth-century England', in L. A. Ferrell and P. McCullough (eds), *The English Sermon Revised: Religion, Literature and History, 1600–1750* (Manchester, 2001); F. Beiser, *The Sovereignty of Reason: the Defense of Rationality in the early English Enlightenment* (Princeton NJ, 1996), 149; I. Rivers, *Reason, Grace, and Sentiment: a Study of the Language of Religion and Ethics in England, 1660–1780* (2 vols, Cambridge, 1991, 2000); M. Heyd, 'The reaction to enthusiasm in the seventeenth century: towards an integrative approach', *Journal of Modern History* 53 (1981), 258–80; Heyd, *'Be Sober and Reasonable': the Critique of Enthusiasm in the Seventeenth and early Eighteenth Centuries* (Leiden, 1995).

18 N. Elias, *The Civilising Process: the History of Manners and State Formation and Civiliza-
tion*, trans. E. Jephott (rev. edn, Oxford, 1997).

19 A. Bryson, *From Courtesy to Civility: Changing Codes of Conduct in Early Modern England*
(Oxford, 1998), 50, 276–7, 283; P. Burke, 'A civil tongue: language and politeness in
early modern Europe', in Burke, B. Harrison and P. Slack (eds), *Civil Histories: Essays
presented to Sir Keith Thomas* (Oxford, 2000); J. G. A. Pocock, 'Post-puritan England and
the problem of the Enlightenment', in P. Zagorin (ed.), *Culture and Politics from Puritanism to the Enlightenment* (Berkeley CA and Los Angeles, 1980); N. Phillipson, 'Politics
and politeness in the reigns of Anne and the early Hanoverians', in J. G. A. Pocock (ed.),
The Varieties of British Political Thought, 1500–1800 (Cambridge, 1993); L. Klein, 'The
political significance of "politeness" in early eighteenth century Britain', in G. Schochet
(ed.), *Politics, Politeness and Patriotism* (Folger Institute Center for the History of British
Political Thought Proceedings V, Washington DC, 1993); Klein, 'Coffee-house civility,
1660–1714: an aspect of post-courtly culture in England', *Huntington Library Quarterly*
59 (1997), 30–51; Klein, 'Liberty, manners and politeness in early eighteenth century
England', *Historical Journal* 32 (1989), 583–604; Klein, *Shaftesbury and the Culture of
Politeness* (Cambridge, 1994); Klein, 'The third earl of Shaftesbury and the progress of
politeness', *Eighteenth Century Studies* 18:2 (1984–85), 186–214; Klein, 'Politeness and the
interpretation of the British eighteenth century', *Historical Journal* 45 (2002), 869–98; S.
Pincus, '"Coffee politicians does create": coffeehouses and Restoration political culture',
Journal of Modern History 67 (1995), 807–34; P. Clark, *British Clubs and Societies, 1580–
1800: the Origins of an Associational World* (Oxford, 2000). But B. Cowan, 'Reasonable
ecstasies: Shaftesbury and the languages of libertinism', *Journal of British Studies* 37
(1998), 111–38, argues that Shaftesbury's 'vision of who should be included in the public
sphere was far more restrictive than that of many of his fellow Whig ideologists' (137);
H. Berry, *Gender, Society and Print Culture in late Stuart England: the Cultural World of the
Athenian Mercury* (Aldershot, 2003); P. McDowell, *The Women of Grub Street: Press, Politics and Gender in the London Literary Marketplace, 1678–1730* (Oxford, 1998); J. Miller,
'Public opinion in Charles II's England', *History* 80 (1995), 359–81; B. Sharp, 'Popular
political opinion in England, 1660–1685', *History of European Ideas* 10 (1989), 13–29.

20 For a stress on the importance of urban civility see J. Barry, 'Civility and civic culture
in early modern England: the meanings of urban freedom', in P. Burke, B. Harrison
and P. Slack, *Civil Histories: Essays presented to Sir Keith Thomas* (Oxford, 2000), and P.
Withington, *The Politics of Commonwealth: Citizens and Freemen in Early Modern England*
(Cambridge, 2004). The latter challenges Habermas's chronology by stressing a cult of
civility in urban society that accompanied rapid urbanization between 1540 and 1640.
He argues that well ruled discourse, honesty, and discretion were all apparent in urban
civility well before 1660. I am very grateful to him for showing me his work prior to its
publication. The essays in J. Richards (ed.), *Early Modern Civil Discourses* (Basingstoke,
2003), from a literary perspective, also stress the 'critical doubleness' of the civil–uncivil
polarity across the early modern period (6). For doubts about the impact of print see T.
Harris, 'Understanding popular politics in Restoration Britain', in A. Houston and S.
Pincus (eds), *A Nation Transformed: England after the Restoration* (Cambridge, 2001). For
reservations about the Habermasian model for the seventeenth century news culture
see J. Raymond, 'The newspaper, public opinion and the public sphere', in Raymond
(ed.), *News, Newspapers and Society in Early Modern Britain* (London, 1999).

21 *Structural Transformation*, 30, 32–3, 42–3.

22 A. Bellany, *The Politics of Court Scandal in Early Modern England: News Culture and
the Overbury Affair, 1603–1660* (Cambridge, 2002); Bellany, 'Libels in action: ritual,

subversion, and the English literary underground, 1603–1642', in T. Harris (ed.), *The Politics of the Excluded* (Basingstoke, 2001); Bellany, 'Rayling rhymes and vaunting verse: libellous politics in early Stuart England, 1602–1628', in K. Sharpe and P. G. Lake (eds), *Culture and Politics in Early Stuart England* (London, 1994); T. Cogswell, 'Underground verse and early Stuart culture', in S. Amussen and M. Kishlansky (eds), *Political Culture and Cultural Politics in Early Modern England: Essays presented to David Underdown* (Manchester, 1995); T. Cogswell, 'The politics of propaganda: Charles I and the people in the 1620s', *Journal of British Studies* 29 (1990), 187–215; Cogswell, *Home Divisions: Aristocracy, the State and Provincial Conflict* (Manchester, 1998); P. Croft, 'The reputation of Robert Cecil: libels, political opinions and popular awareness in the early seventeenth century', *Transactions of the Royal History Society*, 6th ser., 1 (1991), 43–69; Croft, 'Libels, popular literacy and public opinion in early modern England', *Historical Research* 68 (1995), 266–85; A. Fox, *Oral and Literate Culture in England, 1500–1700* (Oxford, 2000); Fox, 'Ballads, libels and popular ridicule in Jacobean England', *Past and Present* 145 (1994), 47–83; Fox, 'Rumour, news and popular political opinion in Elizabethan and early Stuart England', *Historical Journal* 40 (1997), 597–620; Fox, 'Popular verses and their readership in the early seventeenth century', in J. Raven, H. Small and N. Tadmor (eds), *The Practice and Representation of Reading* (Cambridge, 1996); F. Levy, 'How information spread among the gentry, 1550–1640', *Journal of British Studies* 21 (1982), 11–34; R. Cust, 'News and politics in early seventeenth century England', *Past and Present* 112 (1986), 60–90; E. Shagan, *Popular Politics and the English Reformation* (Cambridge, 2002); I. Archer, 'Popular politics in the sixteenth and early seventeenth centuries', in P. Griffiths and M. Jenner (eds), *Londinopolis* (Manchester, 2000); E. Shagan, 'Constructing discord: ideology, propaganda, and English responses to the Irish rebellion of 1641', *Journal of British Studies* 36 (1997), 4–34; A. McRae, 'The literary culture of early Stuart libelling', *Modern Philology* 97 (2000), 364–92. For reservations about the applicability of Habermas to the earlier period see also P. Lake with M. Questier, *The Antichrist's lewd Hat* (New Haven CT, 2002), 324, 360–1, 483, and their 'Puritans, papists and the "public sphere": the Edmund Campion affair in context', *Journal of Modern History* 72 (2000), 590.

23 The best account is G. Holmes, *The Trial of Doctor Sacheverell* (London, 1973).

24 *The Communication of Sin* (preached August 1709).

25 For his sermon *The Perils of False Brethren*, which had become a best-seller.

26 *The Modern Fanatick* (1710), preface, 7–8.

27 *Ibid.*, 7, 21, 22, 27, 31.

28 *A Letter to the Eldest Brother of the Collegiate Church of St Katherine in Answer to his scurrilous Pamphlet entitul'd The Modern Fanatick &c* (1711), 1, 8.

29 W. King, *A Vindication of the Reverend Dr Henry Sacheverell from the False, Scandalous and Malicious Aspersions cast upon him in a late infamous Pamphlet entitled The Modern Fanatick* (1711), 4.

30 *Ibid.*, 11–12. White Kennett, in *The Wisdom of Looking Backward* (1715), 96, described it as written 'in a bantering buffooning stile'.

31 King, *A Vindication*, 43.

32 *Ibid.*, 59, 77, 79.

33 H. Sacheverell, *Dr Sacheverel's True Character of a Low-Churchman drawn to the Life* (1710), an abridgement of a 1702 tract. This tract contained a portrait of Sacheverell depicting

him as the champion of truth and hence complemented the satire reproduced below.

34 W. Withers, *A General Apology* (1711), 14–15.

35 *A Dialogue between Dr Henry Sach—ell and Mr William B—set written secundum usum Billingsgate for the Instruction of Boatmen, Porters, Sailors, and Carmen* (1711), 3–4.

36 *A Letter to the Author of the Vindication of the Reverend Dr Sacheverell* (1711), 21.

37 *Ibid.*, 23.

38 *The Modern Fanatick Part II* (1710), preface. The tract was published in February 1711. Kennett, *The Wisdom of Looking Backward*, summarized it as 'concluding his language is so very course and beastly, as a civil carman would be asham'd to use' (100).

39 *Modern Fanatick Part III* (1714), 13.

40 *The Modern Fanatick Part III*, preface. Mediation avoided a court appearance. Bisset had earlier appeared in an ecclesiastical court for slander, after he claimed that a JP had drunkenly ridden his horse into a dissenting conventicle: *B–ss–t B–sh–t* (1704), 13.

41 *Mr B——t's Recantation in a Letter to the Reverend Dr Henry Sacheverell occasion'd by his Reading the Doctor's Vindication* (1711), 2. The joke here was that the mock recantation warned the reader that print would appear against Sacheverell in Bisset's name but that it would be 'spurious' (5).

42 *A Letter to Mr Bisset eldest Brother of the Collegiate Church in Answer to his Remarks on Dr Sacheverell's Sermon* (1710), 2. The tract was signed 'Amicus' and is usually attributed to Defoe.

43 H. Arendt, 'Judging', appendix to *The Life of the Mind* (New York, 1981), 262.

44 *A Letter to Mr Bisset ... in Answer* (1710), 9–10. Ironically, Defoe was appropriating the title of the earlier anti-Bisset tract and turning it into an attack on Sacheverell. His own work, therefore, looked one way and rowed another.

45 *Ibid.*, 11.

46 *The Works of John Sheffield* (1723) II, 259.

47 This development owed much to Robert Harley, though sponsored publications can be found much earlier: J. Downie, *Robert Harley and the Press: Propaganda and Public Opinion in the Age of Swift and Defoe* (Cambridge, 1979), 117.

48 [J. Rawson?], *A Word to the Wise in a Letter to a City-Clergyman* (1711), 3.

49 This paragraph summarizes issues discussed in my *Representation and Misrepresentation in later Stuart Britain: Partisanship and Political Culture* (Oxford, 2004).

50 D. Zaret, *Origins of Democratic Culture: Printing, Petitions, and the Public Sphere in Early Modern England* (Princeton NJ, 2000); S. Achinstein, *Milton and the Revolutionary Reader* (Princeton NJ, 1994); Achinstein, 'The politics of Babel in the English Revolution', in J. Holstun (ed.), *Pamphlet Wars: Prose in the English Revolution* (London, 1992). Thus whereas Lake and Questier see an opening and closing arena for public discussion, the capacity to close down discussion became severely diminished from the 1640s onwards and attempts by the Restoration regime to regain such control had proved failures by 1678 and at times before then.

51 William Sheppard's *Action upon the Case for Slander* (1662) had a subtitle claiming that 'actions for slander are more common then in times past'. The preface elaborated: 'in these daies they are become almost as natural to men, as their language and discourse'.

Index

Note: 'n.' after a page reference indicates the number of a note on that page.